MIDDOT:
ON THE EMERGENCE OF KABBALISTIC THEOSOPHIES

Middot

On the Emergence of Kabbalistic Theosophies

Moshe Idel

KTAV PUBLISHING HOUSE

MIDDOT:
ON THE EMERGENCE OF KABBALISTIC THEOSOPHIES

KTAV PUBLISHING HOUSE
527 Empire Blvd
Brooklyn, NY 11225
www.ktav.com
orders@ktav.com
Ph: (718) 972-5449 / Fax: (718) 972-6307

Cover design by Shira Atwood
Typeset in Arno Pro by Raphaël Freeman MISTD, Renana Typesetting

ISBN 978-1-60280-440-1

Printed and bound in the United States of America

*"The Attributes of the Holy One,
blessed be He, are one Attribute
versus a [human] attribute"*

R. Baḥya ben Asher,
Commentary on Numbers 16:35.

Contents

Preface

This study is part of a broader type of interest in questions related to te beginning of Kabbalah in the Middle Ages, and its various affinities to earlier Jewish traditions, many of them Rabbinic but also Greek and Philonic ones. Some studies of mine in the past have addressed specific topics, like the theory of three divine attributes, the interpretations of the secret of transmigration of the souls, or the secrets of incest in early phases of Kabbalah, as well as aspects related to the theories of ten divine powers in nascent Kabbalah, all of them to be mentioned in the following chapters.

The present book has been written while I was a member of the Kogod Research Center of Contemporary Jewish Thought at the Shalom Hartman Institute in Jerusalem, and as part of the research done in the framework of the Matanel Chair of Kabbalah at the Safed Academic College. Special thanks are due to my colleagues at the Shalom Hartman Institute, Profs. Israel Knohl, Shlomo Naeh and Adiel Schremer. The conversations with them have been extremely helpful for some aspects of discussions here.

The book has been written some years ago, and I attempted to update it before it went to print, especially after the recent publication of Dr. Avishai Bar-Asher's innovative study "Illusion vesus Reality."

Introduction

Conceived in the popular imagination as the innovator and bearer of an exclusive monotheism, the most widespread theologies in Judaism are, nevertheless, very complex and inclusive ones. The emergence and the fast floruit of a luxuriant theosophy in medieval Judaism in Kabbalah was regarded as an enigma, and sometimes even sharply criticized by more "rationally" – oriented thinkers. Adhering as these thinkers were to a stark exclusive type of monotheism, the inclusive nature of most of the Kabbalistic discussions were even regarded by the opponent to Kabbalah as idolatry, though this lore, in its various forms, has been gradually accepted by the greatest parts of the Halakhic elites since the 13th century.

The present study deals with processes of building growingly more complex and relatively systematic theologies conspicuous in Kabbalistic literature. Those complex theologies, different as they are from each other, will be designated as theosophies. They emerged within the framework of Jewish canonical religious writings that were relatively indifferent toward systematic theology. This relative indifference is evident already in the Hebrew Bible, in the pseudepigraphic literature in antiquity and late antiquity, and in the vast Rabbinic literatures, all of them literary corpora that were more inclined to legalistic and mythical forms of thought. The transition from a non-theological religious modality in those earlier corpora to very complex theologies in the Middle Ages, was triggered by a variety of factors within Judaism and outside it. In the cases discussed here, the process of harmonization between different and sometimes diverging approaches in the Scriptures and in Rabbinic literature was certainly an important factor, though not just a continuation or an elaboration. This is, to be sure, not an apology for Kabbalistic theosophies, neither a critique, since I do not adopt an essentialist vision of Judaism.

The following discussions are part of an historical and phenomenological analysis of some aspects of concatenations between theosophy and theurgy, which passed, for the time being, not sufficiently explored in the field, and sometimes even ignored. This concatenation affected not just the nature of those two topics but also other, more eminently, the nature of what scholars calls Kabbalistic symbolism, and the attention to the belief in efficacy of the rituals. This constitutes one of the main reasons for the reception of this type of Kabbalah in Rabbinic elites since the 13th century. The importance of theurgy and symbolic interpretation – issues that will be dealt with in more details in this study – lays in the pursuit of offering meaning to a certain way of life, namely Rabbinic Judaism, as mainly a ritualist type of religiosity.

The approach adopted here, as in many of my other studies, is a non-Romantic one; namely, an attempt to avoid the glorification of innovations, ruptures, Gnosticism, crises, antinomianism, paradoxes or historical teleologies, that inform much of the scholarship in the field. Instead, I prefer to pay attention to shifts and changes taking place in basic traditional notions, their new or different concatenations, and eventually their reception in Jewish society, in addition to highlighting external influences, and the conceptual tensions the latter triggered.

This does not mean that the categories mentioned as part of the Romantic approach are not pertinent at all. Instead they play, in my interpretation, a much more modest role in a proper understanding of the evolutions of Kabbalistic systems. If the various forms of Kabbalah emerged in conspicuously Rabbinic environments, and many of their exponents were figures that invested time in the study of traditional

Jewish texts, the major effort I propose to invest is in understanding the dynamic or evolution within this type of literature, and afterwards in various intellectual contexts, important as they are. A balanced view should take in consideration both continuities and ruptures, without overemphasizing any of them on the expense of the other. This is the reason why a proper understanding of the emergence of Kabbalah in the Middle Ages should start first with an inspection of those elements inherited from earlier sources that were known, quoted and interpreted by Kabbalists.

This does not mean that in this study I shall try to explain all the complex processes that produced the various forms of theology in Kabbalah. However, I shall try to suggest affinities between different Rabinic models and some Kabbalistic theosophies. In other words, the present study does not attempt to explain the emergence of Kabbalah, since Kabbalah is an umbrella term for various schools and systems, each one having a different history and in some cases different sources. The variety of theories about divine attributes, found in Rabbinic sources, inspired different views in medieval Jewish thought and especially in the various schools of Kabbalah.

The occurrence of several divine names in the various parts of the Hebrew Bible is a fact that triggered a variety of intellectual developments in understanding the Bible. The best known of them is the so-called theory of documents found in the Bible, a theory that opened, dramatically, a new page in the critical study of the Hebrew Bible. Though it takes in consideration a variety of factors that distinguish between the various parts of the Hebrew Bible, either conceptually or terminologically, the occurrence of different divine names constitutes nevertheless a major criterion.[1] In some biblical

1 See, e.g., S.R. Driver, *An Introduction to the Literature of the Old Testament* (Charles Scribner's Sons, New York, 1950), third edition, Jon D. Levenson, *The Hebrew Bible, the Old Testament, and Historical Criticism* (Westminster/John Knox Press, Louisville, 1993), Israel Knohl, *The Sanctuary of Silence: The Priestly Torah and the Holiness School,* (Fortress, Minneapolis, 1995), pp. 124–125, 168–172, 227, idem, *The Divine Symphony,* Baruch J. Schwartz, "The

documents, some of the divine names are used together, as part of an effort to harmonize the discourse about the divinity. The gist of this scholarly approach is to identify various documents that resort to specific divine names that are less evident in other documents and thus to distinguish between them, and analyze each of them in itself.

Basically, those documents stem from different historical periods and what is even more important, from different religious groups that constituted the ancient Israelite societies.[2] Thus, the main vector of modern scholarship insofar as this topic is concerned, is to find out the stylistic differences, the specific conceptual views, which means that this is a theory grounded in a proclivity of separating between the authorship of some documents and that of others. This theory is gravitating around the occurrence of different divine names as one of the blueprints of different ancient authors or groups, as part of the approach of historical criticism.

However, when seen from a traditional point of view, which surmises that the Bible is a document authored ultimately by a divine power and consisting in an overarching conceptual homogeneity, the diversity of divine names reflects not different styles and some human authors, but various divine aspects and their activities.[3] Sometime in late antiquity, most probably before the turn of the millennium,

Pentateuch as Scripture and the Challenge of Biblical Criticism: Responses among Modern Jewish Thinkers and Scholars," in *Jewish Concepts of Scripture: A Comparative Introduction*, ed. B.D. Sommer (New York: New York University Press, 2012), pp. 203–229, and Michael Carasik, *The Bible's Many Voices*, (Jewish Publication Society, Philadelphia, 2014).

2 See Knohl, *The Divine Symphony*, pp. 149–155.

3 See Mordechai Breuer, "Making Sense of Scripture's Plain Sense" and "The Divine Names and Attributes," in his *Pirqei Bereshit*, (Tevunot, Alon Shevut, 1998), vol. 1, pp. 11–19 and 48–54, dealing with what he calls, following the Rabbinic theory of two attributes and the Zoharic views, as well as R. Moshe Cordovero's terminology, evident in the phrase "Torat ha-Beḥinot", and the discussion of his views in Shalom Carmy, "Concepts of Scripture in Mordechai Breuer," in *Jewish Concepts of Scripture: A Comparative Introduction*, ed. B.D. Sommer (New York: New York University Press, 2012), pp. 267–279.

correlations between divine names and some modes of divinity activity can be discerned in some Jewish texts. Those are rather stable correlations and they convey the assumption of the existence of a more complex metaphysical structure than a simplistic exclusive monotheism, assuming a diversity of divine powers that is conveying God's diverse actions and thus the resort to those divine names. Those powers are called in Rabbinic literature by the Hebrew term *middah*, [in plural *middot*], literally measures, while in Philo of Alexandria they are described as *dynameis*, powers.[4]

The earliest dated evidence is found in several of Philo's writings and despite the difference between the specific correlations of divine names and modes of actions in his books, and what is found in Rabbinic literature, the existence of such schemes testify to a prior existence of such a way of thought before the beginning of the first millennium CE. Also the obvious variety of understandings of the nature of the two powers in both Philo, in early Christianity, and in Rabbinic literatures, that will preoccupy us in the first two chapters, militates in favor of an earlier date for the emergence of this theory of two divine powers, sometimes early in the intertestamental period. This variety precludes an essentialistic approach to this topic, in its Rabbinic sources or in their later Kabbalistic avatars.

To be sure: the Hebrew texts resort to the term *middah*, that relates to some form of divine reaction to the human behavior, as the Rabbinic dicta *middah ke-neged middah*, namely one measure against a measure,[5] or "in accordance to the measure you measure, you are

4 See Marmorstein, *The Old Rabbinic Doctrine of God*, pp. 41–53, Naeh, "Philo and the Rabbis on the Powers of God," pp. 91–101, idem, "The Attribute of Judgment and the Attribute of Mercy in Rabbinic Thought', *Maḥanayyim* 5, (1993), pp. 62–68 (Hebrew), Fishbane, *Biblical Myth and Rabbinic Mythmaking*, pp. 99–101, 125–126, 179–180, idem, "The "Measures" of God's Glory," Liebes, *God's Story*, pp. 135–157, as well as ben-Sasson–Halbertal, "The Divine Name YHVH and the Measure of Compassion," Segal, *Two Powers in Heaven*, passim, Kister, "The Manifestations of God," and in particular Abrams, "Chapters from an Emotional and Sexual Biography of God."

5 See, e.g., *BT Shabbat*, fols. 105b, *Nedarim* fol. 32a, *Sanhedrin* fol. 90a. See also

measured."[6] These principles became clues for understanding the relationship between different acts and their results in a long variety of authoritative commentaries of the Hebrew Bible, especially Rashi, Nahmanides and R. Bahya ben Asher. Measuring is also the case even when the topic of creation is engaged, where some form of measure involved in these acts is mentioned.[7] What seems to be missing in the earlier forms of Rabbinic discussions of the *middot* are more general questions, like the immutability of God or the transition from the one to the many. Philo, however, is concerned much more with the issue of hypostatic powers, influenced as he was by Greek philosophers, and much less with an interactive or correlative theology, as it is the case in many instances in Rabbinic thought, as we shall see in detail in chapter 2.[8]

Provided the pair of divine powers includes a benificient and a punitive power, we may ask whether this theory is related in a way or another to the Qumranic dualistic theory of two camps, but at this stage of research it is hard to answer this question in a conclusive manner. In any case, the Rabbinic theory of two – and more rarely three or more – measures had a prominent place both in Rabbinic thought since its inception, and also in those speculative trends that emerged in the Middle Ages under the aegis of Rabbinic authority.[9]

Lorberboim, *Image of God, Halakhah and Aggadah*, pp. 225 n. 216, 2311 n. 241, 264 n. 374, 269, 361, 378–379, 380 n.107.

6 See, e.g., *BT Megillah*, fol. 12a as well as the other Rabbinic sources discussed in ben-Sasson–Halbertal, "The Divine Name YHVH and the Measure of Compassion," p. 63, and Abrams, "Chapters from an Emotional and Sexual Biography of God," p. 278. See also R. Azriel, *Commentary on the Talmudic Legends*, ed. Tishby, p. 34. Compare to, e.g., the commentaries of Rashi and R. Bahya on Numbers 14:37, and R. Bahya on Numbers 16:35, 20:13.

7 See Liebes, *Ars Poetica in Sefer Yetzirah*, pp. 159–166.

8 About correlative theology in Judaism see now the edifying study by Benjamin Sommer, *Revelation and Authority*: *Sinai in Jewish Culture and Tradition*, (Yale University Press, New Haven, 2015).

9 See also my "Notes of Medieval Jewish-Christian Polemics," or *Absorbing Perfections*, pp. 51, 226–230, 260.

Nevertheless, so far only a little has been done in order to examine the richness of the Rabbinic discussions of those divine measures or attributes, and even less the nature of the complex affinities between them and the early Kabbalistic writings, emerging as they were in their vast majority in circles where Rabbinism was a decisive term of reference.

While no scholar would deny the plausible relations between early Kabbalists in late 12th century, and Rabbinism, as some of them were accomplished legalistic figures, an examination of the details of such linkages still wait for a much more detailed scrutiny. I hope that the following chapters will open the door for further and more detailed analyses in this direction. In any case, the discussions of the attributes are an evident case of terminological, and to a great extent also of conceptual continuity, between two types of Jewish literatures that are written mainly in Hebrew that constitutes a fascinating challenge for understanding the precise relationship between those distinct literatures.

This issue is especially relevant for the question of the sources and the beginnings of Kabbalah. What I would like to show is that a type of inclusive theology, found in a more modest manner in the Rabbinic and other Jewish corpora in the first millennium CE, was highly influential in shaping another sort of inclusive theology, namely, several different Kabbalistic theosophies, at the very moment when exclusive theologies of philosophical extraction made the most significant inroads in Judaism in the form of Maimonides' philosophical version of exclusive monotheism.

The existence of many Rabbinic statements about divine attributes, conceived as independent entities, which constitute an inclusive theology, should have, in my opinion, an important role in the emergence of the Kabbalistic theosophical inclusive theology, that deals with many more divine powers, resorting in many cases to the Rabbinic term *middah/middot*. Here we have terms rich in meanings and canonized in authoritative sources that are often quoted by Kabbalists, which can allow a much more secure insight in the processes related to the emergence of Kabbalah in the Middle Ages.

The term encapsulates a variety of meanings but for our purpose it is quintessential to point out that it means, inter alia, also a divine attribute and a mode of activity. In terms to be used in this study: a dynamic theosophy, and even a human way of acting, allowing a reciprocal relationship between the two realms. In my opinion, it is only after elucidating the metamorphoses of this term and its role as a ferment for later theological developments, that we can understand why additional sources, philosophical or other, were added to it, dramatically enriching its meaning.

Indubitably, the problem of the beginnings of Kabbalah is a perennial one in scholarship of the field. Several different explanations have been offered, each reflecting the intellectual concerns of the respective scholar and his generation. I shall mention here only some of them. Heinrich Graetz's assumption was that Kabbalah is an obscurantist reaction to the emergence of the Maimonidean enlightenment.[10] His student, Moses Gaster, was, however, in favor of a totally different explanation that sees in Kabbalah one of the results of the massive migration of earlier material from the Middle East, and even from India, a much more comprehensive move that informed also many of the developments in European culture in the Middle Ages.[11] Though he addressed this issue rather sporadically and in a fragmentary manner,

10 *Geschichte der Juden*, (Leipzig, 1908), vol. 7, fourth edition, pp. 385–402, and the exposition and critique of Scholem, *Origins of the Kabbalah*, pp. 7–8.

11 See, in particular, Moses Gaster, "Cabbala: originea şi dezvoltarea ei," *Anuar pentru Israeliţi*, 6 (1883/4), pp. 25–36, and in more general terms about his theory of transition of knowledge from East to West, see idem, *Ilchester Lectures on Greeko-Slavonic Literature*, (Truebner & Co., Ludgate Hill, London, 1887); idem, *Literatura Populară Română*, ed. M. Anghelescu, (Bucharest, Minerva, 1983²). On his views of Jewish mysticism in general see M. Idel, "Moses Gaster on Jewish Mysticism and the Book of the Zohar," in ed. R. Meroz, *New Developments in Zohar Studies*, (= *Te'uda*, XXI–XXII), (Tel Aviv University, Tel Aviv, 2007), pp. 111–127 (Hebrew), and Abrams, *Kabbalistic Manuscripts and Textual Theory*, pp. 282–285. See also below in *Some Concluding Remarks*.

Let me point out that I do not accept Gaster's rather vague view of the history of Kabbalah as represented, inter alia, by numerical speculations, an

his views require much more attention than they have received so far in scholarship. Gaster's contemporary, David Neumark, conceived of the development of Kabbalah as a phase in the longer process of oscillations that consisted in confrontations between more abstract philosophically oriented views and more mythical ones in the history of Judaism.[12] Scholem regarded this theory as a "total failure."[13]

Gershom Scholem himself formulated another explanation, based on his assumption that there are historical and phenomenological affinities between medieval Kabbalah and late antiquity Gnosticism, and regards Kabbalah as the result of a synthesis between Gnostic and Neoplatonic elements. We shall have more to say about this theory in the following chapters.[14] He is the only scholar who had dedicated intense research and sustained interest in this question, and offered the above answer that was accepted widely by many scholars for decades.

Another approach has been proposed by Yitzhak Baer, who pointed out to significant parallels to Rabbinic and Kabbalistic dicussions in Philo of Alexandria's writings and in ancient Greek sources, without

assumption that allows him to speak about the antiquity of this lore. See his *The Samaritans, Their History, Doctrines and Literature* (London, 1925), pp. 80, 82, 149.

12 *Geschichte der jüdischen Philosophie des Mittelalters* vol. 1 (Berlin, 1907), pp. 179–236, and in a more elaborated manner in the Hebrew version *Toledot ha-Filosofia be-Yisrael* (New York, 1921), vol. 1 pp. 166–354, and see also Scholem, *Origins of the Kabbalah*, pp. 8–11, and Idel, *Old Worlds, New Mirrors*, p. 6, and Wolfson, "The Theosophy of Shabbetai Donnolo," pp. 300–301.

13 *Origins of the Kabbalah*, p. 10. For a combination of Neumark's and Scholem's theory in order to account for the emergence of Kabbalah in Provence see Sendor, *The Emergence of Provencal Kabbalah*, I, pp. 378–379.

14 See, e.g., *Major Trends in Jewish Mysticism*, p. 35, idem, *Reshit ha-Kabbalah*, pp. 96–97, idem, *Origins of the Kabbalah*, pp. 67, 68–97, 119–120, 123, 197–198, 210–211, 231, 236, 245, 247, 316–320, 363–364, 389–390, or Joseph Dan, 'The Emergence of Mystical Prayer', in eds., J. Dan – F. Talmage, *Studies in Jewish Mysticism*, (Cambridge, Mass., 1982), pp. 108–109. See, however, Idel, *Kabbalah: New Perspectives*, pp. 260–262, idem, "Jewish Kabbalah and Platonism," p. 347 n. 37, and idem, "On Binary 'Beginnings' in Kabbalah – Scholarship", *Aporemata*, vol. 5 (2001), pp. 313–337.

however, referring to Scholem's Gnostic hypothesis.[15] More recently, an important topic considered by scholars to be new in early Kabbalah, the feminine perception of the *Shekhinah,* has been attributed to the impact of contemporary Christianity, as we have seen claimed in the writings of Arthur I. Green,[16] and Peter Schaefer,[17] who dealt with the emergence of the feminine aspect of divinity.

I see this shift in scholarship from a Gnostic explanation to a Christian one, for the emergence of the Kabbalistic notion of *Shekhinah,* as operating still within the Scholemian theory of Kabbalah since it postulates a breakthrough within Rabbinism, rather than as a matter of evolution. In the case of Schaefer, this is just one of the topics where he imagines that Jewish mysticism has been impacted by Christian ways of thought, what I propose to call Christotropia.[18] Another issue in early Kabbalah, the image of the cosmic tree, was explained by Elliot R. Wolfson as stemming from ancient Judeo-Christian sources.[19]

Different as Graetz, Scholem, and Schaefer are from each other, their shared assumption is that Kabbalah is basically a rupture with the Rabbinic ways of thought, which can be understood better by assuming a substantial shift, in many cases as the result of the impact of views previously unknown in Judaism, basically due to concepts of an external extraction. This is especially evident in the presentations of Jewish mysticism of Scholem and Schaefer, who embraced an

15 See his "The Service of Sacrifices in the Second Temple," pp. 399–457.
16 Arthur I. Green, "*Shekhinah*, the Virgin Mary, and the Song of Songs: Reflections on a Kabbalistic Symbol in Its Christian Context," *AJS Review*, vol. 26 (1) (2002), pp. 1–52, and see the critique of Yehuda Liebes, "Was the Shekhinah a Virgin?" *Pe'amin*, vols. 101–102, (2005), pp. 303–313 (Hebrew), and his *Studies in Jewish Myth*, pp. 47–54.
17 Schaefer, *Mirror of His Beauty*. This is part of a much wider approach found also in his theories dealing with other aspects of the pre-Kabbalistic Jewish esoteric literature. See now his *The Origins of Jewish Mysticism*. Compare to my different explanation of this phenomenon in "The Triple Family," pp. 91–110.
18 See his *Origins of Jewish Mysticism*.
19 "The Tree that Is All."

approach I would call a Reuchlian approach,[20] namely an axiology that distinguishes quite neatly between the Rabbinic literature as being merely ritualistic, and the Kabbalistic one, conceived of as later in time, more spiritual and essentially different from the former. I do not pass any judgement as to the "hypertrophy of rituals" as Scholem implicitly did, but attempt to integrate the traditional and the new elements that both constitute various forms of Kabbalah. Emblematic for their approach is the neglect of an analysis of the centrality of the Rabbinic theories of two divine attributes, and the theurgical implications of some of them, as significant for the development of Kabbalah. Such neglect is especially evident also in Schaefer's discussions of the sources of the evasive notion in his book "Jewish Mysticism."

On the other hand, the antiquity of some elements found in early Kabbalah has been advocated in some important studies of Yehuda Liebes, who also pointed out the possible impact of pre-Socratic philosophers on *Sefer Yetzirah* and the mythical views of the Rabbis when dealing with *middot* and the impact on Kabbalah. We shall return to his approach and specific discussions in the following chapters.[21]

Since the early eighties of the 20th century, I have proposed an approach that sees in the emergence of Kabbalah in the Middle Ages the restructuring of some older mythologumens, probably stemming from the Middle East, coalescing as a response to the religious challenges posed mainly by Maimonides' influence in Jewish circles.[22] It

20 More on this issue see in *Some Concluding Remarks*.

21 See, e.g., Liebes, *Studies in Jewish Myth*, idem, *The Cult of the Dawn*, idem, "Zohar and Iamblichus," in eds., S. Frunză & M. Frunză , *Essays in Honor of Moshe Idel*, (Provo Press, Cluj-Napoca 2008), pp. 106–111 (= *JSRI* vol. 18, (2008), pp. 95–100), and below n. 550.

22 Idel, "Maimonides and Kabbalah," pp. 31–81, idem, *Kabbalah: New Perspectives*, pp. 250–253. See also idem, *Absorbing Perfections*, pp. 280–289, "On the Theosophy at the Beginning of Kabbalah", Travis, *Rabbi Ezra of Gerona*, pp. 38–48, and see also Hava Tirosh-Samuelson, "Philosophy and Kabbalah: 1200–1600," in eds. D.H. Frank and O. Leaman, *The Cambridge Companion to Medieval Jewish Philosophy*, (Cambridge University Press, Cambridge, 2003), pp. 218–224.

is this response that is one of the factors that triggered the emergence of what I call the "literary platforms" that bring evidence as to the existence of a series of different, though cognate, Kabbalistic schools, since late 12th century.[23] I attempted to foster this explanation in a series of studies,[24] and I return here to some aspects of one of these studies in order to elaborate more on some of its details on the broader basis that has been generated by more recent studies.[25]

Much more radical is the more recent theory based on an examination of the possible ancient traditions of Mesopotamian background on Kabbalah, that has been initiated by Simo Parpola, who claimed the antiquity of the scheme of ten *sefirot* as representing an unified deity, and some efforts to substantiate this line have been made in the wake of the publication of his studies.[26]

23 See my "On the Theosophy at the Beginning of Kabbalah," pp. 147–148.

24 See, e.g., Idel, "The Evil Thought of the Deity," *Tarbiz* vol. 49 (1980), pp. 356–364 (Hebrew), idem, "Sefirot Above Sefirot," pp. 239–280, "Leviathan and Its Consort" and more recently idem, "On the Theosophy in Early Kabbalah," pp. 131–148, idem, "*Be-'Or ha-Ḥayyim*: An Observation on Kabbalistic Eschatology" in eds. I.M. Gafni – A. Ravitzky, *Sanctity of Life and Martyrdom, Studies in Memory of Amir Yekutiel*, (Jerusalem, 1992) pp. 191–212 (Hebrew), "Holding an Orb in His Hand: the Angel 'Anafi'el and a Late Antiquity Helios Mosaic," *Ars Judaica* vol. 9 (2013), pp. 19–44, and "The Triple Family." See also Hananel Mack, "*Midrash Numbers Rabbah'* and the Beginning of Kabbalah in Provence," *Myth in Judaism*, ed. H. Pedayah, (Beer Sheva, 1996), pp. 84–88 (Hebrew). An attempt to deepen the pre-Kabbalistic and Kabbalistic views I dealt with succinctly in the eight pages of "The Evil Thought of the Deity," recently became a four hundred pages' book: *Primeval Evil in Kabbalah: Totality, Perfection and Perfectibility*.

25 As to some of the topics discussed below see especially my *Absorbing Perfections*, pp. 51, 226–230, *Kabbalah: New Perspectives*, pp. 128–136, and even earlier in "Notes on the Judeo-Christian Polemics."

26 See Simo Parpola, "The Assyrian Tree of Life: Tracing the Origins of Jewish Monotheism and Greek Philosophy"' *Journal of Near Eastern Studies*, vol. 52 (1993), 161–208, Amar Annus, *The God Ninurta in the Mythology and Royal Ideology of Ancient Mesopotamia*, (The Neo-–Assyrian Text Corpus Project, Finland, 2002), pp. 156–162, and Pirjo Lapenkivi, *The Sumerian Sacred Marriage in the Light of Comparative Evidence* (The Neo-–Assyrian Text Corpus Project,

Let me clarify from the very beginning: in my opinion Kabbalah in its different forms is a late 12th and much more, early 13th century broad spectrum of religious phenomena: nevertheless, some of the ideas found in early Kabbalistic schools preceded it, perhaps by centuries, though these ideas were independent of each other. What counts, in my opinion, more for understanding the emergence of Kabbalah, are the concrete medieval concatenations of these diverse and sometimes unrelated ideas, which constitute modes of thinking and behavior considered later on to be Kabbalistic. Nevertheless, the different histories of the various pre-Kabbalistic independent themes or of some aspects of Kabbalah found in pre-Kabbalistic material are part of a better understanding of the emergence of these concatenations. Or, to put it in other words: in my opinion, early Kabbalah looks much more as a significant evolution that took place within Rabbinic circles in the Middle Ages, with its various theologies of *middot* and its theurgical components, rather than a Gnostic revolution, as Gershom Scholem thought – under the impact of Hans Jonas – which sometimes display, so he thought, implicit antinomian valences or impulses.

I would like to illustrate my proposal by analyzing in the following pages the Kabbalistic treatments of the Rabbinic, and perhaps also other discussions of divine attributes – *middot*. This choice is a matter of phenomenological approach and by doing it, a different historical picture emerges than when someone is focusing on other aspects of the analyzed material. Nevertheless, early Kabbalistic sources are not one more phase in Rabbinic thought, despite the fact that they drew inspiration from some of them, though reorganizing Rabbinic elements in new manners, inspired by a variety of other, quite different sources.

However, let me emphasize that despite the significant historical and phenomenological differences between my approach and that of Scholem's, I share with him a very important methodological

Finland, 2004), passim. See also now Arieli, *On the Source of the Doctrine of the Sefirot.*

approach: any new understanding of the emergence of Kabbalah should be based first and foremost on a detailed analysis of the available testimonies, some of them still in manuscripts, and only afterwards a different opinion should be formulated.[27]

Scholem did an excellent job in the thirties and forties of the 20th century by unearthing much of the extant documents buried for centuries in manuscripts. He printed many of them and meticulously interpreted them, all this in the adverse conditions of his generation.[28] Without a similar effort that consists basically in a return to the study of manuscripts, those already known and others which still wait for perusal, which are now much more accessible than ever, and by introducing new material in the circuit of modern research, and only then reflecting on Scholem's interpretations, new theories ventilated on fragmentary pieces of evidence. Many of these theses that are related to material already known in the research in the field do not do justice to the magnificent scholarly edifice created by the founder of the modern scholarship of Kabbalah after decades of hard spadework. A fragmentary acquaintance with the pertinent sources is not the best recipe for a significant contribution to such a complex matter as the emergence of Kabbalah or to formulation of theories about its nature.

I shall try to introduce such new material that has not been addressed yet, and reflect also on the details of the interpretations already offered in scholarship, most eminently by Scholem, on the history of nascent Kabbalah. Moreover, on the basis of several of my studies printed solely in Hebrew, Scholem's picture of the treatises and the concepts that are relevant for the understanding of early Kabbalah should change in a significant manner.[29] Those changes

27 *Origins of the Kabbalah*, p. 12.

28 See his *Origins of the Kabbalah* and the collection of the reprint of his studies on the topics of early Kabbalah in *Studies in Kabbalah*, with his additional and updated footnotes.

29 See Idel, "Commentaries on the Secret of Impregnation," pp. 5–14, and "Kabbalistic Prayer in Provence," pp. 265–286, where I proposed to change

are not just bibliographical issues but touch the question as to what is the pertinent material to be taken in account in a more adequate analysis of the emergence of Kabbalah and what not. So, for example, if someone assumes that *Sefer ha-Temunah,* and some other pieces like *Sha'ar ha-Kavvanah of Early Kabbalists* – a short treatise dealing with prayer – the Kabbalistic *Commentary on Midrash Konen* attributed to R. Isaac the Blind, or his *Commentary on Sefer Yetzirah,* are part of early Kabbalah, or were written a century or more later, the results of such an analysis will differ from a picture that ignores them.

I am concerned mainly with some aspects of the history of the concept of two divine attributes, that emerged in late antiquity Judaism, and developed in Philo of Alexandria, in Rabbinic literature and was very important also in early Kabbalah. This is no doubt one of the few and most influential theological contributions of post-biblical Judaism for the later development of this religion, and the exploration of its evolution can contribute much to the understanding of the genesis of important aspects of medieval Kabbalah. It is paralleled by some few new accents on the feminine aspects of the divine realm, especially the emergence of the concepts of *Shekhinah* and *Knesset Isra'el,* that enriched Rabbinic theology in a manner that turned it into a springboard for further speculations in the Middle Ages.[30] In my opinion, binary approaches found in early Kabbalistic documents,

the attribution of some instructions of prayer attributed to R. Abraham ben David (the Rabad) to his Provencal contemporary R. Ya'aqov, the Nazirite of Lunel and vice-versa. This shift substantially affects the analysis of the thought of those figures. *En passant,* in the material that I proposed to attribute to R. Ya'aqov, the attribute of judgment is identified with the last *sefirah,* as it is the case later on in the school of Nahmanides, as we shall see in chapter 6 below. See ibidem, p. 285. This shift in attribution of material has not been adopted by Dan, *History of Jewish Mysticism,* p. 346 n. 38, though he does not offer any explanation for his stance. Let me point out that in the scant material extant so far in the name of R. Ya'aqov discussed in my study, it is only the term *Middah* that occurs in the context of divine powers, but not *sefirah,* indubitably an interesting fact for our point in the present study.

30 See, e.g., Liebes, "De Natura Dei," pp. 278–289.

which are cardinal for understanding the theosophical-theurgical schools of Kabbalah, draw from earlier sources, some of which will be mentioned later. This process of various elaborations is one of the main goals of the present study.

This binary nature of Kabbalistic thought, which started much earlier in Judaism, is evident in the pair of powers described as good and evil, to which I dedicated a separate study.[31] Like that pair discussed elsewhere, here, also the two attributes to be discussed at length are mainly part of what can be called a subordinated pseudo-symmetry, namely a pair that is presented in some cases as symmetrical. But this is a duality that is not becoming a dualism, provided it is subordinated to a higher principle, God, which is not neutral but at least implicitly conceived of as being good. At any rate we may speak about a divine complexity constituted by powers that operate in the extra-divine world, but also include a range of inner divine relationship. The inner and the outer types of dynamism loaded the reciprocal theologies in Rabbinic thought and in many of the medieval Kabbalistic theories, with valences that are absent in the more philosophically oriented theologies dealing with attributes, as it is the case of Philo of Alexandria and Abraham Abulafia, as we shall see in chapters 2 and 9. Moreover, the theurgical component, so vital for many of the schools of Kabbalah that we will survey, is also missing in their worldviews.

Both types of pseudo-symmetries functioned in what is commonly called a monotheistic religion, and their role was to organize religious, and sometimes even secular, information. Provided the historically belated emergence of Kabbalah in circles belonging to the much wider phenomenon called Rabbinic Judaism, the amount of religious data under consideration grew dramatically, and forms of new organizations, or reorganizations, were necessarily in order to make sense of the huge literary corpora and of ritualistic behavior.[32] By subsuming the earlier types of information to the categories of divine attributes

31 See my *Primeval Evil in Kabbalah*.

32 See, e.g., R. Azriel of Gerona, in Scholem, "New Remnants," p. 212, or R. Joseph Alashqar, *Tzafnat Pa'aneaḥ*, a vast commentary on the Mishnah, both

of compassion and judgment, and especially to the structure of the ten *middot* – as we shall see – or ten *sefirot,* some form of logic has been introduced in the welter of the Jewish pre-Kabbalistic disparate material dealing with divine modes of activity.[33] In other words, the very modest constellations of the supernal world in pre-Kabbalistic types of Jewish literature, which contains some micro-myths, became dramatically complex and it gradually constellated some important aspects of Jewish thought in the Middle Ages, especially the Kabbalistic ones, which display what can be called macro-myths. This is especially the case of the some of the literature dedicated to explanations of the ten *sefirot* and in Cordoverian and Lurianic forms of Kabbalah. Thus, we witness a religious phenomenon very similar to those analyzed by the myth-and-ritual schools, as I proposed since my first published books.[34]

related the six tractats of the Mishnah in accordance to the structure of the ten *sefirot.* See ed. M. Idel (Misgav Yerushalayyim, Jerusalem, 1991).

33 For the question of organization or reorganization of earlier religious material in the various forms of Kabbalah see, e.g., my *Kabbalah: New Perspectives,* p. 213, idem, *Studies in Ecstatic Kabbalah,* pp. 136–140, idem, "The Land of Divine Vitality: Eretz Israel in Hasidic Thought," ed. A. Ravitzky, *The Land of Israel in Modern Jewish Thought,* (Yad Izhak Ben-Zvi, Jerusalem, 1998), pp. 256–258 (Hebrew), idem, 'The Kabbalah's "Window of Opportunities" 1270–1290', in eds. E. Fleischer & talia, *Me'ah She'arim; Studies in Medieval Jewish Spiritual Life, in Memory of Isadore Twersky,* (The Magnes Press, Jerusalem 2001), p. 184 n. 96, idem, *Absorbing Perfections,* pp. 22, 50, 117, 248–249, 255, 272–273, 280–284, 442–444, idem, "Some Forms of Order in Kabbalah," *Daat,* vol. 50–52 (2003), pp. xxxi–lviii, idem, "Interpretations of the Secret of Incest in Early Kabbalah," pp. 104–105, idem, "Leviathan and Its Consort," pp. 172–173, idem, *Saturn's Jews,* pp. 18–19, 25, 36–38, 116, and more recently Abrams, *Kabbalistic Manuscripts and Textual Theory,* pp. 591–592.

34 See Scholem, "Mafteaḥ le-Perushim," Oron, "The Literature of Commentaries to the Ten *Sefirot,*" and my *Kabbalah: New Perspectives,* pp. 210–214, or *The Angelic World,* pp. 49–53.

For myth-and-ritual and Jewish mysticism see e.g., my *Kabbalah: New Perspectives,* p. 197, idem, *Messianic Mystics,* pp. 21, 22, 45–46, 111, 252, 289, 314, 319, 331 n. 44, and *Enchanted Chains,* pp. 11, 24–25, 51, 220. On the importance of

The role of the theosophical systems that will concern us is a part of the wider phenomenon that includes also the adoption of astral types of constellations, of a more complex angelology, and as we shall see in chapter 9, also of some philosophical theologies. However, what is quite salient for our discussions is the substantial impact of astronomical/astrological forms of order for understanding the reorganization of knowledge in early Kabbalah.[35] This form of order is evident in *Sefer*

rituals over beliefs see the important article of E. Thomas Lawson, "Cognitive Categories, Cultural Forms and Ritual Structures," in ed., P. Boyer, *Cognitive Aspects of Religious Symbolism* (Cambridge University Press, 1993), especially pp. 194–196. See also Walter Burkert, *Homo Necans, The Anthropology of Ancient Greek Sacrificial Ritual and Myth*, tr. P. Bing, (University of California Press, Berkeley, 1983), pp. 26–29.

35 See, e.g., Reimund Leicht, *Astrologumena Judaica*, (Mohr, Tübingen 2006), idem, "The Reception of Astrology in Medieval Ashkenazi Culture", *Aleph*, vol. 13 (2013), pp. 201–235, Shlomo Sela, *Astrology and Biblical Exegesis in Abraham ibn Ezra's Thought*, (Bar-Ilan University, Ramat Gan, 1999) (Hebrew), Y. Tzvi Langermann, "Some Astrological Themes in the Thought of Abraham ibn Ezra," in eds. I. Twersky and J.M. Harris, *Rabbi Abraham ibn Ezra: Studies in the Writings of a Twelfth-Century Jewish Polymath*, (Harvard University Press, Cambridge, 1993), pp. 28–85, Raphael Jospe, "The Torah and Astrology according to Abraham ibn Ezra," *Proceedings of the Eleventh World Congress of Jewish Studies*, Division C, vol. III (Jerusalem, 1994), pp. 17–24, and Dov Schwartz, *Studies on Astral Magic in Medieval Jewish Thought*, trs. D. Louvish – B. Stein (Brill, Leiden, 2005), and the next footnote.

For connections between astrology and early Kabbalah see, in particular, Scholem, *Origins of the Kabbalah*, pp. 21, 77, 204, 453, 462, 465, Vajda, *Recherches*, pp. 15–17, 49–50, 321–339, idem, *Juda ben Nissim ibn Malka, Philosophe Juif Marocain*, (Paris 1954), pp. 45–46, 136–141, 143, and his 'La Doctrine Astrologique de Juda ben Nisim ibn Malka', *Homenaje a Millás Vallicrosa*, (Barcelona 1956), vol. 2, pp. 483–500. I propose to date the floruit of this Kabbalist around 1250. See also Jacques Halbronn, *Le Monde Juif et l'astrologie*, (Arche, Milano, 1985), pp. 289–334; Ronald Kiener, "Astrology in Jewish Mysticism from the *Sefer Yesira* to the *Zohar*," *JSJT*, vol. VI (1987), pp. 1–42, Haviva Pedaya, "Sabbath, Sabbatai, and the Diminution of Moon, – The Holy Conjunction, Sign and Image," in ed. H. Pedaya, *Myth in Judaism = Eshel Beer-Sheva*, vol. 4 (1996), pp. 143–191 (Hebrew), my *Saturn's Jews*, and "Mongol Invasions and

Yetzirah where correlations between different parts of the universe, including the planets, are evident and via this book it found its way to a large number of Kabbalists.[36] In any case, in the generations preceding the emergence of Kabbalah two main Jewish thinkers, R. Abraham bar Ḥyya' and R. Abraham ibn Ezra were accomplished astronomers, who wrote their books in Hebrew, mostly in Spain, and at least some of them were known by Kabbalists.

Unlike the exegetical and topical nature of the Rabbinic corpora, the Kabbalists introduced several forms of theosophical superstructure, imagined to inform and to distinguish between the welter of details of the canonized information, and thus emerged also the need of much more metaphysical discussions necessary in order to define the powers that constitute that superstructure. The decadic nature of those theosophies should be understood not only as some form of metaphysics but also as part of a larger effort of creating codes for organizing religious knowledge, which means schemes that informed the conceptual valence of both lexical canonical material, and the details of ritualistic behavior, by presupposing the existence of some higher and hidden form of order. Like all the other parts of Judaism, also the codes changed over time. This is also the case with the binary codes of the two attributes and the decadic ones, and their various combinations. However, the codes that inform the religious information are not conceived of as detached from the interpreted material, but are often "contaminated" by it, and the supernal structure is sometimes described by the terms of the religious rituals, like *Torah, Tefillah*, or *Tzaddiq*, as we shall see around n. 178 in chapter 3.

This metaphysical tendency is evident already in the late antiquity

Astrology: Two Sources for Apocalyptic Elements in 13th Century Kabbalah," in eds., A. Quintana, R. Ibáñez-Sperber and R. Ben-Shalom, *Hispania Judaica Bulletin: Between Edom and Kedar, Studies in Memory of Yom Tov Assis*, vol. 10, part 1 (Jerusalem, 2014), pp. 145–168.

36 Meir bar Ilan, *Astrology and Other Sciences among the Jews of Israel in the Roman-Hellenistic and Byzantine Period* (Mossad Bialik, Jerusalem, 2011) (Hebrew).

literary corpus of Philo of Alexandria – but not of classical Rabbinic sources or in the poetic literature during the first millennium CE – as we shall see especially in the two first chapters. The metaphysical turn of medieval Jewish philosophers triggered systemic responses, as mentioned before, which contributed to the emergence of the metaphysical vortex among the Kabbalists. This is a matter of cognitive developments: a continuous process of distinctions, followed by attempts to larger syntheses, which generate at their turn additional distinctions, and so on. This cognitive observation is especially pertinent for the evolutions of theosophical structures, which elaborated more and more on the details of the divine structures, from the point of view of looking at the emergence of theosophical Kabbalah as one more form of organization of religious knowledge in Judaism by a long series of adoptions, adaptations and interpretations, and often times also creative misinterpretation,[37]

Nevertheless, the substantial resort to the Rabbinic terminology of two attributes is evident in all the main forms of Jewish mysticism since the Middle Ages, though in different proportions, and naturally the specific nature of these attributes has been interpreted in different ways. This is not just a matter of just proof-texts, but in many cases much more a matter of a springboard for further theosophical speculations. After all, Kabbalists were earlier in their life students of Rabbinic literature, before they became Kabbalists, and the theories of Rabbinic attributes remained part and parcel of their intellectual apparatus also after they became Kabbalists. They did not think, in their vast majority, that the Rabbinic literature and modes of thought

37 The following pages differ from the basic approach of Abrams, "Chapters from an Emotional and Sexual Biography of God," whose main point is that Rabbis and Kabbalists were basically concerned with understanding the inner life of God, which means a theocentric enterprise. This approach, that is reminiscent of Abraham Y. Heschel's view of the divine pathos, is less concerned with the reorganization of older material in new structures during the Middle Ages as proposed here, and in some other earlier studies. See also more recently his "Divine Jealousy, Kabbalistic Traditions of Triangulation," *Kabbalah*, vol. 35 (2016), pp. 7–54. See n. 33 above and nn. 111, 215 below.

should be superseded, in a way reminiscent of Johann Reuchlin's understanding of the place of Kabbalah[38] but, to use a Christian view, Kabbalah in its various forms was their fulfillment, by revealing and elaborating upon what they believed were the hidden or the ignored esoteric layers, which constitute, allegedly, the essential meaning.

In other words the initial diversity of the biblical narratives, especially the recurrence of many divine names, generated attempts to "rationalize" – basically to reorganize the occurences of these names, by means of a theory of attributes – but these rationalizations elicited further distinctions, as we shall see in chapter 2, and those distinctions or models dealing basically with two attributes interacted with a system of tens – the *sefirot* – and impacted the various perceptions of those *sefirot*, contributing thereby to Kabbalistic theosophy in the earlier phases of this lore. In some cases, the existence of various views of *sefirot* required some forms of harmonization, which triggered more sophisticated theosophical theories, as we can see in Safedian Kabbalah. In other words, in a traditional religious world, which strives toward amalgamation of canonized values and harmonization that attenuates differences, the emergence of distinctions triggers later syntheses, which turn to be more and more complex, multiplying the numbers of the divine powers much more beyond the ten divine powers. This is a spiralic move. Here we shall be dealing with the earlier phases of this comprehensive process of distinctions, that produced smaller and smaller divine units, designated as aspects of the sefirotic worlds, later on called *beḥinot*, and they culminated in a theory of atomization of the divine into many sparks that are found, or fell, in the lower world, according to the views of R. Moshe Cordovero and R. Isaac Luria.[39]

To a certain extent, the present study addresses some few topics of a broader field that still requires a much more detailed attention in scholarship: the emergences and development of the Kabbalistic

38 See more in *Some Concluding Remarks*, and in Idel, *Representing God*, pp. 123–148.

39 See my *Old Worlds, New Mirrors*, pp. 3–5.

theories of ten divine powers better known in scholarship as *sefirot*, but addressed here from the perspective of the term *middot*.[40] This is a vast area of investigation, which is addressed here only in part, namely insofar as the connections between those divine powers and the theories of *middot* are concerned. Interestingly enough, long after the canonization of the theosophical forms of Kabbalah, with their emphasies on *sefirot*, especially since 16th century forms of Kabbalah, in 18th century Hasidism we witness a reversal of the meaning of the term *middot*; it now plays a much more important role than *sefirot*, at least as we can see especially in the traditions related to the Great Maggid of Mezeritch and his school. This oscilation between the alternating roles of the two terms, which were so important for Jewish forms of theologies, is a phenomenon that requires a more detailed analysis.

Another issue that deserves special attention, but will remain beyond the present study, is the parallelism between this atomization of the divinity and that of the soul, especially evident in the Kabbalah in the second part of the 16th century.[41] Neither are the following pages a summary of my previous studies on topics related to early Kabbalah, like the topic of prayer and theurgy, of the ten *sefirot* above ten *sefirot*, for example. Nor do I see the topic of this book as a purely historical discussion of the emergence of Kabbalah in the Middle Ages or its antiquity. Since my view as to the existence of different schools that together resorted to the umbrella term Kabbalah, each of them should be understood as having its own distinct history, though later on in their development they intersected.

My topic here is a picture of certain specific topics, theosophy and theurgy, their sources and their concatenations. However, in order to highlight this concatenation, I shall deal also with Kabbalistic schools that did not adopt it, like the writings from circle of the *Book of 'Iyyun* – chapter 8 – or the ecstatic Kabbalah of Abraham Abulafia,

40 See, meanwhile, Idel, *Kabbalah: New Perspectives*, pp. 136–153 and Wolfson, "The Theosophy of Shabbetai Donnolo."

41 See my "The Secret of Impregnation," pp. 349–368.

in chapter 9. Likewise, the first chapter deals with Philo of Alexandria's theory of divine attributes, divorced as it is from theurgical overtones, because of the profound philosophical impact of Greek thought. The different treatments of the two attributes will serve also as a prism for emphasizing the often deep differences between those Kabbalistic schools, a fact not sufficiently put in relief in modern scholarship of Kabbalah, which is still containing some significant impulses toward harmonization and what I call theologization.

In my opinion, fusing discussions from different schools, because of a deep belief held by a scholar that they must coinncide, or at least correspond, brings about much confusion, even more so because of the conceptual fluidity of Kabbalistic thought, which means that even the same Kabbalist may embrace more than one theology in his books or even in one of them, a phenomenon that can be designated as chronical theological instability.

ONE

Philo of Alexandria's Two Powers and Pre-Socratic Doctrines of Opposites

Philo of Alexandria's writings constitute the first and most systematic attempt to present Judaism as some form of coherent theology, an attempt deeply indebted to a variety of Greek and Hellenistic philosophies. How much Greek and how much Jewish components are to be discerned in his vast opus may be a matter of debate between scholars, but the depth of the impact of Greek thought on his writings cannot be underestimated.[42] His literary corpus includes exegetical writings on the Hebrew Bible, topical ones on religious topics, but also a rather developed effort to offer a consistent metaphysics, and inspite the importance of the two other trends. It is this metaphysical drive, of Greek origin, that triggered the alienation of Rabbinic authors toward Philo's opus, as much as the language in which he

42 See, e.g., the various views of Goodenough, *By Light, Light*, Wolfson, *Philo*, David Runia, "Why Philo of Alexandria Is an Important Writer and Thinker," eds., B. Decharneux and S. Inowlocki, *Philon d'Alexandrie, Un penseur à l'intersection des cultures gréco-romaine, orientale, juive et chrétienne*, (Brepols, Turnhout, 2011), pp. 13–33 and Maren R. Niehoff, "Philo's Role as a Platonist in Alexandria," *Études platoniciennes*, vol. vii, (2010), pp. 35–62. See also Afterman, "From Philo to Plotinus."

wrote.[43] Obviously, the Alexandrine thinkers were not operating in a Rabbinic environment, an anachronism in that period, but in his main speculative bodies of literature he was in an intense dialogue with various Greek philosophers.

This is also the case of a topic that recurs in several of Philo's treatises: the doctrine of two powers – *dynameis* – that are conceived of as opposites, and in some cases also as equal opposites.[44] The emergence of these two opposites – though the divine powers are from time to time more numerous, constituting a sort of pleroma[45] – is sometimes described as the result of a divine act of division. In a series of texts found in his writings, in particular in his *Who Is the Heir of Divine Things, and on the Division into Equals and Opposites*, the division done by the divinity differs from other forms of divisions by its perfect equality of the two emerging parts. The importance of this specific Philonic treatise for understanding late antiquity Judaism has been put in relief in a seminal study of Yitzhak Baer, a study that deserves a much greater attention for the study of the possible sources of Kabbalistic writings.[46] Y. Baer was more concerned with the cultic aspects of Philo's book, and their relevance for understanding of later

43 See Joanna Weinberg, "The Quest for Philo in Sixteenth-century Jewish historiography," *Jewish History, Essays in Honor of Chimen Abramsky* (London, 1988), now translated as "A quête de Philon dans l'historiographie juive du XVIe siècle," in eds., B. Decharneux and S. Inowlocki, *Philon d'Alexandrie. Un penseur à l'intersection des cultures gréco-romaine, orientale, juive et chrétienne*, (Turnhout, 2011), pp. 403–432.

44 For Philo's view of the two powers see, e.g., Segal, *Two Powers in Heaven*, pp. 159–181.

45 See Goodenough, *By Light, Light*, pp. 24–26, and Runia, *Philo of Alexandria, On the Creation of the Cosmos*, p. 386.

46 See his "The Service of Sacrifices in the Second Temple." The quotes are from the later edition. For references to Baer see, e.g., Goldreich, "The Theology of the Iyyun Circle," pp. 146–147, Idel, *Kabbalah: New Perspectives* p. 340 n.185, *Absorbing Perfections*, pp. 135, 414, 498 n. 17, 546, n. 174, 561 n. 56, 562 n. 63, 572 n. 9, 597 n. 90, 600 n. 9, Liebes, *God's Story*, p. 142, and more recently ben Sasson, *The Divine Name*.

forms of Judaism, including the Kabbalistic one. Here I am concerned with questions related to the history of some aspects of doctrines of divine attributes, like the views as opposites in late antiquity and early Kabbalah, especially the equality of the opposites as related to the divine powers and their source, an issue that was secondary for Baer's thesis. This is the reason why I capitalize in the following pages on additional passages, both Philonic and Kabbalistic. He was unaware of or less concerned with their content. This issue was also less important for Yehuda Liebes's very significant contribution to the study of Philo's Platonic sources for his theory of two divine powers.[47]

In Philo's *Who Is the Heir of Divine Things* we learn that

> "XXVII. [133] The subject of a division into equal parts, and on that of opposites, is a wide one, and discussion of it essential. We will neither omit not protract it, but abridge it as far as possible and content ourselves with the vital points only. Just as the great Artificer divided our souls and limbs in the middle, so too, when He wrought the world, did He deal with the being of all that is. This He took and began to divide as follows. First He made two sections, heavy and light, thus distinguishing the elements of dense from that of rare particles."[48]

Equality of what are perceived to be opposites is a leimotif that is relevant for a variety of divisions by the divine. What seems to transpire from this text and others to be adduced below, is a form of moderate exclusive theology that allows some role for intermediary powers, considered to be semi-divine.

Equality is involved also insofar as the division between the male

47 Liebes, ibidem.

48 *Who is the Heir of Divine Things*, vol. IV, p. 349. On equality see the introduction there, pp. 275–278. See also Richard A. Baer, *Philo's Use of Categories Male and Female* (Brill, Leiden, 1970), p. 19. The distinction between rare and dense is reminiscent of one of Anaxagoras' views of opposites. See G.S. Kirk & J.E. Raven, *The Presocratic Philosophers*, (Cambridge University Press, Cambridge, 1971), p. 373 fragment 12.

and female mentioned in Genesis 1, as Philo writes later on in the same treatise:

> "XXXIII. [164] For equality[49] gave day and night, light and darkness their place among the things which are. Equality too divided the human being into man and woman, two sections unequal indeed in strength, but quite equal as regards what was nature's urgent purpose, the reproduction of themselves in a third purpose. "God made man" he says "made him after the image of God." "Male and female He made" – not now "him" but "them." He concludes with the plural, thus connecting with the genus mankind the species which had been divided, as I said, by equality."[50]

Here equality is presented as a term that designates God, at least insofar as He intervenes in the creational process. Especially important is the fact, which seems to be new with Philo, that equality was transposed from the more general cosmological interpretations found in pre-Socratic fragments, to the equality of male and female.[51] This means that the Alexandrine thinker applied the pre-Socratic principle of isonomia, to biblical materials, introducing equality in discussions

49 This kind of reference to the divinity is reminiscent of the medieval Kabbalistic resort to the syntagm *'Aḥdut Shawah,* the equal unity, or *Hashwa'at ha-'Aḥdut,* the equality of the unity, found since early Kabbalah, especially in the writings of R. Azriel of Gerona. See Scholem, *Origins of the Kabbalah,* pp. 312, 439 nn. 174–175, 441. Scholem suggests deriving those terms from the eminent theologian John Scotus Erigena. See, however, the view of Goldreich, "The Theology of the Iyyun Circle," pp. 141–156, who proposes the theology of Ismailyah as a possible source for the early Kabbalistic concepts of equality. See also in chapter 7.

50 *Who Is the Heir of Divine Things,* p. 365.

51 See, however, Aristotle, *On the World,* par. 396b. For the centrality of the act of division in Philo's cosmology see Ursula Fruechtel, *Die Kosmologischen Vorstellungen bei Philo von Alexandrien,* (Brill, Leiden, 1968), pp. 41–52. Compare, however, the much later view found in a Palestinian *piyyut* attributed to Yannay, where God is described as "The Equal and the Equalizer" to be discussed in the next chapter.

which were not concerned with this issue. This is the case also in an additional passage from the same treatise:

> "XXVIII [141] But the text not only says: "He divided" but also "He divided them in the middle"[52]: and it is therefore necessary to make a few remarks on the subject of equal sections, for when anything is divided exactly in the middle it produces equal sections. Now no man can divide anything into equal sections with exactitude, but one of the sections is sure to be either less or greater than the other... No created thing is found to produce equality if tested by the unprejudiced standard of truth. It seems, then, that God alone is exact in judgement and alone is able to "divide in the middle" things material and immaterial,[53] in such a way that no section is greater or less than another by even an infinitesimal difference, and each can partake of the equality which is absolute and plenary...
>
> XXIX [146]... observe how God is "dividing in the middle" actually did divide equally according to the law of equality, when He created the universe."[54]

Equality occurs in Philo in three different forms: as seen above, it stands for God, and here it refers to the manner in which God operates, and finally to the different results of His division of a variety of entities in an equal manner, and in our specific context the division of the first man in male and female that are equal. This mentioning of equality is

52 Cf. Genesis 15:10, which is part of the biblical pericope commented by Philo in this treatise.

53 See above in the passage quoted beside n. 48.

54 *Who Is the Heir of Divine Things*, pp. 353–357. See also Baer, "The Service of Sacrifices," pp. 403–405. Equality of the powers is most probably related to the balance between them. See Runia, *Philo of Alexandria, On the Creation of the Cosmos*, p. 293. This type of equality is not found in early Rabbinic texts. See also David Winston, *Philo of Alexandria*, (Paulist Press, New York, 1983), p. 97 and n. 86, which refers to another aspect of Philo's passage thought not to equality.

especially important since it is considered as a necessary condition in order to have a harmonic universe, in a manner reminiscent of and probably influenced by Anaximander's view of the universe.[55] In Philo the emanation is of one entity and the splitting of the one entity into two opposites is a later phenomenon.

In some cases, especially important for the thesis of this study, Philo discusses this division of the opposites in terms related to biblical themes, especially the two Cherubim. So, for example, he writes in the same book as follows:

> "XXXIV, [166]. And the primary Potencies of the Existent, namely that through which He wrought the world, the beneficent, which is called God, and by which He rules and commands what He made that is the punitive, which bears the name of Lord, are as Moses tells us separated by God Himself standing above and, in the midst of them. "I will speak to thee" it says "above the compassion-seat in the midst of the two Cherubim."[56] He means to show that the primeval and highest Potencies of the Existent the beneficent and the punitive, are equal, having Him to divide them."[57]

Here, again, the equality is evident and it is applied, in a manner absent in the early Rabbinic sources, to a biblical source. Philo was concerned with the problem of governing the world or of providence, which were imagined to depend on some form of equal activity of the

55 See W.K.C. Guthrie, *A History of Greek Philosophy*: vol. 1: *The Earlier Presocratics and the Pythagoreans* (Cambridge University Press, Cambridge, 1962), pp. 78–83, Gregory Vlastos, "Equality and Justice in Early Greek Cosmologies," in eds., D.J. Furley and R.E. Allen, *Studies in Presocratic Philosophy* (London, 1970), vol. 1, pp. 56–91, Freudenthal, "The Theory of the Opposites," pp. 197–228, F.M. Cornfold, *Principium Sapientiae, A Study of the Origins of Greek Philosophical Thought*, ed. W.K. Guthrie, (Harper Torchbooks, New York, 1965), pp. 178–179, 183–185. See also Leonardo Taran, *Parmenides, A Text with Translation, Commentary, and Critical Essays*, (Princeton University Press, Princeton. 1965), p. 161.

56 Exodus 25:21. See Baer, "The Service of Sacrifices," pp. 405–407, 411–412.

57 *Who Is the Heir of Divine Things*, pp. 365–367.

two powers, or of cooperation between them. This is also the case in another Philonic passage:

> "(He indicates that) the limits of the entire heaven and cosmos are secured by the two highest guards, the one in accordance with which God made the entire universe, the other in accordance with which he rules that which has come into being. For their role would be to take care of a possession that was most intimately and closely related (to them), the creative power (doing so) so that what came into being through its agency would not fall apart, the kingly power (doing so) so that nothing would exceed or be exceeded, because things are arbitrated by the law of equality, which ensures that reality lives on forever. After all, excessiveness and inequality are what stimulates war and cause what exists to fall apart, whereas good organization and equality are the seeds of peace, producing safety and a continuing existence which is perpetual."[58]

Again, the law of equality is invoked in order to account for the attainment of the special quality of equality between the two divine attributes. Philo was one of the very few theological thinkers in ancient Judaism who contributed a rather detailed reflection on the nature and modes of action of the divine attributes, symbolized by the two cherubim found in the holy of the holies of the Israelite temple:

> "For it is necessary that the Powers, the Creative and the Royal, should look toward each other in contemplation of each other's

58 *Questiones et Solutiones* in Exodus, II, 66, *Philo*, Supplement II, ed. and tr. Ralph Marcus, (Harvard University Press, Cambridge, Mass., 1953), pp. 110–111, and see also David T. Runia, "A Neglected Text of Philo of Alexandria: First Translation into a Modern Language," *Things Revealed: Studies in Early Jewish and Christian Literature in Honor of Michael E. Stone*, in eds., E.G. Chazon, D. Satran and R.A. Clements, (Brill, Leiden, Boston 2004), p. 203, which I used in the translated passage. See also below chapter 5, R. Azriel of Gerona's description of *Shalom* as equalizing. On Philo and the Cherubim see Fred Strickert, "Philo on the Cherubim," *The Studia Philonica Annual* vol. 8 (1996), pp. 40–57.

beauty, and at the same time in conspiracy for the benefit of things that have come into existence. In the second place, since God, who is One, is both the Creator and King, naturally the Powers, though divided, are again united. For it was advantageous that they be divided in order that the one might function as Creator, the other as Ruler. For the functions differ. And the Powers were brought together in another way by the eternal juxtaposition of the names in order that the Creative Power might share in the Royal and the Royal in the Creative. Both incline toward the Compassion Seat.[59] For if God had not been merciful to the things which now exist, nothing would have been created through the Creative Power nor be given legal regimentation by the Royal Power."[60]

I had the opportunity to deal with aspects of this last passage in more detail elsewhere,[61] and I adduce here the text again in the wider context of Philo's thought, as seen above, as well as for the sake of an analysis of a later Kabbalistic passage on the facial androgyne. The

59 It is evident that also the Cherubs are involved here. See Wolfson, *Philo*, vol. 1, pp. 236–237. In general, there is a connection between the two powers in Philo and worship. See Bréhier, *Les idées philosophiques et religieuses*, pp. 136–144 and Baer, "The Service of Sacrifices in the Second Temple," passim.

60 *Questiones et Solutiones* in Exodus, II, 66, as translated by Goodenough, *By Light, Light*, pp. 25–26. See also Philo, *On the Cherubim*, trs. F.H. Colson – G.H. Whitaker, (Cambridge, Mass., – London, 1979), vol. II, pp. 25–27, pars. 27–29; Margaret Barker, "Temple Imagery in Philo: An Indication of the Origin of the Logos," in ed., W. Horbury, *Templum Amicitiae: Essays on the Second Temple Presented to Ernst Bammel*, (JSTO Press, Sheffield, 1991), pp. 96–98; Patai, *The Hebrew Goddess*, pp. 70–76. See especially Goodenough's salient observation that this passage is reminiscent of Kabbalah, without seeing Rabad's text printed only some few years beforehand – in 1948 in Scholem's book in Hebrew – in *Jewish Symbols in the Greco-Roman Period*, (Princeton, 1954), vol. 4, p. 132. Also Baer's analyses of Philo's views written much later does not relate to this passage of Philo's just as he does not refer to Rabad's Kabbalistic passage to be analyzed in chapter 4, neither to Goodenough's proposal.

61 Idel, *Kabbalah: New Perspectives*, pp. 131–132.

gist of the passage as I understand it is as follows: the two divine attributes coexisted within the divine realm before they were divided, and they regain something of this primordial unity by looking to the Seat of Compassion. By comparison to the passages adduced earlier, it is obvious that those potencies are conceived to be equal and acting in a coordinate or balanced manner. We may assume the existence of three distinct stages: the two attributes found within God, who encompasses them before the division; then the state of division, and then moments of regaining this primeval state, when the attributes, like the cherubim in the Temple, look to each other. It should be emphasized that this division is described as reflecting the divine benevolence.

Unlike some forms of pre-Socratic theories of opposites that assume a struggle between them, Philo is more concerned with cooperation between them. A question that cannot be answered is whether the divisions between the different entities in equal parts: powers, human souls and bodies, or cherubim, also implies some form of affinity between those divided entities.

Of special importance for my later discussions is the sentence: "And the Powers were brought together in another way by the eternal juxtaposition of the names in order that the Creative Power might share in the Royal and the Royal in the Creative." The precise identity of these names is not mentioned in this specific context, but Goodenough surmised, correctly in my opinion, that they are the two names of God, *Theos* – that refers to 'Elohim, stands for the Creative Power, and *Kyrios* – that refers to the Tetragrammaton, stands for the Royal power – which are indeed mentioned explicitly later on in the same treatise II:68. The linkage between the divine names and the divine powers, which differs from the Rabbinic approach, has been dealt with several times in scholarship.[62] However, Philo mentions

62 See Ralph Marcus, "Divine Names and Attributes in Hellenistic Jewish Literature," *PAAJR*, vol. 3 (1931–32), pp. 43–120, N.A. Dahl – A.F. Segal, "Philo and the Rabbis on the Names of God," *JSJ*, vol. 9 (1978), pp. 1–28, Wolfson, *Philo*, vol. 1, pp. 135–137, Baer, "The Service of Sacrifices in the Second Temple,"

here a different juxtaposition than the regular one that he embraced by indicating that he intends to "another way." So far, I did not find a scholarly interpretation of the meaning of his assessment as to "another way."[63] I would, nevertheless, interpret this as referring to the possibility that the difference between the two powers is overcome by assuming that each of them is sharing in some cases also the name of the other. Such an approach is indeed found in early Jewish texts, as we shall see in the next chapter.

Last but not least: Philo was acquainted with doctrines of opposites in pre-Socratic philosophies, but he nevertheless claimed that:

> "Heracleitus, whose greatness they celebrate so loudly, put in the fore front of his philosophy and vaunted it as a new discovery? Actually… it was Moses who long discovered the truth that opposites are formed from the same whole to which they stand in the relations or divisions."[64]

p. 410. For some of the sources of the Rabbinic views of two attributes see Naeh, "Philo and the Rabbis on the Powers of God," pp. 91–101, Liebes, *God's Story*, pp. 135–157, and Marmorstein, *The Old Rabbinic Doctrine of God*, p. 44; See more recently also ben-Sasson–Halbertal, "The Divine Name YHVH and the Measure of Mercy," pp. 65–68 and last but not least ben-Sasson, *The Divine Name* pp. 101–104.

63 See Marcus and Runia in n. 58 above as well as Abraham Terian, *Questiones et Solutiones in Exodus*, (Le Cerf, Paris,1992), pp. 200–201. See also Bréhier, *Les idées philosophiques*, pp. 142–144. Let me point out that Anaximander's view as to the encroachment of the equal opposites is close to this discussion but it is conceived of as negative, while for Philo it is positive and he speaks nevertheless about Divine names. See also below chapter 4.

64 *Who Is the Heir of Divine Things*, XLIV, par. 214, p. 389. This is the earliest testimony of the theme that was treated by Norman Roth, "'Theft of Philosophy' by the Greeks from the Jews," *Classical Folia*, vol. 32 (1978), pp. 53–67. See also Wolfson's discussion of Heraclitus and Philo, *Philo*, vol. 1, pp. 335–336 and Mireille Hadas-Lebel, *Philo of Alexandria, A Thinker in the Jewish Diaspora*, tr. R. Fréchet, (Brill, Leiden, Boston, 2012), p. 67 and Baer, "The Service of Sacrifices in the Second Temple," p. 444 and n. 125. For the list of the Pre-Socratic thinkers mentioned by Philo see Wolfson, ibidem, pp. 93–94. For Heraclitus's

From this passage it is obvious that with Philo the difference between the opposites does not disappear neither are they absorbed in the "whole" but they continue to act in order to maintain creation in an optimal manner. Moreover, it should be pointed out that the doctrine of the equality of the opposites, which is crucial for the Alexandrine philosopher and for some of the Kabbalistic texts to be discussed in the following chapters, is not found explicitly in Heraclitus and he drew it from other pre-Socratics, in my opinion mainly from Anaximander. In fact, from the point of view of the divine activity in the created world, Philo is closer to the Rabbinic doctrine of attributes, which is much more related to divine attributes, and more dynamic, than to the Greek discussions of opposites that is more cosmological, an issue that will preoccupy us in the following chapters. Especially significant is Philo's theory that the world cannot withstand or contain the impact of the infinite divine powers,[65] and this is one of the reasons for their cooperation, a view that is reminiscent of the Rabbinic models [A] and [B], to be discussed in the next chapter. Let me emphasize, the existence of the above discussions does not confer on Philo the title of a Kabbalist, since Kabbalah did not exist by then.

view of God as constituted by opposites see Eva Brann, *The Logos of Heraclitus*, (Paul Dry Books, Philadelphia, 2011), pp. 50–51.

65 See *De Mon* I:6, II:218, *The Creation of the World*, par. 23, *Philo*, vol. I, pp. 19–21, and Bréhier, *Les idées philosophiques*, p. 142.

TWO

Five Models of Relations between Divine Attributes in Rabbinism

Rabbinic literature consists in a huge literary corpus, written over many centuries, in a variety of places, and containing a variety of legalistic schools, active in the land of Israel and in Babylonia. This is the reason why it would be futile to try to discern a unified attitude toward the divine attributes. Though the main role played by the divine attributes in Rabbinic literature has to do with their operations in the lower world, as a measured divine response to human acts, I am concerned here also with the relationship between these attributes, as part of those operations. Thus, it will be better not to expect systemic consistence but some form of conceptual fluidity, and its different expressions converge basically around exegetical ingenuity and attempts to shape and strengthen ritualistic behavior.

Rabbinic literature, written since the centuries immediately following Philo, displays a variety of models as to the relations between the divine attributes, and between them and God. However, important as those attributes are, they are much more a part of an exegetical enterprise, part of the effort of reorganizing knowledge by complex processes of interpretation and reinterpretation, than a topical approach that organizes those models, or a metaphysical approach that clarifies the ontological status of those attributes and their functions, or an attempt to understand the psychology of God, as Daniel Abrams proposed.[66] The absence of the topical type of arrangments is evidence in the brief comments that express all the models, that differ from the systematic treatment of important topics in Greek philosophy, for example, or of Halakhic issues in Rabbinic literature. Neither do I assume that a metaphysics or a unifying ontology transpire beyond the conceptual diversity of those various models. As to the psychology of God, it seems that the Rabbis were relatively indifferent to this subject-matter as they were to the psychology of the human beings, if this is understood as detached from modes of activity. This is obviously different from the Greek philosophical attempts to investigate the structure of human psyche, especially in Plato and Aristotle.

The term *middot,* that is translated here when related to God as divine attributes, namely divine ways of acts – not just a discussion of God's nature – is a multivalent term in Rabbinic literature, both Talmudic and Midrashic, and it occurs also in *Sefer Yetzirah,* as we shall see later, and in several instances in the Heikhalot literature, though the two attributes do not play any significant role in the latter corpus.[67] It refers in those bodies of literature to as disparate topics like the thirteen or thirty-two methods of interpretation of the biblical

66 "Chapters from an Emotional and Sexual Biography of God." See also ben Sasson-Halbertal, "The Divine Name YHVH and the Measure of Mercy," p. 69.

67 See, e.g., *Synopse zur Hekhalot-Literatur,* eds. P. Schaefer et al. (Tübingen, 1981), paragraph 102, pp. 48–49 = (*Heikhalot Rabbati*). For all the occurrences of the term *middah* see *Konkordanz zur Hekhalot Literatur,* ed. P. Schaefer et al. (Mohr/Siebeck, Tuebingen, 1988), pp. 404–405. See also Fishbane, 'The "Measures" of God's Glory," p. 69, Michael Schwarz, "Jewish Visionary Traditions in Rabbinic Literature," *Cambridge Companion to the Talmud and Rabbinic Literature,* eds., Ch. E. Fonrobert – M. Jaffe, (Cambridge University Press, Cambridge, 2007), p. 206, Schneider, *Scattered Traditions of Jewish Mysticism,* pp. 254–255 and the quote from a lost text of R. Nehemiah ben Shlomo's commentary on the divine name of 42 letters, extant in Abraham ben Azriel, *'Arugat ha-Bosem,* vol. 1, p. 39, and in a passage from the same R. Nehemiah's *Sefer ha-Navon,* ed. Dan, p. 125.

texts according to Rabbinic views,[68] to human ways of behavior,[69] or to measures in general.[70] Last but not least, and closer to the topic under scrutiny here, the Rabbis speak about thirteen attributes of compassion, a topic that attracted the special attention of Kabbalists. The divine *middot* were conceived to be the ultimate goal of imitation by humans, and in some few cases also of cleaving to them. [71]

Here we are concerned mainly with discussions dealing with the manner of divine actions, as related to two attributes: *middat ha-raḥamim* and *middat ha-din*, and the various interactions between these attributes. Though most probably there was another type of terminology that was earlier, designated as *middat ha-por'anut* and *middat ha-tov*, it is the former couple that was accepted in later Rabbinic literature and subsequently in Kabbalah.[72] The models to be described below are important not only for understanding the variegated nature of Rabbinic thought but also because they were well-known to medieval Kabbalists, and they served as the starting point of many of their speculations.[73] Though those models were adopted and adapted by

68 See, e.g., *'Avot de-Rabbi Nathan*, chapter 37, 8, ed. S. Schechter, (rpr. Yad ben Zvi, Jerusalem, New York, 1997), p. 110.

69 *'Avot*, V:7.

70 See especially the Talmudic treatise *Middot*.

71 For the thirteen *middot* see Exodus 34:6–7, and for the Kabbalists see, e.g., the treatises on this topic by R. Asher ben David, see Gottlieb, *The Kabbalah in the Writings of R. Bahya ben Asher ibn Halawa*, pp 91–94, and the Pseudo-Hai Gaon epistle, referred below in chapter 8, R. Moshe de Leon, R. Joseph Gikatilla, as well as the Zoharic discussions, all those in the 13th century. See, especially, Afterman, *Devequt*, pp. 34–35.

72 See Marmorstein, *The Old Rabbinic Doctrine of God*, pp. 44–48. For the other discussions in late antiquity of compassion alone see Christoph Markschies, "Compassion: Some Remarks on Concepts of Divine and Human Compassion in Antiquity," *Proceedings of the Israel Academy of Sciences and Humanities*, vol. 8 (Jerusalem, 2002–2014) pp. 91–104.

73 See, especially, the view of Max Kadushin, who considered the divine *middot* as the two out of what he considers to be the four value-concepts in Rabbinic thought. Cf. his *The Rabbinic Mind*, (Global Academic Publishing, New York, 2001), pp. 15, 201–222. See also Martin Buber's view analyzed by Max

Kabbalists, they have rarely been discussed as a separate issue as a whole in scholarship in this field.A more detailed survey will serve the better understanding of the nature of the emerging Kabbalah as different combinations between those models and additional forms of literatures.

Let me suggest the existence of five main and distinct models, dealing with intra-divine situations and processes that are salient for the emergence of many discussions of early Kabbalists. The following typology is not an exhaustive one, since it deals solely with recurring types of relationship between the two attributes. Obviously much of the scattered numerous discussions in Talmud and Midrash have not been addressed in the present framework.

A] The mixture of the two attributes, expressed by using forms of the verb *MZG*. According to a widespread parable in Midrashic literature, God wanted to create the world by means of each of the two attributes, but the world could not bear the presence of the unmitigated acts of either of them alone. This is the reason why God mixed those attributes as two liquids, one hot and one cold, which are poured in a cup, and thus the world has been created.[74] The assumption was that the first intended attempt was done by resorting to the attribute of judgment, since only the name *'Elohim*, the name for that attribute,

Brod, "Judaism and Christianity in Buber's Work," in eds. P.A. Schilpp – M. Friedman, *The Philosophy of Martin Buber*, (La Salle, IL., – London: Open Court, Cambridge U.P. 1967), pp. 335–336, Liebes, "De Natura Dei," pp. 251–278, Fishbane, 'The "Measures" of God's Glory," Idel, *Kabbalah: New Perspectives*, pp. 114, 129–135, "Interpretations of the Secret of Incest in Early Kabbalah," pp. 102–104, and my *Absorbing Perfections*, pp. 228–229. Of special interest is the rarer enigmatic Talmudic discussion in *BT Berakhot*, fol. 27b, and *Hagigah* fol. 12a, where the *middah* of day and that of night are related to prayer, and they should be combined in order to prevent a theological dualism. This statement has been quoted many times by Kabbalists. See also Vajda, *Le commentaire*, pp. 108–109, 113 116, 293–294, 296, 304, for R. Ezra of Gerona's discussion of the topic. See also, e.g., in the texts referred below in nn. 86, 394.

74 *Genesis Rabbah'* 12:15, ed. Theodor-Albeck, pp. 112–113, Abrams, "Chapters from an Emotional and Sexual Biography of God," pp. 271–272.

occurs in the first chapter of Genesis. This understanding of Genesis 1:1, is of outmost importance for some concepts of primordial evil, as we shall see in the appendix. This parable was known already in Philo of Alexandria, as shown by Shlomo Naeh,[75] and may have had some sources in Greek – Platonic and Homeric – sources, as proposed by Yehuda Liebes.[76] The underlying assumption is that it is possible to diluate the extreme nature of each of the attrbutes by their mixture, and the question of cooperation between the attributes is not relevant in this model. We shall have more to say about this model in chapter 10 and in the appendix.

B] The cooperation between the two distinct attributes. According to a similar approach to [A], God wanted to create the world by means of the attribute of judgment but, understanding that it cannot stand it, He preceded to it the attribute of compassion and created by the means of both of them.[77] This is again an exegetical move, that interprets the biblical verses where the divine names *YHWH 'Elohim* occur together and are connected to an act of creation. Those verses are understood to constitute the second attempt to create the world after what has been written in Genesis 1, where only the name *'Elohim* occurs, as if referring to the attempt to create solely by means of the attribute of judgment:

> "R. Hananyah[78] said: when the Holy One, blessed be He, wanted to create His world, He took as partners the two attributes and created it, as it is said [Genesis 2:4], "In the day YHWH 'Elohim

75 "Philo and the Rabbis on the Powers of God," and see also his 'The Attribute of Judgment and the Attribute of Mercy in Rabbinic Thought', p. 62.

76 See his "De Natura Dei," p. 266, *Studies in Jewish Myth*, pp. 27–28.

77 See Abrams, "Chapters from an Emotional and Sexual Biography of God," pp. 275–277.

78 According to other sources it is R. Hanina'. See, e.g., the version found in *Pesiqta' Rabbati*, chapter 40, ed. M. Ish-Shalom (rpr., Tel Aviv, 1963), fol. 166b, where also the creation of Adam is described as the cooperation of the two attributes. See also R. Abraham ben Azriel, *'Arugat ha-Bosem*, ed. Urbach, vol. III, pp. 313 459, 508.

made earth and heaven," and so too in the case of Adam [Genesis 2:6], 'and YHWH 'Elohim created man.'"[79]

The important verb here is *ShTF,* which implies some form of cooperation imposed on the two attributes, not their entering a process in which they are dissolved into an entity, the third liquid that obliterates the independent nature of the two attributes. In other words, the occurrences of the two divine names in biblical texts together as being involved in an act of creation, required an explanation, and the Rabbis resorted to the theme of coordination of the two attributes in order to explain the significance of the two divine names.

In my opinion, this model implies also some correspondence between the two attributes and two hands, which should cooperate in an action in order to be accomplished. In a view attributed to R. Yehudah ha-Nasi', the editor of the Mishnah, God extends his hand in order to receive repentants from the hand of the attribute of judgment.[80] As suggested by Yehuda Liebes, this may be an allusion

79 *Yalqut Shime'oni,* on Psalms 119, par. 877:

אמר ר׳ חנניה: כשבקש הקב״ה לבראות את עולמו שתף שתי המדות ובראו שנאמר ׳ביום עשות ה׳ אלהים ארץ ושמים׳, וכן לאדם ׳וייצר ה׳ אלהים את האדם.׳

See also *Midrash Yelamdenu,* as printed in *Batei Midrashot,* eds. Sh. A. and A.J. Wertheimer, (Mossad ha-Rav Kook, Jerusalem, 1950), vol. I, p. 141, R. Moshe ha-Darshan, *Midrash Bereshit Rabbati,* ed., Ch. Albeck (Mekize Nirdamim, Jerusalem, 1940), p. 37, and R. Abraham ben Azriel, *'Arugat ha-Bosem,* ed. Urbach, vol. III, p. 313 n. 90. For another instance of resorting to the sequal of these two names as if reflecting the two attributes see ibidem, p. 358. See also the quote in the name of Midrash *Bereshit Rabbah',* adduced in R. Jacob ben Sheshet, *Meshiv Devarim Nekhoḥim,* ed. Vajda, p. 156 and see also ibidem, p. 115.

80 *BT Pesahim,* fol. 119a:

אמר רבי שמעון בן לקיש משום רבי יהודה נשיאה: מאי דכתיב [יחזקאל א:ח] ׳וידי אדם מתחת כנפיהם ׳ידו כתיב זה ידו של הקב״ה שפרוסה תחת כנפי החיות כדי לקבל בעלי תשובה מיד מדת הדין.

See also the poem of R. Amitai ben Shefatyah, printed in *Megillat Aḥimaaz,* ed. B. Klar, (Jerusalem, 1974), p. 100 and for earlier material see Schneider, *The Appearance of the High Priest,* p. 151.

to two hands of God and might have an impact on a discussion in the *Book of Bahir* and on theosophical Kabbalah in general.[81]

This model is much better represented in Kabbalistic literatures than [A], especially the schools of Rabad's and Nahmanides, as we shall see in the following chapters. These two models are predicated on the decisive divine intervention that combines the activities of the attributes in one way or another in order to be capable to create a world that subsists, or of Adam. The sovereignity of the divine *vis-a-vis* the attributes are evident, unlike the situation in another case, as discussed in model [E1–2] below.

C] The shift of the activity that is characteristic to the nature of one attribute to that of the other. This change is assumed originally because of an exegetical problem: given the assumption that the Tetragrammaton represents the attribute of compassion and 'Elohim that of judgment, some stark contradictions of these correlations and the content of some biblical texts emerge. So, for example, when describing the destruction of the two famous sinful cities in the Bible it is written: 'Then the Tetragrammaton rained upon Sodom and upon Gomorrah.[Genesis 19:24]' This has been interpreted in a Rabbinic source as follows: 'The Tetragrammaton rained' [means that] He passed from one attribute to another attribute.[82] This is a relatively rare model in Rabbinic sources but nevertheless represented in several Kabbalistic sources.[83] Though less explicit, also in this case the divinity is conceived of as implied actively in the process.

81 Liebes, "De Natura Dei," p. 270, *Studies in Jewish Myth*, pp. 32–33. See also Schneider, "The Myth of the Satan in the *Book of Bahir*," pp. 311–312 and Livie M. Teugels, *Aggadat Bereshit*, (Brill, Boston, 2001), p. 88 n. 349. See also the image of God holding the attribute of justice in his hand, probably the left one, in the poem of Yannai to be discussed later in this chapter and in the late medieval R. Abraham ben Azriel, *Arugat ha-Bosem*, ed. Urbach, vol. III, p. 354. See also R. Todros ha-Levi Abulafia, *Sha'ar ha-Razim*, ed. Kushnir-Oron, p. 123.

82 See *Pesiqta de-R. Kahana'*, ed. S. Buber, (rpr. Jerusalem, 1963), fols. 162a, 164a, *PT, Ta'anit*, fol. 65b, Marmorstein, *The Old Rabbinic Doctrine of God*, p. 44 n. 14, Liebes, "De Natura Dei," p. 267, *Studies in Jewish Myth*, p. 28.

83 See the view of Rabad discussed in the next chapter and R. Asher's *Sefer*

D] The inclusion of an aspect of one of the attributes by the other. My assumption is that this is a certain type of interpretation of the verse in Habaquq 3:2: "In wrath remember mercy." For the time being, the most explicit instance in late antiquity is found in Ephrem the Syrian.[84] Most probably the Christian author reflects an earlier Jewish approach to the nature of the attributes perhaps similar to one alluded in *BT Berakhot*, fol. 27b, where two *middot* are related to God, and the one related to day, "the measure of day" should be recited during night and vice-versa.[85] Even more so since in the Kabbalistic literature, especially in Nahmanides and his school, this model is found many times in a rather explicit manner, and since we find such views also in Ashkenazi

ha-Yiḥud, cf., *Asher ben David*, ed. Abrams, pp. 52, 61, 63, 77, R. Jacob ben Sheshet, *Sefer ha-'Emunah ve-ha-Bitaḥon*, chs. 2, 16 in *Kitvei ha-Ramban*, vol. II, pp. 358, 400, R. Todros ha-Levi Abulafia, *Sha'ar ha-Razim*, ed. Kushnir-Oron p. 101, R. Menahem Recanati, *Commentary on the Pentateuch*, fols. 25ab, 50d, in my *Kabbalah: New Perspectives*, p. 340 note 186, and Wolfson, *Language, Eros, Being*, pp. 60, 445 n. 98 as well as in the Ashkenazi literature to be discussed later on in this chapter.

84 See Naeh, "Philo and the Rabbis on the Powers of God," p. 91 n. 5. See also Abrams, "Chapters from an Emotional and Sexual Biography of God," pp. 272–273.

85 For affinities between the Christian author and Jewish themes see especially the very important article of Nicolas Sed, "Les hymnes sur le paradis de Saint Ephrem et les traditions juives," *Le Museon*, vol. 81 (1968), pp. 455–501; Ephrem the Syrian, *Hymns*, tr. Kathleen E. McVey, (Paulist Press, New York, Mahwah, 1989), pp. 211, 248 note 130, 262 note 6: Wolfson, *Along the Path*, pp. 193 note 17; 195–196 note 23, Tryggve Kronholm, *Motifs from Genesis 1–11 in the Genuine Hymns of Ephrem the Syrian, with particular reference to the influence of Jewish exegetical tradition* (CWK Gleerup, Lund, 1978), pp. 154–163, Kister, "The Manifestations of God," pp. 120–124, 131–132, 136–138, Jean Danielou, "Terre et Paradise chez les peres de l'Eglise," *Eranos-Jahrbuch*, vol. XXII (1953), pp. 434–442, and M. Idel, "Adam and Enoch According to St. Ephrem the Syrian," *Kabbalah*, vol. 6 (2001), pp. 167–218 and see above in a discussion of Philo, beside n. 62. See also ben-Sasson – Halbertal, "The Divine Name YHVH and the Measure of Mercy," pp. 61–62. See also above n. 74 and the important analysis of Naeh, "He does Peace and Creates Everything," pp. 297–298.

authors[86] and in a discussion of R. Abraham Abulafia.[87] Close to this model are some statements found in Midrash as to the fact that the two attributes operate at the same time in different ways, and this mode of activity is designated as *du-partzufin*. In these texts, the term *du-partzufin* relates to the twofold nature of the divine voice.[88] This is a very important and quite clear connection between this anthropomorphic concept as related to God and the divine attributes.

This model differs from the preceding one, since it assumes that the opposite quality is found within each of the attributes, while model [C] assumes the need of a transformation of one attribute into another.

E] Last, but certainly nor least, from the point of view of influence on Kabbalah by Rabbinic views of attributes: The possibility of the ritual to affect the relationship between the divine attributes, which means that the human actions count more than the divine one. This aspect may be designated as theurgy in the manner I define this concept,[89]

86 See R. Abraham ben Azriel, *'Arugat ha-Bosem*, ed. Urbach, vol. II, p. 225, ibidem, vol. III, pp. 416, 459. Compare also to a Midrash on Jonah, printed in *'Aggudat 'Aggadot*, p. 35.

87 See *Mafteaḥ ha-Shemot*, p. 56. See also *Sefer ha-Tzeruf*, an anonymous book from his circle, ed. A. Gross, (Jerusalem, 2004), p. 87.

88 See *Leviticus Rabbah'* chapter I, ed. M. Margaliot, (Jerusalem, 1972), p. 26; *Midrash Exodus Rabbah*, ed. A. Shinan, (Jerusalem – Tel Aviv, 1984), p. 160. See the use of the word *parsopa* by the Syrian theologian John the Solitary. According to A. de Halleux, this term "applique à la maniere d'etre et d'agir du Saveur": see his "Jean le Solitaire," *Le Museon*, vol. 94 (1981), p. 10. This Midrash has been quoted by R. Ezra of Gerona in his *Commentary on Talmudic Legends*, Ms. Vatican 294, fol. 33b. See also R. Azriel of Gerona, *Commentary on the Talmudic Legends*, ed. Tishby, p. 86.

89 See, e.g., Idel, *Kabbalah: New Perspectives*, pp. 173–199, "Some Remarks on Ritual and Mysticism," "From Structure to Performance: On the Divine Body and Human Action in the Kabbalah," *Mishqafayim* vol. 32 (1998), pp. 3–6 (Hebrew), idem, *Absorbing Perfections*, pp. 3, 13, 31, 60, 67, 73–74 etc, idem, *Ascensions on High*, pp. 7, 11, 16–18, 68, 114–115, 120–121, etc., idem, "On the Performing Body in Theosophical-Theurgical Kabbalah: Some Preliminary Remarks," *The Jewish Body: Corporeality, Society, and Identity in the Renaissance*

which is combined here with some form of theosophy, based on the assumption of the existence of a more complex divine realm and the possibility of interaction with powers that constitute it. This model has two variants [E1] and [E2]. Though there is a common denominator between them and [C], given the transformation of one attribute into another, the theurgical emphasis in the models [E] is quintessential though it is absent in [C].

The Rabbinic model [E2] anticipates views found in the *Book of Bahir* – an issue to be discussed in the next chapter – and the much more complex discussions in the main line of medieval Kabbalah I propose to call "the theosophical-theurgical." In this model, in both variants [E1] and [E2], the supreme sovereignty of God versus His attributes has been mitigated or even obliterated. In Rabbinic sources this model is represented by two main versions: One claims that by means of blessing it is possible to affect the relation between the attributes, the other speaks about the reversal of one attribute into its opposite because of an act of a righteous one. In both cases the virtuosi are assumed to be capable to dramatically affect the manner in which the attributes interact or operate.

Lets start with the first version, to be referred to as [E1]: A rather undefined entity designated as *'Akkatriel Yah Tzeva'ot,* plausible a reference to God, tells the Higher Priest officiating in the Holy of the Holies:

and Early Modern Period, eds. G. Veltri and M. Diemling. (Brill, Leiden, 2008), pp. 251–271, idem, "Some Remarks on Ritual and Mysticism," pp. 111–130, especially pp. 23–25, idem, *Enchanted Chains*, pp. 33–34, 47, 215–220; idem, "On the Identity of the Authors of Two Ashkenazi Commentaries," as well as Mopsik, *Les Grands textes de la Cabale*, Brody, Human Hands Dwell in Heavenly Heights, Lorberboim, *Image of God, Halakhah and Aggadah*, Garb, *Manifestations of Power in Jewish Mysticism*, passim, Elliot R. Wolfson, "Mystical-Theurgical Dimensions of Prayer in *Sefer ha-Rimmon, Approaches to Judaism in Medieval Times*, vol. III (1988), pp. 41–80, Afterman, *Devequt*, pp. 43–47, and Maurizio Mottolese, *Dio nel giudaismo rabbinico. Immagini e mito* (Morcelliana, Brescia, 2010).

> "Ishma'el, My son[90], bless Me! I replied: 'May it be Thy will that Thy [attribute of] compassion descend on[91] Thy [attribute of] anger, and Thy compassion overflow over Thy attributes, mayest Thou deal with Thy children according to the attribute of compassion and mayest Thou, on their behalf, stop short of the limit of strict justice.' And He nodded to me with His head."[92]

On the very same page of the Talmud, an important Rabbinic figure, R. Yohanan, reports in the name of R. Yosei ben Zimra, the following question:

> "From where do we know that God says prayers? From the verse [Psalms 56:7] "Even them will I bring to My Holy mountain, and I delighted them in the house of My prayer." [In the verse] it is not written "in the house of their prayer" but "My prayer". Hence the Holy One, blessed be He, says prayers. What does He pray? Mar

90 This phrase is characteristic of God's speaking to other figures in Rabbinic literature. See my *Ben*, pp. 130–155.

91 ויגולו Compare to the verse of R. Shlomo ha-Bavli, 10th century Italy, ed. E. Fleisher, *The Poems of Shelomo ha-Bavli*, (Jerusalem, 1973), p. 294: גלגל מדותיך "You should cause your attributes to circulate." See also below chapter 3.

92 *BT Berakhot*, fol. 7a:

תניא: אמר רבי ישמעאל בן אלישע: פעם אחת נכנסתי להקטיר קטורת לפני ולפנים, וראיתי אכתריאל יה ה׳ צבאות שהוא יושב על כסא רם ונשא ואמר לי: ישמעאל בני, ברכני! אמרתי לו: יהי רצון מלפניך שיכבשו רחמיך את כעסך ויגולו רחמיך על מדותיך ותתנהג עם בניך במדת הרחמים ותכנס להם לפנים משורת הדין. ונענע לי בראשו.

On this passage see Urbach, "The Traditions about Merkabah Mysticism," pp. 21–22, Scholem, *Jewish Gnosticism*, pp. 51–55; Liebes, *Studies in Jewish Myth*, pp. 10–11; idem, "De Natura Dei," pp. 252–253, Green, *Keter*, pp. 62–63, Baer, "The Service of Sacrifice," pp. 134–135, Mopsik, *Les grands textes*, p. 57; Nathaniel Deutsch, *Guardians of the Gate, Angelic Vice-Regency in Late Antiquity* (Brill, Leiden, 1999), pp. 58–59, Idel, *Kabbalah: New Perspectives*, pp. 164–165, *Enchanted Chains*, pp. 167–168, *Ben*, p. 124, Garb, *Manifestations of Power*, p. 36, Fishbane, *Biblical Myth and Rabbinic Mythmaking*, p. 125, R. Azriel of Gerone, *Commentary on Talmudic Legends*, ed. Tishby, p. 9. Compare also to R. Abraham ben Azriel, *'Arugat ha-Bosem*, ed. Urbach, vol. III p. 322 and the interesting parallel cited in Schneider, *The Appearance of the High Priest*, p. 313.

Zutra' bar Tobias said in the name of Rav: "Let it be that My [attribute of] compassion will suppress My [attribute of] anger, and My compassion will overflow My attributes [*middotai*] and I shall act regarding My sons by means of the attribute of compassion, and on their behalf, stop short of the limit of [strict] justice.""[93]

Here again, the attributes are imagined as some form of independent entities that even God has to pray to them. The verb translated in the last two passages as "overflow" is *Yigolu*, – a rare form in Rabbinic literature – which may be understood as the descent of a higher power over the other attributes, and their conquest, especially that of anger, which was considered to be an attribute of the divinity. "Justice" translates in the last two quotes the Hebrew term *din* that is used together with the term attribute in the phrase "the attribute of judgment." Here it is not the cooperation between the two divine attributes that is the ideal type of behavior, like in model [B] but the overcoming of the judgment by compassion. It should be mentioned that in a similar context in Rabbinic literature, the verb *Glgl* is used.[94] The formulation used in the passage: the attribute of compassion versus other attributes in the plural, shows that the divine attributes were more than two, a question that will be addressed.

Another important version of the theurgical model, to be referred in the continuation as [E2] assumes that the righteous are capable, especially by their prayers, to convert the attribute of judgement into that of compassion, while the wicked are capable, because of their sins, to convert the attribute of compassion into that of judgment.[95]

93 *BT Berakhot*, fol. 7a. מאי מצלי? אמר רב זוטרא בר טוביה אמר רב: יהי רצון מלפני שיכבשו רחמי את כעסי, ויגולו רחמי על מידותי, ואתנהג עם בני במדת רחמים, ואכנס להם לפנים משורת הדין.

94 See *BT Pesahim*, fol. 87a.

95 Cf., *Genesis Rabbah*, ed. Theodor-Albeck XXXIII:3, p. 308, LXXX:3, p. 847, *Numbers Rabbah´* X:5, ben Sheshet, *Meshiv Devarim Nekhohim*, ed. Vajda, pp. 155–156, R. Abraham ben Azriel, *'Arugat ha-Bosem*, ed. Urbach, vol. III, p. 439, R. Todros ha-Levi Abulafia, *Sha'ar ha-Razim*, ed. Kushnir-Oron p. 101,

This is a widespread model that left its strong impact on Jewish literature in general. In some of its formulations, it speaks about the transformation of the attribute of judgment to that of compassion by blowing the Shofar on *Rosh ha-Shanah*.[96] The particular importance of this model consists in the explicit conjugation between concepts of divine attributes and liturgical and other acts, performed either by the human or by the divine, as interdependent.

This seminal concatenation is a cardinal nexus that has been elaborated in the main line of Kabbalistic literature. Its recurrence in Kabbalistical literature has much to do with the models described above, though there are also additional Rabbinic sources for the Kabbalistic treatments, especially those dealing with strengthening and diminishing the divine power found on high. However, there is no major difference between midrashic and Kabbalistic theurgy: both assume the centrality of human acts, especially of the Rabbinic rituals, and the response of the divine system to those acts, though the Rabbinic system is scant in comparison to the Kabbalistic luxuriant theosophy. We can conclude that a certain stream of thought about the significance of the commandments, especially prayer, rooted in Midrashic and Talmudic texts, was elaborated upon in the theosophical Kabbalah, which regarded theurgical activity as the main *raison d'etre* of the commandments.[97] Let me point out that the coexistence

Gavarin, "The Concept of Evil," p. 38, Liebes, "De Natura Dei," pp. 267–268, Fishbane, *Biblical Myth and Rabbinic Mythmaking*, p. 100, Idel, "Interpretations of the Secret of Incest in Early Kabbalah," p. 104, nn. 78–79, ben-Sasson–Halbertal, "The Divine Name YHVH and the Measure of Mercy," p. 56, and Porat, "*Founding of the Circle*", p. 130.

96 For a list of Midrashic sources and discussions found in early medieval Jewish poetry and Ashkenazi views see Wolfson, *Along the Path*, pp. 52–59 and the accompanying endnotes and now in the Midrash printed by Ya'aqov Yisrael Stal, "Derashah shel Rosh ha-Shanah we-Nussaḥ Ḥadash shel 'Midrash Mah Rabbu' le-Rosh ha-Shanah," *Moriah*, vol. 34 (2015), pp. 23–24 (Hebrew). See also below chapter 6.

97 See my *Kabbalah: New Perspective*, p. 166.

of a variety of models is a natural situation in Rabbinic literature, which cannot be envisioned as a compact type of Judaism.

The differences between the five models are rather clear despite the scant treatments that characterize Rabbinic theological issues. Nevertheless, I propose not to see in them a result of inner polemics between Rabbis but exegetical efforts to make sense of biblical passages and rituals, like prayer, much less attempts to build up systematic theologies.

It should be pointed out that the two attributes were often times regarded as hypostases, sometimes having some form of seats, like in the following discussion:

> "One passage says [Daniel 7:9]: "His throne was fiery flames" and another passage says: [ibidem.] "Until thrones were placed; and One that was Ancient of days did sit" – there is no contradiction; One [throne] for Him and one for David: this is the view of R. Akivah. Said R. Yossi the Galilean to him: Akivah, how long will you profane the *Shekhinah*? Rather, one for justice and one for mercy [*tzedaqah*]. Did he accept [this explanation] from him, or did he not accept it? Come and hear: One for justice and one for compassion; this is the view of R. Akivah."[98]

The assumption that thrones are occupied by the two attributes shows that the latter were conceived of as superior to angels, and only

98 *BT Ḥagigah*, fol. 14a:
כתוב אחד אומר 'כרסיה שביבין דינור' וכתוב אחד אומר 'עד די כרסון רמיו ועתיק יומין יתיב' לא קשיא: אחד לו ואחד לדוד כדתניא אחד לו ואחד לדוד דברי רבי עקיבא. אמר לו רבי יוסי הגלילי: עקיבא, עד מתי אתה עושה שכינה חול, אלא אחד לדין ואחד לצדקה. קיבלה מיניה או לא קיבלה מיניה? תא שמע: אחד לדין ואחד לצדקה דברי רבי עקיבא.
Daniel Boyarin, "Beyond Judaisms: Metatron and the Divine Polymorphy of Ancient Judaism," *Journal for the Study of Judaism*, vol. XLI, (2010), pp. 323–365, idem, "Once Again: "Two Dominions in Heaven," pp. 95–98, Rowland – Morray-Jones, *The Mystery of God*, pp. 110, 542. See also R. Todros Abulafia, *Sha'ar ha-Razim*, ed. Kushnir-Oron, pp. 94–95, Travis, *Rabbi Ezra of Gerona*, pp. 53, – discussing R. Ezra's commenrary on the Song of Songs, p. 498, and Schneider, *The Appearance of the High Priest*, p. 307.

one of them, Metatron, has been described as possessing a throne.[99] This approach to the attributes is in line with the semi-independent status we have seen in some of the models above, especially in [E1]. That of the attribute of justice is sometimes arguing against humans before God, in a manner reminiscent of Satan, is a common view in Rabbinic thought, though humans are capable to counteract or silence it.[100]

This hypostatic status of the attributes is conspicuous in a relatively late Rabbinic text, that is seminal for understanding of the development of the theory of *Middot* in Kabbalah:

> "There are seven attributes that serve before the throne of the Glory. These are they: Wisdom; Righteousness and Justice; Mercy and Compassion; Truth and Peace – as it is said, 'And I will betrothe you to Me for ever; and I will betrothe you to Me with righteousness and with justice, and with mercy and with compassion; and I will betrothe you to Me with truth; and you will know the Lord' (Hoshea 2:21– 22). R. Meir says: What can the verse 'and you will know the Lord' mean, except to teach that every man who has all these attributes within himself knows the knowledge of the Omnipresent One."[101]

99 See also below in this chapter the text from the anonymous *Sefer ha-Ḥokhmah*. The theme of God as a judge that sits on seats in order to judge is rather widespread in Rabbinic literature and the liturgy of the High Holidays. See, e.g., the Midrash on Jonah, printed in *'Aggudat Aggadot*, pp. 21, 35.

100 See *BT Shabbat*, fol. 55a, discussed in Liebes, "De Natura Dei," pp. 268–269, *BT Sanhedrin*, fol. 94a, R. Abraham ben Azriel, *'Arugat ha-Bosem*, IV, p. 75, and Schneider, *Scattered Traditions of Jewish Mysticism*, p. 184.

101 *'Avot de-Rabbi Nathan*, chapter 37, 8: ed. S. Schechter, (rpr. Yad ben Zvi, Jerusalem, New York, 1997), p. 110:

שבע מדות שמשמשות לפני כסא הכבוד אלו הן חכמה, צדק ומשפט, חסד ורחמים, אמת ושלום שנא׳ (הושע ב 21-22):׳וארשתיך לי לעולם וארשתיך לי בצדק ובמשפט ובחסד וברחמים וארשתיך לי באמונה וידעת את ה׳. ר״מ אומר מה ת״ל וידעת את ה׳ אלא מלמד שכל אדם שיש בו כל מדות הללו יודע דעתו של מקום.

On this passage see Scholem, *Origins of the Kabbalah*, p. 82, Fishbane, 'The "Measures" of God's Glory," pp. 67–69, Wolfson, 'The Theosophy of Shabbetai

We may distinguish here some form of pleromatic structure, composed of the biblical terms, arranged, so it seems in three dyads, and the first attribute standing alone, probably above them. Though the seven attributes are presented as serving before the throne, their knowledge by man is tantamount also to knowledge of God. Implicitly some form of affinity between seven attributes and the nature of God has been articulated.

Other instances where seven *middot* have been mentioned in Rabbinic literature deal with the creations of the world.[102] So, for example, it is said that the seven pillars upon which the divine *Hokhmah* built her house, interpreting Proverbs 9:1, are the seven *middot* of God, probably a parallel to the Hebrew plural form, *Ḥokhmot*, in the biblical verse.[103]

It is evident that seven *middot* have been adopted later on as a significant theological unit in order to refer to the lower seven divine powers in the decadic structure of *sefirot* in both Kabbalah and 18th century Hasidism. Sporadically, also other entities are depicted in Rabbinic literature as hypostatic and as a *middah*, like *berakhah*, blessing, for example.[104]

Let me speculate about the possibility that such a list of seven attributes, could have been combined with the assumption as to the existence of three other attributes, that deal with noetic operations, already found in a Midrash that will be analyzed in chapter 10, and thus generate a view as to the existence of ten divine *middot*, which was the trigger for the list of ten *middot* found in the *Book of Bahir*, as we shall see in the next chapter. Also the plurality of the *middot* in model [E1]

Donnolo," pp. 286–287, 308 n. 67, and Rowland-Morray-Jones, *The Mystery of God*, pp. 548–549. For the earlier theories of seven serving angels before the throne see, e.g., Scholem, ibidem, p. 346 and n. 293. For the symbolism of seven divine powers see Vajda, *Le commentaire*, pp. 352–363.

102 "Interpretations of the Secret of Incest in Early Kabbalah," pp. 102–103.

103 *Yalqut Shime'oni*, on Proverbs, chapter 9 paragraph 943. Compare to *BT Sanhedrin*, fol. 38a, where the term *middotav*, His attributes, does not occur.

104 See *Devarim Rabbah*, ed. S. Liebermann, (Wahrman, Jerusalem, 1974), third edition, p. 228.

may encourage such a reading. In any case, a variety of decads related to the creation of the world have been known since late antiquity in Rabbinic and literatures that are cognate to Judaism.[105]

In a quote in the name of a Midrash cited by the late 13th century Kabbalist R. Todros ha-Levi Abulafia, whose precise source in the Midrashic literature cannot be identified for the time being[106], we read as follows:

> "R. Jacob said: 'We found in the Pentateuch, in the Prophets and in the Hagiography that the Holy One, blessed be He, mentions justice [*Mishpat*], and then He situated *Ḥesed* on one side, and the *Tzedaqah* on the other side. Why did He do so? Because it is harsh. Where is it found in the Pentateuch? [Genesis 18:19] 'For I know him etc., until that which has spoken to him'[107]. What did He speak to him? This is *Ḥesed*, since it is written [Micah 7:20], 'Thou wilt show truth to Ya'aqov, mercy to Abraham etc.,' Where it is found in the prophets? [Jeremiah 9:23]: 'And I am the Lord who exercises mercy, justice and righteousness, on the earth.' Where is it in Hagiography? As it is written [Psalms 89:15]: 'Righteousness and justice are the foundation of Thy throne. Mercy and truth go before Thee.' End of quotation."[108]

105 See my *Kabbalah: New Perspectives*, pp. 112–122, idem, "On the Theosophy at the Beginning of Kabbalah," idem, "Sefirot Above Sefirot," and Assi Farber-Ginnat, ed., *R. Moshe de Leon's Commentary on the Merkavah*, (Cherub Press, Los Angeles, 1998), p. 33 n. 10.

106 The systematic reliance on the three types of scriptural sources is evident in a relatively late Midrash, written perhaps in the 10th century, *'Aggadat Bereshit*, ed. Sh. Buber, (Krakau, 1903), and see the translation of Livie M. Teugels, *Aggadat Bereshit*, (Brill, Boston, 2001), and more recently the study of Ezra Kahalani, *'Aggadat Bereshit* (Ph. D. Thesis, Hebrew University, Jerusalem, 2004), (Hebrew) but our quote is not found in the extant versions of this Midrash.

107 In the middle of the verse, in the part that was not quoted, it is written צדקה ומשפט "to do justice and judgment."

108 R. Todros ben Joseph ha-Levi Abulafia, *Sha'ar ha-Razim*, ed. Kushnir-Oron, p. 123:

The Midrashist is reflecting on the meaning of the recurrence of the pattern of *mishpat*, – justice, between mercy and righteousness. His assumption is that justice is harsh and should be mitigated by inserting it between two other modes of activities. Though the term *middah* is not mentioned at all, I see here a mode of thought that attempts to organize various verses by referring to a common conceptual structure. This structure may imply also some architectural pattern, with the three qualities arranged in a spacial order.

Interestingly enough the two attributes *din* and *tzedaqah*, recur in a late Midrash, apparently written in early Middle Ages, as part of what I would call an eminently correlative understanding of the attributes:

> "The Holy One blessed be He, said to Moses: Moses, tell to the children of Israel: 'my name is *'Ehyeh 'asher 'Ehyeh*, as you are present with me, so I am present with you. I have given to you two good attributes law and justice.[109] If they mete the law, should I not mete the law and emanate good things upon them. But if they do not mete the law, I shall mete the law and destroy the world. Likewise, in the case of *Tzedaqah*: if they open their hands and give [alms] I shall also open for them ... this is why the Holy One said: *'Ehyeh 'asher 'Ehyeh*, as you are present with me, I am present with you. So said David: [Psalms 121:5] 'God is your guardian, God is

מצאתי במדרש: ר׳ יעקב אומ׳ ומצינו בתורה ובנביאים ובכתובים שהקב״ה מזכיר את המשפט וסומך לו את החסד מכאן ואת הצדקה מכאן וכל כך למה? מפני שהוא קשה. בתורה מניין ׳כי ידעתיו וגו׳ עד אשר דבר עליו׳ מה דבר עליו? זה החסד שנא׳ ,׳תתן אמת ליעקב חסד לאברהם וגו׳ בנביאים מנין שנא׳ ׳כי אני יי׳ עושה חסד משפט וצדקה בארץ׳. בכתובים מנין שנא׳ ׳צדק ומשפט מכון כסאך חסד ואמת יקדמו פניך׳ ע״כ.

Compare also to the similar text found in the Cairo Genizah, printed in ed. Peter Schaefer, *Geniza-Fragmente zur Hekhalot-Literatur* (Mohr, Tuebingen, 1984), p. 133, and the discussion of Schneider, *Scattered Traditions of Jewish Mysticism*, pp. 254–255.

109 *Tzedeq*. However, on the basis of both the preceding and the following discussions it seems that the meaning is charity, *Tzedaqah*; see Jeremiah 9:24. See Bernard S. Jackson, "'Law' and 'Justice' in the Bible," *JJS*, vol. XLIX, 2 (1998), pp. 218–229. As charity, *Tzedaqah*, is conceptually closer to compassion.

> your shade on your right hand.' 'As your shade': Just as your shade, if you are laughing to it, it is laughing to you, if you weep to it, it is weeping to you, if you show to it an angry face, it reflects to you likewise, and if your face is welcoming, it also is so, just so the Holy One said, 'as you are present with Me, so I am present with you. This is why Israel must do justice."[110]

This is a fine example of the principle of "measure against measure" mentioned above, and to read this late Midrash literally it assumes more than two types of human behavior and divine response to it. In lieu of the remoteness of the deity the scholars assume, and of its reflection in symbols as the sole mode of perceiving it, I propose a much more correlational theology. My understanding of this term is less related to the presence of God and the dynamism of this presence in things, or to the birth of the new being, as is the case in Paul Tillich's existential theology of correlation, but the possibility of the reciprocal impact of God's and man's deeds on each other, depicted by using the theory of attributes.[111] The Midrash, and to a great extent some Kabbalists following it, was less concerned with the divine transcendence, in Neoplatonic or Gnostic terms, but in a reciprocal type of relationship. However, provided the importance of the rituals this reciprocity is based on a dynamic vision of both God and man as active entities. This move from the theological to the anthropological is obvious in the later stages of Jewish mysticism,

110 *Midrash We-Hizhir*, ed. Y.M. Freimann, (Leipzig, 1873), vol. 1, fol. 43a. See also Nahmanides's quotation from *Midrash 'Aggadah* in his *Commentary on the Pentateuch* to Exodus 3:14, and the significant remark of Menahem Kasher, *Torah Shelemah*, (New York, 1944), vol. 8, p. 153 note 188 (Hebrew) and for additional discussion of this type of correlative theology see Idel, *Representing God*, pp. 76–80 and Mopsik, *Les grands textes*, pp. 11, 35–37. My remarks here and elsewhere in my studies deal with what some few Rabbinic texts have to say, without any attempt to build up a Rabbinic comprehensive theology regarding theurgy. To be sure: I am not attempting to speak about God's need of man, as found in Abraham J. Heschel's books, which constitutes a more dialogical approach, between two types of personality. See also n. 37 above.

111 See my "On the Theologization of Kabbalah," p. 171.

especially 18th century Hasidism, and the understanding of its earlier phase is quintessential for a proper understanding of mai aspects of the phenomenology of Kabbalah.[112]

The existence of such a variety of models in Rabbinic literature considered to be canonical among most of the Kabbalists, encouraged attempts to elucidate their succinct formulations, to combine between some of them, and between them and other discussions of attributes, as found for example those from *Sefer Yetzirah*. Though some of them are rather complex, their existence in a literature that was understood as canonical, compelled some later authors to find out syntheses between them, contributing to the emergence of much greater complexities. Since the canonical status of the Rabbinic literature was much less consacrated than that of the Hebrew Bible, medieval authors, especially Kabbalists, felt free to melt together different Rabbinic discussions, and introduce also other material, from non-Jewish sources, creating thereby further complexities.

There are some affinities between the Rabbinic and the Philonic understandings of the attributes: in both cases they were major tools in the divine creation and the governance of this world. However, the Rabbinic models differ from what we have seen above in Philo, where the basic assumption is that the two powers cooperate without divine or human interventions. Neither do the former include the idea of inherent equality of the two attributes, as it is the case in the writings of the Alexandrian thinker. In other words, while it is possible to find a correlative theology in Rabbinic thought, it is difficult to discern a parallel to it in Philo's much more philosophical orientation, an issue that will be discussed again in another context in chapter 9 below. In other words, preeminently Philo's God is a cosmocrator, and his general religious outlook can be described as a propensity to a cosmic religion, while the Rabbinic one is conceiving God much more as a judge that reacts to the acts of the humans.

I distinguished above between the five main models without making any attempt to harmonize or blur the differences between

112 See also for Rabbinic literature Rosen-Zvi, *Demonic Desires*, p. 5.

them. This disparity is part of a culture that was concerned much more with organizing the communal religious life, especially the synchronic rituals, liturgy and some form of ethical behavior, rather than teaching sublime truths about God, nature, science or psychology. Within such a culture, divine attributes that address the function of the divinity rather than its substance, is quite natural.

Let me turn to the question of equality of the attributes in literatures written in the first millennium CE in Hebrew, which are not necessarily part of the Rabbinic corpus in the strict sense of the term. As already pointed out by Yizhak Baer, in poems of Yannay, a major poet writings in the fifth or sixth century in the land of Israel, the term *Shaweh* occurs several times.[113] Especially relevant for our discussions above and below is the verse found in a poem attributed to him, whose first line is "ha-'Ohez be-Yad Middat Mishpat." Toward the end of the poem that is dedicated entirely to the different qualities of God arranged in an alphabetical order, when dealing with qualities related to the letters *Qof, Reish* and *Shin*, the poet writes, according to a widespread English translation:

"All believe that He hardly gets angry
He is merciful and extends mercy
All believe that He is lightly appeased
He is just and heeds small and great alike."[114]

The first three lines deal with the divine quality of being angry though only for a short time, some parallel to the attribute of judgment, while

113 "The Service of Sacrifices," pp. 454–457.

114 *High Holyday Prayer Book*, tr. Phillip Birnbaum (Hebrew Publishing Company, New York, 1979), pp. 370–372:

הַקְצַר בְּזַעַם וּמַאֲרִיךְ אַף:
וְכֹל מַאֲמִינִים שֶׁהוּא קָשֶׁה לִכְעֹס:
הָרַחוּם וּמַקְדִּים רַחֲמִים לְרֹגֶז:
וְכֹל מַאֲמִינִים שֶׁהוּא רַךְ לִרְצוֹת:
הַשָּׁוֶה וּמַשְׁוֶה קָטֹן וְגָדוֹל:

See also Menachem Zulai, *Piyyutei Yanay*, (Berlin 1938), pp. 136–138 (Hebrew).

the second line deals openly with the divine compassion, and even with is not transparent in the English translation that compassion preceds the anger. The fourth line in Hebrew speaks about God being equal and equalizing. The two words are not explained, and the act of equalizing is related to small and great without any further qualification. Though lines 1–3 can be read together as complementing each other, I propose to separate them from the fourth line and not identify the small and the great as the two divine attributes mentioned beforehand, and leave the fourth verse in its obscurity, or perhaps if we can read it in the context of what is written later in the poem, as dealing with the role of God as a judge. In another instance the two cherubs in the Temple are described as equal, in the context of the service.[115]

However, as we shall see in chapter 7 this was not necessarily the way in which later Ashkenazi commentators understood these verses, who emphasized the issue of the two attributes. Let me emphasize the fact that *Shaweh* is a way to describe God also in another case in Yannay. In another poem God is described rather explicitly as such.[116] According to an anonymous commentary on a Piyyut of R. Eleazar Qallir, the two luminaries have been created as equal.[117] In a poem authored by a renown Ashkenazi poet, R. Shime'on ben Yitzhaq, – second part of the 10th century – God is portrayed as dividing the cosmic waters mentioned in Genesis 1:6, "in an equal manner."[118]

It seems that via the Palestinian *piyyutim*, the concept of equality between entities that are not human, arrived to Ashkenaz. Sometimes during the second third of the 13th century a neglected author in scholarship, known as R. Nehemiah ben Shlomo, known also as R.

115 *The Liturgical Poems of Rabbi Yanai*, ed. Rabinovitz, vol. 2, p. 339.

116 Ibidem, vol. 2, p. 97: הנקדש ושוה

117 See Efraim E. Urbach, "A Commentary on the Silluq of Eleazar Kalir for the Thora-Portion Shekalim, 'Then didst Thou see and count'," in eds., Sh. Abramson – A. Mirsky, *Hayyim (Jefim) Schirmann, Jubilee Volume* (Schocken, Jerusalem, 1970), p. 3: כשבראם הקב"ה שניה' שוין בראם

118 *Liturgical Poems of R. Shim'on bar Yṣḥaq*, ed. A.M. Haberman, (Schocken, Berlin,1938), p. 57: חצה המים בשוה

Troestlin and as the prophet of Erfurt.[119] He wrote a series of commentaries on a variety of earlier treatises dealing with various divine names and liturgical pieces most of them preserved in manuscripts in an anonymous manner. Inter alia, he commented also on Yannay's poem mentioned in chapter 2 above, which I edited recently with its variants.[120] In one of them he writes:

> "The Equal – in gematria ha-Qaftzi'el[121] and also in gematria we-Rapha'el.[122] One of them is the angel of judgment and the other is the angel of compassion.[123] And the Holy One, blessed be He, equalizes the small to the great, since the angel that is replete with compassion belittles himself and that [of judgment] is proud of his great stature, and this is [the reason] why He equalizes him."[124]

The equality referred here is predicated on the size of the bodies of the two angels, representing thereby some form of reverberation of the *Shi'ur Qomah* way of thought. Unlike the original poem, the commentator assumes an initial equality, then the differentiation

119 Idel, "Some Forlorn Writings of a Forgotten Ashkenazi Prophet: R. Nehemiah ben Shlomo ha-Navi'," *Jewish Quarterly Review* vol. 96 (2005), pp. 188–196, idem, "From Italy to Germany and Back, On the Circulation of Jewish Esoteric Traditions," *Kabbalah* vol. 14 (2006), pp. 47–94, "The Anonymous *Commentary on the Alphabet of Metatron* – An Additional Treatise of R. Nehemiah ben Shlomo the Prophet," *Tarbiz*, vol. 76 (2006), pp. 1–10 (Hebrew), "Incantations, Lists, and 'Gates of Sermons' in the Circle of R. Nehemiah ben Shlomo the Prophet – and Their Impact," *Tarbiz*, vol. 77 (2008), pp. 475–554 (Hebrew).

120 Idel, "The Commentaries of R. Nehemiah bar Shlomo to the Piyyut," pp. 165–202.

121 Perhaps it should be read *Qatzfi'el*, the angel of anger, in many earlier sources.

122 *Ha-shaweh = 316 = ha-Qaftzi'el = we-Rapha'el.*

123 See also the secret dealing with the two attributes, printed by Scholem, ed., *Mada'ei ha-Yahadut*, p. 280, attributed to R. Isaac ben Jacob ha-Kohen, where angels of compassion and judgment are mentioned. See also *R. Asher ben David, Complete Works*, ed. Abrams, p. 82.

124 Idel, "The Commentaries of R. Nehemiah bar Shlomo to the Piyyut," p. 182: השוו"ה - גי' הקפציא"ל וכן גי' ורפא"ל, והאחד מלאך דין והשני מלאך רחמים, והקב"ה משווה קטן לגדול כי המלאך מלא רחמים מקטין עצמו ואותו מתגאה בקומתו לכך משווהו

between the two angels, because of their different behavior, and finally a return to the initial equality by the divine intervention. However, it is evident that the couple of attributes, compassion and judgment, though not mentioned as such, nevertheless looms beyond the two angels. In another variant it is said that "He equalizes judgment and compassion in gematria Qaftzie'el and gematria Rapha'el, the small and the great."[125] This technique of transforming a variety of words in the Bible and other earlier texts into angelic names recurs in several writings of R. Nehemiah.[126]

Let me turn to what I consider to be a mid-13th century commentary on the divine name of 42 letters, which contains elements drawn from three different schools: from R. Nehemiah ben Shlomo, the prophet of Erfurt, from the writings of R. Eleazar of Worms, and from early theosophical Kabbalah.[127] My datation here differs from what earlier scholars claimed that it contains proto-Kabbalistic material since the beginning of the 13th century, on the one hand[128]

125 See Idel, "The Commentaries of R. Nehemiah bar Shlomo to the Piyyut," p. 198:

השוה דין ורחמים גי׳ קפציאל וגי׳ רפאל, קטון וגדול

For additional angelic interpretations related to this poem see M. Idel, "On R. Nehemiah ben Shlomo the Prophet of Erfurt and R. Yizhak Luria," in eds. J. Garb, R. Meroz, M. Niehoff, *And This Is for Yehudah, Studies Presented to Our Friend, Professor Yehuda Liebes* (Hebrew University, The Bialik Institute, Jerusalem, 2012), pp. 342–343 (Hebrew).

126 See Idel, "On Angels in Biblical Exegesis," pp. 216–222, idem, "The Commentaries of R. Nehemiah bar Shlomo to the Piyyut," pp. 175, 180, and especially pp. 195–196, where I have shown the impact of this type of interpretation on the late 13th century Ashkenazi author R. Moshe Azriel ben Eleazar ha-Darshan.

127 Idel, *Ben*, pp. 218–235, and my article "On R. Nehemiah ben Shlomo the Prophet's Commentaries on the Name of Forty-Two," pp. 157–261.

128 On this commentary and its preface known as *Sefer ha-Ḥokhmah*, as if containing what was called by some scholars proto-Kabbalistic elements, see already the views of Scholem, *Origins of the Kabbalah*, pp. 125, 184–187, Joseph Dan, *The Esoteric Theology of Ashkenazi Hasidism* (Bialik Institute, Jerusalem, 1968), pp. 68–70, 119–129 (Hebrew), idem, *Studies in Ashkenazi-Hasidic Literature* (Massada, Ramat Gan, 1975), pp. 44–57 (Hebrew), and his "The Ashkenazi

and the more recent claim that it is a mid-16th century forgery, on the other hand:[129]

> "The *Shekhinah* has two thrones, two crowns,[130] and two *'ofanim*, one below and one above, and each of them is 500 paragans higher than the account of creation.... *Davar Yimtza'* in gematria *Mikha'el we-Gavriel*[131], *Mikha'el* is the angel of compassion and Gavri'el is the angel of judgment.[132] And when the *Shekhinah* sits on the attribute of judgment then the crowns and the *'ofanim* recite [the

Hasidic 'Gates of Wisdom,'" in eds. G. Nahon – Ch. Touati, *Hommages a Georges Vajda*, (Louvain, 1980), pp. 183–199, "The Emergence of Mystical Prayer," *Studies in Jewish Mysticism*, eds. J. Dan and F. Talmage, (Cambridge, Mass. 1982), pp. 112–115, Ivan G. Marcus, "Exegesis for the Few and for the Many: Judah he-Hasid's Biblical Commentary," *The Age of the Zohar*, ed. J. Dan, (Jerusalem 1989), pp. 1–24, Idel, *Kabbalah: New Perspectives*, pp. 193–196, Farber-Ginnat, *The Concept of the Merkabah*, pp. 236–237, Wolfson, *Through a Speculum that Shines*, pp. 226–228, 257–259, *Along the Path*, pp. 44–45, 167–168 n. 289, and Sendor, *The Emergence of Provencal Kabbalah*, pp. 363–364. Meanwhile I changed my mind as evident in studies I published later on R. Nehemiah ben Shlomo, to be discussed immediately below.

129 See the interesting, though exaggerated study of David Matatyahu ha-Levi Siegel, *Sefer Sodei Razei Semukhim*, second edition, (Kolel Sha'arei Qedushah u-Tefillah, Jerusalem, 2001) (Hebrew)

130 On two thrones and crowns see Farber, *The Concept of the Merkabah*, p. 247.

131 *Davar Yimtza'* [cf. Proverbs 16:20] = 347 = *Mikha'el we-Gavri'el.*

132 See *BT Shabbat*, fol 55b, and Liebes, "De Natura Dei," p. 269. Compare to the view found in a collectanea of early Kabbalah, perhaps related to a disciple of R. Abraham he-Ḥazan of Gerona, where the two angels are described in a similar manner:

מיכאל כח מדת החסד גבריאל כח מדת הדין.

"Mikha'el is the power of the attribute of *Ḥesed*, Gabri'el is the power of the attribute of judgment." Cf. Ms. Munchen 357, fol 3a. On R. Abraham he-Ḥazan of Gerona as a Kabbalist from the school of R. Isaac the Blind see Scholem, *Reshit ha-Kabbalah*, pp. 243–248. On these two angels as enemies see the Muslim traditions discussed by Schneider, *Scattered Traditions of Jewish Mysticism*, pp. 261–264. In any case, here we have evidence as to the manner in which the theology of two divine attributes impacted angelology.

name of] forty-two letters…since it has the throne of judgment and a crown of judgment, then the crowns and *'ofanim* recite the name of forty-two letters…and the attribute of judgment is moved[133] to the attribute of compassion. Concerning this Isaiah said [26:21], "For lo! The Lord shall come forth from His place," *hinneh YHWH yotze' mi-meqomo*. The word *yotze'* [comes forth] has the numerical value of Mikha'el.[134] [The expression] *hinneh YHWH yotze' mi-meqomo* has the numerical value of [the expression] *YHWH u-mtzptz, kisso' be-raḥamim*[135]. Therefore, we say [Exodus 34:6] *YHWH 'El Raḥum we-Ḥannun*, "the Lord, a God compassionate and gracious" for they are ten letters. Similarly, [the expression] *YHWH YHWH 'El*, "the Lord, the Lord, God" [ibidem]….And He moves the throne of judgment to the throne of compassion. Therefore, we say in the doxography, *hu' yifen be-raḥamim* "He looks with compassion", these are the [same] letters [of the expression] *ha-'ofanim be-raḥamim* "the *'ofanim* in compassion"[136] for the *'ofanim*[137] move the throne of judgment to the throne of compassion and to the crown of compassion."[138]

133 The verb used here is *Glgl*, like in the following sentences. Compare to the use of this verb in *Sefer ha-Bahir*, in a similar context, to be discussed in the next chapter and see the translation of Wolfson, who translated three times the change or the transformation of one attribute in another, in *Along the Path*, pp. 44, 167–168 n. 289. On other uses of the verb *Glgl* in contemporary author, R. Ezra of Gerona see his *Commentary of the Song of Songs*, pp. 476, 510–511 as well as the interesting passage discussed by Weiss, "Most of the Errant Err in *Malkhut*," p. 328. In this period Kabbalists did not use yet this verb in order to refer to metempsychosis. See Idel "Commentaries on the Secret of Impregnation."

134 *Y[o]tze'* in a deficient spelling as it is in the Hebrew Bible, = 101 = *Mikha'el*.

135 *hinneh y[o]tze' mi-meqomo* = *kisso' be-raḥamim* = 387.

136 As Wolfson correctly pointed out in *Along the Path*, pp. 167–168 n. 289, one letter *mem*, is extra.

137 Plausibly some form of angelic wheels that cause the motion from one place to another. See also my discussion in "On R. Nehemiah ben Shlomo the Prophet's Commentaries on the Name of Forty-Two," pp. 181–182, 192.

138 *Sefer ha-Ḥokhmah*, cf. Idel, ibidem, pp. 184–185, where the full text was printed with more accompanying footnotes that have not been reproduced here:

The duality of the two attributes is referred in the context of the two divine names, the two crowns, the two thrones, the two *'ofanim,* and the two angels. In this passage the bringing together of the attribute of judgment with that of compassion is mentioned, resorting to the same verse as found in the Midrash, Isaiah 26:21, just as in model [B]. However, this passage does not work with the assumption of the transformation of the attribute of judgment into compassion, [the Rabbinic model [E2],] or of their being brought together, not by a human act, but by the angelic recitation of a magical name. The affinity between the Tetragrammaton found in the verse and the attribute of compassion is demonstrated by the device of exchange of letters, 'A = T, B = Sh, which results in the syntagm *M Tz P Tz,* whose numerical value is 300 like the word *be-Raḥamim.*[139] Then the anonymous author "decodes" the verb *Yotze'* as referring in gematria to the name of the angel Mikha'el, as both amount to 101. Thus, the lower attribute of judgment is summoned by the recitation of the name to ascent, or to move toward the higher attribute of compassion. This situation differs from the Rabbinic one, as seen in model [E2], where it is the compassion that is conceived of as descending upon judgment.

כי לשכינה יש שתי כסאות ושתי כתרים ושתי׳ אופני׳ אחד למטה ואחד למעלה. וכל אחד גבוה ממעשה בראשית ת״ק ועל זה אמ׳ שלמ׳ ׳משכיל על׳ גי׳ ת״ק, ׳דבר ימצא׳ גי׳ ׳מיכאל וגבריאל׳, ומיכאל הוא שר הרחמים וגבריאל שר של דין. וכשהשכינה יושבת במידת הדין אז מזכירים הכתרים והאופני׳ שם של מ״ב אותיות...לפי שאם יש לו כסא הדין וכתר הדין אז מזכירי׳ האופני׳ של מ״ב אותיות ומגלגלי׳ מידת הדין למידת הרחמים ועל זה אמ׳ ישעי׳ ׳הנה יי׳ יצא ממקומו׳ יצא גי׳ מיכאל ׳הנה יי׳ יצא ממקומו׳ גימ׳ יהוד ומצפץ כסא ברחמי׳ ולכך אנו אומ׳ ׳יי אל רחום׳ לפי שהם אותיות כך ׳יהוד יהוד אל׳ וכך יהוד אל רחום וכן רחום רי״ש חי״ת ו״ו מם, הנעלם אותיות י׳ שמות לפי שמזכירים אותן עם שם של מ״ב, ומתגלגל כסא הדין לכסא רחמים. ולכך אנו אומרי׳ בקדושה ׳הוא יפן ברחמים׳ והן אותיות ׳האופנים ברחמים׳ לפי שהאופני׳ מגלגלין כסא דין לכסא רחמים ולכתר של רחמים.

139 This type of interpretation is found also elsewhere in contemporary Ashkenazi literature. See Wolfson, *Along the Path,* p. 44 and see also the discussion of R. Abraham Axelrod of Koeln's *Keter Shem Tov,* as printed in *'Amudei ha-Qabbalah,* p. 9, and R. Moshe Azriel ben Eleazar ha-Darshan printed by Scholem, *Reshit ha-Kabbalah,* p. 222. See also Herrmann Klaus, "Die Gottesnamen כוזו und מצפץ in der Hekhalot-Literatur," *Frankfurter Judaistische Beiträge,* vol. 16 (1988), pp. 75–87.

It should be pointed out that not all the Jewish literature of the first millennium CA operated with the theology of two attributes. They are almost totally absent in the so-called Heikhalot literature, which was much more concerned with knowing the size of the divine being rather than in the modes of activities.[140] Much less theurgical or concerned with commandments but incomparably more with apotheosis, the theory of two attributes could not contribute much to the mentality of this trend in Judaism, concerned as it is more with a hierarchy and a way to rule over the world, grounded in luxurious angelology.[141] The Rabbis were less concerned with angels and more with the *middot.*

However, a major source for Kabbalistic discussions of attributes is found in the Kabbalistic understandings of some passages from *Sefer Yetzirah*. The time and place of the composition of this seminal text are still a matter of dispute between scholars.[142] However, for the medieval Rabbis – including more speculatively oriented ones as Sa'adyah Gaon or R. Yehudah ha-Levi – it was an authoritative text deserving commentaries, that was often times attributed to R. Aqivah or even to the patriarch Abraham. This is evidently also the case for the perception of many of the Kabbalists. The small treatise did not resort to the terminology or to the theme of two attributes. For our purpose what is essential is to point to the centrality of the structure of ten *sefirot,* whose precise nature is not so clear: are they numbers, spheres, or divine extensions, or some combination between them.[143] They were clearly related to divine names at the beginning of the book in its larger version, and this fact is certainly paramount for later developments.[144]

140 See Idel, *Kabbalah: New Perspectives*, pp. 157–158.

141 See my *The Angelic World*, pp. 19–73.

142 See Hayman, *Sefer Yeṣira, Edition*, Scholem, *Origins of the Kabbalah*, pp. 24–35, Pines, "Points of Similarity," pp. 63–142, Liebes, *Ars Poetica*, passim, Ronit Meroz, "Between *Sefer Yetzirah* and Wisdom Literature: Three Binitarian Approaches in *Sefer Yetzirah*," *JSRI*, vol. 18 (2007), pp. 101–142.

143 See Pines, ibidem, Gedaliahu G. Stroumsa, "A Zoroastrian Origin to the *Sefirot*?" *Irano-Judaica*, vol. III (1994), pp. 17–33, and Idel, *Kabbalah: New Perspectives*, pp. 136–153.

144 Hayman, *Sefer Yeṣira, Edition*, p. 52.

This vagueness elicited a broad spectrum of philosophical and Kabbalistic interpretations, which preoccupied Kabbalists more and more through the history of Kabbalah. They organized much of their discussions around some attempts to clarify their nature and functions, especially as part of the Kabbalistic theogonies, cosmologies and the relationship between them and entities and human acts in the lower world, and especially the various terms found in the canonized writings. Among the Kabbalists the *sefirot* became thereby not only a metaphysical structure, but also a major hermeneutical clue for understanding the allegedly hidden meanings of key words, whose hidden meaning was imagined laying dormant in the sacred texts. As such it absorbed also the Rabbinic discussions of the two attributes, which have been identified with a certain pair of *sefirot* or another, an issue to be discussed in many of the following chapters.

Already in *Sefer Yetzirah* itself (1:2) the *sefirot* were described, according to one interpretation, as infinite, by using the syntagm that can be translated as "their measure is ten that are infinite."[145] There is here an implicit distinction between the *sefirot* themselves that are ten, and their measure, *middatan*, that is infinite. According to some other versions, found in medieval philosophers but representing an earlier view, *middatan* should be understood as pointing to another set of ten *sefirot*, corresponding to the ten cosmic *sefirot* but found within a higher realm, an interpretation found in some pre-Kabbalistic discussions of *Sefer Yetzirah*, like Sa'adyah Gaon and Shlomo ibn Gabirol.[146] Kabbalists, however, conflated sometimes the term *middah* with *sefirah* and thus discussions about the various meanings of the

145 *Sefer Yetzirah*, ed. Hayman, p. 37, 49, no.7, pp. 74–75: מדתן עשר שאין להן סוף Pines, ibidem, pp. 122–126 and compare to the use of the term *middah* in Job 11:9.

146 This is the case of Sa'adyah Gaon, Donnolo, ibn Gabirol and R. Yehudah Barzilai of Barcelona. See my "Sefirot Above Sefirot," p. 278, and Pines, ibidem, pp. 122–126, as well as Wolfson, 'The Theosophy of Shabbetai Donnolo," p. 298, and Sendor, *The Emergence of Provencal Kabbalah*, 1, p. 183 n. 24. See also my "On the Theosophy at the Beginning of Kabbalah" pp. 140–145. The existence pre-Kabbalistic structure of two decads found among these thinkers reinforces my analysis in my two studies mentioned here, and they may

nature of the ten *sefirot* qua divine attributes emerged. In any case, at least implicitly, the term *middah* has been associated here with a certain decad related to the divinity. A perusal of material belonging to early Kabbalah shows, however, that the term *middah* remained in current use for some generations, side by side with the term *sefirot*, as we shall see in more detail in chapter 7 below.

Though conceptually unrelated to each other, the Rabbinic models as we have described them above, and the paragraphs from *Sefer Yetzirah*, conspired together to help articulating several important discussions in the Middle Ages, which departed in a significant manner from those sources. This is the case already in *Sefer ha-Bahir*, though to a very small extent, as we shall see in the next chapter. My point is that the dynamic nature of the *middot* in Rabbinic literature, which are conceived of much less cosmical entities, had impacted the later understandings of the nature of the *sefirot* in *Sefer Yetzirah*, which are related much more to the cosmocratic picture of the divinity, lacking a theurgical valence or an interest in intra-divine processes. In other words, while *Sefer Yetzirah* contributed the picture of the *sefirot* as cosmic and dynamic entities, but not as preeminently interactive powers with performers of rituals, the *middot* contributed the potential of correlative aspects of Kabbalistic theosophies, and this merger between the two independent concepts loaded the dynamic nature of the *sefirot* with quite different dynamic and theurgical valences, after the two concepts have been amalgamated in in the Middle Ages, in the earliest stages of theosophical Kabbalah, triggerring the emergence of more complex kaleidoscopic pictures.

The question that preoccupies me in the following chapters is to discern the various discussions of the two attributes not only as proof-texts, but also as springboards. Though my basic assumption is that simple types of influence of late antiquity Rabbinic material on early Kabbalah are to be found indeed, though what happened

point to a widespread understanding of some aspects of *Sefer Yetzirah*. For the importance of this book in early Kabbalah see Pedaya, *The Name and the Sanctuary*, pp. 37–38.

much more is in fact a series of combinations between the various and diverging models, and other materials, in Jewish and non-Jewish sources. The theological vagueness and the conceptual diversity and fluidity of the Biblical and the Rabbinic materials, and the enigmatic formulations of *Sefer Yetzirah,* constituted a fertile field for further elaborations, interpretations and misunderstanding. Most of the Kabbalists not only tried to clarify the theological valences of the earlier materials and elaborate on them, but also to strengthen their correlative aspects, in the context of the enhancing the significance of the performance of the rituals. What cannot be disputed is the fact that Rabbinic texts, as seen above, not just isolated terms, made their way to early Kabbalists and where quoted verbatim, an issue that is beyond any reasonable doubt. How did some of the Kabbalists, many of whom were also accomplished Rabbis and great experts in Rabbinic literature, understand them is, however, quite a different issue. The understanding of the *middot* differs from one Kabbalistic school to another, a topic that will preoccupy us at length. This is a matter of the articulation of exegetical grids and codes that informed their readings and their reorganization of religious knowledge, which impacted the meaning of the Rabbinic views.

Let me conclude with the observation that most of the Rabbinic authors and others discussed in this chapter, surmised the existence of two divine attributes, but did not address the question as to their emergence out of the ultimate divine realm. They were concerned much more with their functions via an understanding the significance of the occurences of divine names in the biblical accounts, than with their precise metaphysical identity. The more complex mapping of the divine realm, which recourse also to the concept of *middot,* is a development that is characteristic of Kabbalah.

THREE
The Book of Bahir

Polyvalence of terms in canonical writings, a blessing for future religious creativity, is at the same time, a curse for modern philology. This statement is quite appropriate in the plenty of discussions of the term *middot*. At the High Middle Ages, when the first written texts of Kabbalistic literature emerged, Jews had several possible sources for their speculations about the divine attributes: the Rabbinic ones, as discussed above: the Heikhalot literature, *Sefer Yetzirah*, as well as the medieval philosophical speculations on divine attributes in their different forms.[147] As I shall try to show in the next chapters also other sources were possibly available, including Philonic ones. The various choices Kabbalists made by adopting, adapting, elaborating and combining them, tell us a great lesson as to the nature of the medieval

147 See, e.g., David Kaufmann, *Geschichte der Attributenlehre in der Jüdischen Religionsphilosophie des Mittelalters von Saadia bis Maimuni* (Gotha, 1877–1878), Michel Allard, *Le problème des attributs divins dans la doctrine d'al-Ashari et de ses premiers grands disciples* (Imprimerie catholique, Beyrouth, 1965), Harry A. Wolfson's various studies on the topic reprinted together in his *Studies in the History of Philosophy and Religion*, eds. I. Twersky – G.H. Williams, (Harvard University Press, Cambridge, Mass., 1977), vol. II, pp. 161–336, 593–600, M. Idel, "Divine Atributes and *Sefirot* in Jewish Theology," in eds. S.O. Heller-Willensky – M. Idel, *Studies in Jewish Thought*, (Magnes Press, Jerusalem, 1989), pp. 87–112 (Hebrew) and Wolfson, 'The Theosophy of Shabbetai Donnolo."

nascent Kabbalah and the reasons of its conceptual diversity, – part of the dynamic and inclusive theosophies – a situation natural in Rabbinic Judaism much more than in the more exclusive approach to theology in the various forms of Jewish philosophy. In the chapters 3–7, I shall survey distinct types of theosophies found in what I consider to be different Kabbalistic schools that share nevertheless decadic theosophies that were combined at different degrees with theurgical understanding of the commandments.

Sometime at the beginning of the 13th century, full-fleged evidence as to the existence of a treatise that presents itself as the Midrash of R. Nehunyah ben ha-Qanah, a revered first-century CA figure, can be found in some of the writings of Provencal and Gerone Kabbalists.[148] Those are the first evidence to its existence. This attribution is evidently spurious, as it is the case of some references to him in the Heikhalot literature, but they were nevertheless very important in the wide reception of the rather fragmentary and enigmatic text, as one of the pillars of medieval Kabbalah. Also its midrashic form of presentation was helpful in this direction. Modern scholars disputed the time and the locale of its composition between the Middle East[149], Ashkenaz[150],

148 Scholem, *Origins of the Kabbalah*, pp. 35–148, Daniel Abrams, "The Condensation of the Symbol '*Shekhinah*' in the Manuscripts of the *Book Bahir*," *Kabbalah*, vol. 16 (2007), pp. 7–82, and his preface to his edition of the book pp. 1–103, Wolfson, "The Tree that Is All," Fishbane, *Biblical Myth and Rabbinic Mythmaking*, pp. 256–260, Schneider, "The Myth of Satan in the Book of Bahir," or Ben Shalom, "Kabbalistic Circles," pp. 574–576 and Dan, *History of Jewish Mysticism*, pp. 106–299. See also Jordan S. Penkower, *The Dates of Compositions of the Zohar and the Book Bahir* (Cherub Press, Los Angeles, 2100), pp. 138–151 (Hebrew) and Arieli, *On the Source of the Doctrine of the Sefirot*, pp. 276–312.

149 See, more recently, Ronit Meroz, "The Middle Eastern Origins of Kabbalah," *Journal for the Study of Sephardic and Mizrahi Jewry*, Feb. 2007 (http://sephardic.fiu.edu/journal/RonitMeroz. pdf), pp. 39–56, idem, "A Journey of Initiation in the Babylonian Layer of *Sefer ha-Bahir*," *Studia Hebraica* vol. 7 (2007), pp. 17–33, "On the Time and Place of Some Paragraphs of *Sefer Ha-Bahir*," *Da'at* vol. 49 (2002), pp. 137–180, and see now Israel Knohl, "The Chariot, The Righteous Man and Satan, toward Resolving the Puzzle of *Sefer ha-Bahir*," *Jewish Studies*, pp. 1–30 (Hebrew).

150 Scholem, *Origins of the Kabbalah*, p. 99.

Provence[151] or even Gerona.[152] Those different locals evince also different datations from the earlier to the later. It may well-be that the answer is not an either-or one, but a more developmental one, which may allow contributions of the different centers to one degree or another, in a book that has been edited from different sources perhaps through decades or even centuries. In scholarship of Kabbalah it has been often times hailed as the first Kabbalistic document, as part of a history that is rather unilinear.[153]

Though continuing some Rabbinic trends, the content of the book displays nevertheless important elements not found beforehand but shared by some of the others early documents, written roughly speaking in the generations when the written platform of medieval Kabbalah made its first steps.[154] The book is similar to the Rabbinic reticence toward angelology and is concerned more with divine attributes, an observation that holds also for early Kabbalah. Especially important from the point of view of the present study is the fact that a pleromatic picture integrates a Rabbinic theory of two attributes, of three and eventually seven attributes, and of ten *sefirot*, stemming from *Sefer Yetzirah*, but now the latter are designated by a series of abstract terms that will reverberate widely in later forms of Kabbalah.[155] This does not mean that I assume that the *Bahir* invented those terms, but that it

151 See Scholem, ibidem, p. 126, and more recently Schaefer, *Mirror of His Beauty*, and to a certain extent Haviva Pedaya, "The Provencal Stratum in the Redaction of *Sefer ha-Bahir*," in eds., Z.W. Harvey – M. Idel, *Shlomo Pines Jubilee Volume* (= *Jerusalem Studies in Jewish Thought*, vol. IX) (Jerusalem, 1990), vol. II pp. 139–164 (Hebrew).

152 See Adolf Neubauer, *JQR*, (OS) vol. 4, (1891), p. 358, Weinstock, *Studies*, pp. 15–80, and Mark Verman, "Reincarnation and Theodicy: Traversing Philosophy, Psychology, and Mysticism," in ed., Jay M. Harris, *Be'erot Yitzhak; Studies in Memory of Isadore Twersky*, (Harvard University Press, Cambridge, MA, 2005), pp. 399–426.

153 Scholem, *Origins of the Kabbalah*, pp. 35–148.

154 See also in chs. 4–5 below.

155 See Ithamar Gruenwald, "Jewish Mysticism's Transition from *Sefer Yeṣira* to the *Bahir*," in ed. J. Dan, *The Beginnings of the Jewish Mysticism in Medieval Europe*, (Jerusalem, 1987), pp. 15–54 (Hebrew) and Idel, *Kabbalah: New Perspectives*, pp. 123–124, 126–127.

is perhaps the first and most influential document that used them in an explicit and consistent manner. This pleromatic structure of ten divine powers was presented also by resorting to a series of parables, some of them reminiscent of Rabbinic parables, and in any case replete with anthropomorphic terms. The decadic structure absorbed the binary theme of two attributes as part of the broader theosophy. In this book the triad of the attributes *Ḥesed, Din, Raḥamim* occurs already in the form accepted in later forms of Kabbalah though this does not seem to be an innovation of this book, as we shall see below in this chapter.[156] Moreover, even the similar distinction between *Ḥesed* and *Raḥamim*, is not necessarily the invention of the anonymous Kabbalist.[157]

Gershom Scholem has believed that it is possible to discern the historical and phenomenological impact of Gnosticism on this book and via it also on the Kabbalistic literature as a whole.[158] However, he never actually proved his point and in the further development of scholarship this thesis is found in full decline. The alleged gnostic transformation of Judaism in this book has been claimed also insofar as the theory of divine attributes about which it is said that:

> "This symbolism, which in large measure makes use of aggadic motifs, and adds to them a gnostic character, no longer has any connection to the ideas of the *Sefer Yetzirah* concerning the *sefirot*."[159]

Though what he said on both the "aggadic motifs" and *sefirot* is in my opinion to a certain extent correct, what was exactly the contribution of the gnostic elements has not been explicated here or elsewhere. This alleged Gnostic character makes for Scholem the difference between

156 See also below chapter 10.

157 See the discussion quoted in R. Azriel of Gerona, *Commentary on the Talmudic Legends*, ed. Tishby, p. 9.

158 See, e.g., *Origins of the Kabbalah*, pp. 8, 14–15, 18, 21–23, 26, 32–33, 48, 58–61, 66–97, 99, 141, 144, 245, idem, *On the Kabbalah and its Symbolism*, pp. 97–98, and see the critique of Idel, *Old World, New Mirrors*, pp. 138–146.

159 See Scholem, *Origins of the Kabbalah*, p. 144. Compare also ibidem, pp. 87, 137 and see also his *On the Kabbalah and Its Symbolism*, pp. 97–99, 101.

the old and new aspects of Jewish thought. Without explicating it, and without an inventory of what indeed is found in the "aggadic motifs" it is hard to evaluate the explanatory force of such a statement that contains, in a nutshell, Scholem's phenomenology and history of Jewish mysticism. I surmise, however, that the aggadic elements played a much more substantial role in the conceptual structure of many forms of Kabbalah and they were not just motifs artificially embedded in a Gnostic worldview. The major role played by the commentaries on the Talmudic legends and the commentary on the various commandments, especially prayer, in early Kabbalah is prominent, and this is especially evident in the school of Rabad, as his commentary on a Rabbinic statement, that of R. Ezra and of R. Azriel of Gerona, show. It is the new organization of the material, that brings together earlier though disparate Jewish types of thought, that generated indeed something new, and this is one of the reasons why the *deus ex machina* insertion of Gnosticism as a major positive factor for the formation of the early Kabbalah is, in my opinion, superfluous. This is evident, for example, in the case of the term *Male'*, that reflected, according to Scholem's theory, the important Gnostic concept of pleroma, but in more recent scholarship it turns that it is found in earlier Hebrew sources.[160]

For our purpose here a discussion of the nexus between theurgy, as I define this term, and the changes in the divine attributes is of paramount importance and it problematizes the alleged Gnostic valence

160 See Scholem, *Origins of the Kabbalah*, pp. 658–71, and compare to the different explanations found more recently in Idel, "The Problem of the Sources of the Bahir," in ed. J. Dan, *The Beginnings of the Jewish Mysticism in Medieval Europe*, (Jerusalem, 1987), pp. 67–70 (Hebrew), idem, "Mamonides in Nahmanides and His School," pp. 140–147, Yair Lorberboim, *Tzelem 'Elohim in the Rabbis, Maimonides and Nahmanides* (Ph.D. Thesis, Hebrew University, Jerusalem, 1997), pp. 208–218, (Hebrew), D. Abrams' introduction to his edition of the *Book of Bahir*, pp. 5–6, Schneider, "The Myth of the Satan in the Book of Bahir," pp. 339–343, idem, *The Appearance of the High Priest*, pp. 144–165, Yehuda Liebes, "Berakhah u-male be-Sefer ha-Bahir," *Kabbalah* vol. 21 (2009), pp. 123–142 (Hebrew).

of *Sefer ha-Bahir.* Discussing the shape of the Hebrew letter *Ḥet,* the anonymous Kabbalist says that it is open to both good and bad; and two biblical verses were cited in which fire acts in different ways as some form of divine intervention. Then, the question is asked as how is it possible that the same entity displays quite different features? The answer is offered in good Rabbinic terms: The good acts are predicated on the fact that "the people of Israel are performing the will of the Place"[161] – namely of God as Omnipresent – while the negative ones appear when they do not perform the will of God. In the latter case the "fire is close" is indubitable a reference to the attribute of judgment,[162] in the former case "the attribute of compassion is moving and encompassing."[163] Moving and encompassing translate the verbs *mitgalgalet* and *sovevet.* In my opinion, the first verb refers to the passage quoted above from *BT Berakhot,* fol. 7a, where the verb *Yigolu* occurs in the context of the attribute of compassion, while the second one may refer to this attributing encompassing the other attributes, perhaps a parallel to the motif of conquest of one attribute by another.

However, in the book of *Bahir,* it is no more the prayer of God that induces this prevalence of compassion, but the deeds of the people of Israel in general. This type of theurgy related to the performance of the will of God, namely keeping the commandments, is well-known in Rabbinic sources, though not necessarily in the context of the divine attributes.[164] In other words, there is here a combination of

161 This is a well-know designation of God in Philo and in Rabbinic literature. See, e.g, Scholem, *Jewish Gnosticism,* p. 35, Urbach, *The Sages,* pp. 66–79, or Marmorstein, *The Old Rabbinic Doctrine of God,* pp. 92–93.

162 Compare also to ed. Abrams, p. 179 no. 93, where wine, referring to "Fear" namely the *sefirah* of *Gevurah,* is described as being closer to us than the attribute of *Hesed,* symbolized by milk.

163 Ed. Abrams, no. 24, pp. 129–131:

כאן בזמן שישראל עושין רצונו של מקום כאן כשאין ישראל עושין רצונו, בזמן שאין ישראל עושין רצונו אש קרובה, ובזמן שעושין רצונו מדת הרחמים מתגלגלת וסובבת.

See also Scholem, *Origins of the Kabbalah,* p. 144.

164 See Idel, *Kabbalah: New Perspective,* pp. 158–160 and Brody, 'Human Hands Dwell in Heavenly Heights".

two different Rabbinic statements related to theurgy. Though indeed this specific combination is new, it does not constitute a conceptual departure from, or a rupture with the modes of thinking in Rabbinic literature, and we may well-consider this passage from the *Bahir* as part of Rabbinic theurgy, which has been inserted in a series of traditions that possess Kabbalistic concepts.

However, here there is theurgy that is related to the two attributes, when understood in a new way: the activity of the attributes is predicated on the nature of human deeds. Interestingly enough, in another passage from the *Bahir*, the attribute of judgment is described as pouring or flowing from above, in a manner reminiscent of the passage cited above.[165] This vertical hierarchy assumes some form of independence of each of them, though equality is certainly absent in such discussions. This is also the case elsewhere in this book:

> "But at the time that Israel are bringing a sacrifice in front of their Father in heaven, they are uniting together, and this is the "union of the Lord"...And it is said that it is called *Qorban* [sacrifice] because it brings closer the holy powers... and the [divine] delight descends and unites itself with those holy forms and he comes closer because of the sacrifice."[166]

The "holy powers" and the "holy forms" are Bahiric terms for theosophical entities. Two processes are imagined here as connected to

165 Ed. Abrams, p. 147 par. 50.

166 Ed. Abrams, p. 165, pars. 78–77:
דבעת שישראל מקריבין קרבן לפני אביהם שבשמים מתיחדים יחד והינו יחודו של אלהים... ואמר איקרי קרבן. אלא על שם שמקרב הכחות הקדושות ונחת הרוח יורד ומתיחד בצורות הקדושות ההם ומתקרב על ידי הקרבן.

See also Scholem, *Origins of the Kabbalah*, pp. 65, 79, 139, 194, Baer, "The Service of the Sacrifice," pp. 450–451, Fishbane, *As Light Before Dawn*, p. 128 n. 19, and Mottolese, *Analogy in Midrash and Kabbalah*, pp. 234–235. See also *Sefer ha-Bahir*, ibidem, no. 48 p. 145, and Scholem, ibidem, pp. 61, 104, 116,126, 128, 129. See also a quote from the *Bahir* and its interpretation in R. Meir ibn Gabbai, *'Avodat ha-Qodesh*, 1:4, fol. 10a and ibidem 1:6, fols. 11a, 1:9, fol. 13b. See also my discussion in *Kabbalah: New Perspectives*, pp. 161–162.

the effects of the sacrifices: the bringing together of the supernal powers and the descent of divine effluence upon them, as the result of their union.

The *Book of Bahir* scarcely relates to the term *sefirah*, but it nevertheless uses the attributes related to them by Kabbalists later on, resorting to phrases like *middat gevurah, middat mayyim, middat 'esh, middat paḥad, middat 'emmet,*[167] *middat yom ha-Shabbat,*[168] etc. These are phrases that are not found beforehand in Jewish sources, all this in addition to the Rabbinic ordinary terminology of the attributes. Thus, the author of the *Bahir* operates more with the anthropomorphical and attributive codes, than with the sefirotic one, a combination that did not disappear also later on.[169] As I have suggested in the previous chapter, and will reiterate at the end of this chapter, it is possible that a list of ten divine *middot* could emerge from a combination of Rabbinic discussions that dealt, separately, with seven and three *middot*. Let us examine one paragraph of this book in order to demonstrate this observation:

> "[Exodus 17:11] "When Moses lifted his hands, [and][170] Israel prevailed," it teaches us that an attribute named Israel, within it the Torah of truth is found, and what is the Torah of truth? A thing that points to the essence of the worlds and its action in thought, and this is what sustains the world and it is one of them. And He created in man corresponding to them ten [logoi], the ten fingers, and when Moses lifted his hands,[171] and intends a little bit in

167 See Schneider, *Scattered Traditions of Jewish Mysticism*, pp. 254–255 and n. 334.

168 *See Sefer ha-Bahir*, ed. Abrams, p. 177 no. 92, p. 179 no. 94, etc., Scholem, *Origins of the Kabbalah*, p. 146.

169 See the view of R. Joseph of Hamadan translated and discussed in my *Absorbing Perfections*, pp. 72–73.

170 I translated the verse in accordance to the way it was understood by the Kabbalist, which means that the letter waw is not inverting the tense of the verb, as it is the case in the Bible, but is used in order to connect two different actions.

171 He changes "his hand" in the biblical verse to "his hands" in order to establish the ten fingers and the parallelism to be discussed below.

> [his] heart to that attribute called Israel, within which there is the Torah of truth, and he hints at the ten fingers of his hands, that it maintains the ten, and if he will not help Israel the ten logoi will not be sanctified in each and every day.[172] This is why it is written 'and Israel prevailed.'"[173]

The parallelism between the ten fingers and the ten logoi, namely the *ma'amarot* or the utterances by means of which God created the world in accordance to a Rabbinic statement,[174] does not include here the ten *sefirot*, despite the existence of such a parallelism in *Sefer Yetzirah* itself, and in a parallel passage in the *Bahir*.[175] Moreover, at least implicitly, the resort to the term *middah*, – attribute – referring to a supernal power called *Yisra'el*, is a parallel to *Tiferet*, assumes that there are ten of them, probably identical to the creative logoi, as if this is an evident fact. When enumerating some of the cognomens that turned to be classical in theosophical Kabbalah, like *Keter 'Elyon, Ḥokhmah, Binah* etc., the author refers to the ten logoi – *ma'amarot*.[176] This means that the nomenclature that will dominate later on the

172 For the corresponce between a logos and a day see ed. Abrams, p. 189, no. 105.

173 *Sefer ha-Bahir*, ed. Abrams, pp. 179–181 no. 94:

הילכך 'והיה כאשר ירים משה ידו וגבר ישראל' מלמד שהמדה שנקראת ישראל בתוכה תורת אמת. ומאי ניהו תורת אמת, דבר שמורה על אמיתות העולמים ופעולתו במחשבה והוא מעמיד עשרה מאמרות שבהם עומד העולם והוא אחד מהם. וברא באדם כנגד אותם עשרה מאמרות עשר אצבעות ידים, וכשהיה משה מרים ידו ומכוין במיעוט כוונת הלב באותה המדה הנקראת ישראל ובתוכה תורת אמת ורומז לו עשר אצבעות ידיו שהוא מעמיד את העשרה, ואם לא יעזור את ישראל לא יתקיימו העשרה מאמרות בכל יום ויום הלכך וגבר ישראל.

Scholem, *Origins of Kabbalah*, pp. 131, 144–145, Idel, "Sefirot Above Sefirot," pp. 269–270, idem, *Absorbing Perfections*, pp. 116–119, and for the Rabbinic background see my *Kabbalah: New Perspectives*, pp. 157–159, Liebes, "De Natura Dei," pp. 17–18, and Fishbane, *Biblical Myth and Rabbinic Mythmaking*, pp. 180–182. See also Brody, 'Human Hands Dwell in Heavenly Heights" and Sendor, *The Emergence of Provencal Kabbalah*, I, pp. 286–293.

174 See Idel, *Kabbalah: New Perspectives*, pp. 121–122.

175 Ed. Abrams, p. 173 no. 87.

176 Ed. Abrams, p. 181 no. 96.

references to ten *sefirot*, – like *Ḥokhmah, Binah* or *Gevurah* etc., – was found independently of the ten *sefirot*, and the Rabbinic terms *middah, koaḥ* – power – *tzurah*, and *ma'amar*, were considered as being much more important for the terminology of this book, a fact that shows the vitality of the Rabbinic ways of thought at this early stage of the emergence of Kabbalah, more than that of *Sefer Yetzirah*. Moreover, this passage displays some theurgical implications of Moses's act, which are not found in discussions in *Sefer Yetzirah* about the ten fingers. In other words, it is in this Kabbalistic book that the attributive code continues much of the Rabbinic ways of thought, which was not overcome by the sefirotic code, but was the dominant one.

Let me emphasize the significance of the occurrence of the term *Torah* as a reference to a divine power. It is part of a broader phenomenon in this book, a process of constellating the divine realm by means of terms related to the Jewish ritual. This is the case, for example, of the designation of the ninth power, *Yesod*, by the term *Tzaddiq*, the righteous. Its strength is depicted as dependent of the performance of the rituals by the human righteous in the lower world.[177] This type of affinities, which map the divine world by means of ritualistic concepts, became widespread in the theosophical-theurgical Kabbalah already in the 13th century.

The term *middot* occurs in a context that is obscure enough, and the assumption may be that for the readers in his milieu it was evident that it deals with three divine powers:

> "Why is *ZaHa[B]V* [= Gold] called so? Because three *middot* are comprised in it. *Zakhar* [male] which is the latter's [letter of] *Zayn*,

177 Ed. Abrams, pp. 160–161. See the discussions of this important passage in Scholem, *Origins of the Kabbalah*, pp. 152–154, idem, *The Mystical Shape*, p. 95, Wolfson, *Along the Path*, pp. 71–72, and Idel, *Ascensions on High*, pp. 79–83. In more general terms about the ritually constellated supernal realm see my *Enchanted Chains*, pp. 176–180, 215–220. See also below beside n. 498. On righteousness as a supernal attribute and the human righteous as a theurgist, see in the previous chapter and in the text to be referred by n. 195 in this chapter. On hypostatic views of the righteounesness in ancient Israel see Idel, *Ben*, p. 166 n. 23.

> *Ha-Neshamah*, which is the [letter of] *He'* and there are five names for the soul: *Ruaḥ, Ḥayah, Yeḥidah, Nefesh, Neshamah*. What is the deed of *He'*? It is the seat of *Zayin*, as it is written [Ecclesiastes 5:7] 'and there is yet a higher one over them,' and [the letter of] *Bet*, which is their existence, as it is written [Genesis 1:1] *Bereshit Bara*.'"[178]

I am not sure that I can fathom precisely the intention of this passage. It seems plausible that the letter *Z*, in the Hebrew alphabet standing for the figure of seven, refers here to seven last divine powers, over which there are higher entities, represented by the letter *B*, that is represented by the first word related to creation. The letter *H* stands for the soul found in this world, and this is the reason they are a seat for the divine higher powers. It is obvious that we have, maybe for the first time, an identification of the term *middah* with gender distinct issues. As we shall see in the next chapter, this is the case also of an early Kabbalist, the Rabad of Posquieres, though the two discussions are quite different. It should also be pointed out that the Hebrew form *kelulim* or, according to other manuscripts *kelulot*, when related to *middot*, appears also elsewhere in this book,[179] and it will have a long history in Kabbalah, as we shall see especially in chapters 5 and 6, when the relations between *middot* are described by a *middah* being *kelulah*.

Needless to say that also other meanings of the term *middah* occur in this book in the sense of human behavior[180] or referring to the thirteen attributes of compassion.[181] We may surmise that prior to the connection between the ten *sefirot* and the classical cognomens, those cognomens were related to *middot* and *ma'amarot*, and this hypothetic

178 Ed. Abrams, p. 137 no. 36:

ולמה נקרא שמו זהב, שבו כלולים שלש מדות, זכר, והוא זי"ן, הנשמה, והיא הה"א, וחמשה שמות לנשמה רוח חיה יחידה נפש נשמה, מאי עבידתה בה"א. והוא כסא לזיי"ן דכתיב (קהלת ה:ז) 'כי גבוה מעל גבוה שומר', ובי"ת היא קיומם כדאמר 'בראשית ברא'.

See also Scholem, *Origins of the Kabbalah*, pp. 169–170.

179 See e.g., p. 223, no. 139.

180 Ibidem, p. 133 no. 28.

181 Ibidem, p. 175 no. 89.

situation can explain the similarity between some aspects of the theosophy of this book and the earliest of the Provencal Kabbalists who were, most plausibly, not acquainted with this book, and they were much more concerned with *Sefer Yetzirah.*[182]

As I shall try to show, the line of *Sefer ha-Bahir* was followed more by the Kabbalistic school related to Nahmanides, while those who followed the line of Provencal Kabbalah in Gerona, were much more interested in the term *sefirot* than in ten *middot* or *ma'amarot* though they too resort to this term as we shall see in chapter 5. In any case, the unqualified references by modern scholars to *sefirot,* in order to describe the theosophical content of *Sefer ha-Bahir,* is to a certain extent, an anachronistc reading, which should be much more limited in the scholarly discourse. This is also the case of the recurrent use of terms like 'aeons' and 'archonts', terms of Gnostic origins, used by Scholem in order to translate and interpret the views of the *Bahir.*[183] According to another piece of evidence, there is an aposition of *Ḥesed* to *Din,* found in an early Ashkenazi text, which does not display any trace of Kabbalah. In R. Abraham ben Azriel's *Sefer 'Arugat ha-Bosem,* it is written, "There are those who bless over the attribute of judgement just as they bless over the attribute of mercy."[184] This means that the *Book of Bahir* did not invent the dislocation of compassion in the Rabbinic apposition, but it reflects an earlier position in a hypothetic list of ten *middot.* On the other hand, a statement found in R. Eleazar of Worms's *Commentary on Prayers* that assesses that the attribute of judgment is the Satan, is reminiscent of a view found in the book of *Bahir,* as to the identity of the left hand with the Satan.[185]

Let me point out at the end of this chapter that my claim as to the existence of ten *middot* in theological contexts is found already in a

182 See, e.g., my "Kabbalistic Prayer in Provence," pp. 285–286.

183 See, e.g., Scholem, *Origins of the Kabbalah,* pp. 123, 126, 131, 137, 148, 151, 153, 158, 159. For references to aeons see ibidem, pp. 143, 147, 152.

184 ed. Urbach, vol. III, p. 513:

שמברכין על מדת הדין כשם שמברכין על מדת חסד.

185 *Commentary on Prayer,* eds. M. and I. Herschler, (Jerusalem, 1992), vol. 1, p. 16, and compare to Schneider, "The Myth of Satan in the Book of Bahir."

passage that belongs to the so-called Circle of the Special Cherub, where they are conceived as dealing with secret, mainly cosmical, issues,[186] in Nahmanides' *Commentary on the Torah*,[187] and in R. Abraham Axelrod of Cologne's small but quite widespread treatise *Keter Shem Tov*.[188], For the time being I am not acquainted with other earlier examples besides the *Bahir*. I assume that the last two sources written in the sixties of the 13th century do not depend on each other and they probably point to the existence of an earlier source. R. Isaac Todros's use of the phrase "ten *middot*" as part of the thirteen *middot* of compassion, is somewhat later.[189] So is the case in some instances in Abraham Abulafia's writings[190] and in a passage of his anonymous follower, the Kabbalist who authored *Sefer Ner 'Elohim*, to be quoted in chapter 9 below. However, only some of those examples can be derived from each other and a plausible hypothesis would be that they continue earlier traditions about the ten divine attributes. The existence of the phrase "ten *middot*" in non-Kabbalistic sources points to a pre-Kabbalistic tradition, which has been adopted by the Kabbalists since the *Book of Bahir*. It should be mentioned that R. Azriel of Gerona refers twice to "six *middot*" that rule over this world, an uncommon figure in the writings of early Kabbalah.[191] In the same

186 See *Berayyita' de-Yosef ben Uzzie'el*, pp. 169–170, and ben Shahar's footnotes to other parallels from this school, and Abraham Epstein, *Mi-Qadmoniyyot ha-Yehudim*, (Mossad ha-Rav Kook, Jerusalem, 1957), p. 243. On this French-Ashkenazi school see Joseph Dan, *The 'Unique Cherub' Circle. A School of Jewish Mystics and Esoterics in Medieval Germany*, (Mohr, Tubingen 1999).

187 Commentary on Exodus, 34:6, and see also his commentary on Genesis 1:1.

188 *'Amudei ha-Qabbalah*, p. 10. In this text the terms *middah/middot* occur several times.

189 See his *Commentary on the Maḥzor*, Ms. Paris BN 839, fol. 191b. This Kabbalist uses *middot* in theosophical and other contexts also elsewhere in this treatise. See, e.g., fols. 191b, 192b, 198b, 202b, 211b, 222b, 223b.

190 See, e.g., *Matzref la-Kesef*, p. 21, where he identifies the ten attributes to ten *sefirot*, as well as his *'Otzar 'Eden Ganuz*, p. 157, *Shomer Mitzwah*, p. 19, and *Mafteaḥ ha-Sefirot*, p. 72.

191 See Scholem, "New Remnants," pp. 212–213.

text he speaks also about the seven opposites – *temurot* – by which the world is operating, in what seems to be a parallel to the *middot*.[192]

This is, to be sure, not just a pure hypothesis that can better explain the existence of "new" designations for the attributes, as found in the *Book of Bahir* that were mentioned before. Indeed, the list of ten "things" – *devarim* – by means of which the world has been created, found in the Talmud in the name of Rav, consists in quite abstract concepts, "by wisdom, by understanding, by reason, by strength, by rebuke, by might, by righteousness, by judgment, by loving-kindness, and by compassion."[193] This seminal list has been introduced in a mid-13th century treatise of an author active in Italy – most probably in Rome, R. Benjamin ben Abraham "min ha-'Anavim," by the phrase "by ten attributes": *be-Y' middot*.[194] There are good reasons to assume that this author was not influenced by Kabbalistic literature but he preserved an earlier understanding of Rav's ten things. This may be related to the ten powers mentioned as *middatan* in *Sefer Yetzirah*, as discussed in the previous chapter.

Especially important for the arguments I make here is the appearance of the phrase "ten middot" in a passage from the renown Ashkenazi master R. Eleazar ben Yehudah of Worms, an older contemporary of R. Benjamin. In his *Sefer ha-Shem*, when commenting on the "ten sefirot of Belimah" of *Sefer Yetzirah*, he wrote:

> "...restrain your heart to ruminate as to the ten things that were mentioned, if you will think about the Creator of the world, how His presence is upward or downward, or eastward or westward,

192 Ibidem, p. 211.

193 *BT Ḥagigah*, fol. 12a. See Scholem, *Origins of the Kabbalah*, pp. 82–83, Idel, *Kabbalah: New Perspectives*, pp. 115–116. For an ancient anthropomorphic structure of ten powers with a higher entity called Infinite, found in a Gnostic text whose affinities to Judaism has been recognized by several scholars, see my "On the Theosophy at the Beginning of Kabbalah," pp. 144, 146.

194 R. Benjamin ben Abraham Anav, *Perush Alfabetin*, ed. M.H. Schmelzer, printed in H.Z. Dimitrovsky, *Texts and Studies; Analecta Judaica* (New York, 1977), vol. 1, p. 225.

> or northward or southward, or onto the light, which is the air, or in the thickness of the firmament, or on the beginning or on the end, on whatever you will think, restrain your heart, remove your thought and close your mouth, and return to the worship of God, just as the [supernal] beasts do when they want to upright their statues, they run and return and bend their statues and they bow, and on the issue of the ten *middot*, a covenant has been made, so that none of the sages will know the end and the limits of the ten *hawwayot*."[195]

Here the ten *middot* stand for ten types or modes of divine presence in the world, that are conceived to be secret, so that they should not be fathomed, but preferring instead to return to the worship of the divinity, just as holy beasts do, after running. This attitude that attempts to restrain metaphysical speculations, represented here by the ten *middot*, privileging instead the importance of worship, is characteristic of much of Jewish literatures.

Those neglected references to a series of ten *middot* are not necessarily derived from the ten *sefirot* of *Sefer Yetzirah* – though sometimes they are put in relation to each other. I am inclined to attribute to them a substantial contribution toward the emergence of decadic inclusive theosophies in Kabbalah. To be sure: my assumption is not that there was a theosophical structure that sometimes has attracted the resort to the term *middot*, but that a structure dealing with ten *middot* – esoteric or not – has been adopted by Kabbalists and combined more and more with the theory of ten *sefirot* from *Sefer Yetzirah*.

195 *Sefer ha-Shem*, ed. Aharon Eizenbach, (Jerusalem, 2004), p. 2:
"י׳ ספירות בלימה... סתום לבך מלהרהר אחר י׳ דברים הנזכרים שאם תחשב על בורא עולם על חנייתו היאך הוא למעלה או למטה או כלפי מזרח או מערב או צפון או דרום או על האור הוא האויר או בעובי הרקיע או על ראשית או על אחרית על איזה מהם שתחשוב בלום לבך, הסר המחשבה מלבך וסתום פיך מלדבר ושוב לעבודת הקב"ה כחיות כשרוצות לזקוף קומתן רצות ושוב וכופפין קומתם ומשתחווים ועל דבר זה של י׳ מדות נכרת ברית שלא ידעו כל החכמים סוף וקץ לי׳ הויותיו."

This is a reliable edition, and I checked it also against the version of Ms. Moscow-Gunzburg 333, fol. 139b.

Moreover, provided the theurgical overtones of the term *middot* in some cases in Rabbinic literature, as seen in chapter 2 above, the emergence of the vital nexus of decadic theosophy and theurgical valences, quintessential for understanding some of the development of Kabbalistic thought, may be explained without resorting to either Gnostic or philosophical influences on this specific topic. This does not mean, to be sure, that important philosophical influences on this nexus cannot be discerned in early Kabbalah, a fact that I certainly accept, as we shall see immediately in the next chapter, but those issues cannot be dealt with in the present context.

To summarize the point made in this chapter: I would propose to see the existence of a hypothetic list of ten *middot* – occurring in some few cases in non-Kabbalistic brief discussions – as a skeletic structure that was enriched with the passage of time, by additions of different material, including theosophical, philosophical, magical, and astrological concepts, generating different theosophies in different Kabbalistic schools. One way to describe the developments of the different schools of Kabbalah is to point to the various types of interplay between some elements stemming from those domains, though my concern here is to point out the place the theories of divine modes of activity played in the history of Kabbalistic theosophies.

FOUR
R. Abraham ben David of Posquières (the Rabad)

As we shall see below, the theosophical-theurgical Kabbalah, the main trend in Jewish medieval mysticism, is in fact a conglomerate of different schools, and should be described as an attempt to offer detailed correspondences between the cultic acts – the Rabbinic commandments – and divine attributes and the processes taking place between them. As seen in the previous chapter this combination is evident already in *Sefer ha-Bahir*, where the Rabbinic components are evident, especially the theurgical ones. However, this book is not predicated on the act of division of male and female within the divine realm, formulated in the context of the Rabbinic concept of *du-partzufin*. However, in the two other Kabbalistic schools that were active in the very first stages of the emergence of the written platform of Kabbalah, the special interpretation of the creation of the male and female became part of the theosophical speculations.

One of the first Kabbalistic texts, perhaps the first extant extensive passage that represents the theosophical Kabbalah, was attributed to R. Abraham ben David, an inhabitant of the town of Posquières in Southern France, and so far this attribution of the text was accepted by all the scholars.[196] The fact that this may be one of the first extant theosophical texts does not, evidently, mean that necessarily this type of Kabbalah started with this passage.We shall not attribute too great an importance to the fact that this text deals with erotic and sexual issues, since we may assume that sexual and erotic topics were part of a much more comprehensive attitude expressed in the text. The passage is much more a testimony about something already known than a testimony for a beginning. In any case, I assume that some of the aspects of the following passage, especially that of the relations between the divine attributes, are reminiscent of the Philonic views, though Philo's writings are scarcely a plausible direct source for a Provencal medieval master. Nevertheless, the point I would like to make is that such an affinity is quite plausible. Rabad wrote, presumably sometimes around 1175, as follows:

> "[a] The interpretation of the Rabad to the rationale of the creation [as] *du-partzufin*. the reason for the creation of Adam and Eve [as] *du-partzufin*, is that the woman should be obedient to her husband, her life depending upon him, lest he go his [own] way, while she go her [own] way;[197] rather, affinity and friendship will exist between them, and they shall not separate from one another, and [Psalms 122:7] 'peace will rest upon them and calmness in their houses.' [b] Likewise is it as concerns 'the doers of truth' [*Po'alei ha-'Emmet*] 'whose actions are truth.'[198] The rationale of [*du-*]*partzufin*

196 Scholem, *Origins of the Kabbalah*, pp. 205–227, 283. On this author see Twersky, *Rabad of Posquières*, Dan, *History of Jewish Mysticism*, pp. 331–341, 344–348 and Ben-Shalom, *The Jews of Provence and Languedoc*, passim.

197 Compare below, the passage from *Sefer Ba'alei ha-Nefesh* where precisely this type of behavior is attributed to the animals. The evident parallelism between the two claims for the subservient role of the woman to her husband is one of the reasons for Rabad's authorship on this short discussion. However, it should be pointed out that similar views are found also in anonymous Kabbalistic collectanea that preserved material from the 13th century. See Ms. Cambridge, Harvard, Houghton 58, fol. 109a, and Ms. Vatican 202, fols. 58b–59a, to be printed and discussed in chapter 6.

198 Cf., e.g., *BT Sanhedrin*, fol. 42a.

refers to two matters: first, it is well-known[199] that two opposites were emanated,[200] one of them being stern judgment, and its counterpart, complete compassion. And were they not emanated [ve-'illu lo' ne'etzlu] [as] *du-partzufin*, and [if] each were to work out its actions [separately] according to its characteristic, it would be possible to see [them] as if they are two powers acting [separately], without any connection with its partner and without its assistance.[201] [c] But now, since they were created [as] *du-partzufin*, their actions are performed together [*be-yaḥad*], and in an equal manner [*be-shaweh*][202] and in a total uni[s]on, [*bi-yḥud gamur*], without any separation. Furthermore, unless they would be created

199 *ki yadu'a*. On the importance of this phrase for the history of Kabbalistic theosophy see below.

200 The concept of emanation when referring to divine powers is found also in a somewhat younger Kabbalist contemporary of Rabad, R. Yehudah ben Yaqar, in his *Perush ha-Tefillot ve-ha-Berakhot*, ed. S. Ashkenazi, (Jerusalem, 1979), I, p. 100: דרך אצילות as well as in the *'Iyyun* literature. See also Sendor, *The Emergence of Provencal Kabbalah*, I, pp. 346–350. Emanation recurs several times in the literature of the Special Cherub. See, e.g., *Berayyita' de-Yosef ben Uzzie'el*, whose time of the floruit is still open to debate

201 Plausibly this is an attempt to counteract a possible critique that the two attributes may constitute "two powers in heaven." See, e.g., Segal, *Two Powers in Heaven*, pp. 38–39, 44–49, 85–89, 98–108, Daniel Boyarin, "Two Powers in Heaven: or the Making of a Heresy," in eds. H. Najman – J.N. Newman, *The Idea of Biblical Interpretation: Essays in Honor of James L. Kugel* (Brill, Leiden, 2004), pp. 331–370, idem, "Once Again: "Two Dominions in Heaven" in the Mekhilta," idem, "Once Again: "Two Dominions in Heaven" in the Mekhilta," pp. 95–98, and the different view of Adiel Schremer, "Midrash, Theology, and History: Two Powers in Heaven Revisited," *JSJ* vol. 39 (2008), pp. 230–254.

202 Scholem, and following him Wolfson, translated "in an evenly balanced manner." However, my translation of *Shaweh* as "in an equal manner" is well-documented linguistically long before the time of the Rabad, as it has been shown in a study dedicated to this term by Henoch Yalon, *Studies in the Hebrew Language*, (Bialik Institute, Jerusalem, 1971), pp. 213–214 (Hebrew). For *Shaweh* as referring to agreement, that can also be pertinent for our text, see Saul Lieberman's important comments in his edition of *Midrash Devarim Rabbah*, (Wahrmann Books, Jerusalem, 1974) 3th edition, pp. 63–64, 137. Here,

> [in the manner of] *du-partzufin*, no total uni[s]on [*yiḥud gamur*] would emerge from them, and the attribute of judgment would not converge with [that of] compassion, nor would the attribute of compassion [converge] with [that of] judgment. But now, since they were created [as] *du-partzufin*, each of them may approach his/her partner and unite with her/him, and his/her desire is to willingly unite with her/his partner, so 'that the Tabernacle may be one'.[203] [d] A proof[text] for this [view] is found in the [Divine] Names which refer to each other, since *Yod He*[204] refers to the attribute of judgment and *'Elohim* to the attribute of compassion, as in 'Then the Tetragrammaton rained upon Sodom and upon Gomorrah.' [Genesis 19:24] 'The Tetragrammaton rained' [means that] He passed from one attribute to another attribute."[205]

however, the concept of agreement is already implied in the term *be-yaḥad* that occurs earlier in the passage.

203 Cf. Exodus 36:13. The Tabernacle, and sometimes the Temple, became a recurrent symbol for all the powers which constitute the sefirotic realm, which should be unified by the theurgical operation of the Kabbalist. See Idel, *Kabbalah: New Perspectives*, pp. 53–54, especially the quote in the name of R. Isaac Sagi Nahor, Rabad's son. See also Joseph Gikatilla's text, in Charles Mopsik, *Sex of the Soul: The Vicissitudes of Sexual Difference in Kabbalah*, ed. D. Abrams (Los Angeles, CA: Cherub, 2005), p. 184 n. 51. For the symbolism of Tabernacle in Rabbinic and Kabbalistic sources see also the discussions of Pedaya, *Name and Sanctuary*, and Mottolese, *Analogy in Midrash and Kabbalah*.

204 This is a shorter way to refer to the Tetragrammaton, which stands in Rabbinic literature for the attribute of compassion.

205 First printed by Scholem, *Reshit ha-Kabbalah*, p. 79:

[א] פי׳ הראב״ד טעם בריאת דו־פרצופין כי לכך נבראו אדם וחוה דו פרצופין כדי שתהיה אשה נשמעת לבעלה וכי חייה תלויין בו ושלא ילכו זה לדרכו וזה לדרכה אלא שיהיה ביניהם קירוב ואחוה לא יתפרדו ואז יהיה שלום ביניהם ובארמנותם שלוה [ב] וגם כן בפועלי האמת שפעולתם אמת טעם הפרצופין מורה לשני ענינים הא׳ כי ידוע הוא שנאצלו שני הפכים האחד דין גמור וחבירו רחמים גמורים ואם לא נאצלו דו פרצופין ויהיה כל אחד פועל כפי מדתו יראה כשתי רשויות ויפעל כל אחד בלי חבור חבירו ובלי סיוע שלו. [ג] אבל עתה, שנבראו דו פרצופין כל פעולתם ביחד, בשוה, וביחוד גמור, ואין ביניהם פירוד. ועוד כי לולי שנבראו דו פרצופין לא יעשה מהם ייחוד גמור ולא יתעלה מדת הדין ברחמים ולא מדת הרחמים בדין. אבל עכשיו שנבראו דו פרצופין כל אחד ואחד מתקרב

This compact passage drew the attention of several scholars who dealt with various aspects of its content.[206] As far as I know, none

ומתייחד בחבירו וכוסף ומתאוה להתחבר בחבירו "להיות המשכן אחד"[ד] וראיה לזה שתמצא השמות מורים כל אחד לחבירו כי תמצא שיוד הא מורה על מדת הדין ואלהים על מדת רחמים כמו "וד' המטיר על סדום ועל עמורה" המטיר ה' ובא לו ממדה למדה."

Scholem used two 16th century Italian manuscripts, Ms. London, British Library 768, fol. 14a, and Ms. Oxford-Bodleiana 1956, fol. 7a. I identified a third manuscript in Ms. Manchester 11 (olim Ms. Gaster), fols. 39b–40a. The three manuscripts stem from the very same source: an eclectic copyist active in 16th century Italy who relies mainly on Spanish Kabbalistic material in order to compile various Kabbalistic commentaries on the Pentateuch for commercial distribution. There are no significant variants between the three manuscripts. See M. Idel, "R. David ben Yehudah he-Hasid's Translation of the Zohar," *'Alei Sefer*, vol. 9 (1981), pp. 91–98 (Hebrew).

See also my "Androgyny and Equality in the Theosophico-Theurgical Kabbalah," *Diogenes* vol. 52,4 (2005), pp. 27–38; *Kabbalah & Eros*, pp. 53–103, "The Myth of the Androgyne in Leone Ebreo and its Cultural Implications," *Kabbalah*, vol. 15 (2006), pp. 88–90. Let me point out that though discussions of the unity of opposites is found in *Sefer Yetzirah*, a book with which Rabad was certainly acquainted, there is no trace of its terminology in the above quote. See Liebes, *Ars Poetica in Sefer Yetzirah*, pp. 43–44 and the discussion in chapter 6.

206 See Scholem, *Origins of the Kabbalah*, pp. 217–219, 283; Twersky, *Rabad of Posquieres*, p. 291, n. 20; Charles Mopsik, "Genese 1:26:27, L'Image de Dieu, Le Couple Humain at le Statut de la femme chez les premieres Cabalistes," *Rigueur et Passion, Hommage Annie Kriegel*, eds. S. Trigano, B. Courtois, P. Lazar, (Le Cerf, Paris, 1994), pp. 341–361; Mopsik, *Sex of the Soul*, pp. 76–82; Elliot R. Wolfson, "Woman: The Feminine as Other in Theosophic Kabbalah: Some Philosophical Observations on the Divine Androgyne," in eds., L. Silberstein and R. Cohn, *The Other in Jewish Thought and History – Constructions of Jewish Cultural Identity* (New York, NY: New York University Press, 1994), pp. 166–204; idem, *Circle in the Square*, especially pp. 205–206, n. 53, *Language, Eros, Being*, pp. 167–171, Eli Hadad, "Du-Partzufin shel 'Ezer ke-Negdo," in ed., N. Ilan, *A Good Eye – Dialogue and Polemic in Jewish Culture* (Tel Aviv: Hakibbutz Hameuchad, 1999), pp. 476–96 (Hebrew); Mottolese, *Analogy in Midrash and Kabbalah*, pp. 219–222, Pedaya, *Name and Sanctuary in the Teaching of R. Isaac the Blind*, pp. 104–105, the several discussions in Daniel Abrams, *The Female Body of God in Kabbalistic Literature – Embodied*

of them explicitly rejected the authenticity of the text and in my opinion the attribution is quite plausible, since there is a parallel to a writing of this author, to be quoted below, and on the other hand, a Kabbalist at the beginning of the 14th century, mentions, quite briefly, the existence of an interpretation of *du-partzufin* by Rabad, though its details are not mentioned.[207] Another Kabbalist, the anonymous author of a commentary on the Pentateuch written in the circle of the Rashba' in this period, refers also to Rabad as a commentor on the topic of *du-partzufin*.[208]

Let me start with the basic assumption of paragraph [a]: the main reason for the particular way of creating the primordial couple as one entity was to ensure the cooperation between the males and females in the generations to follow the original couple, by means of the latter's subordination to the former. In order to ensure the obedience of a woman to her husband, in fact monogamy – an institution whose status in ancient and even medieval Judaism was not so secure – a certain form of primordial anthropology was envisioned, one that establishes an organic linkage between the two human beings, based on monogyny. The woman's obedience to her husband represents a vision of a social and marital ideal, which was perhaps also a reality, according to the medieval author, for whom she was no more than her husband's limb, as this author formulated elsewhere the relationship between them.[209] What is important in this way of thinking is the fact that an attempt was made to preserve the structure of present

Forms of Love and Sexuality in the Divine Feminine (Magnes Press, Jerusalem, 2004), especially pp. 163–164 (Hebrew), Dauber, "Competing Approaches to Maimonides," p. 83, Porat, "*Founding of the Circle*" p. 66, n. 229. None of these discussions referred to my comparison between Rabad and Philo, an issue to be expanded below. See, however, E.R. Wolfson's summary of the state of the art in n. 476 below.

207 See Scholem, *Origins of the Kabbalah*, p. 216.

208 Ms. Modena-Estense.7.0 (Or. 2,1) (26). On this commentary see M. Idel, "An Anonymous Commentary on the Torah from the Circle of R. Shlomo ibn Adret," *Michael*, vol. 11 (1989), pp. 9–21 (Hebrew).

209 See below beside n. 235.

reality, or the 'order of being,' to use again a Voegelinean phrase, that is reminiscent also of one of Anaximander's fragments, or more precisely a mode of acting, by means of a metaphysical type of explanation. This is a cardinal issue, which should not be overlooked, which means that purely theological readings of the term *Yiḥud*, used in the text as related to unity in the divine world, or of union between two factors, miss the main message of the passage: the explanation of ideal modes of activities. Scholem translated the syntagm *bi-yḥud gamur* – "in a complete unity." However, this Hebrew expression, like the preceding phrases to which it should be linked conceptually, is an adverbial form, and characterizes the type of activity, not an ontological restructuring of the two divine attributes. This meaning returns to and completes the form *Be-Yaḥad*, which occurs beforehand. Such an understanding of one of the meanings of *Yiḥud* is found, for example, also in the *Book of Bahir*, in a passage translated in the previous chapter. [210] Elsewhere

210 ed. Abrams, p. 165, pars. 77–78.

I would say also, by comparing the use of the adverb *meyuḥadim* in another passage by Rabad – see below note 230 – that its meaning is more plausibly 'unison' rather than 'union' or unity. In any case the adverbial reading is supported by the gist of paragraph [d]. This does not mean that the syntagm *yiḥud gamur* does not refer also to complete unity in a theological other, later cases in Kabbalah, especially the 14th century *Sefer ha-Temunah* and in ibn Gabbai's book.

See also Scholem, *Origins of the Kabbalah*, p. 218 that refers to another possible connection between Rabad and the tradition related to the *Book of Bahir*. See also the view of Rabad's grandson, R. Asher ben David's *Commentary on Thirteen Divine Attributes*, in ed. Abrams, *R. Asher ben David*, pp. 64–65: "שמדת הרחמים ומדת הדין מיוחדות היו כשנראה לו למשה בס[נ]ה."

"The attribute of compassion and the attribute of judgment were together when it has been seen [or shown] to Moses in the bush." The question is whether *meyuḥadot* refers to a process of union or to their being together, as mentioned earlier in this footnote. I am inclined to adopt the latter meaning, which seems to fit also the view of R. Azriel of Gerone, in his "Epistle to Burgos," printed by Scholem, in *Madda'ei ha-Yahadut*, vol. II, p. 233: מיוחד בכל תמורה which I propose to translate as "accompanying each opposite." Compare to Porat, *Founding of the Circle*, pp. 102–103, who interpreted *meyuḥad* as "been

in the book of *Bahir* the root *YḤD* means, however, to "unify." Indeed the semantic field of the term *Yiḥud* in early Kabbalah deserves a separate investigation, especially since the importance of performance and cooperation play a greater role than ontological unity, as assumed by scholars.[211]

The anonymous author[s] of the *Book of Bahir* resorted to four terms that define each other: on the one hand, the verb *lehityaḥed,* the adverb *Yaḥad,* together, the noun *Yiḥud,* and on the other hand two verbal forms of the root *QRB,* to bring together, which is presented as the etymology of the *Qorban,* the sacrifice that is interpreted as intended to bring together the holy powers. This operation can be defined as a theurgical one, done by the priest that sacrifices. I propose to understand the two verbal forms as synonymous, which means that the unification is tantamount to bringing close. Such a reading is fostered by the adverbial form *Yaḥad.* [212]

Interestingly enough, with the exception of the term *Qorban,* the linguistic elements that were mentioned here as found in the *Bahir* passage, occur also in the Rabad's passage under scrutiny here. This parallelism is, in my opinion, not a matter of sheer coincidence, neither of the influence of one of these passages on the other, but most probably refers to an earlier tradition that impacted both of them, and is similar to Philo's view adduced above as to the cooperation of

united with". R. Asher's view should be compared to Philo's *On the Cherubim,* p. 27, par. 29: "where God is good, yet the glory of His sovereignty is seen amid the beneficence." In both cases, it is not cooperation that is mentioned here but some form of ontological mixing in the vein of what is going to be found later on in Kabbalah, see below beside nn. 452, 561, 739. See also R. Jacob ben Sheshet, *Sefer ha-'Emunah ve-ha-Bitaḥon,* chapter 1, in ed. Chavel, *Kitvei ha-Ramban,* vol. 2, p. 358. This does not mean that the syntagm *yiḥud gamur* does not refer to complete unity in a theological sense of divine unity in other, later cases in Kabbalah.

211 Ed. Abrams, p. 173 no. 87.

212 Compare also to the view of union or unity, and equality in the context of the two cherubs in the Temple already in *The Liturgical Poems of Rabbi Yanai,* ed. Rabinovitz, vol. 2, p. 339.

the divine powers. According to such a reading, also the noun *Yiḥud* should be interpreted accordingly: not a state of union, unification or unity between those forms, but a bringing closer, or bringing together of the "holy forms."

Let us, therefore, return to the adverbial approach also in the case of the term *du-partzufin* as referring to divine acts as it is evident already in a few Rabbinic sources.[213] Indeed this reference to modes of activities is evident also from the content of paragraph [d]. Let me draw attention to this emphasis: it is not a theological sort of reflection but an attempt to understand the divine mode of action in the world and subsequently a paradigm from human behavior. This is in line with the more general emphasis in Judaism on precise modes of action, as part of the performative approach characteristic of most of the phases of this religion, rather than the precise knowledge of frozen entities, which is a much more theological approach.[214] This

213 See, however, Dauber, "Competing Approaches to Maimonides in Early Kabbalah," pp. 82–84, who speaks about "divine unity" as part of his theory concerning the Kabbalists' appropriation of medieval philosophical – basically R. Baḥya ibn Paquda's and Maimonides' – approaches to divinity. Compare, however, nn. 89, 211 above. More on the actual impact of Maimonideanism on ecstatic Kabbalah see below chapter 9.

214 Idel, *Kabbalah: New Perspectives*, pp. 156–199, *Hasidism: Between Ecstasy and Magic*, pp. 58, 70, 73–74, 76, 79, 93, 105, 114, 116, 121, 126, 128, 140, 155, 164–165, 171–173, 184, 190–192, 195, 197, 204, 274, 288, 305, 310, 314, 327, 344, 363, "From Structure to Performance: On the Divine Body and Human Action in the Kabbalah," *Mishqafayim*, vol. 32 (1998), pp. 3–6 (Hebrew), *Enchanted Chains*, p. 34, *Kabbalah & Eros*, pp. 23–24, and especially my more recent studies "Performance, Intensification, and Experience in Jewish Mysticism," *Archaeus*, vol. XIII (2009), pp. 95–136, idem, "On the Performing Body In Theosophical-Theurgical Kabbalah: Some Preliminary Remarks," in eds. M. Diemling – G. Veltri, *The Jewish Body, Corporeality, Society, and Identity in the Renaissance and Early Modern Period*, (Leiden, Brill, 2009), pp. 251–271. Indeed, our discussion here, as well as elsewhere is part of a broader attempt to modify the more theological propensity for understanding Kabbalah in modern scholarship. See my "On the Theologization of Kabbalah," pp. 123–174. See also above n. 111.

is the reason why cooperation is more important than a metaphysical discourse, and why the concept of *coincidentia oppositorum* is less important than form of activities. Or, to put it in other terms, unison is more important than unity, and the transitive acts of governing over this world are more important than intransitive ones. In some cases, the sexual union between the divine powers is intended to give birth to souls, including in some instances of the later formula about the "unification of the Holy One and His *Shekhinah*" where the noun *Yiḥud* occurs. In my opinion, this major aspect of the role of the sefirotic realm has been neglected in scholarship.

Resorting to several biblical and Rabbinic themes, this early Kabbalist assumes that the first couple had been created as an entity having one body but two faces. This primordial union, which has been separated afterwards, ensures an affinity between male and female, in fact the subordination of the later to the former. In other words, to resort to Erich Fromm's term, Rabad's dynamic theosophy is a fine example of a patricentric-acquisitive culture, which intends to cement the existing social order and type of relationship found in institutions, like marriage. Nevertheless, the recurrence of the theme of delight, including corporeal delight, in a somewhat parallel text of the same author to be dealt with immediately below demonstrates that sexual gratification is indubitably one of the purposes of marriage and of intercourse. To put it in Jungian terms, the search for a cooperation between two opposite attributes in the divine realm, and between the male and female here below, is an act of recurring process of integration, in our case a bodily one, which includes moments of delight.

It should be emphasized that in this Kabbalistic text, just as in the Bible and in the Midrashic sources, the separation between the two parts of Adam has nothing to do with a punishment, as it is the case in the famous Platonic myth of the androgyne in the *Symposium*. The separation between sexes is conceived here as a positive state, an order of being that was intended by God from the very beginning, all this in order to help man by adding to him the woman as an assistant. Man needs the woman, though in the above passage the reason of this need is not explicated. What reflects the ideal state is not the primordial structure, but what happens in 'present' reality, which allows the well being of the male, and indirectly also of the female as his limb, and implicitly also the possibility of procreation. In any case, though speaking about opposites, Rabad uses twice the term *Ḥaver,* which means partner or companion, in order to mitigate the tension between the two members of the couple.

Separation of the male and the female components as described in the biblical story reflects, according to passage [b], not only a mundane event taking place here below, but also a parallel supernal event, namely the separation between two divine attributes, which were conceived of as initially united, though they had opposite qualities. It is not so clear what precisely is the divine power in the sefirotic system, which represents this instance of the primordial *coincidentia oppositorum,* or whether such a sefirotic interpretation is necessary at all. It is possible that in the case of this early stage of Kabbalistic theosophy an attempt to pinpoint one specific *sefirah* may be somehow anachronistic. However, the resort to the description of the two powers as *gamur/gemurim,* points in this direction since such descriptions are extraordinarily rare in Rabbinic literature. Such a theosophical decoding is also necessary because of the resort to the concept of emanation of those attributes. Moreover, we should pay attention that the sort of emanation mentioned here is not a Plotinian and the main types of Neoplatonism which are unilinear, but a more complex one, that assumes two different, in fact, opposite entities emerging together from the same unified source. I would, therefore, opt also for a theosophical decoding of this passage. Thus, the two absolute attributes should be identified with the *sefirot* of *Ḥesed* and *Gevurah,* and their source being the third *sefirah, Binah,* the *sefirah* which has been later on described as a mother[215] that precedes immediately the two attributes of absolute compassion and absolute judgment.

215 It should be mentioned that also Philo's Logos, from which the two attributes stem, is sometimes described as mother. See David Winston, *Logos and Mystical Theology in Philo of Alexandria,* (Hebrew Union College Press, Cincinnati, 1985), pp. 20–21.

Let me address now the Hebrew adverbial form *be-shaweh,* found in Rabad's passage. It designates, in the above context, a certain mode of activity: cooperation or agreement, between two different powers. However, this understanding may have also something to do with a certain degree of equality between the two divine powers which are destined to cooperate. As seen above in Philo and in several 13th century Kabbalistic discussions dealing with the secret of *du-partzufin,* the term *shaweh* is used in order to describe how the separation between the male and female aspects of Adam conceived of as a facial androgyne took place, as we shall see in chapter 5. I assume that this vision of bodily equality is Platonic in its origin, and it may have something to do with its reverberation of the theory of the division of the androgynous soul into two halves, known in earlier sources and then by a Geronese Kabbalist – and perhaps even to Rabad.[216] On the other hand, the theory of equality of opposites points to a pre-Socratic source, most probably mediated by Philo of Alexandria's writings, as mentioned in the previous section. In any case, the various speculations dealing with the equality between the structure and action of the divine attributes, does not mean automatically a simple translation of such a view on the level of marital relationships. It is easier to cultivate equality on high, between divine powers, than implement it on low, just as it is easier to speak about principles than to apply them.

An important observation as to the function of the theory of Aristophanes in Plato's *Symposium* is: The theory of the two halves of bodies was intended to explain the attraction between men and women; as well as homosexuality and lesbian relationships. This quite comprehensive nature of the love-theory found in Platonic text is not represented in the Hebrew sources, which restricted their discussion solely to the male-female attraction. Though homosexuality still remained an option in medieval Muslim culture in Spain with which Jews were well acquainted, and perhaps also influenced by – as it seems to be the fact in some cases in medieval erotic poetry – the Kabbalists

216 See my *Kabbalah & Eros,* pp. 73–75.

seem to ignore the other aspects of the Platonic text. It may well be that this selection is a matter of the intermediary sources to which the Kabbalists were exposed. However, I assume that also the Halakhic propensity of many of the Kabbalists prevented their engagement of the full implications of all the types of sexual relationship in the discourse of Aristophanes in Plato's *Symposium*.

Back to Rabad's passage: The possible identification of the two divine attributes with the two *sefirot* as reflecting a male and female entity described by the term *du-partzufin*, deserves a more detailed analysis. As Gershom Scholem has correctly pointed out, in Rabad's text the symbolism differs from that used later on in Kabbalah, when the *du-partzufin* become the symbol of the eight and tenth *sefirah*, namely that of *Tiferet* and *Malkhut* – sometimes envisioned as identical with the *Shekhinah*, respectively, which will be discussed in chapter 7.[217] Also in other cases when *du-partzufin* is mentioned in his school, very few indeed, the references to these two *sefirot* are missing, as can be seen from the texts of R. Ezra of Gerona, R. Jacob ben Sheshet and R. Azriel of Gerona.[218] However, the identification between the two attributes on the one hand, and the male/female polarity on the other is of outmost importance, given the paramount career this sexual polarity enjoyed in the history of Kabbalah. In fact, there are two different codes implied in such a discussion: the anthropomorphic one, *du-partuzfin*, and the attributive one.[219] The question is whether also the sefirotic code is indeed involved. In his

217 *Origins of the Kabbalah*, p. 217. See also his *Studies in Kabbalah*, p. 30 n. 95, and Baer, "The Service of Sacrifices," p. 408.

218 See R. Ezra's *Commentary on the Talmudic Legends*, Ms. Vatican 294, fols. 33b, 37b, Scholem, "New Remnants," p. 212, and ben Sheshet, *Meshiv Devarim Nekhoḥim*, ed. Vajda, pp. 126, 151.

219 For an interesting example of the organization of religious knowledge by the attributive code see the text printed by Scholem, *Mada'ei ha-Yahadut*, pp. 279–281, attributed to R. Isaac ben Jacob ha-Kohen, which has been translated also to Latin, and printed ibidem, pp. 282–284. Compare also to ben Shalom, "Kabbalistic Circles," p. 580 n. 45.

Commentary on the Song of Songs, R. Ezra of Gerona, who is part of the school of Kabbalah related to the Rabad, writes:

> "I will betake to the mount of myrrh" [Song of Songs 4:6] – this refers to Jerusalem, a blessing in Jerusalem which is on the mount of myrrh. "To the hill of frankincense" – this is Mount Zion. And Jerusalem resembles something which is red, an allegory to the attribute of strict justice, as it is said, "where righteousness dwelt" [Isaiah 1:21], and Mount Zion, on the hill of frankincense, [an allegory] to the attribute of compassion."[220]

R. Ezra undoubtedly alludes to the two *sefirot*: *Ḥesed* [divine mercy; the fourth *sefirah*] – whiteness [*loven*]–the hill of frankincense [*levonah*] – the attribute of compassion; and *Gevurah* [divine power; the fifth *sefirah*] – redness – the mount of myrrh – Jerusalem – the attribute of strict justice. This latter cannot refer to the tenth *sefirah,* so I propose to see the *sefirah Gevurah* as identical to red and Jerusalem. It may reasonably be assumed that the symbols found in this text also possess an erotic connotation; elsewhere in his *Commentary on the Song of Songs,* R. Ezra writes about the sowing of seminal fluid: "For the male comes from the supplement of the male drop which yields white after the female yields red."[221] The colors white and red appear here as symbols of the male and the female, i.e., *Ḥesed* and *Gevurah* respectively.

R. Ezra explicitly claims that the polar understanding of the symbolic and the sexual valences of the terms Zion and Jerusalem as a couple is already known. This is just one of the cases found in his writings wherein he claims to have received symbolic interpretations of biblical terms as some form of key-terms.[222] In this case, however, there is supporting material to confirm it, as seen in the material

220 *Commentary on the Song of Songs,* p. 495.

221 Ibid., p. 534. The discussion also appears in the R. Ezra's *Commentary on the 'Aggadot,* and had influenced R. Baḥya ben Asher. See Gottlieb, *The Kabbalah in the Writings of R. Bahya ben Asher ibn Ḥalawa* pp. 60–61 and note 105. See also Recanati, *Commentary on the Pentateuch,* fol. 61a.

222 See Idel, *Absorbing Perfections,* p. 248.

adduced above, as to the sexual meaning of Jerusalem as a female.[223] It seems that also in another case in the writings of this Kabbalist the two attributes are related to the sefirotic powers *Ḥesed* and *Gevurah*. This is the case in his *Commentary on the Talmudic Legends,* and in a quote in his name by R. Jacob ben Sheshet, where the attributes are depicted as constituting the seat of *Teshuvah,* namely *Binah*.[224]

Let me indicate the possible historical importance of this type of symbolism. According to Rabad's passage and the symbolism of his followers, the feminine element in the divine system is not identical with the last *sefirah,* or *Knesset Yisrael* or *Shekhinah,* as it is in the case of the Nahmanidean and Zoharic schools of Kabbalah and many other Kabbalistic texts afterward, but with another feminine power, the attribute of judgment, *Gevurah*. This means that the sexualizing processes in early Kabbalah took different symbolic forms, in different Kabbalistic schools, each reflecting possible earlier traditions or their interpretations.

In my opinion, as I expressed in a number of studies, from its earliest texts the theosophical-theurgical Kabbalah is related to binitarian or ditheistic conceptions, which are identified with various couples of *sefirot* already in the few remnants of Provencal Kabbalah. This means, for example, that the prayer of Eighteen Benedictions was conceived of bringing together, or uniting, different polarities represented by couples of *sefirot,* as part of a broader enterprise to unify all the ten *sefirot*. This seems to be the gist of the diverging early Kabbalistic traditions adduced in the name of the Provencal R. Abraham ben David and of R. Jacob, the so-called Nazirite of Lunel, in the 12th century, and of 13th century Catalan Kabbalists.[225]

223 See my "On Jerusalem as a Feminine and Sexual Hypostasis: from Late Antiquity Sources to Medieval Kabbalah," in eds. M. Neamtu and B. Tátaru-Cazaban, *Memory, Humanity, and Meaning: Selected Essays in Honor of Andrei Pleşu's Sixtieth Anniversary,* (Zeta, Cluj, 2009), pp. 65–110.

224 See my "Kabbalistic Prayer in Provence," p. 285 n. 107.

225 See my "Kabbalistic Prayer in Provence," "The Mystical Intention of the Eighteen Benedictions by R. Isaac Sagi Nahor," pp. 25–52, *Kabbalah & Eros,* pp. 49–52, *Ascensions on High,* p. 85, *Ben,* pp. 50, 95 note 159, 192 note 312, 201,

To return to Rabad's passage under scrutiny here: what is obvious is that when separated from their primordial form of existence, the two divine powers become the attributes of absolute compassion and stern judgment. Being two distinct and opposite powers, the two attributes could not cooperate would they not have been united ontologically before becoming separated during the act of emanation. However, their later union does not mean a complete reunion, a return to their pristine situation, but a form of cooperation which does not obliterate their independent existence. Nowhere in the text do we learn about an abolishment of the division of the divine attributes, even less so about a transsexual, an asexual or an androgynous situation in the present or in the future. The attributes appointed upon this world were premeditatedly designed in a special manner in order to be able to cooperate and they constitute the paradigm for human condition. I would imagine that a result of such cooperation, like in the case of the human marriage, is another *sefirah, Tiferet,* a median power, often described in Kabbalah as the son.

In other words, cooperation and its offspring, do not regain the original complexity of the higher *sefirah* that once comprised both the male and the female elements. It seems that for the theosophical-theurgical Kabbalists, that primeval situation is a state that can hardly be regained or retrieved, according to my reading of the above text of the Rabad, and of the vast majority of Kabbalistic texts from this school of Kabbalah. This school was concerned less with either the

653, 656–657, 661–662, and Fishbane, *As Light Before Dawn*, pp. 211–213. See also Dan, *History of Jewish Mysticism*, pp. 304, 400–404, where he describes the innovation of early Kabbalists as if dealing solely with theology, namely the creation of a theory of ten divine powers, but ignores both the history of *middot* and their connection to theurgy in R. Jacob and R. Isaac the Blind and earlier in Judaism. Compare also to Vajda, *Le commentaire*, p. 273, who describes R. Ezra of Gerona as "theologian", while elsewhere, ibidem, pp. 381–424, in a very learned appendix, he deals with the "signification théosophique des sacrifices" as if the abstract meaning of sacrifices, not their impact on high, is a main concern of this Kabbalist. See also his somewhat different description on ibidem, pp. 200–201.

primordial or the future ideal, but with the best way to function in the present, which requires first differentiation between two factors and then cooperation between them. Eros, therefore, is less the search for a lost union, like in the Platonic famous myth, but much more part of the fulfillment in the present of the procreative resources generated by a primordial, final and positively conceptualized act of dissection.[226] The above passage does not portray an attempt to escape the result of the divine wrath in the past, but rather an attempt to attain or secure human experiences of bliss in the present. By resorting to the term *du-partzufin*, which means, literarily, two faces, this early Kabbalistic text refers to the corporeal structure, at least insofar as Adam and Eve are concerned, as initially a being possessing, primarily, not only two faces, but most probably two bodies united into one, more comprehensive structure.

However, the binary structure of the primordial couple, which may explain the harmony between the two first ancestors, cannot explain the attraction between male and female in post-Adamic generations. Indeed, there is no way to understand how is someone able to find 'his woman' and why should she cooperate, namely, be subordinated to him, if the two do not stem from the same organism as their ancestors do. Since cooperation in the present – not during the primordial state or in the eschatological future – concerns R. Abraham ben David, without understanding why does a couple function harmoniously now, his text would be no more than an incoherent sermon. If the bodies indeed stem from different families, why should they cooperate? In passage [c] the Kabbalist claims that even now, the male and the female are created *du-partzufin*. This view is to be understood certainly in the framework of a worldview assuming continuous processes in the divine world, which means that the intra-divine processes are not to be understood as a matter of a theogonic development that was accomplished in the past, but of an ongoing emanative event. The

226 This is the difference between the huge majority of Kabbalistic texts and those of the Western occultists, including Mircea Eliade. See my *Mircea Eliade: From Magic to Myth*, pp. 60–103.

Kabbalistic passage is intended to be not only a description of the supernal realm, but primarily, in my opinion, an understanding of the human world in terms relevant also for the divine structure. The above passage is therefore posing a problem whose solution is, perhaps, not found within its details, but understood by persons initiated in the esoteric tradition found in the school which produced this passage.

Nevertheless, let me attempt to address another detail of passage [b], the meaning of the syntagm 'doers of truth.' As pointed out by Scholem, this phrase stems from the Rabbinic texts and was incorporated in the liturgical piece known as the Blessing of the Moon.It refers to the sun and moon, here symbolically alluding to the masculine and feminine divine powers. Thus, not only the divine powers and the first human couple reflect a certain specific type of relations between themselves, but also the two celestial bodies, sun and moon. Rabad is reading, therefore, the sexual dichotomy and the attraction between the two poles on three levels main: the human, the celestial and the intra-divine. Because of the parallel polarities, the different planes of existence not only correspond to each other, but perhaps have an impact on each other, an issue that was emphasized, however, in the theosophical-theurgical schools only later on.

In other words, I assume that not only are the sexual relationship between elements found on the same ontic level, creating a horizontal dynamic between them, but also that such a dynamic generates another, vertical dynamic, which involves different planes of being, which I would call theurgy, or more precisely, erogenic theurgy.

On the basis of the material adduced above, it is hard to decide whether the sympathetic affinities between the different levels of being are only a matter of isomorphism, and becomes obvious in some of the discussions since the late 13th century, or whether also another form of relationship is assumed, a sympathetic one, as it may be the case in Rabad's son, R. Isaac the Blind's view and those of his followers.[227] Or, to put it in terms of the Rabbinic models mentioned

227 See my "The Mystical Intention of the Eighteen Benedictions by R. Isaac Sagi Nahor," pp. 36–39.

in the previous chapter: is there also an impact also of model [E] on Rabad? It is hard to answer this question since as far we know very little about his theosophy.

I would say that for a discussion of some important aspects of medieval Rabbinic Judaism as representing what I called a culture of eros, Rabad's and the many similar passages found in Kabbalistic writings of the 13th and 14th centuries may be very relevant. They represent an effort to telescope the sexual polar structure not only within the divine pleroma, but also in the cosmic order, thus offering a more integral picture of reality, an approach that transcends the ordinary scope of Rabbinic thought. However, I believe that my claim as to the importance of the theosophical scheme for structuring the Kabbalists' present behavior, can be illustrated from an outstanding parallel to this passage found in another writing of this Kabbalist, a Halakhic one. In his introduction to *Sefer Ba'alei ha-Nefesh,* a treatise dealing with the Halakhic purity needed for marital intercourse, he writes:

> "The Creator has created everything for the goodness of man and his pleasure[228] ... Would the male and the female be created out of earth like all the other creatures, the woman would be to man as the female of an animal to the male, which does not accept the rule of the male, and does not stand [ready] to attend him. And every one of the animals is taken by force from another, and they are beating each other, and every one is turning to its [own] way. They [namely the animals] are not consigned to each other[229] because from their beginning they have been created separately. This is the reason why the Creator has seen the need of man and his pleasure,[230] and He created him as a single individual, and He took one of his ribs and built a woman out of it, and He brought her to Adam to be his wife, to be an assistant and a servant to him, because she is considered to be just as one of his limbs, created in

228 *Hana'ato*. This noun can be translated also as delight or gratification.

229 *'Einam meyuḥadim zeh le-zeh*. See above note 211.

230 *Hana'otav*.

order to serve him, and he will rule over her just as he rules over his limbs, because she will be desiring him, just as the limbs are desiring the pleasure[231] of the[ir] body...And this finding[232] was not the result of a search and pursuit, as other findings are, because it is not nice to speak so about the Creator, but it is found in the [divine] primordial thought.[233]"[234]

Here, as in his above cited Kabbalistic passage, we learn about a situation that is described solely in accordance to the common non-mystical criteria. In the first passage, the calmness and peace between a man and a woman is the ultimate reason of the whole structure of the process, and so is it in the second passage. Peace, stability and calmness are the opposites of the struggle between the animals over the female, and the temporality of the relations between them. From this point of view, we have here a reflection of the Greek concept of *isonomia*. On the other hand, there is nothing as a spiritual transformation involved in the description of the two partners. The mystical explanations are attempts to explain the common, rather than to change it. Stability, cooperation – which means in fact, I would like to repeat it, subordination of the wife to her husband and her subservient status – peace and calmness, are the ultimate goals of the Kabbalistic discourse in the passage quoted above. The metaphysical construct validates, therefore, the given order, rather than intends to

231 *Hana'at gufo*. For the wife as a limb see below n. 239.

232 Of the woman by God. The claim is that God did not experiment but He had in mind the entire situation of a unified creation and then separation, from the very beginning.

233 *Ha-maḥashavah ha-qadmonit*. On the possible Platonic background of this term see Idel, *Kabbalah & Eros*, pp. 69–73.

234 *Sefer Ba'alei ha-Nefesh*, p. 14; Twersky, *Rabad of Posquieres*, pp. 86–97; Dan, *History of Jewish Mysticism*, pp. 337–343, Jeremy Cohen, "Rationales for Conjugal Sex in RaBaD's *Ba'alei Ha-nefesh*," *Jewish History*, vol. 6 (1992), pp. 65–78; idem, *"Be Fertile and Increase, Fill the Earth and Master It": The Ancient and Medieval Career of a Biblical Text*, (Cornell University Press, Ithaca and London, 1989), pp. 203–204, 218; David Biale, *Eros and the Jews*, (Basic Books, New York, 1992), pp. 95–100.

change it by offering an alternative ideal. The real is conceived to be also the ideal. The subordination of the physical to the metaphysical, mentioned by Jung, seems to be totally absent here.[235]

In fact, according to the last passage, within the divine thought, the separation has been already adumbrated from the very beginning, because God was conceived not as operating by means of trial and finding: He created the man in the form of *du-partzufin* in a premeditated manner, because only so could He ensure the harmonious relations between them later on. He knew in advance that He must create a two-faced being in order to separate them later, and so to ensure the best relationship thereafter. Woman desires man, and by this general assessment the Kabbalist follows the Biblical verse.[236]

However, while the Bible offers the well known mythical version, which assigns the emergence of the woman's desire to her sin, the Kabbalist sees this desire as the result of a premeditated divine act. Desire, in Hebrew *Teshuqah,* a term that may be rendered as Eros, at least the feminine one, is conceived of by this Kabbalist not as a curse, but much more as a blessing. In other words, while the Genesis episode about sin and curse may invite a metastatic attitude, which will suggest a return to the prelaptic state which will involve the obliteration of the desire, for the Kabbalist this cannot be the case. According to him, more than the satisfaction of corporeal desires, the female's attraction to man is natural because it is part of a divine strategy intended to ensure a stable affinity. Later on in the same text, R. Abraham ben David addresses also the attraction of man to his wife, again invoking biblical connotations, in quite reciprocal terms:

> "She merits to stand with me forever, and I with her, 'and become one flesh' [Genesis 2:24]. This is why man should love his wife

235 See my "Eros in der Kabbala: Zwischen Gegenwaertiger Physischer Realitaet und Idealen Metaphysischen Konstructen," tr. Petra-Susanne Raebel, in *Kulturen des Eros,* eds., D. Clemens and T. Schabert, (Wilhelm Fink Verlag, Munchen, 2001), pp. 59–102 and *Kabbalah & Eros,* pp. 92–94.

236 Genesis 3:16.

> as he loves himself,[237] and honor her and have pity on her and guard her as if he guards one of his limbs.[238] And likewise it is incumbent on her to serve him[239] and honor him and love him as herself, 'because she was taken from him.'"[240] [241]

The reciprocity of the relation of love described here is quite surprising in a religious system that is so male-oriented, conceiving the woman as subservient. Woman is understood not only as an instrument for the well being of the male, as in some of the former passages of the same author, or a ritualistic object for fulfilling a commandment, *ḥeftza' de-mitzwah*. Here, eroticism is part of an almost narcissistic feeling derived from the consciousness of the organic unity between male and female. Rabad is seeing male and female as dimensions that are characteristic not just of the humans but also of other sort of creatures.[242] Sex or reproduction is not mentioned in this context, though no doubt they indeed constituted quintessential dimensions of the author's book quote here.[243] However, in his exoteric book, the two divine attributes have not been mentioned.

The nature of the primordial state is the etiological motivation for present behavior, not an ideal to be cultivated now-a-days. This is the significance of the Kabbalist's resort to the verse from Genesis 2:23, in a new context. Rabad is now portraying Adam not as exclaiming and acknowledging the emergence of a woman out of his body, or dealing with the etymology of her name, but, on the one hand, with the the

237 Cf. *BT Yevamot*, fol. 62b; See also *BT Berakhot*, fol. 24a.

238 On wife as a limb of the husband see above in the other quote from the same book, and in Philo, *Quaestiones in Genesis*, 1:27, and in R. David Qimhi's *Commentary on the Pentateuch*, on Genesis 2:18. Mopsik, "Genesis 1:26–27," p. 358 has pointed out the similarity between this stand and the verse from Ephesians 5:28. See also above n. 232.

239 *Le-'ovdo*.

240 Genesis 2:23.

241 *Ba'alei ha-Nefesh*, p. 15.

242 Ibidem, p. 14.

243 Ibidem, pp. 116–117.

reason for her alleged specific function, and that of Adam's attitude to her on the other hand. It is not the concern with the past, or with genealogy or theosophy that informs the Kabbalist's interpretation, but rather the function of married women in the present and in the future. The myth is again enlisted in favor of preserving a certain type of relationship between husband and wife, this time in service of a basically monogamous type of relationship. Neither does something in the text suggest that in an ideal future, there will be a return to the primordial human state of *du-partzufin*. Neither in Rabad's text, nor in the subsequent numerous Kabbalistic discussions of facial androgyny, is there a proclivity to experience what Eliade has designated a 'ritual androgyny.'[244] The fact that halakhic regulations prohibited the use of female garments by males and vice-versa, forms of bisexual experiences as mentioned by Eliade in the context of other religions, do not occur in the theosophical-theurgical Kabbalah as I know it.[245]

Rabad's Kabbalistic passage should be compared to Philo's discussions of the two attributes adduced above in paragraph 2 for a variety of reasons, one of them being the historical development of theological thought in ancient Judaism and the possible filiation of Kabbalah to earlier sources. In the passages of these Jewish thinkers, the three distinct stages occur: initial state of union, which may be understood as some form of *coincidentia oppositorum*; then the separation between the two powers, and finally their cooperation, which is facilitated by the existence of an initial union between the two divine powers.

It should be pointed out that in each of the three paragraphs [b], [c], and [d], there are different possible relations between the attributes: in

244 See, e.g., *The Two and the One*, p. 117; idem, "Chasteté, sexualité et vie mystique chex les primitifs," in *Mystique et continence, Les etudes carmelitaines*, vol. 7 (Descles de Brouwer, 1952), pp. 48–49; Marie Delcourt, *Hermaphrodite: Mythes et rites de la bisexualité dans l'antiquité classique*, (PUF, Paris, 1958). See also the important material collected by Wayne A. Meeks, "The Image of the Androgyne: Some Uses of a Symbol in Early Christianity," *History of Religion*, vol. 13 (1974), pp. 189–197; Gilbert Durand, *Les structures anthropologiques de l'imaginaire*, (Paris 1993), p. 352.

245 Eliade, *The Two and the One*, pp. 112–113, 116–117.

[d] the attributes change their original type of action into that of the other attribute, in [c] there is cooperation, which differs indeed from [d] and in [b] the negative possibility of independent actions of each of the two is mentioned. As we shall see below, such a distinction is to be found in one of the most widespread treatises in early Kabbalah, in a text autored by a Kabbalist that was influenced by Rabad's son, R. Azriel of Gerona.

The occurrence of the phrase *ki yadu'a* – "since it is known" – in Rabad's first text, which is conceived – so far – to be one of the earliest in the Kabbalistic literature, is quite surprising. If indeed this text has been written by the Rabad – which I think is the case – and if this expression is original, it points to the existence of a certain form of theosophical tradition preceding Rabad, and the similarity between the understanding of *Yihud* in his passage and in the *Bahir*, as claimed above, points in this direction. The occurrence of the same mode of thinking in Philo's passages discussed above, seems to foster Rabad's assessment that the view he exposes is "already known."

Here, however, I am concerned with just one detail: for Philo, the two divine attributes are not related explicitly to the human division between male and female, or their sexual behavior, though behavior of the two equal partners is related to procreation. The Kabbalist is, however, focusing on particularly this practical aspect, which apparently did not attract the attention of the Alexandrine thinker who was concerned more with metaphysics and exegesis.

Let me address paragraph [d] in Rabad's Kabbalistic passage. It reflects a Rabbinic view that is rare, part of an attempt at accounting for the occurrence of a divine name, traditionally related to one attribute, in a context that is pertinent to the other attribute.[246] Therefore, the Provencal Kabbalist claimed that already in the Bible the two attri-

246 See *Pesiqta de-R. Kahana'*, ed. S. Buber, (rpr. Jerusalem, 1963), fol. 162a, Marmorstein, *The Old Rabbinic Doctrine of God*, p. 44, *Sefer ha-Yiḥud*, cf., *Asher ben David*, ed. Abrams, pp. 52, 61, 63, 77, R. Jacob ben Sheshet, *Sefer ha-'Emunah ve-ha-Bitaḥon*, chapter 2, in ed. Chavel, *Kitvei ha-Ramban*, vol. 2, p. 358, R. Menahem Recanati, *Commentary on the Pentateuch*, fol. 25ab, my *Kabbalah:*

butes were convertible, to a certain extent, so as to be able to exercise different divine actions. This is a type of transversti, though neither of the two attributes is reunited with the other in order to recreate the lost broken unit. Indeed, there is a certain reciprocity involved in claiming that each of the two attributes possesses the quality of the opposite one, so that it can cooperate with it. This is the reason why neither of them has to undergo a fundamental transformation while cooperating with the other: it does not import the quality from the other but it possesses it because of the primeval coexistence before their division.

This claim is quite similar to Philo's statement adduced above to the effect that, "And the Powers were brought together in another way by the eternal juxtaposition of the names in order that the Creative Power might share in the Royal and the Royal in the Creative" that we discussed at the end of section 2. This shift in the mode of activity and cooperation is predicated on the shift of names. However, this understanding of the actions differs from the Rabbinic approach to the two attributes, which are not conceived of as cooperating, but as distinct modes. Rabad's view, that is not consonant with the Rabbinic views on the attributes, may be a further indication for the non-Rabbinic source of his view.

Let me summarize the most salient points of similarities between the views of Philo and those of the Rabad:

A] The two authors mention some form of equality of male and female in shape.

B] Both mention equality also of two divine powers. According to the two authors, equality is essential for cooperation and harmony.

C] Both mention opposites that cooperate after they have been separated: divine powers in Philo and in the Rabad, while nothing similar is found in the models surveyed before, related to Rabbinic literature.

New Perspectives, p. 340 note 186, and Wolfson, *Language, Eros, Being*, pp. 60, 445 n. 98.

D] Last but not least: the two authors mention in the same context divine names as the reason for the cooperation between the two different divine names, Rabad's Kabbalistic passage [d] and Philo's quoted passage from *Questions and Solutions* in Exodus II, 66. It is this shared point in particular that prevents the assumption that the theory of the opposites reached Rabad directly from pre-Socratic sources, via quotes in Aristotle's writings, especially his *Physics* and *Metaphysics,* as well as commentaries of his writings which preserved additional traditions, or Simplicius's paraphrasis of Aristotle's *De caelo,* translated in Hebrew, or in various doxographies. The existence of a theory of opposites related to divine powers in Rabad, should be taken into consideration for understanding the reason why his followers were interested in discussions about the unity of opposites stemming from other sources, found in Christian sources, to be discussed in the next chapter.

Last but not least: it is in the Kabbalistic school related to the Rabad that the concept of Infinite, *'Ein Sof,* emerged as a Kabbalistic technical term in Hebrew.[247] It should be mentioned that the term *apeiron,* the boundless or the infinite, is the principle that is characteristic of Anaximander, and it may have an impact on Philo's theory of the divinity as infinite.[248] As I have attempted to show elsewhere, the term *aperantos* – an adjectival form referring to the quality of the infinite – occurs in a late antiquity Gnostic passage that is replete with Jewish themes, together with a structure of two decads situated one above the other, in a manner representative of the structure that consists in *'Ein Sof* and two decads of *sefirot* in early Kabbalah. This

247 Scholem, *Origins of the Kabbalah,* pp. 265–289, 431–444. For a critique of his view see Valabregue-Perry, *Concealed and Revealed.*

248 See, e.g., W.K.C. Guthrie, *A History of Greek Philosophy: Vol. 1: The earlier Presocratics and the Pythagoreans* (Cambridge University Press, Cambridge, 1962), pp. 76–78, 83–87, Freudenthal, "The Theory of the Opposites," pp. 208–210. See also Paul Seligman, *The Aperion of Anaximander, A Study in the Original & Function of Metaphysical Ideas* (University of London, London, 1962). For God as infinite in Philo see Runia, *Philo of Alexandria, On the Creation of the Cosmos,* p. 146, and Wolfson, *Philo,* I p. 222.

double decad is well-represented in the philosophical interpretations of views found in *Sefer Yetzirah,* especially in that of R. Shlomo ibn Gabirol.[249]

249 On those issues see my "On the Theosophy at the Beginning of Kabbalah" and "Sefirot Above Sefirot." See also above n. 147.

FIVE

Attributes, Opposites and Theurgy in R. Isaac Sagi Nahor and His Disciples

Unlike Rabad's scant production in matters of Kabbalah as found in the few quotes in his name, his son R. Isaac Sagi Nahor – namely R. Isaac who is replete with light, a euphemism for his being blind – is known preminently as a Kabbalist and as a teacher of Kabbalah.[250] He is also quoted much more by his disciples than his father was, and

250 Scholem, *Origins of the Kabbalah*, Pedaya, *The Name and the Sanctuary*, Sendor, *The Emergence of Provencal Kabbalah*, Valabregue-Perry, *Concealed and Revealed*, passim, especially pp. 139–143, Gavarin, "The Problem of Evil," Afterman, *Devequt*, pp. 176–210, Idel, "Interpretations of the Secret of Incest in Early Kabbalah," pp. 100–117, idem, "The Mystical Intention of the Eighteen Benedictions by R. Isaac Sagi Nahor," "Did Rabbi Isaac Sagi Nahor Believe in Metempsychosis? Some Remarks on the Study of Provencal Kabbalah," *Romania, Israel, France: Jewish Trails, Volume in Honor of Professor Carol Iancu*, eds. D. Delmaire et alia, (Bucharest, 2013), pp. 51–60, and Dan, *History of Jewish Mysticism*, pp. 361–429 and Ben-Shalom, *The Jews of Provence and Languedoc*, pp. 565–573, 578–581, 600–602, 621–622. See now the important contribution of Avishai Bar-Asher, 'Illusion versus Reality" who casted very significant doubts on R. Isaac's authorship on the *Commentary to Sefer Yetzirah*, attributed by both Kabbalists and scholars to R. Isaac. In the following pages I shall address this commentary as Pseudo-Isaac Sagi Nahor. The datation of this commentary is probably later than early Kabbalah, probably in the second part of the 13th

he was even envisioned as the "father of Kabbalah."[251] The volume of his legacy, mainly quotes in his stidents' writings, transcends the Kabbalistic one written or attributed to his father, though the latter wrote extensively on many other topics related to Rabbinic topics. Whether R. Isaac's Kabbalistic views indeed represent a continuation or a development that started with his father or whether some major changes had been introduced by the son and the latter's disciples, is hard to decide, especially since the passage of the Rabad discussed above, has not been quoted or commented on in R. Isaac's school. In any case, the *Commentary to Sefer Yetzirah* attributed to him has been dealt duly with by several scholars.[252] Far from being a document where hesitations that may reflect a nascent terminology occur, the style of the text reflects the existence of a rather constant and rather specialized terminology, though not always is its meaning evident. However, unlike Scholem, I do not enumerate the book of *Bahir* among his sources,[253] neither Gnostic ones,[254] though they may draw from much earlier common sources. Nevertheless, it seems very plausible that Platonic and Neoplatonic themes did impact the terminology of this Kabbalist.

The passage from the father to the son is, however, more than a generational transition. If the father can be considered part of first elite, especially because of his Halakhic and interpretative opus, while Kabbalah constitutes a hidden part of his knowledge, in the case of the son we may speak about someone belonging to a secondary elite,

century, but it may nevertheless contain some early material that is relevant for the understanding of the development of the *middot* discussions.

251 Scholem, *Origins of the Kabbalah*, p. 260.

252 See Bar-Asher, 'Illusion versus Reality," and the earlier discussions by Sendor, *The Emergence of Provencal Kabbalah*, Pedaya, *The Name and the Sanctuary*, and Scholem, *The Kabbalah in Provence*, ed. Shatz, appendix, pp. 1–18.

253 See Scholem, *Origins of the Kabbalah*, p. 263 and see also his 'The Concept of *Kavanah* in Early Kabbalah', in *Studies in Jewish Thought, an Anthology of German Jewish Scholarship*, ed., A. Jospe, (Wayne University Press, Detroit, 1981), pp. 164–165. See also Idel, preface to *Sefer ha-Bahir*, ed. Abrams, p. 2.

254 Scholem, *Origins of the Kabbalah*, p. 265.

namely about a figure that does not play a major role in a society based on distinction in matter of Rabbinic knowledge. All that remains from the latter deals with Kabbalistic issues alone, namely lore restricted to a small elite. This is also the case of his followers that will be discussed below.

Discussions of the Rabbinic attributes, according to some of the models described above, sometimes combined with treatments of *sefirot* and attributes related to *Sefer Yetzirah,* are evident in his commentary, genuine or just attributed to him. It is this encounter between the Rabbinic attributes and concepts to be found in *Sefer Yetzirah,* that produced a main development in Kabbalistic theosophy, as it was the case also in the *Book Bahir* though in a different proportion. This encounter, however, goes much beyond the mythical speculations of the latter book, and inaugurates some questions that are much more complex and sophisticated, insofar as the nature of the *sefirot* and the attributes are concerned. This is one of the very first beginnings of a metaphysical vortex that will generate some of the complex theories of the *sefirot* conjugated in various ways with that of *middot.* However, let me emphasize that this vortex was deeply connected with both the meaning and the efficacity of the rituals. This means that while the book of *Bahir* is much less reflective as to the nature of the relations between the *middot* and *sefirot,* it is this topic that will be elaborated in a substantial manner by the Provencal Kabbalist, and nourish a long series of developments. Only a few of them will be addressed below.

In other words, while the Bahiric theory of *middot* or *sefirot* is relatively simple, dealing with the manifestation of each of them as a certain divine power or even a divine personality, it seems that with the Pseudo-R. Isaac the Blind it is the more abstract aspects of those powers, especially the contraries between them, external and internal, that he is preoccupied with. I see no reason, however, to assume a development starting with the *Bahir,* that was transcended by someone who knew it, but I assume a separate line of conceptual development, that may share a common, much earlier source, which still has to be uncovered. In any case, the passage of Rabad discussed above that deals with opposites and equality, should be taken into consideration more than done so far, for understanding the view found in the school to be scrutinized in this chapter. Provided my concern here with the history of the term *middah* in Kabbalah, I shall not address below the discussions of the term *sefirah*, which were already engaged by Scholem and Sendor but tangently.

The Pseudo-R. Isaac comments upon the linguistic theory of the late antiquity book, as referring to specific qualities of divine powers. So, for example, two main forms of pronunciation of seven Hebrew consonants are understood as referring to the double nature of each of the seven lower divine powers.He uses in this context the term *middot*:[255]

> "Soft[256] – there is softness that is for good and there is softness for bad. "And hard" – there is hardness for good and there is hardness for evil. And so too, each and every attribute, there is good that is for bad, and there is evil that is for good. This is the reason why it is said that the double [seven consonants] are opposites, since the cause itself that is good is converted in order to operate to him for bad, just as the wicked that convert the attribute of compassion to cruelty, and the righteous invert the attribute of judgment into the attribute of compassion,[257] that correspond to the seven double

255 See Scholem, *Origins of the Kabbalah*, pp. 30–31. For the Pseudo-R. Isaac's theory of *middot* and *sefirot* see Sendor, *The Emergence of Provencal Kabbalah*, 1, pp. 295–315. On pp. 162–163, Sendor proposes to translate in some instances in the Pseudo-R. Isaac's commentary *middah* as dimension, which does not seem to me to be so plausible, though the issue of spaciality is nevertheless important.

256 Cf. *Sefer Yetzirah*, ed. Hayman p. 127. On the contraries of soft and hard in pronunciation of some letters, see Tzahi Weiss, "Soft and Hard: More Comments on the Syrian Context of *Sefer Yetzirah*," *Kabbalah*, vol. 26 (2012), pp. 229–241 (Hebrew). Needless to say that the attributive code added concepts like the soft attribute of judgement and a hard or stern attribute of judgment, as part of the expansion of this code.

257 This is a certain formulation of the Rabbinic model [E2]. See, however, the Pseudo-R. Isaac's view that that the *sefirot* do not invert their function, Scholem, ed., *Commentary on Sefer Yetzirah*, p. 7. The Kabbalist denies that a

that are inner, and the branches that correspond to them, in the likeness of seven days, seven weeks, seven years."[258]

Here we have a combination of two Rabbinic models: one dealing with the coexistence of good and evil elements within each one of the ten divine powers, that is reminiscent of model [D], while the other model, the theurgical one [E], refers to the two attributes. The theurgical possibility is predicated not on a total metanoia of one of the attributes, but on the activation by means of human acts, of one of the two dimensions found in each of those attributes. Let me emphasize that though a *Commentary on Sefer Yetzirah*, a book where the concept of *sefirot* reigns supreme, the Pseudo-R. Isaac's commentary resorts widely to the term *middot*. This is the case, for example, in the following passage:

"The doubles – faces from within faces,[259] powers from within powers. The things that are the attribute of judgment are [found] within the attribute of compassion like a flame connected to the coal. And [just] as they are doing by means of judgment evil, [so] they do by means of judgment good. And when there is no good attribute in that person, the things will separate since they are judgment in order to judge him in a terrible manner, since there is no wicked person that cleaves to the attribute of good in order

sefirah inverts – מתהפכים – as the Rabbis say – despite the fact that he uses it as part of the Rabbinic statement – and I translated his use of the verb הומרה as converted.

258 *Commentary on Sefer Yetzirah*, ed. Scholem p. 15:

רך - יש רכות לטוב, ויש רכות שהוא לרע. וקשה - יש קושי לטוב, ויש קושי לרע. וכן כל מדה ומדה, יש טוב שהוא לרע, ויש רע שהוא לטוב. לכך נאמר כפולות שהן תמורות - כי הסבה עצמה שהיא טובה הומרה לו לפעול לו רע כמו הרשעים שהם מהפכים מדת הרחמים לאכזריות, והצדיקים מהפכים מדת הדין למדת הרחמים, כנגד ז׳ כפולות פנימיות והענפים מהם כנגדן, כעין ז׳ ימים, ז׳ שבועות, ז׳ שנים, ז׳ שביעיות.

See Sendor, *The Emergence of Provencal Kabbalah*, II, pp. 149–150, and Idel, "Interpretations of the Secret of Incest in Early Kabbalah," pp. 104–105.

259 The Hebrew consonants *PNYM* can be vocalized also as referring to *Penim*, namely, interiority. See Scholem, *Origins of the Kabbalah*, p. 272 n. 173.

> that it will emanate upon him, and this is the reason why one of the powers of judgment separated,[260] so that they do not do for them good."[261]

Let me draw attention to the plural forms of the powers and things: not just one power, or attribute is found within another, but many powers are found most probably in each of the last seven divine powers. Their activity takes the shape of the human acts, a clear case of reciprocity. The divine powers are depicted more as a zone wherein many things are found, including opposites, rather than as a personalized entity.[262] This is also the case in another passage from the Pseudo-R. Isaac's Commentary:

> "The doubles – since each and every one of them is double, for two, to benefit and to harm, the good attribute is majoritarian, since it is the principle of everything. And the principle is a cause that is emanated from there and it is an attribute, but there were inner attributes,[263] which did not emerge to light and from there[264] they

260 Namely the element of the compassion attribute is separated in order to allow to judgment full activity.

261 Pseudo-R. Isaac, *Commentary on Sefer Yetzirah*, p. 16:
כפולות - פנים מתוך פנים, כחות מתוך כחות. הדברים שהם מדת הדין בתוך מדת רחמים כשלהבת קשורה בגחלת, וכשם שעושים בדין רע כן עושים בדין טוב. וכשאין מדה טובה באותו האיש, יתפרדו הדברים שהן דין לדונו בשפטים גדולים, שאין הרשע דבק במדת טוב כדי שיתאצל עליו, ולכך יתפרדו אחת מכחות הדין כדי שלא לעשות להם טוב.
This passage has been quoted in the *Commentary on Sefer Yetzirah*, attributed to R. Isaac of Acre, pp. 383–384. See also Sendor, *The Emergence of Provencal Kabbalah*, pp. 170–172. For the view that within each of the *sefirot* there are the two attributes, see a late 13th or early 14th century text, printed by Scholem, *Reshit ha-Kabbalah*, pp. 241–242. Such an approach assumes that *middot* constitute an inner structure of the sefirotic code.

262 See also the passage from *Sod wi-Ysod ha-Qadmoni* – a late 13th century Kabbalistic work to be discussed in chapter 8 – translated and discussed in my *Enchanted Chains*, pp. 176–177.

263 For inner and outer divine attributes see also R. Isaac's nephew, R. Asher ben David's *Complete Works*, ed. Abrams, pp. 68, 77, and in Ms. New York JTS, 1737, fol. 13d.

264 I assume that the act of separation is related to the seven *middot* beneath the

> were separated from one another. Since in one attribute several powers are fixed,[265] and when a bad person is looking at that attribute that is benefiting or harming, that looking is for him for bad, as someone that eats a cooked food, that once it is helpful and another time it is harmful, even if the taste [itself] does not change."[266]

Again, the specific type of the human act of looking activates a certain aspect of the attribute that possesses two opposite qualities. Indubitably, this is a theurgical activity, which depends on the moral qualities of the person, not only on his deeds. A theurgical understanding of the attributes is found elsewhere in the commentary, where the author of pseudo-R. Isaac writes:

> "Favor – since he does not walk in accordance to that attribute from where favor was given, favor is transformed into another attribute that is coming when he is ugly, just like the rich man who does not diminish his wealth by giving charity, finally his wealth will be diminished."[267]

third *middah, Binah*. For the seven *middot* see chapter 2, the passage from *'Avot de-R. Nathan*. The theory of seven *middot* had a significant impact on 18th century Hasidism, where they represent some lower form of divine powers, to be transcended in order to unite with the divine realm. See, e.g., Idel, *Hasidism*, p. 57, idem, 'Higher than Time,' pp. 203–208, and idem, *Enchanted Chains*, p. 189 n. 118.

265 See the passage from R. Isaac of Acre's *Me'irat 'Einayyim*, p. 94, translated in chapter 7, about the existence of a plurality of powers within a certain attribute. See also R. Asher, *Complete Works*, ed. Abrams, pp. 52–54.

266 Pseudo-R. Isaac's *Commentary on Sefer Yetzirah*, p. 16:

כפולות - שכל אחת ואחת כפולה לשנים להיטיב ולהרע, מדה טובה מרובה שעיקר הכל, ועיקר סבה שנאצלת משם היא מדה אלא שהיו מדות פנימיות, שעדיין לא יצאו לאור ומשם נתחלקו. כי במדה אחת קבועים כמה כחות, וכשאדם רע מסתכל באותה מדה שהיא מריעה ומיטיבה כי ההטבה היא לו הרעה, כמי שיאכל תבשיל שיועיל לו פעם אחת ויזיק לו פעם אחרת ואם לאו נשתנה טעמו.

267 Pseudo-R. Isaac's *Commentary on Sefer Yetzirah*, p. 17:

חן - מתוך החן כשאינו הולך באותה מדה שנתנה ממנה החן נהפך למדה אחרת שהיא באה כשהוא כעור, כמו העשיר שאינו מחסר הונו לצדקה סוף שיחסר הונו.

This is a matter of theurgy, though a negative one. Refusing to behave in accordance to the inner logic of a certain attribute, namely because one is given something he should also give, the impact is that the activity of the supernal attribute is inverted and then has an impact on the lower world. This is in principle a variant of the mode [E] in Rabbinic theology. The widespread use of the term *middah* is evident in a seminal passage where the Pseudo-R. Isaac deals with the process that can be depicted as contemplation:

> "*'Adon Yaḥiyd*, refers now to a [certain] *middah* within the Infinite, since it has no end from any point of view, [it is forbidden] to ruminate concerning secrets lest you should be confused since from what one can grasp he can recognize what he does not grasp and this is the reason why the *middot* have been done, since language does not grasp but what comes from it, since a person does not grasp the attribute of speech and of letters, but the attribute alone and there is not *middah* beyond the letters and all the awesome *middot* have been delivered in order to contemplate, since every *middah* is from a *middah* higher than it, and they have been given to Israel in order to contemplate out of the *middah* seen in the heart up to the Infinite, since there is not one way to pray but by means of the limited words a person recieves[268] and ascends in his thought to the Infinite."[269]

268 The verb is *mitqabbel*, and its meaning cannot be precisely determined, though it recurs in the Pseudo-R. Isaac and R. Azriel. My translation is an approximation. Nevertheless, Scholem's rendering "to enter [in their interior]", in *Origins of Kabbalah*, p. 301, does not make sense. Compare, e.g., the Pseudo-R. Isaac's *Commentary on Sefer Yetzirah*, p. 5, in a passage to be translated immediately below: "Since the *middah* is something received by the separated entities" whose context will be brought immediately below, and in n. 329.

269 Ibidem, p. 6:
שאדון יחיד עכשיו רומז מדה באין סוף שאין לה סוף משום צד. מלהרהר מן הנסתרות מן המחשבה פן יטרד, כי מתוך מה שהוא משיג יכול להכיר מה שאינו משיג ולכך נעשו המדות שאין הלשון משיג אלא מה שהוא בא ממנו, שאין אדם משיג מדת הדיבור והאותיות אלא מדתה עצמה ואין חוץ מן האותיות מדה וכל המידות הנוראות נמסרו להתבונן כי כל מדה ממדה שהיא למעלה ונמסרו לישראל להתבונן מתוך המידה הנראית בלב להתבונן

The assumption is that every *middah* is a limited manifestation of the higher *middah*, and the latter can be discerned by a contemplation of the lower *middah*, which is capable to allow some form of mental ascent to the Infinite. However, in addition to this ontological statement concerning the emergence of the *middot*, their reception is described also as dependent on the capacity of the recipients.[270] In any case, what is obvious is the fact that the Kabbalist chose to resort to the term *middah* when describing divine powers, much more than *sefirot*, a fact that is, in my opinion, illuminating in the context of my theory as to the existence of a pre-Kabbalistic theory regarding ten *middot*, as mentioned above at the end of chapter 3. In this context, it would be better to avoid employing unwarrantly an interpretation of *middot* as *sefirot*, as found in scholarship related to the last passage of Pseudo-R. Isaac translated above.[271] This is also the case in another passage of Pseudo-R. Isaac, where he speaks about the term *sibbah*, cause, as a parallel to *middah*:

> "The gazing is when each and every cause receives from the cause that is higher than it, since the drawing *middah* [receives] from the hewn *middah*, and the hewn [*middah*] from the engraved [*middah*] and the engraved [*middah*] from inscribed [*middah*] and the inscribed [*middah*] from the hidden, everything is one

עד אין סוף. כי אין דרך להתפלל אלא על ידי הדברים המוגבלים אדם מתקבל ומתעלה במחשבה עד אין סוף.

See Scholem, *Origins of the Kabbalah*, pp. 300–301, Sendor, *The Emergence of Provencal Kabbalah*, 1, pp. 182–183, 224–230, Wolfson, *Through a Speculum*, pp. 169–187, Travis, *Rabbi Ezra of Gerona*, p. 82, and Afterman, *Devequt*, pp. 216–217.

270 *Commentary to Sefer Yetzirah*, p. 5: "Since the prophets have seen the *middot* in accordance to their intellectual capacity." This view is found also in R. Asher ben David. See Idel, *Kabbalah: New Perspectives*, p. 55 and Valabregue-Perry, *Concealed and Revealed*, p. 142. A similar view is found also in the anonymous *Commentary on Ten Sefirot*, Ms. Paris BN 837, fol. 116a. On this commentary see Idel, *R. Menahem Recanati*, 1, pp. 192–195, 197, where I identify the author as Recanati.

271 See, e.g., Scholem, *Origins of the Kabbalah*, p. 301.

> within another, and one from the other, and everything is linked with each other, and to one another... since the *middah* is something received by the separated [entities], since the prophets have seen the *middot* in accordance to their intellectual capacity, and by their[272] reception of their power they were broadening their thought more than other persons, since they had a breath of mind so that it expands through the particulars to the infinite."[273]

In my opinion, the ontology reflected here, and also elsewhere in R. Azriel's writings to be discussed in this chapter, is based on an infinite starting point, called *'Ein Sof*, the Infinite, within which a series of processes of limitations took place. Naturally, the limitation in this case is not an act of withdrawal of the divine from a certain place, but of creating smaller ontological units within it.[274] This is the reason why equality is mentioned: the Infinite and the smaller units coincide ontologically, as well as the higher limited units do so with the smaller ones. For this sake I would not necessarily translate the term *Shaweh* as indifferent, as Scholem proposed, which did not take into account the occurrence of this term in Rabad's passage discussed in the previous chapter. This is the conceptual framework that allows passing from the contemplation of the limited divine power to contemplate or to intuit the larger, higher stages, up to the Infinite, which comprises all

272 Of the prophets.

273 *Commentary on Sefer Yetzirah*, p. 5:

והצפייה היא שכל סבה וסבה מתקבלת מסבה עליונה ממנה, כי מדה שואבת ממדה חצובה וחצובה מחקוקה והחקוקה מן הרשומה והרשומה מן הנעלמת, הכל זה בתוך זה וזה מתוך זה והכל קשור זה בזה וזה עם זה... כי המדה דבר המתקבל לנפרדים, כי הנביאים ראו מדות כפי השגתן וע״י קבלת כחם היו מרחיבים מחשבתם יותר משאר בני האדם שהיה להם בשביל זה רחב הנפש להתפשט בפרטים באין סוף.

See also Scholem, *Origins of the Kabbalah*, p. 290, Afterman, *Devequt*, p. 213, Gottlieb, *The Kabbalah in the Writings of R. Bahya ben Asher ibn Halawa*, pp. 196–197, Sendor, *The Emergence of Provencal Kabbalah* I, pp. 178–181, 296, II, pp. 258–60, and Travis, *Rabbi Ezra of Gerone*, p. 83 and Idel, *Enchanted Chains*, pp. 172–173.

274 On this issue see Idel, "Zimzum," pp. 102–104.

the limited entities, divine or otherwise, and such a view is held also by R. Azriel of Gerona.[275]

Last but not least: Toward the end of Pseudo-R. Isaac's *Commentary on Sefer Yetzirah* we read:

> "There is a [kind of] death that is a mercy, in order to honor him [the dead] in the world to come, so that the attribute of punishment [*middat ha-por'anut*] which is prone to expand [in this world] [*lehitpashshet*] will not hold strength over him. The attribute of peace [*middat ha-shalom*] draws him, as it is written [Isaiah 57:1]: 'Because of the evil, the righteous is collected [upwards], he will come in peace.' And it is written [Psalms 116:15]: 'Precious in the eyes of the Lord, is the death of his pious ones.'"[276]

I read this passage as dealing with three attributes: mercy, punishment, and peace, a tripartite view is conceived of by the Kabbalist as reflected also in the Isaiah 57:1 verse, where righteousness, evil, and peace occur. That Peace is understood in this Kabbalistic school as a separate, third attribute, we learned also from a text of R. Azriel of Gerona, to be discussed later on in this chapter, and also from *Sefer ha-Bahir* as discussed in chapter 3 above, as well as from the theosophical discussion found in R. Yehudah ben Yaqar's *Commentary on the Blessings and Prayers.*[277] In short: the Pseudo-R. Isaac the Blind's resort to the

275 See Idel, "Jewish Kabbalah and Platonism," pp. 339–340, Sendor, *The Emergence of Provencal Kabbalah*, II, pp. 173–174, Valabregue-Perry, *Concealed and Revealed*, pp. 229–232.

276 *Commentary on Sefer Yetzirah*, ed. Scholem, *The Kabbalah in Provence* appendix, p. 17:

יש מיתה שהיא חסד כדי ליקרו לעולם הבא, כדי שלא ישלוט בו מדת פורענות העתידה להתפשט, ושואבת אותו מדת השלום כ"ד [ישעיה נז:א], "כי מפני הרעה נאסף הצדיק יבא שלום" כו', וכתיב [תהלים קטז:טו], "יקר בעיני ה' המותה לחסידיו."

See also Afterman, *Devequt*, pp. 218–219, Idel, "Some Remarks on Ritual, and Mysticism," p. 120, *Ben*, pp. 655–656 and R. Ezra of Gerona, *Commentary on the Song of Songs*, p. 504 and *R. Asher ben David*, ed. Abrams, p. 55.

277 I, p. 101. See also below n. 462. Since I assume that ben Yaqar was not acquainted with the *Bahir*, they probably draw independently the phrase *middat shalom*

term *middot*, and his theurgical understanding of some aspects of *Sefer Yetzirah*, parallel to a certain extent views found in the *Book of Bahir*, and diverge from the philosophical sources. It is especially theurgy, in the manner defined above, that differs profoundly from the theology of the Neoplatonic sources and this is the reason why it requires a special attention, which was not accorded yet by scholars dealing with this text. Even more so, since this seminal religious category is found also other Kabbalists, as we shall see further in this chapter.

Some of the theosophical concepts found in the Pseudo-R. Isaac have parallels in the writings of R. Asher ben David, the nephew of R. Isaac the Blind, its alleged author. R. Asher speaks about the *middot* many times in all his writings, and describes them as dwelling *vis-a-vis* one another, but also as linked to each other[278] and adopts the theurgical metanoia of the Rabbinic models [E1–2].[279] Of special importance is his claim that human activity should imitate the divine one, which means that when acting in accordance to one attribute, also others, especially two others of the three attributes, should be included.[280] It should be mentioned that this Kabbalist uses often times the term *middah*, even when dealing with theosophical issues, and special attention should be paid to his view, according to which God "comprises in each *middah* all the others and He will operate one thing and its opposite concomitantly, since the power of this is found in the other, since every *middah* is comprised [*kelulah*] in the [all the] other."[281] This means that theosophy should be understood

from a common source. This additional type of *middah* is part of the more complex structure of the attributive code, that evolved early in Kabbalistic theosophies. See also below n. 723.

278 See *R. Asher ben David*, ed. Abrams, pp. 61–72.

279 Ibidem, pp. 55, 66, 192.See also Vajda, *Le commentaire*, pp. 198–199.

280 *R. Asher ben David*, ed. Abrams pp. 61, 66, 72, 74. See especially ibidem, pp. 52, 54, 63, 65, 74, 155, where God's three attributes of the forefathers are mentioned as a paradigm for human behavior in general. This Kabbalist speaks several times about three *middot*, perhaps following the book of *Bahir*, as discussed in chapter 3. See also the view of R. Bahya ben Asher, adduced in chapter 6.

281 See ed. Abrams, p. 119:

in a more relational manner, than as a realm of isolated powers, like Platonic ideas or separate cosmic intellects, that define the supernal realm in itself in philosophical forms of metaphysics.

However, what is interesting is the recurrence of formulations, according to which, each of the attributes, and now the intention is that each of the ten attributes is included within the others. He resorts several times to the plural form *kelulot*.[282] This theory will have a long and distinguished career in some Kabbalistic theosophies, as we shall see also in the next chapter. Interestingly enough, in one case R. Asher speaks about the equality of the two attributes, of compassion and judgment.[283] In the vein of his uncle he speaks about the fact that a divine *middah* operates a thing and its opposite.[284] In some cases he regards the meaning of *middah* as referring to our limited perception of what is actually an infinite realm.[285]

The Kabbalist who was more explicit about equality of the divine attributes, described sometime as opposites was, however, R. Azriel ben Shlomo of Gerona, active there in the second third of the 13th century.[286] From many points of view he belongs to the circle of

לפי שהוא אחד מתאחד בכלן והוא הפועל בכלן כאחת או באחת מהן וכולל בה את כלן וגם באחת פועל דבר והפכו כאחד.

and compare to the parallel versions in ed. Abrams, pp. 64 151 174–172 and the discussion on p. 27. See also ibidem, p. 182, e.g., ibidem, pp. 51, 52, 53, 54, 55, 60. See also below n. 563. However, it is only in the above passage that the opposite operations are explicitly mentioned. See also Valabregue, *Concealed and Revealed*, pp. 144–148.

282 Ibidem, pp. 52, 55, 61, 64, 70. In the latter page the term חכמתה should be corrected for חברתה. The inclusive nature of each of the *middot*, that is found also in other early Kabbalistic theosophies, as important ramificatios for the understanding of the gender-theory in Kabbalah, an issue that cannot be addressed in this framework. See, for the time being, in chapter 8.

283 Ibidem, p. 54: מדת החסד ומדת הגבורה שניהם בשוה במעון אחד

284 Ibidem, p. 56, 64 119 151 174–172

285 See Scholem, *Origins of the Kabbalah*, pp. 284–285.

286 Scholem, *Origins of the Kabbalah*, passim, idem, *Kabbalah*, pp. 391–393, "New Remnants," Tishby, *Studies*, vol. 1, pp. 17–30, 31–35, Sed-Rajna, *Azriel de Gérone, Commentaire sur la liturgie quotidienne*, Pachter, *Roots of Faith and*

Kabbalists related to R. Isaac the Blind. From some other points of view, he is close to themes found in another Kabbalistic school, as reflected in a literature related to the *Book of 'Iyyun,* whose views will be discussed below in chapter 7. His writings display a variety of ideas on the same topic, not always consistent to each other, as they were formulated in his various treatises.The following discussions will help us in suggesting some form of developments in his thought. Indubitably the thought of this Kabbalist constitutes one more step in the metaphysical vortex, beyond what we have seen in the case of R. Isaac the Blind.

This Kabbalist was especially interested in the concept of equality of divine powers,[287] and he refers several times to the root *ShWH* in his *Commentary on the Daily Prayer.* The most important one is the act of equalizing the attribute of compassion and that of judgment as part of the act of praying the prayer of Eighteen Benedictions:

> "Since He has seen that the world does not subsist by [when created by the attribute of] judgment, He preceded and took as a partner the attribute of compassion to that of judgment.[288] and this is the reason why we are causing the precedence of the attribute of compassion to that of judgment and unify and say "*YHWH 'Eloheinu,*" in order to equalize the attributes, namely that the Special Name [the Tetragrammaton] is [equal to] *'Eloheinu,* as it is said [Psalm 100:3] that "*YHWH* is *'Eloheinu* and He created us." "[289]

Devequt, pp. 13–45, Mark Verman, "Reincarnation and Theodicy: Traversing Philosophy, Psychology, and Mysticism," ed. J.M. Harris, *Be'erot Yitzhak; Studies in Memory of Isadore Twersky,* (Harvard University Press, Cambridge, MA, 2005), pp. 399–426, Valabregue-Peri, *Concealed and Revealed,* pp. 148–154, Afterman, *Devequt,* pp. 265–285, and Altmann, "The Motif of the "Shells."

287 See Tishby, ibidem, p. 18.

288 See model [B] in Rabbinic literature in chapter 2.

289 See R. Azriel of Gerona's *Commentary on Daily Liturgy,* ed. Gavarin, p. 2, cf. Ms. Ferrara 1:

לפי שראה שאין העולם מתקיים בדין הקדים ושתף מדת הרחמים למדת הדין ולכך אנו מקדימים מדת הרחמים למידת הדין ומייחדים ואומרים יי אלהינו ולהשוות המדות, שהשם המיוחד הוא אלהינו כדכ׳ דעו כי יי הוא האלהים הוא עשנו

The cooperation between the two attributes is here explicit, and the assumption is that during the prayer someone should be aware of the equality between these attributes. Earlier in his commentary, Azriel explained the meaning of the equalization:

> "The prayer should say *'Attah,* because of [the verse], "I always put *YHWH* in front of me" [Psalm 16:8] and the meaning of putting is equalization [*ha-hashwa'ah*] since this[290] is a word[291] that is equal to every name and every praise, and it is a hint at the power of existence.[292]"[293]

The biblical verse resorts to the root *SHWH,* in order to describe a certain spiritual operation related to the Tetragrammaton or to God. The general meaning of the verse is the creation of an awareness of the divinity in front of a person. This root has been interpreted by the Kabbalist as related to the relationship between the Tetragrammaton and other linguistic units: names, perhaps divine ones, or praises of God. The question is what the meaning of the root in this context is: is it equality, as I propose, or is it identity, as Scholem would say. Both meanings would fit the first quote above, where the Tetragrammaton is described in the context of the name *'Eloheinu.* Nevertheless, I assume that mentioning the Rabbinic view of partnership between the attributes, equality would make a better sense than identity. This

For a French translation, notes and introduction of the text see Sed-Rajna, *Azriel de Gérone, Commentaire sur la liturgie quotidienne,* p. 29.

290 Namely the Tetragrammaton.

291 I assume that he refers to the Tetragrammaton.

292 Compare also to ed. Gavarin, p. 4, where Azriel writes that *'Attah* refers to "His existence."

293 See ibidem, p. 1, and Ms. Paris BN 595, fol. 4a:

המתפלל צריך שיאמר אתה משום שויתי יי׳ ופי׳ שויתי השוואה שזו היא מלה שוה לכל שם ולכל שבח והוא רמז לכח המציאות.

Sed-Rajna, *Azriel de Gérone,* p. 26 and n. 4. This passage has been discussed in Goldreich, "The Theology of the Iyyun Circle," p. 147. See also the detailed analysis in Valabregue-Peri, *Concealed and Revealed,* pp. 232–244.

latter understanding is supported by a passage found in R. Azriel's *Commentary on Sefer Yetzirah*:

> "*Face and back*[294]: Face is compassion, back is judgment. *And a sign for it*: this is a sign that all the creatures from superiority to inferiority and from inferiority to superiority, in order to equalize their attributes, according to the way of unity, since they are the essence of their equality."[295]

It is not clear what is the affinity between the two attributes and the states of superiority and inferiority. It seems that the ascent is generating the situation of equality because of returning to the source of everything. Here, the equality is achieved by a cosmic process and not by a theurgical act, but it is hard to see here a matter of "indifference."

To return to the passage from the *Commentary on the Prayer*: The pronunciation of the word *'Attah* in the Eighteen Benedictions, which means "Thee," is the reason why the verse from the Psalm is quoted: this is a matter of the divine presence.

The question may be asked: what is the precise meaning of equalization: is it an act of the awareness of an objective situation, an act of recognition, or is it a theurgical act, that generates equality of the opposite attributes during prayer? At the end of his commentary he explains the term *Shalom,* peace, a word found in the text of the prayer:

> "It equalizes between the opposites, since it is [stemming] from the "equal root" that there is nothing outside it. This is the reason

294 *Sefer Yetzirah,* II:4.

295 *Kitvei ha-Ramban,* II, p. 459:

פנים ואחור, פנים זה רחמים אחור זה דין. וסימן לדבר: סימן זה לכל הנבראים מעילוי לגריעות ומגריעות לעילוי כדי להשוות מדותיהן בדרך האחדות שהן עיקר השוואתן.

Some few generations later, the terminology of *'illuy* and *geriyy'ut,* had a significant impact on R. Joseph ben Shalom Ashkenazi, a Kabbalist to be discussed in chapter 8.

why all the attributes are sealed within it, and from it they receive what they lack and their perfection."[296]

The term *shaweh* is related to two different entities: one is called *Shalom,* the other is its source, which is most plausibly the Infinite that is recurrently described by R. Azriel, as the entity that there is nothing outside it.[297] I assume that to this higher level the Kabbalist refers in the second part of the above quote. This is also the case also in another treatise of R. Azriel, widespread in manuscripts and in print. In his *Sha'ar ha-Sho'el* he speaks about the power of *'omen,* that is identified by scholars with the first *sefirah,* that there is within it "an equal power[298] to equalize a thing and its opposite."[299] If so, than the divinity is referred to as both equal and equalizing, as we have seen above in Philo and in the verse from the poem attributed to the abovementioned early medieval poet Yannay: "*shaweh u-mashweh*" as they were discussed in chapter 2 above.

The activity of the attribute called *Shalom,* which in some Rabbinic sources designates God,[300] is described in the same way as the effect of the prayer in the first quote as generating a state of equality, but this time attributes are not mentioned, but opposites. In this case, the

296 Ed., Gavarin, p. 46:

שהשלום משוה בין ההפכים לפי שהוא מעיקר שוה שאין חוץ ממנו ולכך כל המדות חתומות בו שממנו כל מחסורם ושלמותם.

Sed-Rajna, *Azriel de Gérone*, p. 123. It should be mentioned that the affinity between isonomia and peace may reflect a pre-Socratic approach.

297 See the view found in Scholem, "New Remnants," pp. 207–208.

298 See also in *Sha'ar ha-Sho'el,* pp. 33:

הספירה הראשונה שהיא שוה לכולם

299 *Sha'ar ha-Sho'el,* pp. 35–36:

לשון אומן יש בו כח שוה להשוות דבר ותמורתו

See also Porat, *Founding of the Circle",* pp. 109–110 and Tishby, *Studies,* vol. 1, pp. 28–29. Similar formulations are found later on in Kabbalistic literature. See, e.g., the anonymous *Commentary on Ten Sefirot,* Ms. Paris BN 837, fol. 115b, no. 26 in Scholem's list, and above n. 271.

300 See, e.g., Marmorstein, *The Old Rabbinic Doctrine of God,* pp. 104–105.

stronger act of inducing equality, not its recognition, is more plausible. Interestingly enough, in one case in this treatise, R. Azriel explicitly claims that the two attributes have been divided.[301] In any case, the nexus between peace and the divine act of equalizing is found already in Philo, following the Pre-Socratic concept of isonomia.[302]

Let me distinguish between three stages implied here: the first is related to the "equal root" – *ha-'Iqqar ha-Shaweh* – namely the Infinite,[303] which assumes the existence of things that are equal in the highest divine level: then the existence of opposites as separate, – when they were divided, as mentioned above – and finally the stage when they were equalized or reunited. The third state is, however, in need of explanation: what is the specific identity of the entity called *Shalom*? What is it doing: causing a change in the relationship between the opposites, namely creating a balance between them, or perhaps integrating them in a way that they are equal?

For an attempt to answer those questions let us turn to some other, quite brief, references of R. Azriel's to the root *ShWH* in his *Commentary on the Daily Prayer.* When commenting on the phrase "The King of the World": the Kabbalist writes in one instance: "Since the King has all that He has in Himself, more than them and equal to them, His hands have created."[304] This means that while within the Infinite there are zones that were created and thus identical to the divinity, other zones of the Infinite transcend those where the created universe is to be found. This sort of reading may explain the meaning of equalize and equalization, against a background of an earlier tradition, a threefold scheme of the opposites that is reminiscent of

301 Ed., Gavarin, p. 27:
אומרי קדוש כנגד כח הרחמים אומרי כנגד כח הדין ולפי שחלק ביניהם

302 See above chapter 1, the passage from *Questiones et Solutiones* in Exodus, II, 66.

303 For this term see also Scholem, "New Remnants," pp. 209, 212. See also ibidem, p. 208: עיקרם.

304 Ed., Gavarin, p. 2: ".שהמלך כל מה יש בו יותר מהם ושוה להם ידיו יצרו", Sed-Rajna, *Azriel de Gérone*, p. 29.

the scheme we have seen above in the case of the divine attributes of Philo and Rabad.

A perusal of the *Commentary on the Daily Prayer* shows that the special interest in the two divine attributes – and sometimes also their equality – should be understood against the minimal role played by the sefirotic system. Names of *sefirot* occur quite rarely and certainly do not constitute the significant scheme for understanding R. Azriel's thought. This is also the case in some brief but very important treatises identified and published by Scholem for the first time that deal with questions of faith and heresy.[305] Let me turn to some aspects of the short treatises. When dealing with the different ten theological errors, or heresies, regarding the nature of the Infinite and the opposites, he writes insofar as the seventh one is concerned:

> "The seventh [heretical] path: whoever acknowledges that it[306] is more than everything and [also] equal to all, and there is nothing outside it[307] – but according to the path[308] he believes that within it there are opposites [*hafakhim*] and contraries [*temurot*], just as they are divided in the visible [realm], they are also divided in the innermost part of their essence."[309]

There are two ways to interpret this passage: the first one sees heresy in introducing opposites within the realm of the Infinite, while the other assumes that within the infinite, the division is different from that found in the manifest reality. Those are different meanings: the one denies the existence of opposites in the supernal zone altogether, the other assumes that they exist in a manner different from what is visible in this world. Let me compare the last passage to another one found in

305 See his "New Remnants," pp. 207–214, and the detailed analyses in Pachter, *Roots of Faith and Devequt*, pp. 13–46.
306 Probably the Infinite.
307 This formula is parallel to what we have quoted above from his *Commentary on the Daily Prayer*, ed. Gavarin, p. 2.
308 Namely this path, the seventh type of heresy.
309 Scholem, "New Remnants," p. 208.

a variant of the quoted treatise. R. Azriel refers to various "attributes" seen by the prophets according to their mind,[310] and then writes:

> "All of them are comprised in *'Emmet* and *Tzedeq*[311] and *'Emmet* and *Tzedeq*, despite the fact that they seem to be as two [different] attributes are not but one, and the judgment is but for [the reason] of validating *'Emmet* and *'Emmet* is appropriate to subsist from the judgment [*din*] and the judgment is appropriate when this is a judgment of truth, and whoever says that truth is one attribute different from [that of] *Tzedeq* and *Tzedeq* is another attribute than truth, it is found on another path, and it is called *meqatztzetz bi-netiy'ot*[312]... namely everything is truth and everything is judgment, namely these two attributes are one since none of them is without the other[313] since both emerge from one root and return to one principle... all have one root and there is nothing outside it."[314]

The assumption is that though there are two attributes, because they are stemming from the same principle, they are intertwined and cooperating, and should not be conceived of as totally different. It should be pointed out that in this small parallel treatise, the concept of equality does not occur at all: the root or the principle is not qualified by the term *shaweh*, and the two attributes are not depicted so, neither does the concept of opposites occur in this specific context. However, the scheme that we discuss above is implied also in the last passage: the stemming of the two attributes from one source is invoked as the reason for the cooperation that should not be separated.

Even when declaring that the two attributes are one, he nevertheless resorts to the plural form. This means that unlike the separation of entities in this world, which can act independently, within the divine sphere the powers are interconnected. To learn from this passage as

310 See the Pseudo-R. Isaac's *Commentary on Sefer Yetzirah*, p. 5, discussed above.
311 See *Commentary on the Talmudic Legends*, ed. Tishby, p. 38.
312 See the texts referred in below nn. 382, 460.
313 This view is also reflecting an earlier approach. See chapter 2 model [D].
314 Scholem, "New Remnants," p. 214. See also Tishby, *Studies*, vol. 1, p. 29.

to the interpretation of the opposites in the earlier discussion: they exist in a state of union that differs from their state in their ultimate source on the one hand, and from the visible separation between them as dominating this world. This kind of union implies the existence of each of the attributes within the other, though it is plausible that admixture does not obliterate the uniqueness of the attributes. This approach, found already in R. Asher ben David, as seen above, and in Nahmanides and his school, became a widespread theory in Kabbalistic theosophies for centuries.

The translation of *shaweh* as equal or balanced or united, differs from the dominant understanding of R. Azriel's views, as referring to indistinction, a reading that assumes the impact of John Scotus Erigena. This interpretation has been introduced by Gershom Scholem, in 1942, and elaborated in his later studies, and adopted, for example, in Sed-Rajna's French translation of the commentary on R. Azriel's *Commentary on the Daily Prayer,*[315] as well as some other scholars following them.[316] It is based on the manner in which Johann Reuchlin understood a passage from one of R. Azriel's short treatises that has been identified, printed, and analyzed by Scholem.[317] There are, nevertheless, scholars who doubted the relevance of some aspects of Scholem's introducing the eminent Neoplatonic theologian Erigena as a significant source for R. Azriel's metaphysics.[318] This is

315 See Sed-Rajna, ibidem, on the pages mentioned in the footnotes above, especially on pp. 160–161, eadem, "L'influence de Jean Scot sur la doctrine du kabbaliste Azriel de Gerone," in *Jean Scot Erigene et l'histoire de la philosophie* (Paris, 1977), pp. 453–463.

316 See, e.g, Tishby, *Studies,* vol. 1, p. 18, and Wolfson's translations of texts of R. Azriel in *Language, Eros, Being,* pp. 97–99 and *Along the Path* pp. 65, 191 n. 14. See also Sendor, *The Emergence of Provencal Kabbalah,* I, pp. 194, 221, 228–229, 258–259, 310–311.

317 See e.g., "New Remnants," pp. 204–205, 207, *Reshit ha-Kabbalah,* p. 146, *Origins of the Kabbalah,* p. 318, *ha-Kabbalah be-Provence,* pp. 24–26. See also below *Some Concluding Remarks.*

318 Goldreich, "The Theology of the Iyyun Circle," pp. 141–144, Verman, *The Book of Contemplation,* pp. 108 n. 242, 181–181.

especially evident in Scholem's understanding of the Hebrew terms *'Aḥdut Shawah, hashwa'ah* or *shaweh,* as referring to the Erigenean theme of *indifferentia* or *indistinctia.*[319] In the vein of this proposal he understands R. Azriel's treatments – and those of the texts from the *'Iyyun* literature that will be discussed in chapter 8 – as, for example, in the following translation of a Hebrew text of the Geronese Kabbalah. The pertinent Hebrew terms translated below will be added in the footnotes:

> "The eighth [erroneous] path is that of him who believes that He [*'en-sof*] has a superesse[320] above everything and that nothing exists outside of him, but that he is not *indifferent [indistinct]*[321] in relation to everything, and also that he draws the substance of the effluence that comes from him only as far as the potency of the emanating, which always preexisted, but not to the potency of the emanation, which originates from it, and still less to the potency of the emanated; and in this way he posits a lack in his power. For if he wants to explain the power of the emanating as indistinct[322] from the mysterious darkness[323] from which it comes, he is unable to do so since he does not recognize this principle according to which, both in the visible and in the hidden, he [the *'en-sof*] is without distinction[324] "equal" in relation to Nought and to Being, in the simplicity and complete nondifferentiation[325] that is called unity.[326]"[327]

319 *Origins of the Kabbalah*, p. 439 and n. 174 and Tishby, *Studies*, vol. 1, p. 18. Compare, however, to Valabruege-Pery, *Concealed and Revealed*, pp. 210–221, 232–243.

320 יתר על הכל

321 אך אינו שוה. My proposal is, however, to see this verb as referring to equality or agreement.

322 להשוות

323 סתר התעלומה

324 מבלי הפרש

325 השוואה

326 אחדות

327 Cf. Scholem, *Origins of the Kabbalah*, p. 441, cf., idem, "New Remnants," pp. 208 209.

On the other hand, the role of the two attributes and of equality, according to two other main writings of R. Azriel, the *Commentary on the Talmudic 'Aggadot* and his *Commentary on Ten Sefirot*, display an inverse situation: they do not deal with opposites, but adopt the view of *sefirot*. In the latter treatise we read:

> "And what you asked whether there is a recipient and what is received.[328] You should learn from the holy cherubim, as the sages said:[329] "That are like the admixture of a man and his partner, see the love of God for your"...and sometimes one of them acts by itself and [other times] another acts by itself, and sometimes they are equal in their action. And sometimes one is acting the action of the other, and vice-versa, and sometimes they invert[330] their actions."[331]

It is obvious from this list of relations between the attributes, that there is not ontological identification between the attributes, neither a functional one. One of the options is cooperation, like in the passage from R. Azriel of Gerona's *Commentary on Daily Liturgy*, ed. Gavarin, p. 2 that was quoted above, the other is the shift of one of an attribute's action to the action that is characteristic of the other, as in the Rabbinic model described in chapter 2 as [C] and in Rabad's passage in chapter 4 in paragraph [d]. The two sorts of action differ from each other. In addition, the possibility of independent actions is mentioned and this is the case in a lengthy discussion in his commentary on Talmudic legends, where only also the attribute of compassion is mentioned in the various divine activities.[332] This is a clear example for the side by

328 מתקבל For this term see also the texts referred in nn. 269, 270, 274.

329 *BT Yuma'*, fol. 54b.

330 See above the passage referred by n. 259.

331 *Sha'ar ha-Sho'el*, pp. 43–44, corrected according to Ms. New York, JTS 1878, fol. 74:

ועל מה ששאלת אם יש מקבל ומתקבל. תשובה: צא ולמד מכרובים הקודש [!] שכתוב בהם 'כמער איש ולוית' ואמרו חז"ל 'ראו חיבתכם לפני המקום'...ופעמים שזה פועל לעצמו וזה לעצמו, ופעמים שהם שוים בפעולתם, ופעמים שזה פועל פעולתו של זה וזה של זה, ופעמים מהפכים פעולתם.

332 See p. 119. The view that it is only the attribute of compassion that is involved

side coexistence of several Rabbinic models in the writings of a single Kabbalist, in fact in the same passage.

According to several other texts authored by this Kabbalist, each *middah* comprises both the attribute of compassion and judgment,[333] and computations as to the numbers of the *sefirot* that emerges because of this view are given in different Kabbalistic treatises. This comprisal is an example of the combination of the theory of *sefirot* with that of *middot*: the latter refer to an inner dimension of the former. This view differs from model [D] in the Rabbinic models, where each attribute contains also some dimension of the other, an issue to be reiterated in the next chapter. It is plausible that this compounded nature of the *middot* or *sefirot* can explain R. Azriel's critique of Christians that are described as if they conceive all the *middot* as being compassion alone.[334]

Conceptually speaking, privation is regarded here as being its precise opposite according to the Aristotelian physics: it means fullness of forms and hence of Being. Elsewhere, in R. Azriel, the realm of *'Ayin* is described as the place of *coincidentia oppositorum* – a conception which completely demolishes the philosophical understanding of privation as absence or potentiality.[335] In any case, according to

in the act of creation is found in an independent contemporary source. See R. Abraham ben Azriel, *'Arugat ha-Bosem*, ed. Urbach, vol. III, p. 313.

333 See, e.g., R. Azriel, *Commentary on the Talmudic Legends*, ed. Tishby, p. 34, and see also ibidem, p. 15, where sefirot are mentioned in a similar context and n. 2 or Idel, "Kabbalistic Material," p. 182 and n. 65. Compare also *Zohar*, III, fol. 262b, and the quote from the *Zohar* as extant in Recanati's *Commentary on the Pentateuch*, fol. 549c: "There is no crown [= *sefirah*] in all the crowns of the King that is not comprised of judgment and compassion… good and evil."

לית כתר מכל כתרין דמלכא דלא אתכליל דינא ורחמי׳... טב וביש.

334 See Scholem, "New Remnants," p. 209, building on a discussion in *BT Megillah*, fol. 25a.

335 Scholem, "New Remnants," p. 207. By resorting to the term 'realm of *'Ayin*' I assume some form of pre-sefirotic space, which is the source of some later developments. In Kabbalistic literature, views regarding "the depths of *'Ayin*"

this Kabbalist "everything is one, in a simple manner, in an absolute equality."[336] Though the most philosophically oriented Kabbalist in R. Isaac's school, also R. Azriel's approach displays an interest in theurgy, as seen in several instances above. In other words, even in his case, the Neoplatonic metaphysics did not obliterate the inner dynamic aspects of Kabbalistic kaleidoscopic theosophies.

Let me shortly address another major figure in the school of R. Isaac the Blind, R. Ezra of Gerona.[337] He avoids the concepts of opposites and the presence of the two attributes within each of the *sefirot*, but he probably considered the lower seven ones to be vessels for the presence of the divine power.[338] I assume that the term *keliy*, vessel, is reminiscent of the meaning of *middah* as a measure, namely a limited entity serving as a container, like in Pseudo-R. Isaac the Blind's theosophy. Indeed the two terms occur together, under the impact of R. Ezra,[339] in the early part of the second half of the 13th century Kabbalist R. Abraham Axelrod's *Keter Shem Tov*. [340]

In any case, in his writings the term *middah* recurs many times[341] and especially interesting is what he writes in a responsum to a query, as to the reason of using the term *middah* in the sense of measure insofar as the divine powers are concerned. His response is based on the passage from *Sefer Yetzirah* about the view of the *sefirot* as infinite. He claims that the *middot* are infinite in number and in quality.[342] He

are found, but not in contexts that deal with primeval evil, but with evil that is done by humans, namely by their sins. See Idel, *Kabbalah: New Perspectives*, pp. 184–185.

336 Scholem, ibidem, and Valabregue-Peri, *Concealed and Revealed*, p. 221.

337 See Vajda, *Le Commentaire*, Travis, *Rabbi Ezra of Gerona*, and Idel, "Some Remarks on Ritual and Mysticism."

338 See his *Commentary on Song of Songs*, p. 511, and Vajda, *Le commentaire*, pp. 273–274.

339 idem p. 482.

340 *'Amudei ha-Qabbalah*, p. 11.

341 Scholem, ed., *Studies in Kabbalah*, pp. 30, 31, 32, 33 and his *Commentary on Song of Songs*, pp. 482, 496–497, 499, 511.

342 See Scholem, ed., *Studies in Kabbalah*, p. 31.

uses the phrase *rashei ha-middot,*[343] namely the heads of the *middot,* that is to say the principle attributes, while the numer of the attributes is in fact as many as "the sand of the sea."[344]

In a responsum he gave to a question addressed to him, he uses the term *middah* in a context that would stand for *sefirah* in other cases.[345] In his commentary on the commandments, where he uses many times the term *middah,* he adopts the Rabbinic model [E2] in order to explain the theurgical effect of the various blowings of the Shofar has on the attributes by inverting them.[346]

Last but not least in this Kabbalistic school are R. Jacob ben Sheshet's writings.[347] He was acquainted with R. Isaac the Blind's view and those of R. Ezra as well as the book of *Bahir.* He speaks about the inversion of the attribute of judgment into that of compassion and vice-versa,[348] and it seems that he assumes that this type of change is related to the seven double letters that refers to the seven lower *sefirot.*[349] In this context he refers explicitly to the concept of opposites, reflecting a stance close to model [D].[350] In this context he refers to the Rabbinic model [E2], conjugating the theosophy of opposites with a theurgical approach, depicted by the Rabbinic view that someone is retributed in a manner he behaves.[351]

343 Scholem pointed out, ibidem, that this term is taken over from Pseudo-R. Isaac the Blind's *Commentary on Sefer Yetzirah.*

344 Ibidem. See also the view of R. Azriel, "New Remnants," pp. 212–213, according to which the six or seven *middot* that rule over the world in the pre-Messianic times, are the "principle" – *kelal* – of the thirteen *middot.* For innumerable middot see already the material in Wolfson, "The Theosophy of Shabbetai Donnolo," p. 308 n. 67.

345 See the epistle printed by Scholem, *Studies in Kabbalah,* p. 30: אור השכל היורד על המדות

346 See Travis, *Rabbi Ezra of Gerona,* p. 262 and Hebrew part p. 44.

347 On this Kabbalist see in particular Vajda, *Recherches,* pp. 11–113, and 321–326.

348 *Sefer ha-'Emunah we-ha-Bitaḥon,* in *Kitvei ha-Ramban,* II, pp. 399–340, and his *Meshiv Devarim Nekhoḥim,* pp. 155–156, 165.

349 Ibidem, pp. 155–156.

350 Ibidem.

351 Ibidem, p. 156. He refers in this context to a view found in *BT Shabbat,* fols 105b, *Nedarim* fol. 32a, *Sanhedrin* fol. 90a.

He also refers to the cooperation of the two attributes, as everything in the world depends on the two attributes, in the vein of model [B], though immediately afterwards he speaks about three attributes, in a more theosophical manner.[352] He identifies the attribute of compassion with the male and that of judgment with the female.[353] In another discussion we may discern a more detailed effort of ben Sheshet to use the two attributes as some form of code that organize his interpretation of several issues.[354] It should be emphasized that in his *Sefer ha-'Emunah we-ha-Bitaḥon*, he uses more the term *middah*, and only very rarely *sefirah*. Once he refers to the possibility that the same term, including the Tetragrammaton, may designate both the attribute of compassion and that of judgment, a view reminiscent of Rabbinic model [C],[355] while elsewhere he adopts a view similar to model [D].[356]

Interestingly enough, this Kabbalist compares the situation of opposite acts stemming from the very same sefirotic source, to the astronomical theme that assumes that two persons born under the aegis of the same planet may suffer different effects that stem from it.[357] It is hard to know to what extent his acquaintance with astronomy represents an intellectual concern with this type of lore in R. Isaac the Blind's circle in general.

The five Kabbalists mentioned in this chapter are sharing major topics, though not all of them – R. Azriel being the most diverging in his thought – and it is relatively easy to distinguish between them both stylistically and conceptually. Nevertheless, each of them differ much more from the Kabbalists that constitute another school, active in Catalunia, the school of Nahmanides. We shall address this in the next chapter.

352 See *Meshiv Devarim Nekhoḥim*, pp. 156, 162, 165.

353 Ibidem, p. 141.

354 Ibidem, p. 187.

355 Chapter 16, ibidem, p. 399. See also the interesting discussion on *middah* in chapter 3 of this book, p. 360.

356 Ibidem, p. 400.

357 *Meshiv Devarim Nekhoḥim*, p. 156, and Vajda, *Recherches*, pp. 321–326.

SIX

Divine Attributes and Du-Partzufin in Nahmanides' Kabbalistic School

Contemporary and somewhat later to the circle of Kabbalists related to Rabad – that disappeared as a distinct school around 1260 – as another Kabbalistic school emerged, active in Gerona and Barcelona, whose major figure was R. Moshe ben Nahman – known as Nahmanides [1196–1270].[358] This later school flowered mainly in Gerona and

358 On his thought see, e.g., Chaim Henoch, *Nachmanides: Philosopher and Mystic* (Jerusalem, 1976), (Hebrew), Pedaya, *Nahmanides*, Yair Lorberbaum, 'Nahmanides' Kabbalah on the Creation of Man in the Image of God,' *Kabbalah* 5 (2000), pp. 287–326 (Hebrew), David Novak, *The Theology of Nahmanides Systematically Presented* (Scholars Press, Atlanta, Georgia, 1992), and Halbertal, *By Way of Truth*, in particular pp. 145–146, 202–203. See also the studies of Shlomo Pines, "God, the Divine Glory, and the Angels according to a Second Century Theology," in J. Dan, ed., *The Beginnings of Jewish Mysticism in Medieval Europe* (Jerusalem, 1987), pp. 11–12 (Hebrew), and my "*Zimzum*," pp. 67–68, as to the possibility that Nahmanides preserved a late antiquity theory of divine contraction, and see also Elliot R. Wolfson, "By Way of Truth: Aspects of Nahmanides' Kabbalistic Hermeneutic," *AJSR* vol. 14 no. 2 (1989), pp. 103–178, Ben Sasson, *The Divine Name*, pp. 249–277, 289–291, Joseph Stern, *Problems and Parables of Law: Maimonides and Nahmanides on Reasons for the Commandments (Ta'Amei Ha-Mitzvot)* (SUNY Press: Albany, 1998), as well as in the following footnotes.

Barcelona between 1240–1330. Given the temporal overlapping of the floruit of these two Kabbalistic schools, both were active in Catalunia. The contact between Nahmanides and R. Isaac the Blind, Rabad's son,[359] scholars in the past conflated between them, assuming that they constitute a rather homogenous Kabbalistic school.[360] However, an examination of the details of their Kabbalistic views concerning a long series of topics, shows that they differ in quite a significant manner.Those discrepancies are very important for what I see as a proper historical understanding of the dynamics of the emergence of early Kabbalah.

The beginnings of distinction between the schools were made in scholarship in the early eighties.[361] This distinction is the case of their different attitude to the nature of ten *sefirot*,[362] to the nature of the soul,[363] to the meaning of the secret of the soul-impregnation, known as *sod ha-'Ibbur*,[364] to the theory of *Tzimtzum*,[365] to the view

359 See, e.g., Scholem, *Origins of the Kabbalah*, pp. 393–404, Abrams, "Chapters from an Emotional and Sexual Biography of God," pp. 281–283, idem, *Kabbalistic Manuscripts and Textual Theory*, pp. 199–223, and my study, "Nahmanides: Kabbalah, Halakhah, and Spiritual Leadership," in eds. M. Idel and M. Ostow, *Jewish Mystical Leaders and Leadership in the 13th Century*, (Northvale, N.J., 1998), pp. 15–96.

360 See, e.g., Scholem, ibidem, or Joseph Dan, *Jewish Mysticism and Jewish Ethics* (Northwale, New Jersey, 1996), pp. 34–41, idem, 'The Emergence of Mystical Prayer', in eds., J. Dan – F. Talmage, *Studies in Jewish Mysticism*, (Cambridge 1982), pp. 108–109, etc., and n. 371.

361 See the important study of Bezalel Safran, "Rabbi Azriel and Nahmanides: Two Views of the Fall of Man," *Rabbi Moses Nahmanides (Ramban): Explorations in His Religious and Literary Activity*, ed. I. Twersky, (Cambridge, Mass. 1983), pp. 75–106.

362 Idel, *Kabbalah: New Perspectives*, pp. 137–144.

363 Idem, "*Nishmat 'Eloha*, The Divinity of the Soul in Nahmanides and His School," in eds. S. Arzy, M. Fachler, B. Kahana, *Life as a Midrash: Perspectives in Jewish Philosophy* (Yediot Aharonot, 2004), pp. 338–382 (Hebrew).

364 See my "Commentaries on the Secret of Impregnation," passim, and "The Secret of Impregnation," pp. 349–366.

365 Idem, "*Zimzum*," pp. 60–68, 102–106.

of Leviathan and Behemot,[366] to the topic of esotericism,[367] to the view of the post-mortem fate of the soul,[368] to the different contents of their Kabbalah,[369] and we shall see also an additional example pertinent to our subject-matter here, related to the different forms of treating the *du-partzufin*. Needless to say that there are scholars who still believe that Nahmanides was a student of R. Isaac the Blind, of R. Ezra or of R. Azriel as it was the case more than fifty years ago.[370] Some

366 Idem, "Leviathan and Its Consort," pp. 159–170.

367 Idem, "We Have No Kabbalistic Tradition on This," pp. 51–73.

368 Idem, "Some Remarks on Ritual and Mysticism," p. 121.

369 Idem, "The Jubilee in Jewish Mysticism," *Millenarismi nella cultura contemporanea*, in ed. E. Rambaldi, (F. Angeli, Milano, 2000), pp. 209–232, and the Hebrew larger version of this article printed in *Shilhei Me'ot – Qitzam shel 'Idanim*, ed. J. Kaplan, (Merkaz Shazar, Jerusalem, 2005), pp. 67–98. For a detailed analysis of the cosmic cycles in Nahmanides' school see Pedaya, *Nahmanides*. See also Vajda, *Le commentaire*, p. 349 n. 29.

370 See Tishby, *Studies*, vol. 1, pp. 3, 17, Scholem, *Origins of the Kabbalah*, p. 368, Yahalom, *Between Gerona and Narbonne*, pp. 284–285, Travis, *Rabbi Ezra of Gerona*, pp. 25, 301–325 – see especially pp. 323–325, where the same passages were pasted twice. See, however, R. Meir ibn Sahulah's *Commentary on Nahmanides' Secrets*, where the Kabbalist from Nahmanides' school was sensitive enough to see the differences between R. Ezra and Nahmanides, and reject the views of the former. See already Tishby's preface to his edition of R. Azriel of Gerona's *Commentary on the Talmudic Legends*, p. 36. See also ibidem, p. 11 n. 1 and Sendor, *The Emergence of Provencal Kabbalah*, 1, pp. 346–347.

More recently, the pathetic attempt of Joseph Dan to portray R. Azriel as the teacher of Nahmanides, in "Rabbi Azriel of Gerona: One Enigma or Two," in ed. Y. Ben-Naeh & alia, *Studies in Jewish History Presented to Joseph Hacker*, (Zalman Shazar Center, Jerusalem, 2014), pp. 59–68 (Hebrew). Without knowing it, Dan follows the mistake made already by the 16th century Kabbalist R. Meir ibn Gabbai, who regarded R. Azriel as Nahmanides' teacher, on the ground of a bibliographical error. See *Derekh 'Emunah*, p. 80, as well as R. Ḥayyim Vital's *Sha'ar ha-Gilgulim* (Jerusalem 1971), p. 117, and even a scholar like Adolph Jellinek already thought once so. See Tishby, *Studies*, vol. 1, p. 17 and Travis, *Rabbi Ezra of Gerona*, pp. 319–321. For several other reasons, this view of R. Azriel as influencing Nahmanides is a blantant mistake, and an examination of their views presented here and in the prior chapter shows the

others accepted the distinction I proposed between these schools.[371] However, let me emphasize, sharp as the distinction between the two schools is, it should not be misunderstood as necessarily covering all the topics shared by these schools, and some overlappings are more than plausible. Let me analyze the divergent opinion of Nahmanides and his school on *middot*, in comparison to those surveyed in the previous chapter.

Nahmanides himself embraced a rather strict form of esotericism when dealing with those topics that constitute, according to his view, his Kabbalah.[372] Not everything we as scholars or other Kabbalists, consider to be Kabbalah, was necessarily for him part of an esoteric tradition that he claimed he received. However, we may guess the content of his esoteric views from several writings from his circle written at the end of the 13th century and early 14th century. However, let me start with a statement found in the sermon to the New Year, written at the end of Nahmanides' life:

> "Provided that it was at the beginning of the conquest of the land of Israel, the Holy One, blessed be He, wanted that the attribute of judgment was present over them, and this is the reason that was a forfeited property, and Onqelos hinted at it when he translated [Numbers 23:21]: "And the trumpet blast of a king among him" as "and the presence[373] of their king is found amidst them, since the trumplet blast, [*teru'ah*] is the attribute of judgment, and he

stark differences. I cannot enter here in the details of the evidence brought in order to make these claims, and I find it sufficient for my discussions below to refer to the conceptual divergences that were pointed out in the detailed studies mentioned in the earlier footnotes and in the material to be discussed further on in this chapter.

371 See, e.g., Oron, "The Literature of Commentaries to the Ten *Sefirot*," pp. 218–219 and Afterman, *Devequt*, pp. 287, 324.

372 This includes in particular the theories of cosmic cycles and of the secret of the impregnation of the soul by another soul, two important theories not found in the circle of Rabad's followers, at least not in the way Nahmanides and his school understood them. See my studies referred in the previous footnotes.

373 *Shekhinah*, considered by Nahmanides to be the attribute of soft judgment.

> said, it is said [Psalms 89:16]: "Happy is the nation that knows the quavering blast" that it brings close to it knowledge, since knowledge is said about cleaving as it is written [Genesis 4:1]: "And Adam knew Eve" and [Genesis 24:16]: "A virgin neither had any man known her." And the meaning of the verse is that the day of judgment [is] in compassion, and it is said, 'Happy is the nation that knows the quavering blast' since [Psalms 89:18]: 'For You are the glory [*Tiferet*] of their strength ['*Uzzamo*]' since *Tiferet* is the attribute of compassion, and strength ['*Oz*] is the attribute of judgment. Those are things belonging to the secrets of the Torah, and it is not appropriate to speak about them in public, and even not to every one of the elite."[374]

Nahmanides regards the trumpet blast or the quavering blast, as referring to the attribute of judgment and to the Day of Judgment – symbolized also by the *Shekhinah* in the Targum – and he alleges the need to bring it together with the attribute of compassion, referred as *Tiferet*.[375] This can be understood as some form of inducing union between the two attributes in the vein of model [B]. It is very plausible that the knowledge should be understood in sexual terms, as the two verses from Genesis show. However, the question is why such a view is considered to be so esoteric? As seen above, in his passage analyzed

374 *Kitvei ha-Ramban*, vol. I, pp. 220–221:

ולפי שהיא היתה תחלה בכבוש הארץ רצה הקב"ה שתהיה מדת הדין מתוחה כנגדם ולכך היתה חרם, ואונקלוס רמז זה שתרגם ותרועת מלך בו ושכינת מלכהון ביניהון, ולפי שהתרועה מדת הדין אמר אשרי העם יודעי תרועה שמקרבת אליה הדעת כי הידיעה תאמר על הדבקות כמו 'והאדם ידע וגו", 'בתולה ואיש לא ידעה', ואמר 'יום תרועה יהיה לכם' כי היום יהיה לנו, ולא הוצרך להזכיר שופר כי השופר רמז ביום והתרועה בו, והנה פירש הכתוב כי הוא יום דין ברחמים, והוא שאמר 'באשרי העם יודעי תרועה' כי תפארת עוזמו אתה כי תפארת מדת רחמים ועז מדת הדין, ואלו דברים מסתרי התורה הם ואין ראוי לדבר בהם ברבים וגם לא לכל היחיד.

See also ibn Gaon, *Keter Shem Tov*, Ms. Paris BN 774, fol. 89b, that sees the phrase *Tiferet 'Uzamo* as *du-partzufin*.

375 *Tiferet* recurs in similar contexts. See Nahmanides' commentary on Deuteronomy 34:12, ed. Chavel, vol. II, p. 505. See also the text from Ms. Christ Church College 198, to be discussed at the end of this chapter.

inchapter 4 above, the Rabad already construed the relations between the two attributes as male and female. Indeed, the sexual dimension was not put in relief though it is hardly peripheral, since he deals with a married couple. In my opinion, the precise concatenations between the divine attributes and the performance of the ritual constitute Nahmanides' secrets. Or, to translate the formulation of one of the followers of Nahmanides' esotericism, the anonymous sage that commented on Nahmanides' secrets: "that a person activates those attributes that activate him and he [activates] them."[376] It is the details related to theurgy, which are the core of his esotericism, not just the details of theosophy *per se*. At the same time, it is a correlative type of religiosity, explicated here in the clearest terms.

For a better understanding of the above passage let us compare it to a parallel discussion found in Nahmanides' *Commentary on the Pentateuch*:

> "The trumpet blast hints at the attribute of judgment... and it is victorious in a war... and it is said [Joshu'a 6:20]: 'The nation blasted the horn loudly and the wall fell down.' And this is the reason for the forfeited property, and when the community that merits [to hear] the blow [of the horn] was gathered, since the sustained blast [*teqiy'ah*] refers to the attribute of compassion, since His right hand is extended to receive the repentants[377]... since the war is to the quavering blast, and the holidays and the joy is [referring] to [the attribute of] compassion... the sustained before it [the quavering blast] and afterwards and the quavering blast in the middle,[378] so that one should not cut down the branches[379] during the [the day of] New Year and the Day of Atonement, and when sacrificing.[380]

376 Cf., *Ma'or va-Shemesh*, fol. 40b:
פועלות באדם כי הוא פועל למדות הללו שפועלות בו והוא בהם.

377 See above n. 81.

378 See *BT Rosh ha-Shanah*, fol. 34a.

379 For this famous syntagm see Scholem, *Jewish Gnosticism*, p. 16 n. 6.

380 See R. Shem Tov ibn Gaon's *Keter Shem Tov*, ed. *'Amudei ha-Qabbalah*, p. 63, where he claims that Nahmanides hinted also to *du-partzufin*, and in Ms. Paris

But the intention is one to the sustained and the other to the quavering blast. And the illuminated will understand."[381]

Again, according to the last phrase, Nahmanides hints at a secret teaching. In a rather complementary manner, in the last passage he speaks about the interdiction of cutting, reminiscent of the cleaving in the first quote. In both cases the attributes are treated in a context that assumes a theurgical interpretation: by performing the rituals, the union between the attributes is induced. In my opinion, the secret has to do with the specific concatenation between divine attributes and particular rituals, a concatenation that is not explicated in detail in the Rabbinic literature, as we have surveyed above.

However, it seems that the simple, unifying theurgy does not exhaust Nahmanides' intention. So, for example, in the quote from his sermon he speaks about "the day of judgment in compassion" which means that the day of New Year is related not just to judgment but also to compassion. What is the possible meaning of such a statement: does it follow the Rabbinic model [B] about the cooperation between two attributes? Or perhaps we have a version of model [D], which assumes the existence of one attribute within the other? Indeed, in another passage in his *Commentary on the Pentateuch* he speaks about the blowing of the horn during the day of New Year, he uses again the formula we mentioned earlier: "This is the day of judgment in [or within] compassion.," Immediately afterwards he repeats the Talmudic formula about the quavering blast found between the two sustained blasts, then he wrote that the quavering blast is "comprised from compassion." Then he writes:

BN 774, fols. 80b, 81a, 84b, 89a. More on *du-partzufin* in this school see below in this chapter.

381 Nahmanides on 10:6, ed. Chavel, vol. II, p. 228:
כי התרועה רמז למדת הדין... 'ויריעו העם תרועה גדולה ותפול החומה, ולכך היתה חרם ובהקהיל את הקהל ראויים לתקיעה, כי הפשוטה רמז למדת רחמים 'כי ימינו פשוטה לקבל שבים'... כי המלחמה לתרועה והמועדים והשמחה לרחמים... פשוטה לפניה ופשוטה לאחריה ותרועה באמצע, שלא יקצץ בנטיעות בראש השנה ויום הכפורים ועל הקרבן, אבל הכוונה זו לתקיעה וזו לתרועה, והמשכיל יבין.

"And according to the path of truth... In the New Year He unites with the attribute of judgment and rules over His world, and in the day of Atonement [He unites] with the attribute of compassion... the New Year is the day of judgment [with]in compassion, and the Day of Atonement is the day of compassion [with]in judgment."[382]

Each of the two High Holidays are conceived of as governed by one of the two attributes, which, however, cooperates with its opposite. This means that some form of cooperation or perhaps mutual inclusion of the two attributes is conceived to be necessary in order to have a proper rule. This is the meaning of the comprised attribute – *middah kelulah* – mentioned above, as well as elsewhere, where God says to Moses that, "I shall not behave with you by the stern attribute of judgment but by [means of the] attribute that is comprised in the attribute of compassion."[383] The two High Holidays reflect, therefore, two different variants of the inclusion of one attribute into another.

382 Nahmanides, Commentary on Leviticus 23:24, ed. Chavel, vol. II pp. 153–154:
ועל דרך האמת... והנה הוא יום דין ברחמים... ומפני שהיא כלולה מן הרחמים תקיעה לפניה ולאחריה... אלא בראש השנה מתיחד במדת הדין ומנהיג עולמו, וביום הכפורים במדת הרחמים... ראש השנה יום דין ברחמים ויום הכפורים יום רחמים בדין.

383 Commentary on Exodus 33:14, ed. Chavel, vol. I p. 520:
שלא אתנהג עמך במדת הדין עזה, אלא במדה כלולה במדת הרחמים
This view is quoted as the opinion of the anonymous Sage printed as glosses to R. Shem Tov ibn Gaon's *Keter Shem Tov*, in ed. Koriat, *Ma'or va-Shemesh*, fol. 40b, העטרה הכלולה מהתפארת and compare to R. Menahem Recanati, *Commentary on the Pentateuch*, fols. 50d, 51c. See also the view expressed by R. Shem Tov ibn Gaon, *Keter Shem Tov*, in ed. *'Amudei ha-Qabbalah*, p. 34: רחמים כלולה בדין and see also his teacher, R. Isaac Todros, *Commentary on the Maḥzor*, Ms. Paris BN 839, fol. 211b. About the meaning of the verb *KLL* in the Palestinian *Piyyut* and in early Kabbalah see Idel, *Kabbalah: New Perspectives*, pp. 330–332 nn. 37, 45, 47, 50. On the concept of *middah kelulah* see also Mottolese, *Analogy in Midrash and Kabbalah*, p. 215, and in chapter 10. On the inclusion of the two attributes in each and every *sefirah* see also the view of R. Moshe Cordovero, e.g., *'Or Yaqar*, vol. 11, (Jerusalem, 1981), p. 174. See also below n. 502.

Thus, inclusion or comprisal is the answer to the potential heretical understanding that attributes a certain act of one attribute as if it is independent of the other. It therefore does not refer to a specific *sefirah* but to a mode of divine activity, in which two powers are involved. Indubitably this is an attempt to mitigate the possible accusation of a belief in two dominions on high, which implies a separation between two powers that are actually united or at least cooperating.[384]

This is also the case when Nahmanides describes God's answer to Moses concerning His name that he is "the emissary to them [the people of Israel] by the [dint of] attribute of judgment that is [found] [with]in the attribute of compassion."[385] The recurrence of the syntagm "attribute X within [or alternatively comprised] attribute Y" is therefore a way to describe sometimes the divine action. The traditional, mythical Rabbinic picture of God as sitting on the seat of justice or judgment or alternatively on that of compassion, when judging the world, is therefore conceived of as inadequate for the conceptual approach as embraced by Nahmanides.[386]

Though Nahmanides uses from time to time the cognomens of the *sefirot*, and in the passages above the term *Tiferet* occurs several times, the wider theosophical implications of the above discussions are not evident, and the Kabbalist preferred to adopt the traditional Rabbinic terms of the two attributes. The question is whether beyond those statements and his claims that there is a secret, there was indeed a more comprehensive explication that was formulated in more technical theosophical terms. In any case, let me point out that in the above passages, Nahmanides resorts to the term *middah*, while the term

384 This approach differs from that of R. Ezra in his commentary on the commandments, where it is the transformation of judgment in compassion that is referred to in the vein of the Rabbinic model [E2]. See Travis, *Rabbi Ezra of Gerona*, p. 262 and Hebrew part, p. 44, and n. 226, where Nahmanides' view is adduced but he does not specify the differences between the two.

385 Nahmanides on Exodus 3:13, ed. Chavel, vol. 1 p. 293: הודיעו שהוא שלוח אליהם במדת הדין אשר במדת הרחמים

386 See, however, the discussion in Travis, *Rabbi Ezra of Gerona*, p. 262 and Hebrew part p. 44.

sefirah is rare in his writings, with the exception of his *Commentary on Sefer Yetzirah*.[387]

In order to answer this question, let me address some discussions about *du-partzufin,* as found in the school of Nahmanides, which includes several Kabbalists that were active as a school for at least two generations. Like in the case of the Rabad, the specific manner in which Adam was created as a facial androgyne helps understanding the relationship between the two attributes, though the details differ. For the further development of the theosophical understanding of the term *du-partzufin* in Nahmanides's school, its identification with the *sefirot* of *Tiferet* and *Malkhut* is crucial, while it is absent in the writings belonging to Rabad's school.[388] This interpretation is evident in the supercommentary on Nahmanides' secrets that he hinted to in his *Commentary on the Pentateuch,* entitled *Keter Shem Tov,* authored by R. Shem Tov ben Abraham ibn Gaon, a student of Rashba' and R. Isaac Todros, Nahmanides' main disciples. He identifies the two attributes to the *du-partuzfin,*[389] and the latter with the first and the second days of the seven days of creation,[390] while elsewhere he identifies this syntagm with two cherubim and the words *Zot* – the tenth power that is feminine, and the sixth power that is masculine.[391] This identification has something to do with the initial higher status of the Feminine, found on the same level like *Tiferet,* or perhaps part of it, or construing together a common entity, that changed afterwards by the descent of the Female to the lower place, as a result of Her transgression, as we shall see below. In any case, it is possible to discern

387 See Scholem, *Studies in Kabbalah,* pp. 87–96, especially p. 92, where the ten *sefirot* are described as divided between the two attributes.

388 See Idel, "The Mystical Intention of the Eighteen Benedictions by R. Isaac Sagi Nahor," pp. 28 n. 22, 30 n. 39, 49, Pedaya, *Nahmanides,* pp. 220–223, and Weiss, *Cutting the Shoots,* pp. 66–76.

389 Ms. Paris BN 774, fols. 76b, 77b, 78b.

390 Ms. Paris BN 774, fol. 74a. See also below beside nn. 403, 425.

391 Ibidem, fol. 76b. See also fol. 89b. See also R. Isaac of Acre, ed. Goldreich, *Me'irat 'Einayyim,* pp. 175, 188, 189 and Goldreich's discussion on pp. 364–365.

an attempt to organize biblical and Rabbinic material by means of the attributive code, together with the anthropomorphic one.

More explicit is the discussion where ibn Gaon identifies the two attributes to *du-partzufin* with the Rabbinic theme of white and black fires, and explicitly to *Tiferet* and *Shekhinah*.[392] He also identifies this syntagm with "day and night," terms which again are widely understood as referring to these two *middot*.[393] Especially important for our discussions above is the fact that ibn Gaon speaks about the *du-partzufin* as *shawin*, namely as being equal.[394] Interestingly enough the Kabbalist describes the *sefirah* of *Tiferet* as "the equal line."[395] Other references to *du-partzufin* in his book are easily discernable, but they are less explicit insofar as their symbolic reference is concerned.[396] According to some indications it seems that this topic has been discussed orally by the teachers of ibn Gaon.[397] In a book of his written several years later, ibn Gaon writes in a poetic manner: "Adam and Eve/ were created equally/, *du-partzufin*/ intertwined in one another, as symbolized by the form of the cherubim."[398]

392 Ms. Paris BN 774, fols. 76b, 77b and see also fols. 78ab, 81a, 85a, and in *'Amudei ha-Qabbalah*, p. 8. Let me point out that many of the discussions of *du-partzufin* in ibn Gaon's book have been appropriated in the anonymous classic of Kabbalah stemming from the circle of Nahmanides' followers, *Ma'arekhet ha-'Elohut*. See also Gottlieb, *The Kabbalah in the Writings of R. Bahya ben Asher ibn Halawa*, pp. 249–259 and in the appendix below. However, this book adopted exoteric views of the school of Rabad, Nahmanides, and Rashba.' See, e.g., fols. 88b, 93b, the first one to be discussed below in this chapter.

393 Ms. Paris BN 774, fols. 88b–89a. See also the anonymous letter addressed, in my opinion, to R. Shem Tov ibn Gaon, printed by Scholem, *Reshit ha-Kabbalah*, pp. 249–250. Scholom thought that the addressee was Nahmanides.

394 Ms. Paris BN 774, fol. 78b. This view is found in all the good manuscripts of *Keter Shem Tov*.

395 הקו השוה ibidem, and fol. 88a, in *Ma'or wa-Shemesh*, ed. Koriat, fol. 47a and in the edition of *'Amudei ha-Qabbalah*, p. 7.

396 Ms. Paris BN 774, fol. 91ab, 98a, 112a. See also below in n. 429.

397 *Ma'or va-Shemesh*, ed. Koriat, fols. 33b, 35ab, 45a.

398 *Baddei 'Aron*, Ms. Paris BN 840, fol. 6a, Idel, *Kabbalah: New Perspectives*, p. 131: אדם וחוה/ בגזירה שוה נברא/ דו־פרצופין/ זה בזה מעורין/ רמוזים בצורת הכרובים.

Similar views are found also in some glosses that have been integrated in the printed version of *Keter Shem Tov*, authored by an anonymous Kabbalist referred to as the "opinion of the Sage"[399] – *da'at he-Ḥakham* – and he too claims the equality of the two dimensions of *du-partzufin*.[400] Similar views are found also in another supercommentary, authored by R. Meir ibn Avi Sahulah or perhaps by R. Joshu'a ibn Shu'aib, and by other members of the school of Nahmanides' students.[401]

Let me turn to the reference to the two *sefirot: Tiferet* and *Malkhut, 'Atarah* or *Shekhinah* as equal, that occurred once in one of the above-mentioned books. In a collectanea of Kabbalistic traditions stemming from Nahmanides' school it is written that:

> "God, blessed be He, created a subtle creature in [the manner of] *du-partzufin*, an equal power [*be-koaḥ shaweh*], and they are *'Ateret Tiferet*, and they served the [first] three days until the fourth.[402] And when God has seen that the world is not worthy of such a great light He did by the light of *du partzufin*[403] the lights of the spheres, which are sun and moon and they are the similitude of the lights of the first ones. And the sun and moon served until the sixth day when Adam and Eve were created also [as] *du-partzufin*, after the creation of the world. And since she did not accuse, namely the *'Atarah* in that legend that the moon said: is it possible that two kings will use the same crown, namely the equal power. Her Creator, namely the Blessed be He, that is the *Teshuvah* answered her: "Go and diminish yourself." Immediately the twins separated themselves a little bit. And this was in the eve of Sabbath, in the twilight, and also the sun and the moon separated themselves, and Adam and Eve, which are the emanation of the first ones.[404]

399 See *Ma'or va-Shemesh*, ed. Koriat, fols. 28ab, 29b.
400 Ibidem, fol. 28b
401 See ed. Warsau, 1875, fol. 4abc, 5d, 10c, 19a, 24a, etc.
402 See also below n. 429.
403 Namely the two *sefirot* mentioned earlier.
404 Namely *Tiferet* and *Malkhut*.

You should understand from this the legend according to which Sabbath said to the Holy one blessed be He, namely the *Tzaddiq* said about this: "You have given to all a partner and to me you did not give one." Then the Holy One blessed be He said: "*Knesset Yisrael* will be your partner". Immediately the two unite to each other and became both Sabbath. And you should rejoice and be glad like the joy of bridegroom and bride. And to this issue the Rabbi[405] intended when he spoke about division, as it is written in the case of R. Simon[406]: they divided to it, namely the *Teshuvah*. And this is the reason why [it is written], "you should bring a ransom for me, namely to me[407] ... Know the secret of the first light namely for it *'Ateret Tiferet* said, in order to show how that they were *du-partzufin* and in one union.[408] And when they said to *'amusei beten*, it refers to [the secret of] storage. And there are some people[409] who say that the influx was separated by *Teshuvah* [going only] to *Tiferet*."[410]

405 Namely Nahmanides.

406 Cf., *BT Hullin*, fol. 60b.

407 This is a demythization of the Midrashic stance: It is not God that should be forgiven because of a mistake He made, but the sacrifice should be intended to Him, referred here by the *sefirah* of *Binah*, symbolized by *Teshuvah*.

408 See ibn Gaon, *Keter Shem Tov*, ed., *'Amudei ha-Qabbalah*, p. 22.

409 I guess that those are the Kabbalists from the school of R. Isaac the Blind.

410 Ms. Oxford-Bodeliana 1610, fols. 90a–90b, Ms. Cambridge Or. 2116.8, Ms. Parma-Palatina (1285) 2270, fol. 113b, or Ms. New York, JTS 191, p. 94, part of which has been printed now from the last manuscript in Weiss, *Cutting the Shoots*, pp. 82–83:

השי״ ברא בריאה אחת דקה בדו־פרצופין בכח שוה והם עטרת תפארת ושמשו בעולם הג׳ ימים הראשונים עד יום ד׳ ובראות השי״ שאין העולם ראוי לאור גדול כזה עשה באורם של דו פרצופין מאורות הגלגלים והם חמה ולבנה והם נובלות מאורם של ראשונים ואלו חמה ולבנה שמשו עד יום ששי עד שנברא אדם וחוה ג״כ דו פרצופין לאחר בריאת העולם. ולמה שלא קטרגה כלומר העטר׳ באותה הגדה שהי׳ אמרה הלבנה: אפשר לשני מלכים שישמשו בכתר אחד כלומר בכח שוה. ענה לה יוצרה כלומר ית׳ שהוא התשובה: לכי מעטי את עצמך, ומיד נפרדו מעט התאומים. וזה היה ערב שבת בין השמשות וגם כן נפרדו חמה ולבנה ואדם וחוה שהם אצילות הראשונים. ומכאן תבין הגדה שאומר אמרה שבת לפני הקב״ה כלומר אמרה הצדיק ועל כן אמר: לכלם נתת בת זוג ולי לא נתת. ואז

The "subtle creature" mentioned at the beginning of the translated passage is not the human Adam but a divine entity that incorporated two entities that had an equal power, namely two *sefirot* as symbolized by the two luminaries. The syntagm "equal power" in the singular occurs again in the same collectanea in order to refer to the zone of *Tiferet*.[411] However, while in the quote attributed to Rabad, it is plausible that those powers are the *sefirot* of *Ḥesed* and *Gevurah*, here those powers are identified in an explicit manner as the couple of feminine and masculine divine attributes *Malkhut* and *Tiferet*.[412] This identification is persistent in this Kabbalistic school, as we shall see more below.

The expression "equal power" seems to qualify the term *du-partzufin*: they were not just two powers found within one body but also two divine powers that are equal insofar as their power is concerned. Also the resort to the form "in [the manner of] *du-partzufin*" refers to an adverbial formulation. The resort to the word *koaḥ*, power, is interesting since it may point both to an entity, and to a form of operation. The latter meaning is obvious in another passage that reflects Nahmanides' Kabbalah. In R. Isaac of Acre's *Me'irat 'Einayyim*, where earlier Kabbalistic traditions have been preserved, we read that:

> "Again the Kabbalistic tradition of Saporta: "Know that they were *du-partzufin*, and when they were operating equally there was a fear that provided that their rule was equal, lest the people will err and say that there are two powers [in heaven], God forbid."[413]

א"ל הקב"ה כנסת ישראל יהיה בת זוגך ומיד נתחברו שניהם ונעשו שתיהם שבת 'וישישו ושמחו כמשוש חתן וכלה'. ולזה כיוון הרב באומרו ענין הבדלה שכתוב ב"ר סימון 'הבדילו לו' כלומר התשובה ולפי זה 'הביאו עלי כפרה' כמו אלי... תדע סוד אור הראשון ר"ל בשבילו אמרו 'עטרת תפארת' להורות שהיו דו פרצופין ודבוק אחד. וכשאמרו 'לעמוסי בטן' מורה על הגניזה. ויש אומרים כי השפע הבדילו התשובה לת"ת.

For cognate material see also Ms. Oxford-Bodleiana, 1610, fol. 91a, and nn. 430, 563.

411 Ibidem, fol. 91a: כי כשהמלכות היתה מתאמצת בכח שוה

412 See Scholem, *Origins of the Kabbalah*, p. 217.

413 This view is found in the name of the anonymous Sage, in the version of ibn Gaon's book *Keter Shem Tov*, as printed in ed., Koriat, *Ma'or va-Shemesh*, fol. 28b. See above n. 384.

> End of Quote. But the opinion of the sage[414] was that it is possible to say that *du-partzufin* is from the perspective that in the sun the power of the moon was comprised,[415] and also that this power of the moon has been then consonant to the sun, and was not mixed to the sun, but was distinguishable... in any case it is possible to say that the power of the moon is consonant in the sun at that moment, and was exercising also the act of compassion,[416] as it seems to be from the Kabbalah of Saporta."[417]

The Kabbalist quoted by R. Isaac of Acre as "Saporta," is someone very close to Nahmanides' thought who preserved his Kabbalistic, esoteric views.[418] He offers an explanation for the distinction made between the two powers that were initially equal: it is the fear of a theological error that necessitated the diminution of one of the two powers –all this in order to prevent misunderstanding as to the existence of two powers on high. Earlier in the same book, R. Isaac appropriates a discussion found in R. Shem Tov ibn Gaon's book, writing that:

> "[a] This is the reason why *Tiferet* and *'Atarah* are called *du-partzufin* since at the beginning they were emanated from *Teshuvah* [as] *du-partzufin*, and they receive [from there] in an equal manner [*be-shawweh*], [b] but the sins of Israel caused that they are in exile,[419] and this is the reason that it is necessary to bring

414 It is not clear who this *Ḥakhum* is, and it is not certain that he should be identified with the Sage who authored the glosses printed within ibn Gaon's text mentioned above. See Gottlieb, *The Kabbalah in the Writings of R. Bahya ben Asher ibn Halawa*, pp. 221–224. See also above n. 384.

415 In some instances, in Nahmanides' school, *du-partzufin* is related to the *sefirah* of *Tiferet*, which includes also the *sefirah* of *'Atarah*. See, e.g., the opinion of the "Sage," printed in *Ma'or va-Shemesh*, fol. 28b, and in the anonymous *Ma'arekhet ha-'Elohut*, fols. 106b, 160a. See also below n. 430.

416 Compare the view about the cooperation between the two powers in Rabad, in the Kabbalistic passed, especially paragraph [d].

417 R. Isaac of Acre, *Meirat 'Einayyim*, ed., Goldreich, pp. 8–9.

418 See Gottlieb, *The Kabbalah in the Writings of R. Bahya ben Asher ibn Halawa*, pp. 216–221, Goldreich's introduction, ibidem, pp. 76–89.

419 This is a rather obscure statement. It may point to the separation between the

atonement, and this is the meaning of the Prosecution. [c] This is the secret meaning I received:[420] Know that the *Teshuvah* is the king of the kings of kings. How is it? *Teshuvah* is king, kings are the arms of the world, namely *Ḥesed* and *Gevurah*,[421] [the second] kings are *du-partzufin*, that are two kings that serve and use one crown, which is the *Teshuvah*, which is the Holy One, blessed be He. When the *'Atarah* stood and accused[422] and said to *Teshuvah*: "It is impossible that two kings will use the same crown,"[423] because you know that the *du-partzufin* were equal, since during the six days of creation the light of one [of them] was like the light of another, since *Tiferet* was the first day and *'Atarah* is the second one[424]... and *Knesset Yisra'el* slandered and demanded good for herself, and so too, the moon in relation to the sun, and Eve in relation to Adam,

two entities, a separation that is induced by the sins of men, which causes the exile. In any case, this is an explanation for the diminution of the feminine power different from that he offered elsewhere in passages to be discussed below. For a discussion in which the separation between *Tiferet* and *Malkhut* is related to a sin that is not done by *Malkhut*, see *Zohar* III, fol. 44b. In any case, this is another instance of demythization of the Midrashic view, since the onus of the responsibility has been removed from the divinity and put on the sins of the people of Israel.

420 The source is not clear, but it may be traditions related to the name of Saporta – Nahmanides' Spanish name – since some lines later one, in the passage quoted above, R. Isaac formulated his quote "again the Kabbalistic tradition of Saporta." "Received" here probably points to an oral reception, characteristic of Nahmanides' school. See Idel, "We Have No Kabbalistic Tradition on This," pp. 51–73.

421 See above, beside n. 225.

422 This situation is reminiscent of the Rabbinic picture of the attribute of judgment functioned as an accuser. See, e.g., *Midrash Tanhuma'*, Mishpatim, par. 7.

423 Cf. *BT Ḥulin*, fol. 60b, *Genesis Rabbah'*, 3:6, 12:6. For the Midrashic background of the myth of the diminution of the Moon see e.g., Liebes, *Studies in Jewish Myth and Jewish Messianism*, pp. 47–54. Pedaya, "Sabbath, Sabbatai, and the Diminution of Moon," pp. 143–191, Halbertal, *By Way of Truth*, pp. 144–148, 234–237, 348 n. 495, and Weiss, "Most of the Errant Err in *Malkhut*," pp. 329–330 and n. 42, idem, *Cutting the Shoots*, pp. 63–64.

424 See above n. 225.

> and all is the same matter, but one is the holy and consecrated spirit of God,[425] blessed be He, and the other have been created in a corporeal manner."[426]

Paragraph [a] represents an interesting parallel to the theory of the emanation of the two opposites found in Rabad's Kabbalistic passage, however, without resorting to the term opposites, which is not found in this school also in the parallel texts brought in this chapter. The comprehensive attitude to the duality as referring to a variety of realms, found at the end of this quote, is reminiscent of the passage of the Rabad and implicitly in that of Philo's views as expressed in various places if they are read together. However, while the Provencal Kabbalist is concerned with maintaining the *isonomia* in a family, the traditions related to Nahmanides' Kabbalah describes the cosmic disturbance of the *isonomia* depicted in terms of a primordial crisis provoked by one of the two powers, on the various levels of existence. Some kind of symmetry that has human, celestial and intra-divine components is evident here, and one can learn as to the structure from one plane of existence as to the other, without attempting to claim a special status of the divine world from the point of view of the cognitive possibility to understand what happened there. This symmetry is part of the reorganization of diverse micro-myth in Rabbinism, into more comprehensive discussions, which may culminate in a

425 Namely the sefirotic couple versus the human one.

426 See *Me'irat 'Einayyim*, ed. Goldreich, p. 22, drawing from *Keter Shem Tov*, Ms. Paris BN 774, fol. 76b–77a, and in *Ma'or va-Shemesh*, fol. 26b, and compare also ibidem, fol. 3b. This passage represents a hypersemantic approach to a Rabbinic statement, by interpreting meticulously each word as pointing to a certain sefirotic power. For a similar approach of R. Isaac of Acre to another Rabbinic statement see Idel, *Absorbing Perfections*, pp. 449–460. See also the anonymous tradition preserved in the Kabbalistic collectanea preserved in Ms. Paris BN 859, fol. 10b and Recanati's *Commentary on the Pentateuch*, fol. 44c. For a combination of Nahmanides' view and what is attributed to Rabad, see *Ma'arekhet ha-'Elohut*, fols. 86b–87a, 88b, where *Ḥesed* and *Gevurah* are regarded as *du-partuzfin*, and immediately afterwards also *Tiferet* and *Malkhut* are understood so. See also Weiss, *Cutting the Shoots*, pp. 66–67.

macro-myth. Let me point out that the Nahmanidean emphasis on secrecy is evident in this passage, an approach that is absent in Rabad's passages.

The theme of equality is evident also in a later work of R. Isaac of Acre:

> "At the beginning they[427] were equal [*shawim*]…as they were created [as] *du-partzufin,* back to back, no one has any priority to the other, this being the reason why Adam and Eve were equal [*shawim*]."[428]

The theory of the primordial equality between the two luminaries, symbolizing here the *sefirot* of *Tiferet* and *Malkhut,* is found already in the above-mentioned book of ibn Gaon, where the myth of the diminution of the supernal Female is found in a rather explicit manner.[429] Here Anaximander's and Philo's view of *isonomia,* that assumes the importance of equilibrium between the two powers, has been combined with a critical view of the divine and extra-divine order, taken over from the Rabbinic myth. Nevertheless, this and other Kabbalistic texts, imply the importance of the primordial equality

427 Namely the two luminaries.

428 R. Isaac of Acre, *'Otzar Ḥayyim,* Ms. Moscow-Ginsburg 775, fol. 95b, ed. Gross, p. 96. This view recurs also in R. Isaac's earlier *Me'irat 'Einayyim,* ed. Goldreich, pp. 81, 83. Let me point out that the primordial equality of Adam and Eve, and the two luminaries in the context of *du-partzufin,* has been mentioned several times by a mid-14th century author close to Rashba's followers, R. Yehudah Campanton, in his treatise *Leqaḥ Tov,* extant in a unique manuscript Ms. Oxford-Bodleiana 1642, fols. 16b–17a, 18b–19a, etc., without resorting, however, to an overt theosophical symbolism in this context. The syntagm *du-partzufin* is mentioned also in other contexts in the same book and his views deserve a separate discussion. See also beside n. 403 above.

429 See the version of the anonymous Sage printed in *Ma'or va-Shemesh,* fol. 28b and also the lengthy discussion in the collectanea in Ms. Oxford-Bodeliana 1610, fols. 90b–91a. The two discussions are very close and deserve an additional inquiry in order to establish the nexus between the Sage and the anonymous collectanea. See also *Ma'arekhet ha-'Elohut,* fols. 86b–87a, 92b and above n. 416.

but are operating with a view that such a cosmic order has been disturbed and consequently one of the two members of the couple, the feminine one, has fallen.[430] In the Nahmanidean Kabbalistic tradition, there are other elements found in Philo's texts discussed above, in a more explicit manner. So, for example, we may read about a more explicit mentioning of equality and the identification of the two divine attributes with the *cherubim*, as seen, for example, in ibn Gaon's books. However, this school does not operate with the explicit assumption that the equal divine powers are also opposites, as Rabad and R. Azriel did.

Let me turn to another discussion of the emergence of the human male/female couple, as formulated by Nahmanides and in his chief follower, the Halakhic and Kabbalistic figure, R. Shlomo ben Abraham ibn Adret, known by the acronym Rashba' (died c. 1310). Both were quoted together by the latter's disciple, R. Baḥya ben Asher Ḥallewah.[431] Theirs are exoteric discussions, reminiscent of that of the Rabad in *Ba'alei ha-Nefesh*, reflecting a view according to which the human male is superior of and the source for the female entity. Nothing like equality that was mentioned in the context of the divine couple, as illustrated above by the esoteric traditions from Nahmanides' school. Those three major figures, the writings of Rabad, of Nahmanides and of Rashba', may be seen as part of the interesting interplay between esotericism and exotericism that characterizes

430 In this context I cannot enter the important issue of the sources of the equilibrium male/female for the theories that emerged one generation later in the Zoharic literature.

431 *Commentary on Genesis* 2:18, ed. Ch. Chavel, (Mossad ha-Rav Kook, Jerusalem, 1966), vol. 1 pp. 72–73. This view is reverberated in a mid-14th century book by R. Yehudah Ḥallewah, (most probably a descendant of R. Baḥya), in his book *'Imrei Shefer*, Ms. Oxford-Bodleiana 281, fols. 24b–26a, 40a, 130b, 137a, Ms. Paris BN 264, fol. 93a. The exoteric views of Rabad, Nahmanides, and Rashba', reverberate also in the discussion of the 19th century Hasidic author, R. Tzvi Elimelekh Shapira of Dinov, *Derekh Piqqudeikha*, (Lemberg, 1921), fol. 101ab. See also below the discussion of the passage from the anonymous *Ma'arekhet ha-'Elohut*, fol. 88b.

figures that belong to what I call "first elite" in Kabbalah.[432] They allow the possibility of an equalitarian relation between divine male and female, but do not allow such an approach insofar as the human couple is concerned.[433] This discrepancy reflects, in my opinion, the existence of an esoteric tradition that does not necessarily fit their exoteric approach or social reality. In other words, Kabbalists belonging to the first elite were not attempting to subordinate the human behavior to their theosophical speculations, thus ignoring equality in the case of human relationship.

As mentioned in chapter 2 above, Philo's insistence on the equality of the two divine powers has no correspondence in the classical Rabbinic literature as it reached us. Nevertheless, some claims as to their equality are to be found in texts that, though related to Rabbinic figures, Rabad and Nahmanides, they deal with two powers within the supernal world, but they do not make claims as to the male/female equality in this world. When dealing with the members of the human couple, let me insist, equality disappears or is obscured.

Let me turn to an anonymous passage found in two manuscripts, where the creation of the human and divine powers is related explicitly to the two divine attributes under scrutiny here:

> "And what you inquired as to the two ribs,[434] why were they called so, you should pay attention to the emanation.[435] And you should not inquire why, and your eyes should be enlightened on this

432 See my "Kabbalah and Elites in Thirteenth-Century Spain," *Mediterranean Historical Review*, vol. 9 (1994), pp. 5–19, idem, "The Kabbalah's Window of Opportunities', 1270–1290," in eds. E. Fleisher, G. Blidstein, C. Horowitz, B. Septimus, *Me'ah She'arim, Studies in Medieval Jewish Spiritual Life in Memory of Isadore Twersky*, (The Magnes Press, Jerusalem, 2001), pp. 171–208.

433 See also my *"Male and Female": Equality, Female's Theurgy, and Eros – R. Moshe Cordovero's Dual Ontology*, appendix N.

434 The Kabbalist refers to Genesis 2:21: "He took one of his ribs" in the context of the creation of Eve.

435 *Hishtalshelut*. This specific term for emanation is widespread in Nahmanides' school but not in that of Rabad.

reason. But insofar as the divinity is concerned, no one should inquire why it is appearing so, since so did His wisdom. And from there the rationales for [the topics of] all [your] inquiries emerged. And it has already been said: "that He could create by one utterance [alone]."[436] Moreover, you know that that He took as partner the attribute of judgment together with the attribute of compassion,[437] since they are the rulers of the lower beings. And know that unless Adam and Eve were created [as] *du-partzufin,* linked to each other, at the beginning of creation, they would be like the animals and would not listen to each other.[438] Indeed, the woman[439] is the essence of the man's house as it has been said [Psalms 113:9]: "He sets [the woman] as the essence of the house," and [Proverbs 32:15]: "She rises also while it is yet night, and gives food to her household, and a portion to her maidens." [Proverbs 9:9]: "Give instruction to a wise man and he will be yet wiser," [ibidem 3:5] "and do not lean upon thy understanding,"[440] since [II Samuel 1:23] "the beloved ones in their lives, and in their death they were not divided." This suffices to everyone who understands.[441] However, you should concentrate your attention on the 'Aggadah at the beginning of the chapter 'Osin Pasin,'[442] and pay attention to its words and to

436 *'Avot* 5:1.

437 The underlying assumption differs from the Rabbinic model [B] which speaks about an inverse sequel. This is, however, consistent with the emphasis on the *sefirah* of *Tiferet,* as seen earlier in Nahmanides' passages. This is a characteristic of Nahmanides' Kabbalah, while R. Isaac the Blind prefers the third *sefirah, Binah.* See the text cited in Idel, "The Mystical Intention of the Eighteen Benedictions by R. Isaac Sagi Nahor," pp. 42–47.

438 This argument is found in Rabad as seen in chapter 4, and in the circle of ibn Adret, as discussed in this chapter.

439 In Ms. Vatican it is written היא.

440 Again, this conservative approach is reflecting a Nahmanidean attitude to religious information he conceives to be Kabbalah.

441 In the Harvard manuscript it is written ימיני and in the Vatican one it is לב ימיני but I think it is an error for מבין as I translated.

442 *BT 'Eiruvin,* fol. 18ab.

the problems and [their] solutions,[443] and your eyes will be open and your heart will rejoice."[444]

The tone of the passage betrays the existence of a secret meaning underlying the topics: the tone of the anonymous inquirer is characteristic of Nahmanides' school, but not of that of Rabad, as we have seen in chapters 4–5. Here the questions concern several topics, but it is obvious that it involves in particular the meaning of *du-partzufin* as related to the two attributes. This is obvious at the beginning of the translated passage, but also from the hint at the end, since the Talmudic 'Aggadah the Kabbalist has in mind deals with *du-partzufin*, in fact it is one of the longest treatments of this topic in Rabbinic literature.

The underlying theory is, nevertheless, very similar to that of Rabad: the initial linkage between male and female is intended from the very beginning in order to ensure their cooperation. However, this explanation, conceived to constitute the plain sense of the Bible, and of the Rabbinic discussion of *du-partzufin*, is conceived of as related to the divinity and to the realm of emanation, and this is the nature of the secret: it refers to a process within the divine world, but its details are, however, not disclosed. Nevertheless, the participation of the two divine attributes in the process of creation, rather than of

443 The Talmudic masters try to accommodate the fact that God created the two first humans in one body and then He had to separate them, a process that assumes a change in the divine mind.

444 Ms. Cambridge, Harvard, Houghton Heb. 58, fol. 109a, and Ms. Vatican 202, fols. 58b–59a:

ומה ששאלת בענין שתי הצלעות למה נקראו כך שים דעתך להשתלשלות ואל תשאל למה ויאור עיניך על מה ועל מה, אבל באלהות אין לשאול למה נדמה כי כן חייבה חכמתו. ומשם יצאו טעם כל שאלות. וכבר אמרו והלא במאמר אחד יכול להבראות. ועוד ידעת שתף מדת הדין עם מדת רחמים כי אלה הם מנהיגים את השפלים. ודע שלולי שנבראו אדם וחוה דו פרצופין מחוברים בתחלת הבריאה היו כעין הבהמות ולא ישמעו זה לזה. אמנם האשה היא עקר ביתו של אדם כענין שנאמר: 'מושיבי עקרת הבית', 'ותקם בעוד לילה ותתן טרף לביתה וחק לנערותיה'. 'תן לחכם ויחכם עוד' 'ואל בינתך אל תשען' 'כי נאהבים בחייהם ובמותם לא נפרדו' ודי בזה לכל ימיני [!]. אמנם תדקדק באגדה של ראש פרק עושין כסין ותדקדק במלותיה ובקושיות ובתירוצין יפקחו את עיניך וישמח לבך.

one of them alone, is presented in explicit terms. What remains to be disclosed are the sefirotic details.

Let me draw attention to the theory of the cooperation of the two attributes as formulated in this passage. It does not have a verbatim parallel in the classical Rabbinic literature,[445] but it most plausible drew from Rabbinic sources, and from Nahmanides's commentary on Leviticus 23:17, where the commentator says that "at the creation of the world He took as a partner the attribute of compassion with the attribute of judgment, and He created it."[446] In his school, another commentator on the Pentateuch, R. Baḥya ben Asher, uses this formula several times but in one of them he adds an interesting element, probably under the impact of R. Asher ben David:[447]

> "That a person should accustom himself to behave according to the attribute of compassion . . . and by doing so he will take as a partner the attribute of compassion with that of judgment, since cooperation is the existence of the world, and it is impossible to subsist without the two."[448]

This view is described immediately afterwards as related to the union of *Knesset Yisra'el* and the king, namely *Tiferet*, and it seems plausible from the context that this union has a sexual overtone.[449] This is an interesting case of theurgy grounded in distributing alms, which is informed by the manner in which God created the world. This cooperation is therefore not just a matter of human male and female, but also of the two attributes in the vein of the approach of Rabad, though

445 See above, chapter 2, in the discussion of model [B].

446 See ed. Chavel, vol. II, p. 150 שיתף מדת רחמים במדת הדין ובראו בבריאת העולם

447 See Gottlieb, *The Kabbalah in the Writings of R. Bahya ben Asher ibn Halawa*, p. 90, Afterman, *Devequt*, pp. 216–218.

448 On Deuteronomy 15:19: ed. Chavel, (Mossad ha-Rav Kook, Jerusalem, 1968), vol. 3, pp. 34–341:

שירגיל האדם עצמו במדת הרחמנות שיתן מברכתו צדקה לעני, ובעשותו זה ישתף מדת רחמים עם מדת הדין, שהשיתוף ההוא הוא קיום העולם ואי אפשר להתקיים מבלעדי שניהם.

449 Ibidem.

the details differ. In other words, unlike the Rabad, Nahmanides and his school conjugated the *du-partzufin* myth with another Rabbinic myth, that of the diminution of the moon, and applied both the the intra-divine processes, related also to another Rabbinic topic, that of the two attributes. In a somewhat different way, R. Baḥya sees the mixture of compassion and judgment insofar as the *sefirot* of *Gevurah* and *Ḥesed* are concerned, as we learn from his commentary on Genesis 3:22. When discussing the nature of the angel Gabriel, he writes that:

> "despite the fact that it is the angel of *Gevurah*,[450] the attribute of compassion is found in it, in order to acquit the innocent, and the power of compassion is not separated from it, as the garment of the grasshooper, that is identical with it and does not move away from it."[451]

It seems that it is an expression of model [D] in Rabbinic typology offered in chapter 2 above. The image of grasshooper will become a major metaphor in later Kabbalah for the identity between two distinct divine entities.

The above texts dealing with a dynamic structure of divine powers and theurgical acts, generating a series of kaleidoscopic pictures, do not address the question of divine perfection and immutability. However, in the atmosphere of the controversy with philosophers, Maimonides and his followers, such a question emerged, and its trace can be discerned in Nahmanides' school, including Nahmanides's two main disciples who were also Kabbalists, R. Shlomo ben Abraham ibn Adret and R. Isaac Todros. So, for example, the latter writes that:

> "He is united [with]in His names, and in the ways of His *middot*, and despite the fact that there are distinct [or separated] names

450 See above chapter 2, the text of R. Nehemiah ben Shlomo.

451 Ed. Chavel vol. 1, p. 87:
אף על פי שהוא שר הגבורה כח הרחמים יש בו לזכות הזכאי ואין כח הרחמים נפרד ממנו כלבוש החגב הזה שהוא מעצמו ואינו זז ממנו לעולם.

and distinct *middot* He is united in all of them, and all are united in Him and they are the signs of His in accordance to His acts."[452]

From our point of view, the phrase *darkhei middotav* – the ways of His *middot* – is quite interesting. It refers to divine acts, not to a certain sort of theosophy alone. This syntagm is rather rare and it may refer to Maimonides' *Guide of the Perplexed* I:38. The philosopher interprets this phrase as walking in the path "of His actions and to behave in accordance to His *Middot*." Moreover, in the intellectual milieu of R. Isaac Todros, it occurs in a significant context. R. Yom Tov Ashvili, a student of ibn Adret, another student of Nahmanides, has written a defense of Maimonides against the critiques of Nahmanides, entitled *Sefer ha-Zikkaron*.[453]

The penetration of the philosophical terminology dealing with the negation of corporeality, plurality, and change from the divinity is evident in R. Isaac Todros's student R. Shem Tov ibn Gaon, who claims, as his teacher did, that by attribution of names, attributes, and *sefirot*, he does not differentiate between them, but only related to them. God is conceived of as being one, united with all of them.[454] This statement nevertheless does not prevent him from offering theosophical and theurgical components of the divinity, as seen above.

Let me address at the end a small passage preserved in a unique manuscript that deserves special attention in the context of the symbolism of attributes in Nahmanides's school:

"[a] 'Since by a forceful hand YHWH took out' [Deuteronomy 7:8]. Commentary: since they did not realize but the 'hand' alone that

452 *Commentary on the Maḥzor*, Ms. Paris BN 839, fol. 222b:
מיוחד בשמותיו ודרכי מדותיו אע״פ שיש שמות חלוקים ומדות חלוקות הוא מיוחד בכולן וכולן מיוחדים בו והמה אותותיו לפי מעשיו.

453 See ed. K. Kahana, (Mossad ha-Rav Kook, Jerusalem, 1982), second edition, p. 82.

454 Introduction to his *Keter Shem Tov*, Ms. Paris BN 774, fol. 73b:
כי אע״פ שנזכיר מדות ושמות לספירות לא להחליק רק להתייחס אבל הוא אחד מיוחד בכולן.

corresponds to *Ḥametz* that is judgment, He said to him that they should not cut the branches, and He interdicted the *Ḥametz* to them, in order to say that He and His Court were there. And they paid attention also to the *Matzah* and this is 'Since by a forceful hand YHWH took them out' in order to say that not by means of the hand alone but by the forceful hand, since the power is in the right [hand] and by means of its force you exited from there not by the hand alone, and this is the reason why they will not eat *Ḥametz*. And this is the reason why it is said, "and the second Passover we should eat *Matzah*, but *Matzah* and *Ḥametz* is with him in his house,'[455] since by means of both[456] the miracle happened, compassion to Israel and judgment to the Egyptians,[457] and He and His court agreed on this verdict and [b] this is [the meaning] 'I, but not an emissary'[458] as it was interpreted by Nahmanides, blessed be his memory. [c] And this is a rationale I found in the name of the sage R. Isaac ben Abraham, blessed be his memory: *Matzah* is neither sweet nor bitter but intermediate, and this refers to *Tiferet*, because it receives from both of them."[459]

455 See Rashi on Numbers 9:10.

456 Namely the two divine attributes, referred to by *Matzah* and *Ḥametz*. See also below in this chapter the reference to the anonymous text from Ms. Vatican 236.

457 See above n. 89.

458 The version found in the Passover Haggadah.

459 Ms. Christ Church College 198, (Oxford, Catalogue Neubauer, 2456), fols. 11b–12a:

"כי ביד חזקה הוציא יי׳ וגו׳ פי׳ בעבור כי לא השיגו כי אם היד בלבד שהוא כנגד החמץ שהוא דין א"ל שלא יקצצו בנטיעות ואסר להם החמץ לומר כי הוא וב"ד היו שם ונתנו לבם גם למצה וזהו כי בחוזק יד הוציא יי׳ אתכם לומר לא ביד לבד יצאתם אלא בחוזק היד שהכח בימין ובכחו יצאתם משם לא ביד לבד ולכן לא יאכל חמץ. ומפני זה אמר ובפסח שני שנאכל על המצה אלא שמצה וחמץ עמו בבית כי בשניהם נעשה הנס, רחמים לישראל והדין על המצרים והוא וב"ד הסכימו בדין, וזה אני ולא שליח כמו שפי׳ הרמב"ן ז"ל. טעם זה מצאתי בשם החכם ר׳ יצחק בר אברהם ז"ל מצה אינו לא מתוק ולא חמוץ אלא בינוני ולזה רמז לת"ת שהוא מקבל משניהם."

The possibility of a tradition found in R. Isaac ben Abraham, R. Yehudah ben

There are two different approaches in this passage: [a] claims that the religious danger is the separation between two attributes: that of judgment – *Ḥametz* – and that of compassion, *Matzah* – referred to by the right hand. The perception of the redemptive act as related to the former alone generated the interdiction of the *Ḥametz* during the Passover. I assume that if interpreted symbolically, [a] reflects a view similar to the school of Rabad, related to *Ḥesed* and *Gevurah*. In paragraph [c] however, what is important is the synthesis that is related to another power, *Tiferet*. I would, therefore, not attribute [a] as authored by Nahmanides, as implied in [b], because this master endorses an approach closer to [c] as seen above in the cases when *Tiferet* has been mentioned in texts adduced above.

Paragraph [c] is adduced in the name of R. Isaac ben Abraham, probably, a French authority active in late 12th and early 13th century. He is known to have been in contact with R. Yehudah ben Yaqar, a Barcelonese Rabbi who was one of the masters of Nahmanides.[460] If we accept the reliability of [c] and its textual integrity, we have a possible source for Nahmanides' s specific theosophical symbolism.[461]

Yaqar and then in Nahmanides and his circle of students, should be seen as part of the existence of different Kabbalistic circles that can be identified by their distinct terminology and theosophical concepts. Compare also to the discussion of *Matzah* related to Nahmanides' view in R. Shem Tov ibn Gaon, *Keter Shem Tov*, in ed. *'Amudei ha-'Avodah*, p. 55, and R. Isaac of Acre, *Me'irat 'Einayyim*, ed. Goldreich, pp. 163–164.

See, however, the doubts cast recently by Judith Weiss, "Kabbalah in Gerona in the Thirteenth Century: Azriel and Nahmanides, a Re-evaluation," *Tarbiz*, 87 (2019), pp. 69–97 (Hebrew), as to the existence of different circles of Kabbalists in Gerona.

460 Yahalom, *Between Gerona and Narbonne*, pp. 245–247. See also Sendor, *The Emergence of Provencal Kabbalah*, 1, p. 346, where ben Yaqar is described as teaching Nahmanides in Barcelona in 1173, roughly twenty years before the latter was born!

461 Scholem, *Origins of the Kabbalah*, p, 251 n. 107, who referred to fol. 129 instead of fols. 11b–12a. Scholem, who was the first to refer to paragraph [c], doubted whether the last words that include a theosophical identification, are part of the original quote, and he surmised that they are an accretion of a later copist.

However, it is also possible that this Isaac ben Abraham stems from Narbone and was a student of Nahmanides and even of R. Shlomo ibn Adret. He is mentioned also elsewhere in the Kabbalistic collectanea as R. Isaac, who was in contact with R. Isaac Todros.

With the emergence of the two different theosophical-theurgical schools surveyed above, also some syntheses between them are conspicuous, especially in the manner in which the school of Nahmanides's traditions have been combined with those stemming from the school of Rabad, late in the 13th century and early 14th century. This is evident in particular in the content of various collectanea of Kabbalistic traditions that have been mentioned in various footnotes in this chapter, but also in the contents of full-fleged books – mainly commentaries on the Pentateuch – like those of R. Baḥya ben Asher, R. Isaac of Acre or R. Menahem Recanati, all of them written at the end of the 13th and early 14th centuries. These three Kabbalists have combined views found in the two earlier Kabbalistic schools also with those found in the Zoharic literature. This synthetic approach will be continued in the later forms of Kabbalah, most eminently in the writings of the mid-16th century R. Moshe Cordovero in Safed.

Let me emphasize again that what is more conspicuous in the Nahmanidean school is the importance of the nexus between the *middot* and the commandments, in comparison to other Kabbalistic schools in his generation. This is obviously a matter of the stronger exegetical propensity of this school and its more conservative

If the attribution of the last phrase to R. Isaac ben Abraham is nevertheless genuine, as I think it is, then already a teacher of R. Yehudah ben Yaqar was acquainted with a Kabbalistic view in the vein of Nahmanides' form of Kabbalah. See, however, Oded Yisraeli, "A Kabbalist Despite Himself: R. Judah ben Yaqar – A Historical Figure and His Image," *Kabbalah* vol. 31 (2014), pp. 281–309 (Hebrew), especially p. 281. The whole question as to the Kabbalistic valences of ben Yaqar's thought should start with a definition of Kabbalah as consisting in a much broader realm of concepts since its very beginning. See, meanwhile, my "Defining Kabbalah" and above n. 278. Elsewhere I shall deal with the question of ben Yaqar and Kabbalah on the basis of additional material.

approach. As seen in the last quoted passage, the syntax of the ritual is the conceptual center that dictates the details of the interpretation rather than the flexible logic of the theosophical structure. This is also the case in an anonymous short treatise which cites Nahmanides, where it is claimed that the exodus from Egypt took place by the dint of the cooperation between the two *middot*.[462]

Let me point out that beside those two major theosophical-theurgical schools, there is plenty of Kabbalistic material found anonymously in manuscripts – entitled *sodot*, or *ṭeʿamin* – secrets, few of them printed so far, and a mapping of this material is still a desideratum for articulating a more adequate picture of the history of the early stages of Kabbalah.

462 See Ms. Vatican 236

SEVEN

Binitarianism/Ditheism, Dual Ontology and Medieval Beginnings

We have dealt in the four previous chapters with views that constitute schools that are part of what I call the main line in Kabbalah, the theosophical-theurgical one. The impression from analyzing the salient texts is that they display much more complex traditions concerning the divine powers than what transpires in the available scholarship, and this fact is hardly a sign of a sudden explosion of Gnosticism in the bosom of medieval Rabbinic Judaism. I would opt for seeing some of the above texts as the result of a process of gestation, which took place before the emergence of the platform of Kabbalistic literature in the High Middle Ages. In its various manifestations, Kabbalistic theosophy is conjugated to theurgy, as I defined it, a major factor in the phenomenology of Kabbalah, but not in Gnosticism or Neoplatonism, and this conjugation was inherited from Rabbinic sources and elaborated in many details. The encounters between Gnosticism and Neoplatonism stipulated by Gershom Scholem, could contribute to theosophy, not to Kabbalistic theurgy that is grounded in Rabbinic views, as seen above in chapter 2. This is the reason why I see the complex processes that generated medieval Kabbalah more as an evolution, grounded in reorganization of earlier, material than a matter of revolution.

Before turning to two other forms of Kabbalah in the next two chapters, actually two schools that both differ from the conceptual point of view from the theosophical-theurgical Kabbalahs, let me attempt to reflect on some aspects of the two Kabbalistic schools discussed earlier. As seen above, the earliest texts related to theosophical Kabbalah, written in the 12th century: the book of *Bahir*, Rabad, and at least implicitly his son R. Isaac ben Abraham, share a special concern with two divine attributes. This is the case later also with Nahmanides. This common denominator has been overlooked in scholarship of early Kabbalah and I would like not only to put this fact in sharp relief but also to interrogate its religious significance, phenomenologically, but also from the historical point of view.

The two different symbolic interpretations of the meaning of the Rabbinic syntagm *du-partzufin* in the context of the two atributes, discussed in the three previous chapters, reflect, in my opinion, two distinct Kabbalistic traditions, though they were connected earlier between them at some point, or diverged from a hypothetical common source. Nevertheless they should be better understood as part of the wider religious phenomenon, I proposed above to call dual ontology, represented in early Kabbalah by the phenomenon of ditheism or binitarianism.[463] This means that not only may we speak about the centrality of two powers on high – to be sure in a framework of a monotheistic scheme – but also about a linkage between them and the ritual. Meanwhile, the resort to the concept of ditheism/binitarianism insofar as Jewish mysticism is concerned has been accepted by a variety of more recent studies. [464] This nexus is related to the ideal of

463 See my studies referred above in n. 226, and see also below nn. 465, 564. For ancient Christianity, see the important study of Larry W. Hurtado, *One God, One Lord: Early Christian Devotion and Ancient Jewish Monotheism*, (SCM, London, 1988). On ancient Rabbinic ditheism see now Peter Schaefer, *Two Gods in Heaven, Jewish Concepts of God in Antiquity* tr. A. Brown, (Princeton University Press, Princeton, 2020), Schaefer was not aware of some of the studies mentioned in the next two footnotes, printed long ago.

464 See also, e.g., Schneider's groundbreaking contribution *The Appearance of the High Priest*, Adam Afterman, *The Intention of Prayers in Early Ecstatic*

unifying two divine powers – especially during prayer – which I call the unitive theurgical operation, though the theosophical identity of these pairs differ from the school of the Rabad to that of Nahmanides, as well as from the earlier view of the late 12th century R. Jacob the Nazarite of Lunel.[465]

This theme constitutes what I propose to call "unitive theurgy" and this ideal stands in opposition to Philo's speculative approach, which does not allow an impact of the human action on the divine structure of powers or the theory of sefirot in *Sefer Yetzirah*. However, the unification of divine powers is related to their cooperation when functioning as governing over the processes in this world. This is the reason why the adverbial understanding of some of the texts above is important, as they refer to an interactive understanding of the relations between the two planes of existence: the divine and the human. Indeed, this is the case in the passage from the book of *Bahir* discussed above, and in Nahmanides' school, where the cultic meaning of these two *sefirot* is evident, especially in R. Shem Tov ibn Gaon's book.

My assumption is that this difference between traditions emerged as the result of different symbolic interpretations of an earlier, perhaps inchoate, tradition, which was originally ditheistic, though not necessarily part of theosophical systems of ten *middot* or *sefirot*.[466] This hypothetical pre-Kabbalistic tradition, most probably related to ten *middot*, is somewhat reminiscent of the traditions found in a variety of dual ontology found in late antiquity.[467] It seems that this hypothetical

Kabbalah (Cherub Press, Los Angeles, 2004), pp. 138–151 (Hebrew), Fishbane, *As Light before Dawn*, pp. 211–213 and n. 81. See the most updated list of bibliography in the various footnotes of Weiss, "Most of the Errant Err in *Malkhut*," pp. 319–334, especially pp. 320–321 n. 4, as well as his more recent monograph *Cutting the Shoots*.

465 "The Mystical Intention of the Eighteen Benedictions by R. Isaac Sagi Nahor," pp. 30, n. 39, 42–47, and my "Kabbalistic Prayer in Provence," pp. 268–269.

466 See also the manner in which I dealt with another late antiquity tradition and its resurge in early 13th century writings in my "Holding an Orb in His Hand: The Angel 'Anafi'el and a Late Antiquity Helios Mosaic."

467 See my "*Male and Female*."

earlier ditheistic tradition is not dependent on the role and history of the *Shekhinah* in Jewish pre-Kabbalistic texts, though already in 13th century Kabbalah *Shekhinah* has been grafted on concept[s] of ditheism, as discussed in Tzahi Weiss's book. Given the fact that the Rabad's passage about sexual polarity within the divine as discussed in chapter 4, is unrelated to a development related to the erotization of the *Shekhinah*, we should look for types of describing the history of theoeroticism different from Gnostic theory of Gershom Scholem,[468] or from the historicist theory of Arthur I. Green and Peter Schaefer that analyzed the ascendancy of the feminine understanding of the *Shekhinah* in the book of *Bahir*, as the result of the impact of the nascent cult of Maria in Western Europe.[469] In both cases scholars concentrated solely on the feminine aspect of the divinity without taking into account that such a dimension is actually discussed as her being part of a sexualized divine couple.[470]

However, in my opinion, as I attempted to substantiate it elsewhere in some detail, the concept of the *Shekhinah* has been attributed some feminine dimensions long before the emergence of Kabbalah.[471] At any rate a rejection of this latter historicist explanation done on a philological ground insofar as the reliable versions of the book of *Bahir* are concerned, is found in a more recent analysis of Daniel Abrams.[472] To the best of my knowledge his quite detailed arguments, which contradict the claims of the two scholars, first printed already in 2007, have not yet been addressed by these scholars. It is part of a larger tendency in recent scholarship of Kabbalah, and also of Hasidism, that

468 See *Origins of the Kabbalah*, p. 236.

469 See above nn. 16–17.

470 See Idel, *Ben*, pp. 377–399.

471 See my "Triple Family," and "Limbs of the *Shekhinah*": On the Ascent of the Divine Feminine in Kabbalah and Her Decline in Modern Scholarship," in catalogue of the exhibition *Art and Ritual, The Female Side of God*, eds. Eva Atlan, Michaela Feurstein-Prasser, Felicitas Heimann-Jelinek, Mirjam Wenzel (Frankfurt Jewish Museum, Kerber Christof Verlag, Bielefeld, 2020), pp. 77–110.

472 See Abrams, *Kabbalistic Manuscripts and Textual Theory*, pp. 122–198.

I call Christotropia, that emphasize some form of impact without a proper analysis of the available sources – an intellectual phenomenon, part of what I call the "transfer of categories" – that deserves a separate and elaborate discussion. [473]

On the other hand, the insistence on the emergence of the opposites together and their cooperation, and sometimes their equality, in early Kabbalistic texts, represents a non-Maimonidean speculative approach. It has some mythical valences in Philo and in the two Kabbalistic schools mentioned above. Without embracing a theory of a significant or comprehensive impact of Philo on Kabbalah,[474] it seems nevertheless plausible that first Kabbalists were in possession of a tradition about the emergence and cooperation of opposites that were understood as divine powers, similar to Philo's adoption and adaptation of earlier views of two attributes in Judaism, and it is plausible that he was the author that mediated pre-Socratic theories of opposites into Jewish thought. Some views found in late Midrashim, like *Midrash Tadshe'*, indicate that such a Philonic tradition, or a cognate one, entered Hebrew texts in Provence long before the emergence of Kabbalah.[475]

473 "The Condensation of the Symbol '*Shekhinah*' in the Manuscripts of the *Book Bahir*," *Kabbalah*, vol. 16 (2007), pp. 7–82, idem, *Kabbalistic Manuscripts and Textual Theory*, pp. 185–198. For Christotropia see, meanwhile, M. Idel, "The Divine Female and the Mystique of the Moon: Three-Phases Gender-Theory in Theosophical Kabbalah," *Archaeus* 19/20 (2015/2016), pp. 151–182.

474 See, e.g., Goodenough, *By Light, Light*, pp. 359–369, Patai, *The Hebrew Goddess*, pp. 70–76, Samuel Belkin, "The *Midrash ha-Ne'elam* and Its Sources in the Old Alexandrian Midrashim," *Sura* vol. 3 (1958), pp. 25–92 (Hebrew), and the critique of Belkin's approach by R.J. Zwi Werblowsky, "Philo and the Zohar," *JJS* vol. 10 (1959), pp. 23–44, 113–135. See also Scholem, *Origins of Kabbalah*, pp. 6 n. 1, idem, *On the Kabbalah and Its Symbolism*, pp. 33–34, 40, 45–46, 62–63, 160, and his *Major Trends in Jewish Mysticism*, pp. 114–115, and in particular Liebes, *Ars Poetica in Sefer Yetzirah*, pp. 303–304 nn. 1–2.

475 See Abraham Epstein, "*Le Livre des Jubilés*, Philon et le *Midrasch Tadsché*," *REJ*, vol. 21 (1890), pp. 80–97, Bernard Bamberger, "Philo and the Aggadah", *HUCA*, XLVIII (1977), pp. 153–185, Samuel Belkin, "Midrash Tadshe' or the Midrash of R. Phinebas ben Yair, an Hellenistic Ancient Midrash', *Horev* 11

Let me emphasize: I discussed a very specific topic and my conclusions are significant solely for that topic alone and my explanation of its history does not intend to attribute a Philonic or an Alexandrine origin for Kabbalah,[476] or even less for Jewish philosophy as Harry A. Wolfson did.[477] Nevertheless let me point out that though historically there is scarcely one single significant document in medieval Judaism

(1951), pp. 1–52, especially 10–14 (Hebrew) or his 'The Symbolic Midrash in Philo', in *Harry Austryn Wolfson Jubilee Volume* (American Academy for Jewish Research, Jerusalem, 1965), Hebrew Part, pp. 33–67, Patai, *The Hebrew Goddess*, pp. 76, 82 119–120 Idel, *Kabbalah: New Perspectives*, pp. 132–134, *Ben*, p. 247 n. 6, and Runia, *Philo of Alexandria, On the Creation of the Cosmos*, pp. 37, 173, 196, 307. For the possible affinities between *Sefer Yetzirah* and Philo see Liebes, *Ars Poetica in Sefer Yetzirah*, passim, cf., index, under items, "Philo," p. 368, the list of discussions of his writings pp. 362–363 (Hebrew) as well as his "The Work of the Chariot and the Work of Creation as Mystical Teachings in Philo of Alexandria," tr. J. Jacobson-Maisels, in eds. D.A. Green and L.S. Lieber, *Scriptural Exegesis: The Shapes of Culture and the Religious Imagination. Essays in Honour of Michael Fishbane*, (Oxford University Press, Oxford, 2009), pp. 105–120. See also Elliot R. Wolfson's survey of additional claims of connections to Philo in other scholars, in his "Traces of Philonic Doctrine in Medieval Jewish Mysticism: A Preliminary Note," *Studia Philonica* vol. 8 (1996), pp. 99–106, especially p. 103, where he judiciously summarized my discussion in *Kabbalah: New Perspectives*, pp. 131–132, 190.

For reverberations of some of Philo's views of mystical union in the Middle-Ages via Plotinus see Afterman, "From Philo to Plotinus," pp. 177–196, and Avraham Elqayam, "Nudity in the Sanctus Sanctorum: Philo and Plotinus on Nudity, Esthetics and Sanctity," *Kabbalah* vol. 28 (2012), pp. 301–321 (Hebrew). Let me highlight also Gershom Scholem's paramount observation in *Reshit ha-Kabbalah*, p. 207, as to the similarity between a late 13th century Ashkenazi text and a view of Xenophanes.

476 For a totally different explanation for the emergence of another topic in Kabbalah see, for example, my claim as to the importance of Zurvanic thought in my *Primeval Evil in Kabbalah*, passim. See also, e.g., M. Idel, "Hermeticism and Kabbalah," in eds., P. Lucentini, I. Parri, V.P. Compagni, *Hermeticism from Late Antiquity to Humanism*, (Brespols, 2004), pp. 389–408.

477 Steven Harvey, "Islamic Philosophy and Jewish Philosophy," in eds. P. Adamson and R.C. Taylor, *The Cambridge Companion to Arabic Philosophy*, (Cambridge University Press, Cambridge, 2005), pp. 349–350.

where a passage from Philo is quoted[478] we should better adopt a panoramic view as to the variety of sources that nourished the various schools that constitute early Kabbalah.[479] Important contributions in the direction of including Philo in the orbit of research of Jewish mysticism have been made in some studies of Yehuda Liebes that have been mentioned above.[480]

Let me turn to some other forms of binary thought, found in the authors that were contemporaries of the early Kabbalists, who were active in the Ashkenazi provinces. Much more than the Provencal and Spanish Jewish communities, the Ashkenazi ones adapted Palestinian poetry as part of the liturgical rituals as well as a series of late Midrashim, like *Midrash Tadshe'*, whose affinities to late antiquity material has been recognized by scholars.[481] Needless to say that some of them share with the early Kabbalists also a deep interest in *Sefer Yetzirah*. However, though the Jewish sources used in their writings overlap to a great extent the basic approaches to these materials differ immensely.

The early Kabbalists as discussed above, adopted what is known in scholarship as a symbolic approach, which actually means, in my opinion, not a Romantic type of approach to symbolism as adopted

478 See the later addenda to the *Book of Yosefon*, printed by David Flusser, ed., *The Josippon, [Josephus Gorionides]*, (Mossad Bialik, Jerusalem, 1981), vol. 1, pp. 434–435 (Hebrew), where Philo is mentioned in Hebrew as well as the titles of some of his writings. According to Flusser, this passage is drawn from a late antiquity Latin text and it cannot be an evidence of the acquaintance of Jews with Philo's writings. See, however, for the different view of Liebes, *Ars Poetica in Sefer Yetzirah*, pp. 304–305 n. 8, who drew attention to this text and assumes that the Hebrew passage is not entirely dependent on the Latin one. To be sure: this reference does not solve the problem, for which I do not see for the time being an historical solution, as to how exactly Philo's views on the two divine powers could reach Jews in the Middle Ages Europe or Rabad.

479 See, e.g., Idel, *Hasidism: Between Ecstasy and Magic*, pp. 9–15, *Messianic Mystics*, p. 23.

480 See, more recently, his "Clothed Nudity: The Esoteric Cult of Philo," *JSJT*, vol. 24 (2015), pp. 9–28 (Hebrew).

481 See n. 476.

by scholars, but that the theosophical structure was envisioned as supplying the meaning of the interpreted terms, functioning as a code. This understanding of semiosis is far away from approximating a situation presupposed by what scholars who adopt a German Romantic approach understood as symbolic,[482] which is grounded in reverberations of the classical negative theologies in the realm of art and literature in late 18th and early 19th century.

However, instead of adopting this view that symbols represent the ineffable or a realm that cannot be presented, namely serving as an answer to a human noetic insufficiency, some avatars of apophasis, my assumption is that the theosophical system is functioning as an exegetical code that is capable of reorganizing as much of the religious material as the Kabbalists would like, and attribute a special valence to its components. Symbols have a pedagogical function of shaping a theosophical understanding of texts and rituals.[483] My view of the manner in which early Kabbalistic authors operated is much closer to the organization of knowledge since late antiquity astrology, which attributed relations between each of the seven planets on the one hand, and a variety of entities in this world, on the other.[484] This

482 See my *Old Worlds, New Mirrors*, pp. 83–108.

483 See Idel, *Absorbing Perfections*, pp. 272–313, and especially my *Kabbalah: New Perspectives*, p. 232. See, especially, Umberto Eco, *Semiotics and the Philosophy of Language*, (Indiana U.P. Bloomington 1984), p. 153 and his *Limits of Interpretation*, (Indiana U.P., Bloomington 1990), pp. 14–15, and Morlok, *Rabbi Joseph Gikatilla's Hermeneutics*, pp. 212–213. See also Yehuda Liebes, "Myth vs. Symbol in the Zohar and Lurianic Kabbalah," in ed. L. Fine, *Essential Papers on Kabbalah*, (New York University Press, New York, London, 1995), pp. 212–242, my "Symbols and Symbolopoiesis in Kabbalah," in eds. Flavia Buzzetta – Marco Golfetto (eds.), *Il Simbolismo. La grammatica del sacro*, (Officina di Studi Medievali, Palermo, 2016), pp. 197–233, and Oron, "The Literature of Commentaries to the Ten *Sefirot*," pp. 215–220. Compare also to Abraham Elkayam, "Between Referentialism and Performativism: Two Approaches in Understanding the Kabbalistic Symbol," *Daat* vol. 24 (1990), pp. 5–40 (Hebrew) and Sendor, *The Emergence of Provencal Kabbalah*, pp. 230-242.

484 See, especially, my *Saturn's Jews*, pp. 19–20.

type of hierarchical reorganization was well-known in the Middle Ages by means of Arabic, Latin and Hebrew translations of [Pseudo-] Ptolemeus's *Tetrabiblos* and its various reverberations in astro-magical literature, like another widespread book, *Picatrix*, for example.[485] In other words, emphasizing codes, grids, reorganization of salient knowledge, I presuppose that many Kabbalists embraced a predominantly more positive theology, which could be studied from what were then famous and available texts.

To formulate my proposal in different terms: the vertical referential relationship involved in what scholars designate as symbolism can be interpreted in two different directions: the first, the upward one assumes that by a contemplation of the lower entities or words, someone is capable to intuit the supernal structure, with is hardly accessible by a direct type of contact or act of cognition. Here the move is from the particular to the more paradigmatic, comprehensive, and transcendent entity that presides over a certain set of particulars. Unlike this Romantic move regarding the manner in which the symbols of the infinite operate, my proposal assumes the preponderance of a downward move, which means that the higher structure acts as a grid or a code, informs meaning to a variety of lower entities, and organizes them according to categories that are independent of the particulars. The downward move, based on the previous acquaintance with the code or the grid, is known by the Kabbalist from oral tradition or by studying Kabbalah from books, not as the result of a discovery grounded in some kind of insight as a result of an act of contemplation or illumination. Meaning is therefore intuited not from the contemplation of the particular by induction or extrapolation, in a Platonic style, but by means of deduction, which starts with the code whose meaning and structure is transparent to the Kabbalist before the exegetical or contemplative acts, and he then imposes it on the particular details of the texts or of the commandments.

This distinction does not mean that Kabbalists were aware or admitted it, or that they did not adopt the Platonic *ascensio mentis*, but

485 See, e.g., ibidem, pp. 69–70.

that the ascent was done to a supernal realm that was rather mapped in their studies prior to their experience of ascent. This is more evident in philosophically inclined Kabbalists, like R. Azriel as seen above. It should be emphasized that the emphasis I put on theurgy also assumes a previous mapping of the divine world that allows the impact of the human rituals on the supernal realm. To a significant extent, the theurgical and the symbolic understanding may be seen as in conflict. In Nahmanides's school the code was not so much part of the esoteric aspects of Kabbalah, as it is its specific application to details, which often times involves the theurgical dimension.

The Ashkenazi authors, however, were less concerned with exegetical codes grounded in one type of theosophy or another, but used complex linguistic manipulations in order to demonstrate some themes related to other topics. We have exemplified this propensity in chapter 2 above, in the context of their treatments of the attributes. Such a kind of discourse was alien to early Kabbalists but will be introduced in Kabbalah in the last third of the 13th century in the writings of Abraham Abulafia and his circle, as we shall see in chapter 9. Nevertheless, in late 13th century R. Moshe Azriel ben Eleazar ha-Darshan, Abulafia's contemporary, speaks about the attributes, presumably ten, as depending on the ten *sefirot* and they play in this text a role reminiscent of the angels.[486]

Many of the discussions above are predicated upon the various combinations of three main codes: the attributive one, dealing especially with two or three and in some instances ten attributes, reflecting mainly the interactions between God's attributes and human behavior; then the sefirotic code, dealing with the functions of the theosophical and cosmic systems and its relations to the attributes; and last but not least the anthropomorphic code, represented in many cases above by the concept of *du-partzufin*, or by the anthropic nature of the theosophy, like the various views of the sefirotic system as supernal or primeval Anthropos, or by the couple of male and female, or the ten

486 See Scholem, *Reshit ha-Kabbalah*, pp. 214–215. See also my *Angelic World*, pp. 26–27.

fingers. So, for example, the three codes are found together in a view that was quite widespread in most of the extant Kabbalistic theosophies, which assumed that it is from the divine manifestation, the fifth *sefirah, Gevurah,* which may be translated as Might, or Strength, or the attribute of Stern Judgment, *Middat ha-din ha-qashah,* or the left hand of God.[487] In many cases also divine names are involved in connection to each of these three codes, as seen above in many cases and it becomes central for the theosophies in the writings of the later R. Joseph Gikatilla. It is in the writings of this Kabbalist and of his contemporaries, R. Moshe de Leon and R. Joseph of Hamadan, that the doctrine of the ten *sefirot* transpires as a decisive code in the history of Kabbalah, and the genre of *Commentaries on Ten Sefirot* to which all the three contributed more than one commentary, turns to be a leading genre in this kind of literature.[488]

My basic concern here was to delineate the contours of the attributive code, while the other two played only secondary role in the present analyses. However, it is evident that elements belonging to each of the three codes influenced the perception of elements found in the other two codes. Those interchanges generated complexities, and in some cases obscurities, related to the manifold types of interference, and created semantic polivalences. So, for example, the understanding of the 613 commandments as divided between two main categories, each related to one of the two attributes, as proposed in R. Ezra of Gerona[489] that conflicts his view of the commandments as related

487 Discussions of this theme are legion in the Kabbalistic literature. See, e.g., R. Ezra of Gerona, *Commentary on the Song of Songs,* p. 497, Scholem, *On the Mystical Shape,* pp. 46–47, 55, Tishby, *The Wisdom of the Zohar* II, pp. 459–460, 465, Gottlieb, *Studies in the Kabbalah Literature,* p. 343, and especially, on the book of *Bahir,* see Farber, "The Shell Precedes the Fruit," p. 119 n. 4, Schneider, "The Myth of the *Satan* in the *Book Bahir,*" pp. 309–315, and Elliot R. Wolfson, *Luminal Darkness: Imaginal Gleanings from Zoharic Literature* (Oneworld, Oxford, 2007), pp. 31–32. For later examples see R. Moshe Cordovero, *'Or Yaqar,* vol. VIII, (Jerusalem, 1976), fol. 241b.

488 See above n. 34.

489 *Commentary on the Song of Songs,* p. 497.

to one of the ten attributes.[490] Both of them differ from the view of the parallelism between the human and the divine limbs and the corresponding commandments on the one hand, and the supernal anthropos on the other hand, as found especially in treatises of the late 13th century R. Joseph of Hamadan.[491] This means that different schemes for reorganizing the meaning of the rituals, worked parallelly or synthetically in variegated theosophical Kabbalistic literature, sometimes even in the same Kabbalistic treatise, creating multivocality or polysemic discourses which preclude simplistic generalizations or essentialist approaches to these theosophies.

The ascent of the two other codes, the sefirotic and the anthropomorphic, that competed with the attributive one, did not however obliterate the importance of the latter, even in later forms of Kabbalah. This is obvious in R. Abraham Axelrod of Koeln's *Keter Shem Tov*,[492] and especially in great parts of the Zoharic literature that avoid the resort overtly to a sefirotic code. This is the case also of the writings of R. Joseph of Hamadan. Even later, in the 14th century, there are texts that continue the earlier attributive code. So, for example, we read in R. Isaac of Acre:

> "The essence of our faith is to unify the Blessed Name [i.e., God] that is to say, to unify the Attributes – the Attributes of Strength with the Attributes of Mercy – namely all kinds of judgment with all kinds of compassion. But by adherence of this Attribute called Faith [*'Emunah*] to the Attribute called Truth, Truth is the line that receives from Mercy [*Ḥesed*] and from that which is above *Ḥesed*, the line emanates to *Yesod* that emanates onto Faith [*'Emunah*].

490 Ibidem, p. 496, referring to the affinities between commandments and *middot*: "it is incumbent upon us to interpret, in accordance with our way, from what [divine] attribute each and every *mitzvah* is [emerging]." See my *Absorbing Perfections*, pp. 289–290 and *Enchanted Chains*, pp. 215–220 and also Travis, *Rabbi Ezra of Gerona*, p. 49.

491 See Idel, *Absorbing Perfections*, pp. 298–299.

492 See R. Abraham Axelrod, *Keter Shem Tov*, in *'Amudei ha-Qabbalah*, p. 10, where the three codes occur on the same page.

And prayer is directed to the Foundation of the Building, that is *Binah*, that is the king and enters through the line of Faith, that is the gate of the things [namely the *sefirot*]."[493]

Here two different attributive codes are found together: one of Rabad's, dealing with the *sefirot* of *Ḥesed* and *Gevurah* and the importance of the third *sefirah*, and the other one of Nahmanides, dealing with the couple of *Tiferet* – Truth – and *Malkhut*, – Faith, an example of organization of earlier forms of Kabbalah into more integrated structure, a strategy characteristic of R. Isaac of Acre's writings in general. Of some importance is the recourse to a plural form of each of the two types of *middot*. This plurality is reminiscent of another seminal statement of this Kabbalist, who claims in the *Commentary on Sefer Yetzirah* attributed to him, that the *middot* are the active aspects of the ten *sefirot*, and the former are limitless upwards and downwards and they are renewed every day.[494] Here the distinction between the two sets is conspicuous, as it is the dynamic nature of the *middot*.

493 *Me'irat 'Einayyim*, ed. Goldreich, p. 94:

עיקר אמונתינו לייחד השם יתברך ר"ל לייחד המדות :מדות הגבורה עם מדות החסד כלומר כל מיני דין עם כל מיני רחמים. ובהתחבר זאת המדה שהיא אמונה עם אמת שהוא הקו המקבל מן החסד וממה אשר למעלה הימנו והקו משפיע ליסוד המשפיע לאמונה .והתפלה היא ליסוד הבנין שהיא הבינה שהוא המלך ונכנסת לו דרך אמונה שהיא שער לדברים.

See also Fishbane, *As Light before Dawn*, pp. 128 and 220. For the use of the term *middah* in the later composition of R. Isaac of Acre see is *'Otzar Ḥayyim*, ed. Gross, pp. 77, 80, 113, 123, 157, 167, 170, 176.

494 Ed. Scholem, p. 388:

ואלו עשר ספירות אינם כן, כי הם דבר אחד כולם אין בהם פירוד כלל, אלא על פי המדות אשר מהם יוציא פעולתם הם. ואלו עשר מדות אין להם גבול לא למעלה ולא למטה, כי יחדשו בכל יום, ובכל עת דברים יולדו מהם. ולשון מדה הוא כמו שרגילים לומר חז"ל, "כך מדתו של פלוני".

Compare to an anonymous text, authored in my opinion, by R. Isaac of Acre, extant in Ms. New York, JTS 2324, fol. 158a, where the *middot* are described as the lower nine *sefirot* beneath *Keter*, and the lower realm where the corresponding opposites are found. Though Bar-Asher, "Illusion versus Reality," made an interesting point concerning the absence of conclusive evidence

In a somewhat later book of this Kabbalist we find an interesting mixture of two codes:

> "I have seen before me the tree of flowers that emanate a good odor and their name is called in Arabic jasmine... and in Hebrew it is called *ḥavatzelet* [Song of Songs 2:1]... and I contemplated... its color and the essence of the leaves of its bud, namely its branches, and I have seen the hint at the ten *sefirot* of *Belimah*... and I have seen that its whiteness is not absolute but it is mixed with a little redness... so is the color of this flower. And while it is stored within its shell, you may find it red, a very sharp redness, namely on its shell, since its redness is sharp, but it itself exited white, as said above, and despite the fact that it is white, its tail remains red. And now listen to the secret to which all this alludes: the nine leaves hint at the nine *sefirot* from *Ḥokhmah* [second *sefirah*] to *Ḥokhmah* [tenth *sefirah*], and the flower itself hints at the *Keter*, since from the *Keter* [the attributes of] *Din* and *Raḥamim* [Judgment and Compassion] are emanated, external ranks and divine ranks. The redness of the flower that preceded by their existence [sic] the existence of the ten pure and holy *sefirot* of *Belimah*, and the precedence of the evil urge to the good urge, as it is said [Genesis 8:21]: 'Since the urge of the heart of man is evil since his youth,' and its whiteness hints at the divine holy attributes. This is what I have seen in this flower."[495]

This is indubitably an outstanding passage in the entire Kabbalistic literature dealing with contemplation and symbolism. Evidently, the Kabbalist does not identify the *middot* with the *sefirot*, which are

as to R. Isaac of Acre's authorship of this commentary, the text printed by Scholem includes' nevertheless, several elements characteristic of R. Isaac's thought an issue that deserves a more detailed discussion.

495 *'Otzar Ḥayyim*, Ms. Moscow-Ginsburg 775, fol. 100ab, ed. Gross, p. 99. Thanks to Dr. Amos Goldreich, who drew my attention to this passage. For more on this text see my *Primeval Evil in Kabbalah*, pp. 204–205. On divine attributes מידות אלוהיות see also, e.g., ibidem, ed. Gross, pp. 99, 185.,

part of two different codes. While mentioning the "holy *sefirot*," R. Isaac of Acre also alludes to the existence of "holy attributes" and specifically refers to Judgment and Compassion as emanated from the first *sefirah*, *Keter*, an important issue that has some parallels in early Kabbalah and to be discussed in details in the appendix. In fact, the colors he mentions, white and red, fit also the oppositive between the two attributes. In such a manner each of the nine lower *sefirot* are divided as related to the two attributes and to the two colors, though more details are not mentioned. Moreover, the distinction between holy and impure, or good and evil, refers to another type of code that does not concern us here. This synthetic or eclectic approach is part of the "mosaic" sort of writing that became widespread at the turn of the 13th century, as mentioned above. Nevertheless, let me point out that R. Isaac of Acre is a main source for the development of the most systematic structure of four decads of *sefirot* found in what is going to become the classical theory of four-fold cosmic worlds.[496] This means then even the most systematic treatments of the structure of *sefirot* in early Kabbalah did not exclude the importance of the Rabbinic term *middot*.

Last but not least in the context of R. Isaac of Acre's multifaceted thought: in a *Commentary on Sefer Yetzirah* attributed to him, the Kabbalist contributes an interesting example for what I call the ritually constellated theosophy, by interpreting the meanings of some form of commandments, the *Huqqim*, namely those rituals that have no explanation, as referring to the root *ḤQQ*, that means engraving,

496 See Gershom Scholem, "The Development of the Doctrine of the [Cosmic] Worlds in Early Kabbalah," *Tarbiz*, vol. 3 (19320, pp. 33–66, (Hebrew), Idel, *Studies in Ecstatic Kabbalah*, p. 88 n. 47. It should be mentioned that R. Isaac of Acre was fond of treatments of ten *sefirot*, as his copying the different commentaries on ten *sefiro*t found in his introduction to *Me'irat 'Einayyim*, show. He was instrumental in one way or another with the composition or elaboration of commentary no. 26 in Scholem's list *"Mafteaḥ le-Perushim,"* to be mentioned below in n. 500. As I shall try to show elsewhere, some few pages of an unidentified commentary on ten *sefirot* are extant in a manuscript.

referring to the term *Ḥaqiqah,* an intra-divine process within the sefirotic realm.[497]

The use of the term *middah* in the context of the theosophical structure, together with the reference to the two attributes, is evident in the anonymous Kabbalistic compilation *'Ohel Mo'ed,* probably written in the 15th century Spain.[498] Also in an anonymous commentary on ten *sefirot,* the Kabbalist refers to the *middot* as "The Order of the Ten Sefirot", "*Siddur ha-'Eser sefirot*".[499]

Let me turn to another major Kabbalist's treatment of the *middot.* R. Moshe Cordovero compiled at the very beginning of his theosophical book *Sefer Shi'ur Qomah* a list of terms that describe the decad of divine powers. The first category on this list is *middot,* and Cordovero distinguishes between four main meanings of this term: measure, extension and garment,[500] and the fourth, to which he devoted the lengthiest discussion, refers to spiritual qualities like "anger, anxiety, compassion, joy". One of the main functions of this type of *middot* is to express changes taking place within the divine sphere that cannot be attributed to the Infinite.[501] It is in this last context that the *middot* are conceived also as being vessels for the infinite light that expands

497 Ed. Scholem, p. 381. See also above n. 178. On the conceptual and textual complexities related to various forms of transmission of Kabbalistic traditions by this Kabbalist see my "R. Isaac ben Shmuel of Acre and His Attitude to Prophetic Kabbalah and its Implications for Scholarship," (forthcoming) (Hebrew).

498 See ed. J.E.E. Porush, (Jerusalem, 2002), pp. 76–77. See e.g, also pp. 68–69, 72–73, 115, 116, 117, 118, 119, 142, 143.

499 Ms. Vatican 214, p. 256, = no. 87 in Scholem's list "Mafteaḥ le-Perushim". See also the anonymous *Commentary on Ten Sefirot,* Ms. Paris BN 837, fols. 116a–117a and see above n. 271.

500 *Shi'ur Qomah,* fols. 3a–4a. See also the very beginning of his introduction, fol. 1a.

501 Ibidem, fols. 3d–4a. See, especially, the statement in *'Or Yaqar,* (Jerusalem, 1983), vol. 12 p. 8:

> "This is the path of the supernal *middot,* the quintessence of their operation is to mix *Ḥesed* in *Gevurah.*"
>
> כך דרך המדות העליונות שכל עיקר הנהגתם להמזג החסד בגבורה

downward. Only afterwards Cordovero speaks about the ten *sefirot*,[502] about ten creative logoi, ten commandments, etc. Needless to say that the Safedian Kabbalist is aware also of the difference between the sefirotic code and the more anthropomorphic one, as we learn from a rather explicit distinction he makes between them.[503]

My insistence on the centrality of codes of the divine world for understanding theosophical Kabbalah, prioritizes a much less symbolic understanding of the role of the *middot*. The code, which includes mainly the ten sefirot and their different arrangements, generates the meaning of the particular words to be commented or clarified, as much as their semantic content does. In general, the theosophical codes were rather simple to acquire and understand in a short period of time. It is only rarely that the Romantic view of the symbol adopted by scholars, is adequate for understanding the Kabbalistic discourse.[504] Compassion and judgment are, after all, attitudes that someone can experience in ordinary life, though their meaning differ from one person to another, and so I assume it is the case of Kabbalists. Nevertheless, the divine power that is part of a code anchors the importance of one topic or another as if reflected in processes within the supernal world. Much more than intuited by the Kabbalists, the supernal powers organize the variety of words, rituals and objects here below, in meaningfull patterns.

Moreover, continuity between the language of the Rabbis and that of the Kabbalists, Hebrew and Aramaic, attenuates dramatically a semantic rupture between the manner in which the terms for the two attributes functioned. In any case, in the material analyzed above,

See also ibidem, p. 19 the syntagm "the mixing of the *middot*": המזגת המדות that reflects some Rabbinic impact. For more on the use of the verb *MZG* in the context of these two divine powers, see below in chapter 10, especially n. 741, and above n. 384.

502 *Shi'ur Qomah*, fols. 4a–5a.

503 See Bracha Sack, ed., *From the Fountains of Sefer Elimah by R. Moshe Cordovero and Studies in His Kabbalah*, (Ben Gurion University Press, Beer Sheva, 2013), pp. 184–186 (Hebrew).

504 See my *Old Worlds, New Mirrors*, pp. 83–108.

continuity is not just a matter of using earlier material as proof-texts but also a significant starting-point for further conceptual developments. Indeed, the widespread reception of the theories about two or three attributes in Kabbalah, stands in contrast to its marginality in philosophical circles.In chapter 9 we shall see strategies of allegorical interpretations of the attributes that intended to remove the mythical sting from the Rabbinic modes of thought. Seeing divine perfection as a matter of stasis, Jewish philosophers were reluctant to operate with dynamic intra-divine powers. Let me exemplify this reticence by analyzing a topic that has been addressed only tangently above.

Written mainly in a century when great parts of the Jewish elites in Europe were engaged in one form or another in the Maimonidean controversies, the treatises of the Kabbalistic authors mentioned above did not adopt his principle of the one simple entity emerging from the higher one that is regarded as simple. They postulated a bifurcated type of emanation from the very beginning, which assumes the existence of opposites already within the highest levels, and their subsequent separation.

The theories of opposites that are related in so many cases to the two divine attributes, did not hesitate to describe the emergence of pair from the Infinite or from *Keter.* This is evident in the writings of Rabad, R. Azriel of Gerona, in the literature related to the *Iyyun* circle, to be discussed in the next chapter, as well as in the passage of R. Isaac of Acre cited earlier in this chapter. Moreover, the presence of the two attributes within the Infinite is evident in Lurianic texts to be analyzed in the appendix below. The split that generated the two distinct attributes differs starkly from the continuous nature of the Neoplatonic type of emanation, which has been adopted in a way or another also by many Kabbalists. However, I am concerned here with the awareness of many of the Kabbalists as to the discrepancy between the Kabbalistic and the philosophical approaches. Kabbalists adopted philosophical visions of perfections and thus a split which produces also a negative type of divine quality, turns to be a quandary for them. So, for example, we learn from R. Shem Tov ben Shem Tov, an early 15th century Kabbalist that was active in Spain:

> "Since the Lord of All is absolutely perfect, and from His essence everything is found, and from the influx that is emanated from Him, how did the opposites and the *Temurot*, and the evil things, and the composite matter, emerged out of an [entity]?"[505]

The opposites, *hafakhim*, and the evil dimensions were considered to emperil the divine perfection. R. Shem Tov's first answer is fidestic: just as it is impossible, he writes, to know the thought of the perfect God, so is it impossible to know how the evil stems from the absolute good. In principle, the two powers were created as corresponding to each other, in order to allow retribution of human actions. The symmetry is expressed by resorting to the Ecclesiastes verses and to Solomon in quite a clear manner, as well as to *Sefer Yetzirah*. He resorted also to the theory of the precedence of the Edomite Kings, thus subordination is quite evident[506] as the emergence of the opposites is from inscrutable "depth of the supernal wisdom."[507]

It is, however, only R. Joseph ben Shalom Ashkenazi that displays an open polemic with Maimonides, and with similar attempts to naturalize Judaism. So, for example, he writes:

505 *Sefer ha-'Emunot*, fols. 47b–48a. For the formula "The Lord of . . . all the *temurot*" see the text of R. Azriel, printed in Scholem, "New Remnants," p. 215. Compare also to R. Shem Tov's text printed by G. Scholem in the name of R. Shem Tov ibn Gaon, but belonging actually to R. Shem Tov ben Shem Tov, (as shown by Gottlieb, *Studies in the Kabbalah Literature*, p. 348), printed in *QS*, vol. 8, p. 542.

506 Ibidem, fol. 48ab. Solomon is described as the author of a *Book of Features, Sefer ha-Tekhunot*, dealing with matters and their opposites. See *Commentary on Ten Sefirot*, in David Ariel, *Shem Tob ibn Shem Tob's Kabbalistic Critique of Jewish Philosophy in the Commentary on the Sefirot* (Ph. D. Thesis, Brandeis University, 1981), p. 115, and *'Amudei ha-Qabbalah*, p. 67. See also Ms. New York, JTS 1822, fol. 11a and the text printed by Scholem, *QS*, vol. 8, p. 538.

507 *Sefer ha-'Emunot*, fol. 48b. An interesting parallel, which mentions thought rather than wisdom, is found in the other text of this Kabbalist printed in Scholem, *QS*, vol. 8, p. 538. See also for another partial parallel to *Sefer ha-'Emunot*, see this author's anonymous text extant in Ms. Florence-Laurenziana, Plut. II, 18, fol. 97b, printed in Idel, "Zimzum," pp. 84–85.

> "You should know that those that are going to interpret the Torah according to the way of nature, and say that the [human] intellect is cleaving to God, this is no more than a joke and a theft that they attempt at stealing the mind of the sons of religion."[508]

In more than one way, their positions reflect appropriations of views found in pre-Socratic thinkers, whose views have been explicitly rejected by Maimonides.[509]

This is also the case in many other topics in the literature of the emerging Kabbalah, especially the appropriation of Pythagorean, Platonic and neo-Platonic views,[510] or Zurvanic theories as to the

508 See, e.g., his *Commentary on Sefer Yetzirah*, fol. 6a: ולכן יש לך לדעת כי ההולכים לפרש התורה ע״ד טבע ואומרים כי השכל נדבק בשם, אין זה רק היתול וגנבה שגונבים דעת בני הדת.

See also his *Commentary on Genesis Rabbah*, ed. Hallamish, p. 250:

אלא שגם קמו בעדתנו אנשים נקראו חכמים בעיני מי שאינו יודע דתו וסבור שעלתה בידו אמונתו והנם מפרשי התורה על דרך הטבע עד שפירשו את התורה על הקדמות.

"But in our community appeared persons who are called sages by those who do not know what is his religion but thinks that his faith was understood by him, and they are commenting on the Torah in accordance to the path of nature, so that they will comment on the Torah according to pre-existence." See also ibidem, pp. 146–147. For Ashkenazi the philosophers are almost tantamount to heretics, *epyqursim*.

509 See Maimonides's famous epistle as to reliable types of philosophy studied by Steven Harvey, "Did Maimonides's Letter to Samuel ibn Tibbon Determine Which Philosophers Would Be Studied by Later Jewish Thinkers?" *JQR*, vol. 83 (1992), pp. 51–70. See also more recently Doron Forte, "Back to the Sources: Alternative Versions of Maimonides' Letter to Samuel Ibn Tibbon and Their Neglected Significance," *JSQ*, vol. 23 (2016), pp. 47–90.

510 See, e.g., Gershom Scholem, "The Traces of ibn Gabirol in Kabbalah," reprinted in *Studies in Kabbalah*, pp. 39–66, my "Maimonides and Kabbalah," idem, "Jewish Kabbalah and Platonism in the Middle Ages and Renaissance," in ed. L.E. Goodman, *Neoplatonism and Jewish Thought* (SUNY Press, Albany, 1993), pp. 319–321, 325–331, or "Anamnesis and Music, On Kabbalah as Renaissance before the Renaissance," *Rivista di Storia e letteratura religiosa*, XLIX.2, (2013), pp. 383–405 and see also below n. 519.

origin of evil.[511] Moreover, the theurgical elements that were conjugated with their various theosophies, generated structures of religious literatures and interpretations of ways of life, sometimes diametrically opposite to those of the Great Eagle and his followers,[512] including the approaches of a Kabbalist like Abraham Abulafia and some of his followers.[513] Though disparate elements from the philosophical sources of Maimonides and from his own writings may, eventually, enter those structures, their meaning may change dramatically,[514] just as his figure has been often times distorted when Kabbalists attempted to "convert" him to Kabbalah.[515]

Interestingly enough, when the interest in Pre-Socratic philosophers became more evident than ever in Judaism, in the writings of the 17th century R. Joseph Shlomo del Medigo, known as ha-Yashar of Candia,[516] some of R. Joseph ben Shalom Ashkenazi's passages

511 See my *Primeval Evil in Kabbalah.*

512 Compare, however, the very different views found in Elliot R. Wolfson, "Beneath the Wings of the Great Eagle: Maimonides and Thirteenth-Century Kabbalah," in eds. G.K. Hasselhoff and O. Fraisse *Moses Maimonides (1138–1204): His Religious, Scientific, and Philosophical "Wirkungsgeschichte" in Different Cultural Contexts,* (Würzburg, 2004), pp. 209–237 and, in keeping with him, in Dauber, "Competing Approaches to Maimonides in Early Kabbalah," who dealt with what are in my view, Maimonidean elements that are marginal in the basic structure of the various Kabbalistic theosophical systems.

513 See, e.g., "Abraham Abulafia: A Kabbalist "Son of God" on Jesus and Christianity," in ed. N. Stahl, *Jesus Among the Jews* (Routledge, London, New York, 2012), pp. 60–93, and "The Pearl, the Son and the Servants," pp. 103–136 and my monograph *Abraham Abulafia's Esotericism.*

514 See my "Maimonides in Nahmanides and His School, and Some Reflections," *Between Rashi and Maimonides,* in eds., E. Kanarfogel – M. Sokolow, (Yeshivah University Press, New York, 2010), pp. 131–164. See also in the next footnote.

515 See Gershom Scholem, "Maimonide dans l'oeuvre des Kabbalistes," *Cahiers juifs* vol. 3 (1935), pp. 103–112, and M. Idel, "Some Images of Maimonides in Jewish Mysticism," in *Studia Judaica,* vol. 17 (2009), pp. 36–63 and chapter 9 above.

516 See, e.g., *Novelot Ḥokhmah,* (Basle, 1631), fols. 11a, 47b, 56b, 66b, 201b, some of which has been translated in M. Idel, "Differing Conceptions of Kabbalah in

from his *Commentary on Sefer Yetzirah* that have been mentioned above,[517] that deals with opposites, have been presented as one piece of evidence for his own interest in philosophy.[518]

the Early 17th Century," in eds. I. Twersky and B. Septimus, *Jewish Thought in the Seventeenth Century*, (Harvard University Press, Cambridge, Mass. 1987), pp. 188, 194–195 and "Conceptualizations of *Tzimtzum* in Baroque Italian Kabbalah," in eds. M. Zank – I. Anderson, *The Value of the Particular: Lessons from Judaism and Jewish Modern Experience, Festschrift for Steven Katz on the Occasion of His Seventieth Birthday*, (Brill, Leiden, 2015), pp. 43–44. Del Medigo mentions several times the names of Empedocles and Anaxagoras.

517 The book was printed in Mantua, 1562, under the name of Rabad.

518 *Sefer Matzref la-Ḥokhmah*, chapter 5, (Warsau, 1890), p. 42. Interestingly enough, "Rabad" is mentioned as a philosopher together with the Catalan R. Hasdai Crescas, the author of an incisive philosophical critique of Aristotelianism, which returns in at least one case, to a pre-Socratic view. See Carlos Fraenkel, 'From the Pythagorean Void to Crescas, God as the place of the world', *Zutot*, vol. 5, (2008), pp. 87–94. See also *Matzref la-Ḥokhmah*, p. 107, where he prefers the views of the "ancient philosophers" to those of Aristotle's. See also David B. Ruderman, *Jewish Thought and Scientific Discovery in Early Modern Europe* (Wayne State University Press, Detroit, 1995), pp. 117–153.

CHAPTER EIGHT

The 'Iyyun Literature: Emanation of Two Opposites from One Simple Entity

Let me turn to some other instances of discussions of opposites, in the formative period of Kabbalah. As seen above in Rabad's Kabbalistic passage, two opposites are described as emanating from one entity, and similar views continued in his school, as seen in chapters 5–6. The phrase *shnei hafakhim* in the context of emanation from the highest level stands in clear contrast with a view found in Aristotle and elaborated in medieval Neo-Aristotelianism, including Maimonides, which claims that from one simple entity, only one simple entity can emerge, as shown in a seminal study of Arthur Hyman.[519] Let me point out to some reverberations of this anti-Maimonidean view in Kabbalistic literature, which are most plausibly independent of Rabad's Kabbalistic passage or Nahmanides' school, but close to views of R. Azriel of Gerona.

In addition to the two main Kabbalistic schools we dealt with above, another type of Kabbalah is known in the 13th century, described in scholarship as the circle of *Sefer ha-'Iyyun*, a title translated as the *Book*

519 See his "From One and Simple," pp. 111–135. See also Pachter, *Roots of Faith and Devequt*, p. 29 and n. 43 and R. Shem Tov ibn Falaquera, *Sefer ha-Ma'alot*, ed. L. Venetianer (Berlin, 1894), p. 70.

of Speculation.[520] The precise period of the floruit of these writings is disputed among scholars some of whom claim that it started already in the 12th century, others claiming a later date like mid-13th century.[521] This literature has been studied recently by Oded Porat, and his careful studies and editions of its texts are most helpful for dealing with the issues to be addressed below. He proposed to see the decades of mid-13th century as the time of the floruit of this literature, namely contemporary to the students of R. Isaac the Blind. For the purpose of our discussions here it is important to mention the assumption as to the emergence of two opposites from the "Primordial Air." In one of the major compositions belonging to this circle, perhaps the first one, entitled *Ma'ayan Ḥokhmah*, namely *The Spring of Wisdom*, it is said that:

> "prior to all these things that we mentioned above, there was there nothing but the Air[522] and it was obscured[523] by two things,

520 For descriptions of the writings belonging to this circle see Scholem, *Origins of Kabbalah*, pp. 309–346, Verman, *The Book of Contemplation*, idem, 'The Evolution of the Circle of Contemplation', in eds., P. Schäfer and J. Dan, *Gershom Scholem's "Major Trends in Jewish Mysticism" 50 Years After; Proceedings of the Sixth International Conference on the History of Jewish Mysticism*, (Tübingen 1993), pp. 163–177, Menachem Kallus, *Two Mid-13th Century Kabbalistic Texts from the 'Iyun Circle', with Commentaries*, (M.A. Thesis, Hebrew University, Jerusalem, 1985), Porat, *"Founding of the Circle"*, Dan, *History of Jewish Mysticism*, pp. 11–104, For the recent publication of all the pertinent sources belonging to this circle see the excellent edition of Porat, *The Works of Iyyun, Critical Editions* (Cherub Press, Los Angeles, 2013), (Hebrew), that will be used in the following discussions.

521 The various views are surveyed in the three studies mentioned above.

522 Verman translated the Hebrew אויר , a term recurring in this circle, as Ether but I prefer to keep air, especially since the discussions refer to the three elements. See Gad Freudenthal's important study *"Ha-Avir Barukh hu u-Varukh Shemo in Sefer ha-Maskil of R. Shlomo Simhah of Troyes," Da'at*, vol. 32–33 (1994), pp. 187–234, ibidem, vol. 34 (1995), pp. 87–129 (Hebrew), and idem, "Stoic Physics in the Writings of R. Sa'adyah Gaon al-Fayyumi and Its Aftermath in Medieval Jewish Mysticism," *Arabic Science and Philosophy* vol. 6 (1996), pp. 133–136, and Porat's comprehensive survey in *"Founding of the Circle,"* pp. 309–322, of pre-Socratic and some later discussions of the status of the air. See also below n. 167.

523 The Hebrew form *neḥshakh* should be understood as referring to the obscurity

> pertaining to two springs. From the first flowed an undefinable light, infinite and incommensurable…Afterward one fountain was emanated from which darkness was emanated."[524]

The Hebrew term translated as spring is *maqor*, and in medieval Hebrew it may have more than one meaning. However, from the specific context, it definitely stands for a well, since the term *mabo'a* – fountain – is used as a synonym, qualifying one of the two springs. Though the term "opposites" does not occur, I assume that the opposition of light and darkness are conceived so. The passage reverberates later in the same book, where it is written: "two springs, one flows light and the other flows darkness."[525] In any case the primordial darkness is described as stemming directly from the Air[526] allowing a picture that assumes symmetry between the two springs. A very similar view is found also in the Pseudo-R. Isaac the Blind's *Commentary on Sefer Yetzirah* and in Azriel of Gerona's *Commentary on the Talmudic Legends*.[527]

This theory of two springs, one of light and one of darkness, is

that surrounds the higher levels of the divine world preventing its contemplation.

524 Ed. Porat, *The Works of Iyyun*, p. 70:

> קודם אלו הדברים שזכרנו למעלה לא היה שם אלא אויר שאמרנו והוא היה מחושך בשני עניינים של שני מקורות הא׳ נובע אורה עד לאין חקר ולאין מספר...ואחריו נמשך מבוע האחד שממנו נובע החשך.

See also *Origins of the Kabbalah*, pp. 332–333, and Verman, *The Book of Contemplation*, p. 57, Porat, "*Founding of the Circle*", p. 43.

525 Porat, *The Works of Iyyun*, p. 73: שני מקורות האחד נובע אורה והשני נובע חשכה For another mentioning of the two springs see also ibidem, pp. 79, 85. See also ibidem, p. 86 as well as the discussion in idem, "*Founding of the Circle*", p. 322 and on R. Isaac the Blind, see Sendor, *The Emergence of Provencal Kabbalah*, II, p. 70 n. 192.

526 See idem, *The Works of Iyyun*, p. 70: החשך הקדמון שיצא מן האויר. In general, the primeval air is described as a light that is becoming dark, or occultated, so it cannot illumine:

> מהאור הנחשך מהאיר שהוא האויר הקדמון

Thus, the two elements that are connected to the two springs, light and darkness, are found in a way already before their bifurcation. See *Ma'ayan Ḥokhmah*, in Porat, ibidem, pp. 85, 260–261.

527 Pp. 100–101. As Tishby pointed out ibidem, n. 16, this is also the view of

reminiscent of a theory found in the so-called *Manual of the Discipline*, which is part of Qumran literature:

> "And [he] placed within him[528] two spirits so that he would walk with them until the moment of his visitation: they are the spirits of truth and of deceit. From the spring of light stem the generations of truth and from the source of darkness the generations of deceit."[529]

The "spring" translates *Ma'ayan*, the "source" translates the Hebrew *maqor*. However, let us remind the reader that the above quote is found in a Kabbalistic book entitled in Hebrew *Ma'ayan Ḥokhmah*. Therefore, despite the slight lexical difference and the huge conceptual one, the two passages share two important points: a] the existence of two metaphysical springs, which b] are then described in an identical manner: one of light and the other of darkness. It should be mentioned that in R. Azriel's discussion, the term *ma'ayanot* is mentioned.[530]

Though the direct connection between the two literary corpora is hardly plausible, it is nevertheless not totally impossible. It should be

[Pseudo-] R. Isaac the Blind's *Commentary on Sefer Yetzirah*, ed. Scholem, p. 15. See also the discussion in R. Azriel, ibidem, p. 85. See below, appendix.

528 There is a certain ambiguity here: it is not totally clear whether each person was given two spirits, like the two urges in Rabbinic literature, or whether each spirit is given only to one person, creating the dichotomy between the children of light and of darkness. It seems that the latter alternative is more plausible.

529 See III, 18–19, in ed. Licht, *The Rule Scroll*, p. 91:

וישם לו שתי רוחות להתהלך בם עד מועד פקודתו הנה רוחות האמת והעול. במעין אור תולדת האמת וממקור חושך תולדות עון

Cf., *The Dead Sea Scrolls, Study Edition*, eds. and trs. F. Garcia Martinez and E.J.C. Tigchelaar, (Brill, Eerdmans, Cambridge, Grand Rapids, Michigan, UK, 1997), vol. I, pp. 74–77. See Herbert G. May, "Cosmological Reference in the Qumran Doctrine of the Two Spirits and in Old Testament Imagery," *Journal of Biblical Literature*, vol. 82, No. 1 (Mar. 1963), pp. 1–14. Compare also to Naeh, "He Does Peace and Creates Everything," pp. 297–298.

530 *Commentary to the Talmudic Legends*, ed. Tishby, p. 101.

mentioned that some parts of the Qumran literature had a significant impact on Karaism, as many of scholars agree,[531] parts of it have been preserved in the Cairo Genizah, and copied as late as the 13th century, while Gershom Scholem pointed out to a striking similarity between a passage found in the library of the Qumran sect and a medieval book of magic.[532] As I suggested elsewhere there is a possible connection between a motif found in a Qumran text and the *Book of Bahir.*[533]

Let me turn to another occurrence of the syntagm "two springs" in another important treatise belonging to this literature entitled *Sod Yediyʿat ha-Metziyʾut,*:

> "The lightning that was made in the Air, when it split[534] and two springs emerged out of it, *Ḥashmal* and *ʿArafel*, that were divided

531 See Naftali Wieder, *The Judean Scrolls and Karaism* (East and West Library, London, 1962). For the quite plausible possibility that Karaite literature was the tradent of other ancient traditions – the most outstanding example being the theories of the Great Angel, including Philonic ones – see Bernard Revel, "The Karaite Halakhah and Its Relation to Sadducean, Samaritan and Philonian Halakhah," in ed., Ph. Birnbaum, *Karaite Studies*, (Hermon Press, New York, 1971), pp. 1–88, Yoram Erder, "The Prince *'Mastemah'* in a Karaite Work," *Meggilot*, vol. I (2002), pp. 243–246 (Hebrew), *The Karaite Mourners of Zion and the Qumran Scrolls, On the History of the Alternative to Rabbinic Literature* (Hakibutz haMeuchad, Tel Aviv, 2004), and Shlomo Pines, "The Oath of the Physician," in *Completed Works*, vol. IV, ed. G.G. Stroumsa, (Magnes Press, Jerusalem, 1996), pp. 170–171.

532 See Scholem, *Devils, Demons and Souls*, pp. 175–176 notes 123, 124, 125. See also ibidem, p. 172, note 103, where he points out to another striking parallel, this time between *1 Enoch* and the medieval book of magic entitled *Havdalah de-R. Aqivah*, known mostly in the Ashkenazi regions, to judge from the manuscripts in which it has been preserved. See also my *Ben*, pp. 71, 106, n. 211 and my Hebrew monograph *Fallen Angels, the Metamorphosis of a Myth in Jewish Thought* (in preparation) (Hebrew).

533 "On the Problem of the Study of the Source of the *Book of Bahir*," in ed., J. Dan, *The Beginning of Jewish Mysticism* (The Hebrew University, Jerusalem, 1987), p. 64 (Hebrew).

534 *BQʿ*. On this verb in the context of cosmogonic processes in Kabbalah and in earlier sources see the discussion and the parallels in Porat, *"Founding of the*

> from one another, and changed during their motion, and from them all the emanated powers proliferate."[535]

We may assume that *Ḥashmal* stands for what has been described in the passages above as the spring of light, while *'Arafel* – literally fog – stands for darkness. Though reflecting quite a dynamic theosophy, those discussions do not mention, however, cooperation between the two springs. Again, we have an example of a dual type of metaphysics, which has nevertheless one common source.

The relation between the two designations of the two springs is described in another treatise in this literature, (quite probably later on), which brings together motifs from earlier discussions, though in the framework of the system of ten *sefirot*, which is missing in the earlier stratum of this Kabbalistic literature. When dealing with the *sefirah* of *Gevurah* the anonymous Kabbalist wrote:

> "The two parts that separate from [the *sefirah* of] *Gevurah*, the one is called *'Arafel*, and it is the *'Arppilei Ṭohar*,[536] and it is seized from the side of *Binah*, and this is why it is a light that is enlightening and occultating itself within *Binah*. The second is called the attribute of judgment, is similar to darkness that is darkening the eyes of every

Circle," pp. 39, 244, 269, 320–334 and the printed version in his "The Linguistic Form 'And the Air was Established' in *Sefer Ma'ayan Ha-Ḥokhmah*: Its Jewish Sources and the Non-Catastrophic Figuring of the First Stage of Emanation," *Daat* vol. 78 (2015), pp. 11–54 (Hebrew).

535 Porat, *The Works of Iyyun*, p. 44:
הברק שנעשה באויר כשנבקע ויצאו ממנו שני מקורות חשמל וערפל שהן מתחלקים זה מזה ומשתנים בתנועתם כשמתפשטין מהם כל הכחות הנאצלים מהם.
See also *Sod Yediy'at ha-Metziy'ut*, in Porat, ibidem, p. 51, where these two entities are described as emerging from the primeval Air, one of them *Ḥashmal* adhering to its right side and the other, *'Arafel*, to its left side. To be sure: the symbolism of spring as dealing with the divine world is found in early Kabbalah but it is related to solely one spring. See Nahmanides' *Commentary on Sefer Yetzirah*, ed. Scholem, in his *Studies in Kabbalah*, pp. 89–90.

536 Literally "the fogs of purity," a syntagm found in the Mussaf prayer of Rosh ha-Shanah according to the Sefardi rite.

> creature so that it will not be capable to realize the *mamashut*[537] of *ʿArafel*. And you should understand that *Ḥashmal* and *ʿArafel* are two forms [found] one beside the other, the one I called by the language of male and it is the *Ḥashmal*, and this is "the beasts of fire that speak"[538] and the other is [called] by the name of female. The difference between them is that *ʿArafel* has a receptacle[539] that the *Ḥashmal* enters within it. And they are compound one beside the other… the water is called by language of male, and the fire by the language female."[540]

Thus, though divided from a higher unity, the two lower manifestations of the two springs are depicted as cooperating.[541] Thus we have some examples of a binary type of thought, as has been pointed out by Porat, though in this literature the term *hefekh*, for the concept of opposite, is quite rare.[542] In this circle of Kabbalistic writings, the term *ʾAḥdut Shawah*, the equal unity, occurs many times and it is,

537 This term, whose meaning is not clear, perhaps referring to the essence of something, occurs in this literature in many places. See, e.g., *Sefer ha-Yiḥud*, cf. Porat, *The Works of Iyyun*, pp. 183, 184 and *Sod ve-Yesod ha-Qadmoni*, ibidem, p. 170.

538 Cf. *BT Hagigah*, fol. 13b.

539 See also *Sefer ha-Yiḥud*, cf. Porat, *The Works of Iyyun*, p. 184. Let me point out that the precise meaning of *Yiḥud* in this *Sefer ha-Yiḥud* is far from being clear. See also above n. 44.

540 *Sod ve-Yesod ha-Qadmoni*, cf. Porat, ibidem, 175.

ב׳ חלקים מתחלקים מהגבורה. האחד נקרא ערפל הוא ערפלי טוהר והוא אחוז מצד הבינה, ועל זה הוא אורה מאירה מתעלמת תוך הבינה. השני נקרא מדת הדין דומה לחשך מחשיך עיני כל בריה כדי שלא יהיו יכולין להשיג ממשות הערפל, והבן כי חשמל והערפל שתי צורות זו בצד זו. האחד נאמר בלשון זכר והוא החשמל וזהו חיות אש ממללות. והשני בלשון נקבה. הבדלה שיש לערפל בית קבול שהחשמל נכנס בתוכו והם מורכבים זה בצד זה... שהמים נקראים בלשון זכר והאש בלשון נקבה.

On male and female, see also *Sefer ha-Yiḥud*, ibidem, p. 184 and *Sefer ha-Yiḥud ha-ʾAmmiti*, ibidem, p. 123. Compare also to *Sod Yediyʿat ha-Metziyʾut*, ibidem, p. 45

541 See Porat, *"Founding of the Circle,"* pp. 26–28, 49, 52, 228–229.

542 See ibidem, and idem, "The Linguistic Form," pp. 52–53..

together with R. Azriel's writings, one of the major sources for the later Kabbalists.[543]

A part of this Kabbalistic literature, though perhaps belonging to a later layer, is an influential responsum attributed to Rav Hai Gaon, dealing with thirteen attributes of compassion.[544] The anonymous Kabbalist creates a parallel between ten *sefirot* and ten attributes, described as some form of offspring of the former, while the first three are conceived of as a special triunitarian entity, a fact that attracted the special attention of many Christian Kabbalists. However, despite the resort to the thirteen *middot,* there is no interactive understanding of these entities.

Some of the views from this circle nourished a passage found in a commentary on *Sefer ha-'Iyyun,* found in an anonymous manner in many manuscripts, (which I proposed to identify his author as R. Joseph ben Shalom Ashkenazi), which refers explicitly to the concept of opposites as *hafakhim*:

> "*Ha-Keter,* is his equal unity, namely the Cause of causes, and how from this power the power of all the emanated and separated and created[545] ... water and fire emerged from air[546] and you should know that this Air is the Primeval Air that is mentioned in the book *Midrash Ḥokhmot,*[547] and the proof [of it are] heaven and earth,

543 See, e.g., Porat, *The Works of Iyyun,* pp. 39, 45, 50, 89. See also above n. 49. Compare, however, Wolfson, *Language, Eros, Being,* p. 98 who translated *Shawah,* or *ha-Shwa'ah* as indifferent/indifference, equal or identical.

544 See Porat, ibidem, pp. 240–245. On this text see Scholem, *Origins of the Kabbalah,* pp. 347–364, Vajda, *Recherches,* pp. 179–181 and the bibliography mentioned by these scholars. It should be mentioned that the English translation of Scholem's book on p. 350, where the epistle is rendered, mistranslated *kaf zekhut, kaf hovah,* as shell instead of scale.

545 This triad of entities occurs again in this small treatise. See *Perishat Sefer ha-'Iyyun,* printed now in *Sifrei Qabbalat ha-Ge'onim,* ed. Y.M. Erlanger, (Jerusalem, 2006), p. 113.

546 Such a view is not found in *Sefer Yetzirah.*

547 Perhaps a reference to R. Yehudah ibn Matka's still inedited encyclopedia with the same title written in mid-13th century in Toledo.

> those two opposites emerged from the Simple Primeval Air... that from Him these opposites come... and there is in the power of the Primeval Air that fire and water... that are two opposites, [emerging] from the One Simple, of outmost simplicity."[548]

Here the opposites are mentioned explicitly, as emerging from the Primeval Air. This air is described in this specific context as determining or preponderating – *hakhra'ah* – between the two opposites, a view reminiscent of *Sefer Yetzirah* III:3. We have therefore a combination of a theory from the *'Iyyun* circle theory with *Sefer Yetzirah*. This nexus between the Air and two elementary opposites is reminiscent of Anaximenes' emphasis on Air as playing a role similar to that played by the *Apeiron* in Anaximander. As part of the earlier quote the Kabbalist wrote that "[even] the material air is capable to link with fire or with water."[549] Moreover, the claim of the end of this passage to the effect that opposites emerge from a simple entity seems to be

548 *Perishat Sefer ha-'Iyyun*, ed. Erlanger, p. 115:
הכתר אחדותו השוה, ר"ל של עלת העלות .וכיצד נאצל מכל כחו כל הנאצלים והנפרדים והנבראים... אויר מים אש פי' האויר יצאו ממנו מים ואש ודע כי האויר הזה הוא האויר הקדמון הנזכר בספר מדרש החכמות, והמופת שמים וארץ שני הפכים הללו שיצאו מאויר קדמון הפשוט... כי יצאו ממנו אלו ההפכים... שאויר הקדמון יש בכחו לצאת ממנו אש ומים שני הפכים מתוך פשוט בתכלית הפשיטות.

See also Verman, *The Book of Contemplation*, p. 155. On this anonymous booklet and various views as to the possible authorship of R. Joseph Ashkenazi see Gershom Scholem, "The Remnants of R. Shem Tov ibn Gaon's Book," *QS*, vol. 9 (1932), p. 126 n. 1 (Hebrew), my "The Image of Man Above the *Sefirot*: R. David ben Yehuda he-Hasid's Theosophy of Ten Supernal *Sahsahot* and its Reverberations," *Kabbalah*, vol. 20 (2009), pp. 194–195, Hallamish in R. Joseph Ashkenazi in his *Kabbalistic Commentary on Genesis Rabbah*, ed., Ḥallamish, p. 16, Giulio Busi, "The Early Kabbalistic Exegesis on the Book of Contemplation," in eds., R. Elior – P. Schaefer, *Creation and Re-Creation in Jewish Thought: Festschrift in Honor of Joseph Dan on the Occasion of His Seventieth Birthday* (Mohr/Siebeck, Tuebingen 2005), pp. 97–101 (Hebrew part), and Porat, *The Works of Iyyun*, p. 273, idem, *"Founding of the Circle"*, pp. 92 n. 96, p. 136, n. 352, 157 n. 505. See also below n. 552.

549 *Perishat Sefer ha-'Iyyun*, ed. Erlanger, p. 115: האויר הזה הגופני הוא יכול להתחבר עם

a silent controversy with the view of the Aristotelians, mentioned at the beginning of this section.

Another opponent to the Aristotelian philosopher, and probably the author of the anonymous commentary discussed earlier, is capitalizing on views found in the *'Iyyun* literature. In a *Commentary on Sefer Yetzirah* by R. Joseph be Shalom Ashkenazi, a late 13th century Kabbalist,[550] we read as an explanation of the three letter *'MSh* mentioned in that book:

האש או עם המים Compare to the view of R. Joseph Ashkenazi in his *Kabbalistic Commentary on Genesis Rabbah*, ed., Ḥallamish, pp. 173–174:

ואל תתמה איך מכח אחד הפשוט הגמור יתפשט ממנו דברים רבים ויהיו בציור קדמותו ויקראו אחדות השוה על שם שבו ישתוו כל התמורות כי אפי׳ במוגשמים תמצא זה.

"You should not wonder how from one totally simple power many things will emanate, and they were within the conceptualization of his primordiality and will be called the equal *'Aḥdut*, because there all the contradictions will be equalized since even in the corporeal things you can find this."

This parallel should be one of the significant proofs for Ashkenazi's authorship on this small treatise. Moreover, the opening of this passage: "you should not wonder" recurs several times in Ashkenazi's *Commentary on Sefer Yetzirah*. See, e.g., fols. 13c, 18b, 22c, etc, or his *Commentary on Bereshit Rabbah*, ed. Hallamish, p. 243. See above n. 549.

550 On this Kabbalist see the groundbreaking studies of Gershom Scholem, "The Real Author of the *Commentary on Sefer Yetzirah*,attributed to R. Abraham ben David and His Works," *Studies in Kabbalah*, pp. 112–136, Georges Vajda, "Un Chapitre de l'Histoire du Conflit Entre la Kabbale et la Philosophie: la Polemique Anti-intellectualiste de Joseph b. Shalom Ashkenazi," *AHDLMA*, vol. XXIII (1956), pp. 45–143, idem, "Ninety-Four Principles of the Philosophers Cited by R. Joseph Ashkenazi," *Tarbiz*, vol. 27 (1958), pp. 290–300 (Hebrew), Liebes, *Studies in the Zohar*, pp. 93–95, as well as Ḥallamish's introduction to his edition of the *Commentary on Genesis Rabbah* and his "Remnants from the Commentary on Psalms by R. Joseph ben Shalom Ashkenazi," *Da'at*, vol. 10 (1983), pp. 57–70 (Hebrew), as well as Pedaya, "Sabbath, Sabbatai, and the Diminution of Moon," pp. 150–153, and Brian Ogren, *Renaissance and Rebirth, Reincarnation in Early Modern Italian Kabbalah* (Brill, Leiden, Boston, 2009), pp. 18–21, 187, 193–194, 216–219, 279–280, idem, "The Law of Change and the Nature of the Chameleon: Yosef ben Shalom 'Askenazi and Giovanni Pico della Mirandola," in ed. F. Lelli, *Giovanni Pico e la cabbalà* (Olschki, Firenze,

"When we shall come to inquire how two opposites like fire and water were emanated from one simple power, and the minds are precluded from understanding this cause and this is the reason that they called [in *Sefer Yetzirah*] a secret, which means a hidden thing... and even [the *sefirot* of] *G[edullah]* and *G[evurah]* and *Binah* do not understand the truth as to the reason of the opposites, how they were within the supernal *Keter*, in an equal unity."[551]

The gist of this passage is that lower *sefirot* are unable to comprehend the manner of existence of opposites together within the same higher zone. However, I do not see the necessity to understand this type of existence as a coincidence of opposites but as equality between them, when they are found together, before their bifurcation, as seen in sections 2 and 3. The resort to the plural when referring to their supernal existence should be understood as implying some form of distinction between them. While the coincidence of opposites is an attempt to overcome diversity, as seen above in the discussion of Mircea Eliade's approach, as part of transcending diversity, the texts we discussed in this study are an attempt to account for the emergence of diversity.

Here the concept of the Air was substituted by a "simple power," which is also a "hidden thing." Fire and water are mentioned in the passage from *Sefer Yetzirah*, III:2, where these elements are identified with male and female. Air, mentioned in *Sefer Yetzirah* III:3, together fire and water is, however, not presented in this late antiquity book as the source of these two opposites, but as preponderant between them. It should be mentioned that R. Joseph Ashkenazi refers to opposites as *hafakhim* that cooperate, while the term *temurot*, that stems from

2014), pp. 121–133, and my "Ashkenazi Esotericism and Kabbalah in Barcelona," *Hispania Judaica Bulletin*, vol. 5 (2007), pp. 100–104 and *Saturn's Jews*.

551 *Commentary on Sefer Yetzirah*, fol. 44b:

פירוש כשנבא לחקור איך נאצלו שני הפכים כמו אש ומים מכח פשוט נמצא שהדעות נלאו מהשיג סבה זו. ולפיכך קראו סוד פירוש דבר נעלם. גדול מגדולה ומופלא מגבורה ומכוסה מבינה. פירוש אפילו ג"ג ובינה נעלם מהם אמתת סבת ההפכים איך היו בכ"ע באחדות השוה.

Sefer Yetzirah, stands, in many cases in his writings, for the ontological opposites that constitute a symmetrical type of opposition, namely demonic powers that parallel the divine powers.[552]

This is also the gist of another discussion in this book, where three components of every being are described as the substratum, privation and generation. The two latter are conceived of as opposites that are sustained by the substratum.[553] However, pertinent for our discussions is also the view found elsewhere in the same book, where he describes the eight *sefirot*, with the exception of *Keter* – depicted as "simple" – and *Malkhut*, as composed of the attributes of compassion and judgment, this being the reason why they are not to be conceived of as opposites.[554] Like in the case of the quote from the anonymous commentary on *Sefer ha-'Iyyun*, the terms *Keter* and "simple" occur in the context of opposites. A similar view is found in another book of Joseph Ashkenazi:

> "Since each and every *sefirah* has been created *du-partzufin*, namely male and female, the light and its shining, thus on the right side male and on the other [side] female, so that they should be able to link to each other and separate... also in the ten *sefirot*, also in Adam, [and] also in Eve."[555]

552 See, e.g., R. Joseph Ashkenazi, *Kabbalistic Commentary on Genesis Rabbah*, ed., Ḥallamish, pp. 43–44, 174, 252, 266, and my "The Meaning of "Ta'amei Ha-'Ofot Ha-Teme'im" of R. David ben Yehuda He-Hasid," in ed., M. Hallamish, *'Alei Shefer, Studies in the Literature of Jewish Thought Presented to Rabbi Dr. Alexander Safran* (Bar-Ilan University Press, Ramat Gan, 1990), pp. 11–27 (Hebrew). For earlier pre-Kabbalistic and Kabbalistic resorts to the term *temurah* see Porat, *"Founding of the Circle"*, pp. 128–131, 218 ff. and his footnotes.

553 *Commentary on Sefer Yetzirah*, fol. 18b. The three Hebrew terms are הויה, הפסד, נושא

554 Ibidem, fol. 23a.

555 See Ashkenazi, *Kabbalistic Commentary on Genesis Rabbah*, ed., Ḥallamish, p. 224:

כי כל ספירה וספירה נבראת ד"ו פרצופין ר"ל זכר ונקבה, אור וזריחתו, אם כן צד אחד זכר והשני נקבה...גם בי"ס גם באדם גם בחוה.

There are four other references to *du-partzufin* in this book. See pp. 33, 124, 130,

The comprehensive inner bisexuality does not, however, recourse to the language of opposites.[556] Indeed, the main concern for Ashkenazi, just as in the case of the Rabad's passage, is the possibility of cooperation, an issue that is depicted as found on the entire range of cosmic beings.

Moreover, in a response dealing with the secret of *du-partzufin*, authored by R. David ben Yehudah he-Ḥasid to a query of one of his students, he employs phrases from Ashkenazi's commentary on *Sefer Yetzirah* together with specifically Zoharic terminology.[557] This is a second phase of synthesis that added to the pre-Zoharic theosophies used by Ashkenazi together with the *ʿIyyun* views, also the Zoharic one. This synthetic approach is quite characteristic of R. David's writings in general and left an indelible impact on a major Kabbalist like R. Moshe Cordovero. Though the precise meaning of some hints in this response is far from clear, it must include the assumption that the common source of the opposites – related in the response to categories of male and female as emerging from the supernal world within the divine realm – includes a phase when they are not yet separated – though they were distinguishable – found within the Primeval World, described as *ʿOlam Qadmon*, identical to

132. In the first of these four the assumption is that *Tiferet* and *ʿAtarah* have been emanated together, in a way reminiscent of the Nahmanidean views surveyed above. See Hallamish, p. 33 n. 24 and in n. 107 above.

556 About supernal actions that operate a thing and its opposite see the view of Philo, in nn 62, 64, R. Abraham ibn Ezra's commentary on Amos 4:13, R. David Qimhi, on Amos 9:6, or Nahmanides' Commentary on Exodus 15:26, 17:5, ed. Chavel vol. 1, pp. 360, 371, and R. Bahya ben Asher, in many places in his commentary on the Pentateuch, and following them many other commentators. See, especially, R. Meir ibn Gabbai's *ʿAvodat ha-Qodesh*, III:68, fol. 111c. See also Cordovero's *Tefillah le-Moshe*, fols. 244b, 252b, the divine powers operate a thing and its opposite, and compare also to his *Pardes Rimmonim*, IV:9. According to his *Sefer Shiʿur Qomah*, fol. 33b, all the entities – *hawayyot* – are in the form of *du-partzufin*. See also above nn. 39, 173. This is part of the broader phenomenon I describe as dual ontology.

557 Idel, "Kabbalistic Material," pp. 194–197. On this text see also Liebes, *Studies in the Zohar*, pp. 132–134.

the *sefirah* of *Keter*, and a later one, when they are separated, in the lower *sefirot*, designated as the "world of the innovated ones" – *'Olam ha-meḥuddashim*.[558] Moreover, R. David h-Hasid capitalizes on the view mentioned above that *sefirot* are a mixture of the attributes of compassion and judgment, which he associates with the theory that those *sefirot* possess also male and female aspects.[559] This type of theosophy is of paramount importance for an understanding of a widespread theory of gender in theosophical Kabbalah: bisexuality is a pervasive aspect of many forms of Kabbalistic theosophy – including the Zoharic one – which means that neither the male nor the female aspects of a *sefirah* can be obliterated, nor is the male *sefirah* lacking a feminine aspect for attaining a state of perfection, since the male and female dimensions are omnipresent, as part of what I call dual ontology. This view about theosophical bisexuality had a deep impact on Safedian Kabbalah, and I discussed its various reverberations in my monograph mentioned above "*Male and Female*."

Interestingly enough, it is especially in the two theosophical Kabbalists that the question of cooperation is addressed in a direct manner, in order to overcome the problem of the opposites. In fact, both Joseph Ashkenazi and R. David, as well as the author of *Perishat Sefer ha-'Iyyun*, which is to be identified with the former Kabbalist, adopted also another view that ensures the possibility of cooperation between *sefirot*: they share the view that in each *sefirah* there are also other *sefirot*, a theory that allows interaction of all the *sefirot* with the others.[560] This theory is found also in Rabad's and Nahmanides'

558 Idel, ibidem, p. 195 nn. 141, 142. See Goldreich, "The Theology of the Iyyun Circle," pp. 155–156, n. 59.

559 Idel, ibidem, p. 196. See also above nn. 334, 558.

560 Gershom Scholem, "R. David ben Yehuda he-Hasid, Grandson of the Ramban," in his *Studies in Kabbalah*, p. 145, Tishby, *The Wisdom of the Zohar*, I, p. 291, my "An Anonymous Commentary on *Shir ha-Yiḥud*," in eds. K-E Groezinger – J. Dan, *Mysticism, Magic and Kabbalah in Ashkenazi Judaism*, (Walter de Gruyter, Berlin, New York, 1995), p. 147, and see also the anonymous *Perishat Sefer ha-'Iyyun*, in ed. Busi, p. 100. See also Scholem, *Kabbalah*, pp. 113–114 and the next footnote.

schools.[561] Also the passage about male and female translated above from *Sod ve-Yesod ha-Qadmoni* stems from a treatise that is structured according to the order of ten *sefirot* that have been understood in a theosophical manner. Though some of the theosophical Kabbalists were well-acquainted with the *'Iyyun* texts, what dominates in their writings is nevertheless the issue of the cooperation and complementarity of the two opposites. This is part of the integration of the sefirotic theosophy with theurgical approaches, or with the transformation of a binary approach into a binitarian one, namely a view of a binary couple of powers as important for the religious cult.

However, the other texts adduced in this section, representing mainly the first layer of the *'Iyyun* literature, are concerned with a binary structure that intends to safeguard the epistemological

561 See *R. Asher ben David*, ed. Abrams, pp. 61, 77. See also above n. 282. The earliest most explicit mentioning of this theory I am acquainted with is found in a short remark of R. Isaac Todros in his *Commentary on the Maḥẓor*, Ms. Paris BN 839, fol. 215b, written sometimes in later decades of the 13th century in Barcelona. Following him it can be discerned also in his disciple's commentary on Nahmanides's Kabbalistic secrets, entitled *Keter Shem Tov* by R. Shem Tov ibn Gaon, printed in *Ma'or va-Shemesh*, ed. Koriat, fols. 26b and 45a, or in the parallel discussions in Ms. Paris BN 774, fols. 76b, 104a of this work, and in traditions from Nahmanides' school, as found anonymously, e.g., in Ms. Oxford-Bodleiana 1610, fol. 86b or in R. Menahem Recanati's quotation of some Kabbalists in his *Commentary on the Pentateuch*, fol. 25ab and ibn Gabbai, *Derekh 'Emunah*, p. 82. In some Nahmanidean texts mentioned earlier in this footnote, the presence of judgment within compassion and vice-versa is mentioned, as it is the case also in chapter 5 of R. Joseph Gikatilla's *Sha'arei Tzedeq*, and *Sha'arei 'Orah*. My assumption is that the theory as to the comprisal of the ten *sefirot* within each of the ten *sefirot*, is a development of an earlier tradition according to which if there are two attributes, each of them also comprises something of the other. Indeed, in some of the texts referred to above, the two traditions are mentioned together. See Wolfson, *Language, Eros, Being*, p. 445 n. 98. For an ancient view according to which everything is found in everything see already Anaxagoras' fragment 6, in Kirk-Raven, *The Presocratic Philosophers*, pp. 375–376, and following him a variety of Neo-Platonic formulations about all being in all.

transcendence of the Primeval Air and not with binitarian views. This binary structure serves as a veil, and is concerned not with the manner in which the world is governed but most plausibly represents an independent theme, related to some form of negative theology, which has been conjugated later on with the decadic structure, in a manner reminiscent of the two different interpretations of the two theosophical schools discussed in chapters 3–5 above. This does not mean that it was the same tradition that is shared by those two theosophical schools, and by the one discussed in this section, but we may discern a similar phenomenon of conjugation, that took place in the two different cases.[562] This conjugation introduced in this synthesis with the *'Iyyun* material views of reciprocal containment of judgment and compassion, of female and male, and the views about the ten *sefirot* that are found within the other ten *sefirot*.

Interestingly enough, none of the Kabbalists mentioned here refers to the passage of Rabad, analyzed in chapter 4.

562 See Porat, "*Founding of the Circle*", pp. 22–23, 27–29, 68. For binary phenomena that are sometimes also binitary, according to additional sources of Ashkenazi extraction see my "The Mystical Intention in Prayer at the Beginning of Kabbalah: Between Ashkenaz and Provence," in eds., B. Safran – E. Safran, *Porat Yosef, Studies Presented to Rabbi Dr. Joseph Safran*, (Ktav Publishing House, Hoboken, New Jersey, 1992), pp. 8–14 (Hebrew).

NINE

The Interiorization of the Two "Divine" Attributes in Ecstatic Kabbalah

"The soul's attribute and its nature are changes."
Abulafia, *Ḥayyei ha-'Olam ha-Ba'*

Since the seventies of the 13th century, another type of Kabbalah emerged, mainly in the writings of R. Abraham ben Shmuel Abulafia [1240–c. 1292].[563] It differs on many points, from the earlier Kabbalistic schools that were surveyed above, as I have remarked in several studies.[564] From our point of view here, Abulafia is a Kabbalist that,

563 For full-fledged monographs see on this Kabbalist, see Idel, *The Mystical Experience in Abraham*, idem, *Language, Torah, and Hermeneutics in Abraham Abulafia*, tr. M. Kallus, (SUNY Press, Albany, 1989), *Abraham Abulafia's Works and Doctrine*, idem, *Ben: Sonship and Jewish Mysticism* (Continuum, London, New York, 2008), pp. 276–375, idem, *Le porte della Giustizia*, idem, *Abraham Abulafia's Esotericism*, Wolfson, *Abraham Abulafia*, Harvey J. Hames, *Like Angels on Jacob's Ladder: Abraham Abulafia, the Franciscans, and Joachimism* (SUNY Press, Albany, 2007), and Sagerman, *The Serpent Kills*. For separate studies see also in the following footnotes.

564 See, e.g., Idel, "Defining Kabbalah," pp. 97–122, idem, "On the Secrets of the

though active in Rabbinic environments, in more than one country in Europe, his attitude to Rabbinic lore, as it is to the Hebrew Bible, is strongly informed by a philosophically allegorical approach, that often times misinterprets the texts he commented upon, and in some cases, it is possible to discern a strong critical approach to Rabbis. From this point of view, he differs from the earlier Kabbalists we addressed above. Due to his many books and oral teachings in a variety of countries in Southern Europe, especially in Sicily, it became a separate Kabbalistic school, designated by him as "prophetic Kabbalah" or as "Kabbalah of names," sometimes labeled in modern scholarship as ecstatic Kabbalah. This brand of Kabbalah differs substantially from all the major contents of Kabbalistic schools mentioned above on more than one essential point, and this is the case also in the manner in which his understanding of the topics under scrutiny here is articulated in his writings and those of his followers.

Writing under the spell of Maimonides' Neoaristotelian metaphysics, an author whose major philosophical book he studied and even taught over several years, also long after he became a Kabbalist, Abulafia adopted neither the Rabbinic nor the theosophical visions of the relationship between the divine attributes, in the manner they have been presented above. Interestingly enough, though not totally surprising, in his philosophical writings, Maimonides himself

Torah in Abraham Abulafia," in eds. B. Brown, M. Lorberbaum, A. Rosnak, Y.Z. Stern, *Religion and Politics in Jewish Thought, Essays in Honor of Aviezer Ravitzky*, (The Israel Democracy Institute, Merkaz Z. Shazar, Jerusalem, 2012), 1, pp. 371–458 (Hebrew). See also my studies 'Inner Peace through Inner Struggle in Abraham Abulafia's Ecstatic Kabbalah,' *The Journal for the Study of Sephardic & Mizrahi Jewry* 2 (2008), pp. 62–96, idem, "*Milhemet ha-Yetzarim: Psychomachia* in Abraham Abulafia's Ecstatic Kabbalah," in ed. A. Bar Levav, *Peace and War in Jewish Culture* (Merkaz Shazar, Jerusalem, 2006), pp. 99–143 (Hebrew), and "Higher than Time," pp. 179–210. For some of Abulafia's special type of narrative see also my "Multilingual Gematrias in Abraham Abulafia and Their Significance: From the Bible to Text to Language," in eds. M. Bar-Asher & I. Meir, *Nit'ei 'Ilan, Studies in Hebrew and Related Fields Presented to IIan Eldar* (Carmel, Jerusalem, 2014), pp. 193–223 (Hebrew).

avoided any significant discussion of the two divine attributes as part of quite an exclusive type of theology.[565] I would say that in general, also other Jewish philosophers took little interest in the two divine attributes. Provided the unique manner of interpretation Abulafia and his followers offered to the two attributes, and the fact that his interpretation has been misinterpreted in scholarship, I shall dwell on their discussions, in order to illustrate the diversity of Kabbalistic attitudes to these major Rabbinic theologumena.

Abulafia interpreted the canonical texts, the Bible and Rabbinic statements, as well as Kabbalistic theosophical-theurgical topics, in accordance to his allegorical approach inspired mainly by Maimonides' exegetical techniques, but also in accordance to linguistic exegetical techniques, that flowered in the Ashkenazi provinces. However, he preferred certain types of allegories over others: while the center of gravity of the philosophical interpretations of the Jewish tradition was strongly inclined to its naturalization, dealing with cosmic processes as well as psychological ones, Abulafia prefered the latter to the former, accentuating what can be called "spiritual allegorization." This is also the case of his treatments of the two attributes, which occur dozens of times in his writings. I had the opportunity to refer to some of those discussions elsewhere but this is the place to elaborate on some of the other occurrences of the two attributes.[566] In the following parts of this chapter I shall try to show that the two attributes served as a code of interpretation in Abulafia's system, understood as dealing not with the divine acts as changing entities but with two modes of human behavior.[567]

In *Get ha-Shemot*, Abulafia's very first book – at least in the domain of Kabbalah – he wrote: ''Divine names change the nature, [as they]

565 See also Chanah Kasher, "The Myth of "the Angry God" in the *Guide of the Perplexed*," in ed. H. Pedayah, *Myth in Judaism*, (Ben Gurion University Press, Beer Sheva, 1996), pp. 95–111 (Hebrew).

566 See, e.g., Abulafia's passage translated and analyzed in my *Absorbing Perfections*, pp. 439–442, 444.

567 See ibidem, p. 444.

are the throne, and this is the secret of [the verse] [Exodus 8:9]: 'the finger of God,' namely the finger changes nature by virtue of the mentioned 'Elohim, which is the attribute of judgment.''[568] This is a very compact passage, similar to many other in his writings, which differ in form and content from the discourse of the theosophical-theurgical Kabbalists. He hints at the Rabbinic views that connected between divine names, attributes – here the attribute of judgment – and thrones, as seen in the Ashkenazi text discussed at the end of chapter 2. However, he introduces themes that are absent in the Ashkenazi type of thought during the first part of the 13th century, especially the concept of nature, *Teva'*. Operating with the device of gematria he establishes a nexus between some of the concepts: *'Elohim* = 86 = *ha-kisse'* = *ha-Teva'*. This seems to be the first documented instance that introduced the gematria *'Elohim* = *ha-Teva'*, which entered the circuit of Kabbalah, also by means of the early writings of R. Joseph Gikatilla, Abulafia's student, and influenced ultimately Spinoza's famous formula *Deus sive natura*.[569] Mentioning the divine name and the finger of God as changing nature may, in principle, be understood as a magical approach. However, this would be a sharp misunderstanding: the book where the passage is found is entitled *Get ha-Shemot*, namely the divorce of the Names, which means the divorces of the magical understanding of names. I propose to understand it more in a naturalistic way. So, for example, Abulafia writes several years later:

568 Ms. Oxford, Bodleiana 1682, fol. 101b:

וכולם הם אלוהיים משנים הטבע שהם הכסא, וזהו סוד "אצבע אלהים הוא" (שמות ח:ט), כלומר האצבע משנה הטבע בכח אלהי"ם הנזכר שהוא מדת הדין.

On this work by Abulafia see Idel, *Abraham Abulafia's Works and Doctrines*, pp. 4–5. See also *Absorbing Perfections*, pp 260–261, and below at the end of this chapter, the passage cited from R. Nathan's *Sha'arei Tzedeq*.

569 See M. Idel, "*Deus sive Natura*, The Metamorphosis of a Dictum from Maimonides to Spinoza," *Maimonides and the Sciences*, eds. S. Cohen and H. Levine, (Kluwer Academic Publishers, Dordrecht, 2000), pp. 87–110, idem, *Abraham Abulafia's Esotericism*, pp. 186–208.

"You should know that from the nature that operates [or generates] the attributes, you should recognize the *middot,* since just as the elements are four, and their qualities are eight and all have one matter, also the *middot* are, in principle one, and from them there was generation and decay, that are incumbent from the opposites. And the witness is that the opposites and the decay that is inverted, are equal, and all generation is from KW,[570] and all the decay is from KB.[571]"[572]

The language of attributes as opposites and their equality is very reminiscent of the various theosophical discussions as seen in chapters 4 and 5 above. There can be no doubt that Abulafia was acquainted with at least some of them since his studies of Kabbalah in Barcelona in 1270–1271.[573] However, here they describe processes related to *middot* as taking place in nature, not in the divine world. He adopts concepts of Aristotelian physics in order to interpret it in his special way.[574] Abulafia interprets it by means of manipulations of letters, including the Tetragrammaton. The nature of the change refers either to the linguistic permulations by the humans, or to the the Aristotelian concepts of generation and decay, taking place in nature.

Let me start with a clearcut denial of possibility of changes in the divine world or in the divine attributes, in the vein of the Great Eagle.

570 The gematria of the Tetragrammaton.

571 These are the twenty-two letters that everything is created by their permutations and everything disappears by the change of those permutations, as we learn from the context of this discussion.

572 *Commentary on 'Ish 'Adam,* p. 47:

ודע שמהטבע שהוא פועל המדות תכיר המדות, כי על היות היסודות ארבעה ואיכותיהם שמונה ולכולם חומר אח"ד, היו המדות גם כן בכללם אחד. והיה מהם הויה וההפסד חויב מן ההפכים, והעד כי ההפכים וההפסד הנהפך שווים, וכל הויה מן כ"ו וכל הפסד מן כ"ב.

573 See my "*Sefer Yetzirah* and Its Commentaries." See e.g., his epistle *Matzref la-Kesef,* p. 6, where the impact of the theory of R. Azriel of Gerona can be discerned, when he speaks of the *sefirot* consisting in "a thing and its opposite," though his view nevertheless differs.

574 Compare also to *Commentary on 'Ish 'Adam,* p. 49.

In one of his commentaries on what he thought were the secrets of Maimonides's *Guide of the Perplexed*, Abulafia wrote:

> "And the secret is that He was in the past, as He is now, and as He will be in the future, without change, for none of His actions change in relation to Him and in accordance with His knowledge. All the more so as He himself does not change and inasmuch as His attributes are naught [else] but His essence, [also] His attributes do not change.[575] And the change that is thought by us that is found in our world is not a change in His operation, blessed be He, but [only] the revolution of the sphere. And the revolution of the sphere is not a change in the substance of the sphere, not in general and not in particular."[576]

This categorical denial of changes when related to divine attributes, or to their relation to God, which fits Abulafia's more general metaphysical stances about the immutability of God and of the "separate" cosmic intellects, even of the supra-lunar world, is far from being an isolated discussion, and should serve as the cornerstone for understanding his other discussions of attributes.[577] So, for example, we read in an untitled treatise authored by the ecstatic Kabbalist:

575 Compare to *Perush Sefer Yetzirah*, ed. Weinstock, p. 19, where he speaks about the eternity of the genera.

576 *Ḥayyei ha-Nefesh*, p. 72:

הסוד היה לשעבר, כאשר הוה עתה, וכאשר יהיה לעתיד בלא שנוי, שאין דבר ממעשיו משתנה אצל עצמו ולפי דעתו, כל שכן שלא ישתנה הוא בעצמו וגם אחר שאין מדותיו אלא עצמו לא ישתנו מדותיו. והשנוי הנחשב אצלנו שהוא נמצא בעולמנו, אינו שינוי אצל פעולתו יתע׳ כי אם גלגול הגלגל. וגלגול הגלגל אינו שנוי בעצם הגלגל, לא בכלל ולא בפרט.

See also Wolfson, "Kenotic Overflow and Temporal Transcendence," p. 187. This denial of change even in the substance of the sphere, despite its motion, should be compared to a passage from *'Or ha-Sekhel*, p. 29, and see Wolfson's quite different interpretation, ibidem, p. 187.

577 See also, e.g., *Mafteaḥ ha-Ra'yon*, p. 5, and the passage from *Sitrei Torah*, p. 111, to be discussed below.

> "And you should not think that I believe that the separate intellects are under the hands of man,[578] since this is impossible to say and [even] to address it in one's thought at all, but when he changes the nature, the world is delivered under man's hands."[579]

Equally explicit is a passage found in one of the earliest books of the ecstatic Kabbalist, who wrote: "It is totally impossible that changes will occur in the separate intellects."[580] Elsewhere he wrote: "You should know in truth that the attributes change at fixed dates, without change and shift, [but] because of the rule of the creatures. But the change is in the causatum not in the cause, because of the necessity of the entities."[581] Nota bene: Abulafia uses the term *middot* but in

578 I assume that the term "man" covers here both Jews and gentiles. Like in many other cases, Abulafia does not create a stark difference between Jews and gentiles, provided his universalist approach, that transformed the Jews or Israel into allegories of intellectual powers or processes. See also my "The Pearl, the Son and the Servants," and *Abraham Abulafia's Esotericism*, pp. 125–142. Compare, however, Wolfson's general view of Abulafia's thought as if particularist in his *Venturing Beyond Law*, p. 72, and Sagerman, *The Serpent Kills*, pp. 54, 68.

579 Untitled Treatise, Ms. Firenze-Laurenziana Plut. 11, 48, fol. 83b:

ואל תסבור שאני מאמין שהשכלים הנפרדים תחת יד האדם כי זה לא יתכן לאומרו ולא להעלותו על הלב כלל אמנם כשהוא משנה הטבע העולם המתנהג תחת ידם נמסר לאדם.

For Abulafia's authorship of this treatise see my "A Unique Manuscript of an Untitled Treatise of Abraham Abulafia in Biblioteca Laurenziana Medicea," *Kabbalah*, vol. 17 (2008), pp. 7–28, a text published meanwhile by Ohad Turjeman, under the title *Pardes ha-Sefar*, (Jerusalem, 2018), p. 63. See also Abulafia's discussion of the 'measures of the world" – namely, מדות העולם when dealing with a variety of units of time. See his *Sefer ha-Hesheq*, p. 70.

580 See *Mafteaḥ ha-Ra'yon*, p. 5: כי לא ימצא שינוי בשכלים הנפרדים כלל Compare the quite different approach in Nahmanides' school as, e.g., formulated in the passage quoted in n. 377 above.

581 "Sheva 'Netivot ha-Torah," p. 25:

דע באמת שהמדות מתהפכות לקיצים ידועים בלי שנוי ותמורה מפני הנהגת הנבראים. והשנוי הוא לנפעל לא לפועל מצד הכרח ענין הנמצאים

See also *Sefer ha-Ḥesheq*, p. 28.

his nomenclature they do not stand necessarily for divine attributes. Those denials of changes means at the same time that theurgy as understood in the previous chapters should not constitute the clue for attempting to understand the meaning of התהפכות המידות namely the inversion of the attributes, a phrase that E. Wolfson understands it as fraught with theurgical valence.[582] To judge from the subtitle of his book on Abulafia and its content, the ecstatic Kabbalist was substantially concerned with both theurgy and theosophy. Though he was aware of one of the texts where such a phrase is allegorized,[583] Wolfson assumes that there is just a tension between two views excluding, implicitly, the possibility that Abulafia had a basic conceptual approach that negates theurgy in principle. Moreover, some of the quotes adduced above and their possible implications have not been discussed at all in his treatment of Abulafia's alleged theurgy. Theosophy, like theurgy, has been allegorized, as Abulafia does even to names of the towns he lived in, in order to extract a meaning that is totally divorced from the original term and its context.

However, provided the explicit cases of negation of the change in the intellectual world, including the divine attributes, as adduced above, the question can be asked: what was, after all, Abulafia's view as to the nature of those attributes and the claim of their inversion. In a seminal passage from his *Sefer ha-Melammed* written in 1276,[584] we read that:

> "It is known that these two attributes are changed always in accordance to the nature of creation, into each other. And the secret is that the attribute of compassion is always prevailing, because the numerical value of *YHVH* is 26 while that of the name *'Elohim* is 86, namely when someone will add 86 to 26, and when someone will write 26 in its *plene* form, *kaf vav*, the concealed [name of] 86 under the name of 26 will be found. This means that the attribute

582 *Abraham Abulafia*, pp. 82–83, 172–173 and n. 21. See also Sagerman, *The Serpent Kills*, p. 186 n. 26, 210.

583 Ibidem, p. 175.

584 On this treatise see my *Abraham Abulafia's Works and Doctrines*, pp. 15–16.

> of judgment is concealed while that of compassion is revealed. Both are, however, 26, which means that these two attributes are [or constitute] but one attribute."[585]

Prima facie, Abulafia refers to a sort of Rabbinic discussion similar to what I described in model [E]. However, the theurgical aspect of this model is obliterated as he mentions the "creation" as related to the change of the attribute and not human acts. The change is interpreted by means of a linguistic technique: the attribute of compassion is related to the Tetragrammaton, which amounts in gematria to 26, in Hebrew letters כו referring to the attribute of compassion. The plene spelling of these two letters is כף וו which are understood as constituting two linguistic units: כו and פו. The second unit amounts in gematria to 86, like the name *'Elohim,* that is related to the attribute of judgment. In other words, the attribute of compassion, or the Tetragrammaton when it is written in a plene manner as mentioned above, includes also the name of the attribute of judgment.

Therefore, though Abulafia spoke first about two different attributes, they are considered in fact as being only one, which manifests itself in different forms in accordance to the preparation of the recipients. Opposite, or even diametrically opposite as the two attributes are in Rabbinic literature, in his views they do not exist as separate or unrelated. The attributes are, according to this Kabbalist, therefore not two independent powers, but actually only one, whose different acts are revealed in an alternating manner, depending on the different preparations of the lower beings. These different results are not related to a complexity of opposites as found within each divine power as we

585 Ms. Paris, Biblioteque Nationale 680, fol. 308a. See also above the quote from the *Commentary on Sefer 'Ish 'Adam,* where the oneness of the *middot* is mentioned. See also the Abulafian treatise *Sefer ha-Marde'a,* Ms. Oxford-Bodleiana 1649, fol. 204a, where he uses the letter *KW PW* in order to refer to the two *middot.* See also the passage of Joseph Gikatilla's *Ginnat 'Egoz,* as analyzed by Morlok, *Rabbi Joseph Gikatilla's Hermeneutics,* p. 65 where, however, the *middot* are not mentioned.

have seen especially in R. Asher ben David, R. Azriel and Pseudo-R. Isaac the Blind.

However, the question is if indeed there is a change on high, that takes place in history, or in time, or if this change is a matter of how the Kabbalist understands a certain situation, by using the linguistic techniques. Let me turn to another discussion of the "inversion of the attributes." In one of his most important books, *'Or ha-Sekhel*, he writes:

> "Behold you already found that from the [plene spelling] of *Yah MaLe', YHWH 'Elohim* emerge. And this is the meaning of the "inversion of the attributes" since YHWH is the attribute of compassion but 'Elohim is the attribute of judgment, since 'Elohim is judge."[586]

Here the shift of the *middot* is described explicitly as related to numerical calculations alone: *YH* when written in a plene manner, *YWD H'* amounts to 26, like the Tetragrammaton. The syntagm *YH ML'* – which means literally *YH* written in a plene manner – however amounts in gematria to 86, like *'Elohim*. Moreover, the addition of 26 to 86 amounts to 112 while *HPWKh* – namely inversed – = 111. This means that inversion, or *hippukh*, is related to the operations connected to the numerical values of the divine names, not essential changes in the activity of the two attributes. In both cases, the inclusion of the attribute of judgment within that of compassion represents a major Kabbalistic claim, thus obliterating the theological innovation of the Rabbis concerning the existence of two separate attributes that operate by acting at the same time, as it is the case of Rabbinic model [B], or a coexistence of the two attributes according to model [D].

This is also the case in one of Abulafia's commentaries on the secrets allegedly found in Maimonides' *Guide of the Perplexed*:

586 P. 83:
והנה כבר מצאת שיצאו מן י״ה מלא יהו״ה אלהים, והוא הוראת הפוך המדות, כי יהו״ה מדת רחמים, אבל אלהי״ם מדת הדין, כי אלהים הוא דיין.

"The issue of the instruction as to the transformation of the sphere of the attributes,[587] namely the transformation of the attribute of punishment in its entirety, to the extremity of its degree, and the height of its existence, into the attribute of compassion that determines redemption and true and complete salvation. And on this issue the beginning of the mission of the angel to the prophet is "the angel of YHWH" and it is called "YHWH is 'Elohim," as it is written [Exodus 3:2]: "And the angel [of] YHWH revealed to him in the flame of fire out of the midst of the bush." And this is the flame of YH that is born out of perfect love."[588]

Here again Abulafia's approach assumes a complete metanoia of the attribute of judgment into that of compassion, predicated on an exegetical move: the angel – in Hebrew *mal'akh* – equals 91 in gematria, like *ha-'Elohim*. It appears first in the verse, and then the occurrence of the Tetragrammaton is interpreted as the result of the transformation. This means that there is no cooperation between two attributes, but there is only one type of activity alone that alternates in one of its dimension or the other, though this is quite a nominalistic approach depending on the reception or preparation of the lower beings. The attributes are conceived of as exclusive of each other. Extremely important for the understanding of the ecstatic Kabbalist is the redemptive significance of this transformation that has put in relief an important issue to be discussed in more details below.

How do those transformations of the attributes fit the assumption as to the immutability of God? *Prima facie* there is here a deep contradiction between these two attitudes. In the scholarship about this topic the assumption is that Abulafia's writings reflect both theosophical and theurgical elements, ignoring thereby the more general statements

587 Compare below the passage translated from *Ḥayyei ha-'Olam ha-Ba'*, pp. 64–65.

588 *Ḥayyei ha-Nefesh*, p. 62:

והעניין הוראת הפוך גלגל המדות כלומר שוב מדת הדין בשלמותה ובתכלית מעלתה ובגבהות מציאותה אל מדת רחמים הגוזרת גאולה וישועה אמיתית שלימה. ובא על זה תחילה שליחות מלאך לנביא הוא מלאך יי' והוא נקרא יי' והוא אלהי"ם. ככתוב "וירא מלאך יהוה אליו בלבת אש מתוך הסנה. והיא שלהבת י"ה הנולדת מאהבה שלימה.

adduced above about divine immutability.[589] In fact, the scholarly theory of the ontological existence of the two attributes on high is part of a larger view attributed to Abulafia, as to the existence of an alleged bipartite vision of the nature of the Agent Intellect, as claimed by Elliot R. Wolfson and, following him, also Robert J. Sagerman.[590] Though the latter kindly attributes this view also to me, as if I was one of the first who allegedly pointed out to this phenomenon, I must confess that this is a very weird understanding of what I actually wrote insofar as Abulafia's thought is concerned.[591]

In my opinion, some of the Abulafian texts adduced to substantiate the so-called bipartite structure of the Agent Intellect, may be much better understood not by resorting to a complex theosophical approach designated as integration of opposites, but by a philosophical assumption that the same supernal body, like the sun, for example, may have two different effects, in accordance to the preparation of the recipients.[592] In any case, this philosophical view, (which he most probably found in Maimonides' *Guide*), is adduced explicitly by Abulafia in one of his epistles.[593] He applies it to the theory of

589 See especially Wolfson, *Abraham Abulafia*.

590 See Wolfson, ibidem, pp. 155–156, pp. 172–173 note n. 12, and Sagerman, *The Serpent That Kills*, pp. 265, 361 where he calls the bipartite theory a "prevalent thesis" in Abulafia's writings.

591 Sagerman, ibidem, pp. 107–108 and n. 3. Nowhere in the two studies of mine referred to there, or elsewhere; to my best knowledge, I insinuated the existence of such a vision in Abulafia's own thought. Neither is the reference to Scholem indeed supporting such a view. This "prevalent thesis" constitutes hardly a hypothesis to be examined.

592 Maimonides, *The Guide of the Perplexed* 1:53. See also R. Baḥya ben Asher, *Commentary on the Torah*, Leviticus 26:1, ed. Ch.D. Chavel, (Jerusalem, 1967), vol. II, p. 572, *Ma'arekhet ha-'Elohut*, chapter 2, R. Meir ibn Gabbai, *'Avodat ha-Qodesh*, 1:12. Compare also the full and corrected text, different from what was adduced by Wolfson, *Abraham Abulafia*, pp. 172–173 note 213, from Abulafia's *Sefer ha-Melitz*, as it has been printed in ed. Gross, pp. 28–29.

593 See "Sheva' Netivot ha-Torah," p. 8. For another philosophical description of the polarity in the intellectual realm as a matter of the recipients on low, see also in *Sitrei Torah*, pp. 58–59. Compare, however, the resort to alchemical

divine attributes, whose multiplicity is explained as depending on the recipients, not on a duality or multiplicity within the supernal source, as he claims in one of his major writings:

> "This secret comprises, in accordance to thought of the soul, the *Ḥokhmah*, and the *Binah* and the *Da'at*, since the Wisdom of God is His Understanding and His Knowledge, and His Understanding is His Wisdom and His Knowledge, and His Knowledge is His Wisdom and His Understanding, since none of them is [found] without the others,[594] but the Names were witnessing and teaching us that all the matters of God are not in addition to God but they are the essence of God. And even what appears that He has attributes [*te'arim*] and measures [*middot*] that change, [it is] in accordance to the recipients that refers to composition, or on plurality or on change, this is [however] not so with Him, blessed be He, but with us they are so because of the shortage of our wisdom, and accordance to our scant understanding and the deficiency of our knowledge since our intellect was not perfected such perfection that we shall comprehend this divine matter as it is."[595]

Let me emphasize the paramount importance of the syntagm "in accordance to the recipients" for understanding the approach of the

material in order to substantiate Wolfson's claim "Kenotic Overflow and Temporal Transcendence," pp. 155 n. 84, as to the bipartite nature of the Agent Intellect. Needless to say, I prefer Maimonides's book as a much more plausible and authoritative source for Abulafia's thought.

594 Compare also to Abulafia's commentary to his prophetic *Sefer ha-Melitz*, p. 8.

595 *'Imrei Shefer*, p. 71:

וזה הסוד כולל לפי מחשבת הנפש החכמה והבינה והדעת, כי חכמת השם היא בינתו והיא דעתו ובינתו היא דעתו והיא חכמתו דעתו היא חכמתו והיא בינתו. ואין זו זולת זו והיו השמות מעידים ומודים ומעידים ומורים לנו שכל ענייני השם אינם נוספים על השם. אבל הם עצם השם ואפי׳ מה שנראים לו תארים או מידות מתחלפות לפי המקבלים אשר יורו על הרכבה או על ריבוי או על שנוי אינם אצלו יתב׳ כן. אבל אצלנו הם כן לפי קצור חכמתנו ולפי מיעוט בינתנו ולפי חסרון דעתנו. כי לא נשלם שכלנו שלמות שנשיג זה העניין האלהי כאשר הוא.

See also ibidem, p. 128, in a passage to be discussed immediately below.

ecstatic Kabbalist. This is a well-known theme in Jewish medieval thought of philosophical extraction – though its formulations differ slightly from time to time – which conveys the relativity of the human perceptions of the unchanged divine action, that is based on the differences existing solely below, but not in the higher realm.[596] In some cases this theme reflects an impact of astrology.[597] This is the case also elsewhere in another book of Abulafia's:

> "I have hinted by means of sublime hints concerning the issue that emanates from God, Blessed be He, and how that influx is emanated in accordance to the path of legality and justice and many other attributes that operate in accordance to that influx onto the one selected, that comes from Him, blessed be He, that changes in accordance to the recipients, not in accordance to His influx, as the Rabbi [Maimonides][598] allegorized concerning the attributes of fire, and the recipients in the vast majority receive the changes of the influx, as it is the matter of water that satiates several kinds of animals, and the satiation differs in each of them, and the recipents change in according to it."[599]

596 See, e.g., *'Or ha-Sekhel*, p. 29, *Shomer Mitzwah*, pp. 26, 27, 114.

597 See, e.g., R. Abraham ibn Ezra's Commentary on Exodus 18:25, and Deuteronomy 31:16, or R. Baḥya ben Asher, Commentary on Exodus 3:13, and on Numbers 23:4. See aso his discussion in his *Kad ha-Qemah*, p. 446: "This is the explanation: since the one who does those things [dons *tefillin*], draws upon himself the supernal attributes [*middot*], as one who brings an offering." See also his interesting phrase סדור המדות – the order of the attributes, ibidem, p. 350.

598 *Guide of the Perplexed* 1:53, tr. Pines, vol. 1, p. 120. For other occurrences of Maimonides' discussion in Abulafia's milieu see Gottlieb, *Studies in Kabbalah Literature*, p. 115.

599 *Sitrei Torah*, p. 111:

רמזתי רמזים מעולים בעניין השופע מהשם ית׳ ואיך השפע ההוא נשפע על דרך משפט וצדקה ומדות רבות אחרות פועלות על פי השפע ההוא באחד המיוחד הבא מאתו ית׳ שמשתנה לפי המקבלים לא לפי שפעו כאשר המשיל הרב בתארי האש והמקבלים לפי רוב שנויים קבלו השפע בשינויים כעניין דמות המים המרוים כמה מינים מבעלי חיים, והריווי משונה בהם, והמקבלים נשתנו בעדו.

This means that while on high, within God, and in each of the spiritual entities including the Agent Intellect, there is no duality or polarity at all; the impact of the supernal entity here below, is conditioned by the different constitution of lower entities, which receive it in different ways. Abulafia should be better understood by assuming a functional, rather than structural, differentiation in a hypostatic entity. The differentiation is, however, the result of the defficient human intellect. In according to this passage, the assumption as to the independent of existence of attributes is wrong and the significant center of the speculations should be the divine names, especially the combinations of their consonants and their gematrias.[600] This is the case also in another important discussion of attributes found in Abulafia's *Commentary on the Genesis*:

> "Indeed, every Kabbalist will invoke the Name in all places[601] it occurs, as instructed by means of any of the divine attributes, because this is true and right; and this is the reason why it is necessary to inquire into names and to know about each and every one of them to what attribute it points, because the attributes change in accordance with each and every topic. And it is known that God does not possess at all attributes that will change from one to another, but that the attributes change in accordance with the nature of the creatures that are necessarily emanated from them."[602]

Again, the recipients, represented here by the creatures, are the reason for a change, but the Kabbalist denies the change in the divine attributes. In my opinion, it would be more plausible to adopt another approach since a reading of the transformation or inversion of the

600 See, e.g., *Mafteaḥ ha-Shemot*, p. 56:
רחם בדין דין ברחם... כל שדי רחמים בדין דין ברחמים. וידעתי שדי לך בידיעה זו שגיליתי לך סוד שתוף הכחות במדות.

601 Compare to Exodus 20:21.

602 *Mafteaḥ ha-Ḥokhmot*, Ms. Moscow-Ginzburg 133, fols. 23b–24a, discussed also in my *Kabbalah in Italy*, p. 71.

attributes does not deal with divine attributes but with human perceptions related to human development.[603] Unlike the realist understanding of the two attributes as powers having an independent status in relation to the divine, in my opinon, Abulafia's view is nominalistic.

Interestingly enough, in one passage Abulafia describes the status of the Agent Intellect, a cosmic power that plays a central role in his religiosity, as the "fount of reward and punishment".[604] Unlike the split found in the *'Iyyun* literature, or the emergence of the opposites as the result of a double emanation stemming from one source, which produces two springs, here there is one spring alone that emanates a homogenous stream of intellectual overflow that is perceived differently by different recipients. This is also the case elsewhere:

"You should know in truth that the blessing and the curse, good and evil, and life and death, are dependent on the explicit Name. Those three attributes are found from God, blessed be He, and always they come and they are the good, and the blessing and the life, the Torah is replete of them and they are the promises that prophets always promised to those that walk in the ways of God. And behold, the three negations that correspond to them have no existence but in the calling of the names alone, and they are evil, and curse and death, and they are not found but in thought [alone]."[605]

This is a rather Parmenidean or Neoplatonic understanding that assumes that only the existence exists, while negations have names and can be conceptualized in thought, but nevertheless they have no

603 Compare to Sagerman, *The Serpent Kills*, p. 159, who assumes the existence of the attribute of judgment as an entity external to the humans in Abulafia.

604 p. 165, and Ms. Paris, Biblioteque Nationale 774, fol. 164b.

605 *'Imrei Shefer*, p. 128:

תדע באמת כי נתלו על השם המפורש הברכה והקללה והטוב והרע והחיים והמות ואל שלש מדות נמצאות מהשם ית' תמיד באות. והן הטוב והברכה והחיים והתורה מלאה מהם והם הייעודים שיעדום הנביאים תמיד להולכים בדרכי השם. והנה שלשת ההעררים שכנגדם אין להם מציאות כי אם בכנוי שמות בלבד והם הרע והקללה והמות ואינם נמצאים כי אם במחשבה.

ontological status. Unlike the duality of the Rabbinic and theosophical-theurgical Kabbalistic theories as to the two divine attributes, here the negative counterpart is considered to be inexistent, as some form of meontology.[606] As such there is no possibility to have a change on high, in the vein that the Rabbinic and Kabbalistic theories indicate. Though there are instances where he seems to have another stance, related to the divine attributes and individual providence, I propose to understand this as an exoteric way of speaking, different from his esoteric view that is represented by the earlier passages:[607]

> "You should know that in a person there are three issues that are created by three matrices *'MSh* that are combined with the *YHW*, and they are the angels of fire, and wind, and water... and fire is the scale of guilt, and water is the scale of acquittal, and the wind is preponderating between them.[608] And the higher *middah* is hard, and the lower is soft, and so too, the opposites of the *middot* in accordance to Kabbalah, and this will teach you how to rotate the wisdom of the attributes of the Name.[609]"[610]

I translated the Hebrew form "attributes of the Name" as I did, since the letters of the Tetragrammaton have been mentioned earlier, *YHW*,

606 See also the untitled treatise found in Ms. Firenze-Laurenziana, Plut. 11 48, fol. 74a. In general, it should be emphasized that Abulafia did not believe in the existence of external demons, which are for him solely figments of human imagination. See his *Mafteaḥ ha-Ra'yon*, p. 5, *'Otzar 'Eden Ganuz*, p. 56, or *Mafteaḥ ha-Sefirot*, p. 90. Compare, however, to Sagerman, *The Serpent Kills*, p. 159.
607 See, e.g., *Mafteaḥ ha-Sefirot*, p. 52. On the two ways of writing in Abulafia, see Idel, "The Pearl, the Son and the Servants," and my *Abraham Abulafia's Esotericism*, especially pp. 167–168.
608 Cf. *Sefer Yetzirah* ed. Hayman, par. 23 p. 50.
609 Or of God.
610 *Ḥayyei ha-'Olam ha-Ba'*, pp. 64–65:
דע כי יש באדם ג׳ עניינים נבראים בג׳ אמות אמ״ש מצורפות עם יה״ו והם מלאכי אש ורוח ומים... והאש כף חובה והמים כף זכות והרוח מכריע בינתיים. ומידה של מעלה קשה ושל מטה רפה וכן הפכי המידות כפי הקבלה ויודעך לגלגל חכמת מידות השם.

in the context of permulations. The wisdom of the attributes in the context of rotation, most probably of a wheel or a circle, is reminiscent of Abulafia's conception of his Kabbalah as a form of superior form of knowledge, an inner, higher logic based on combinations of letters.[611] On the other hand, the rotation of divine attributes is also reminiscent of Ramon Lull's use of concentric circles where letters pointing to divine attributes, *dignitates*, are found.[612] In any case the circles were described, following *Sefer Yetzirah*, as moving back and forth, sometime described as inversion.[613]

While for a mythical vision of invertion of attributes from one another the result is univocal, and a matter of one type of activity, for Abulafia inversion is conceived of as a process that goes on on many phases, like his view of permutation of letters as an ongoing practice. This permutation is conceived of as worship of God:

> "One should circumcise his heart in order to understand the secrets of the revolution of letters and their inversion, for the sake of worship of God, blessed be He, alone, and he always recites them. This is the man that adheres to God alone. This is the reason why you should understand that the inversion of letters is the essence of every creature and speech.[614]"[615]

611 See M. Idel, "Ramon Lull and Ecstatic Kabbalah," *Journal of the Warburg and Courtauld Institutes*, vol. 51 (1988), pp. 170–174, and Hames, *The Art of Conversion*, pp. 122–124. See also below chapter 10. See now Saverio Campanini, 'Una fonte trascurata sul rapporto tra *qabbalah* e combinatoria lulliana in Pico della Mirandola: il commento alle preghiere di Yehudah Ibn Malka', *Studia Lulliana*, vol. 55 (2015), pp. 83–127.

612 See M. Idel, "*Dignitates* and *Kavod*: Two Theological Concepts in Catalan Mysticism," *Studia Lulliana*, vol. 36 (1996), pp. 69–78.

613 See *Commentary on 'Ish 'Adam*, p. 49: וגילו סתרי גלגל בהפכו

614 Cf. *Sefer Yetzirah*, ed. Hayman, p. 100 no. 19.

615 *Hayyei ha-'Olam ha-Ba'* third edition, p. 34:
מל את לבבו להבין סודות גילגול האותיות והפוכם לשם עבודת ה׳ ית״ש לבדו ומדבר בם תמיד. הוא האיש הדבק בה׳ לבדו על כן תבין כי היפך האותיות הוא אמיתות כל יצור וכל הדיבור.

Abulafia writes under the impact of the Rabbinic statement that encourages the ongoing study of the Torah, by using the verb *HPKh*, הפוך בה והפוך בה, which means in the original context to turn the Torah continuously, but in Abulafia's interpretation it refers to the ungoing permutation of the letters of the Torah.[616]

However, what is even more important is the main purpose of Abulafia's Kabbalah. According to his views, it is solely the human spiritual evolution that counts, since only the inner human changes are relevant as there is no change in the divine realm on high. Let me turn to a passage found in another commentary on the secrets of the *Guide of the Perplexed*:

> "When you shall know within yourself that you have been perfected in the knowledge of those attributes, which witness to the form of the power of imagination and the truth of its essence in you, and when you will know that you have achieved perfection in knowledge of the attributes of the Name by which the world is always governed, and let your mind pursue your intellect to imitate it according to your ability, always, and you shall know with your intellect that you have obliterated the powers within you that are superfluous, and your entire intention is [solely] for the sake of heaven."[617]

The center of attention shifts dramatically from the intra-divine powers in theosophical-theurgical Kabbalah to the extra-divine ones: the cosmic and the human ones: the manner in which the world is governed on the one hand, and the imagination and the intellect on

616 See my *Absorbing Perfections*, pp. 439–441.

617 *Sitrei Torah*, pp. 138–139, Ms. Paris BN 774, fol. 155a:

בעת שתדע בעצמך שנשלמת בשלמות המדות הטובות המעידות על צורת הכח המדמה ועל אמיתת מהותו אצלך, ותדע שנשלמת בידיעת מדות השם הידועות שבהם העולם מתנהג תמיד ותרדוף דעתך אחר שכלך להדמות לו בהם כפי יכולתך תמיד, ותכיר בשכלך שכבר בטלת הכוחות הנקראות מותרות ממך וכל כוונתך לשם שמים .

See also Idel, *The Mystical Experience*, pp. 119–120, 162 n. 171, and compare to Sagerman, *The Serpent Kills*, p. 166.

the other hand. Here, God is actually less relevant since the attributes of the divine Name that are conceived of as ruling over the world namely in the vein of philosophical types of speculations. In my opinion, Abulafia relates the attributes to imagination because of a pun: *Middot – demut – dimyon,* which mean that the attributes are related to *demut,* interpreted in many cases in his writings with imagination.[618] The first two Hebrew terms are compounded from exactly the same consonants. Interestingly enough, in one case Abulafia speaks about *Demut 'Adam* as *hem middot* as amounting to 495.[619] This is done in the context of a recurring triad Angel, Adam, Satan, and the median place of Adam shows that the *middot* are not the highest possible value. In any case, it is implausible to assume that according to Abulafia there is an intrinsically demonic dimension of the influx descending from the Agent Intellect.[620] The demonic impact is solely the result of the inferior nature of the recipient, just as the intellectual dimension is determined by the intellectual capacity of the human person.

Let me turn to Abulafia's interpretation of theosophical symbolism related to the divine attributes:

> "There are two attributes, truth and fear, the former comprises the knowledge of God that is the knowledge of truth, and the latter comprises the fear of God that is the attribute of fear. And behold, after you will conceptualize the two extremities mentioned insofar as faith is concerned, that are not dependent on deeds, you should conceptualize that the Torah is median [*'emtza'it*][621] between the two, just as the study of the Torah announced to you the path of

618 See e.g., Idel, *Absorbing Perfections,* pp. 442, 444.

619 *Mafteaḥ ha-Tokhehot,* p. 120. Compare also to the similar pun in his epistle *Matzref la-Kesef,* ed. A. Gross, (Jerusalem, 2001), p. 6.

620 Compare Sagerman, *The Serpent Kills,* p. 166.

621 See also a very similar discussion in R. Nathan's book, *Le porte della giustizia,* p. 462, where the term *'Emtza'it,* refers to the third attribute, is depicted again between two divine attributes, in the context of the occurrence of the form תורה. However, it is possible that this form may be understood as *toreh,* namely as referring to the third, and not as *Torah.*

> the appropriate deeds that you should walk on it, and the path of the inappropriate ones that you should stray away from them.[622] And provided that all the commandments are following faith, they amount in gematria[623] to 'the knowledge of God.'"[624]

It is obvious that the gematria of 611 is again implied but not explicated. And again the Torah is mentioned after a series of pairs: the two attributes of truth and fear, and knowledge of God and fear of God. It is plausible that the attribute of truth corresponds to the intellectual sense in the passage from *Get ha-Shemot*, and by default, the attribute of fear to that of sensual realm. As Warren Zev Harvey pointed out to me, these pairs correspond to the first two commandments, reducing the 613 to 611 standing in the middle.

However, in this passage the terminology points in an obvious manner to theosophical imagery, especially when the attribute of fear, expressed by the Hebrew *Paḥad*, is used. In the common theosophical

622 See also below the passage from *Shomer Mitzwah*, p. 37.

623 This is a widespread calculation of the number of the commandments 613, from the numerical valences of words in Exodus 3:15 mentioning the divine name – *shemi* – and the rememberance of God *zikhri* and letters of divine name, as mentioned by Abulafia immediately afterwards on the same page.

624 *'Or ha-Sekhel*, p. 20:

והם ב׳ מדות אמת ופחד, האחת כוללת ידיעת השם שהיא מדת האמת, והשנית כוללת יראת השם שהיא מדת הפחד. והנה אחר שתצייר שתי הקצוות הנזכרות באמונה אשר לא נתלו במעשים, תצייר היות תורה אמצעית בין שתיהם, מפני שתלמוד תורה מודיעך דרך המעשים ההגונים שתלך בה, ודרך המגונים שתתרחק מהם. ומפני היות כל המצות נמשכות אחר האמונה, עלו כן במספר שווה לידיעת השם.

On the possible relation of the median role of the Torah and the Aristotelian and Maimonidean concept of Golden Mean, see my *Language, Torah and Hermeneutics*, p. 165 n. 47. For this theory in general see Marvin Fox, "The Doctrine of the Mean in Aristotle and Maimonides: A Comparative Study," in eds. S. Stein – R. Loewe, *Studies in Religious and Intellectual History Presented to Alexander Altmann on the Occasion of His 70th Birthday* (University of Atlanta Press, University, Atlanta, 1979), pp. 98–120, rpr. in his *Interpreting Maimonides*, pp. 93–123, and Herbert A. Davidson, "The Middle Way in Maimonides' Ethics," *PAAJR* vol. 54 (1987), pp. 31–72.

scheme, the attribute of *Paḥad* is found on the left side, while that of truth, *'Emmet*, is found in the middle between two "higher" attributes, corresponding to Jacob, just as *Paḥad* corresponds to Isaac, as it is mentioned before the quoted passage. However, here it is obvious that the attribute of truth is conceptualized as opposite of that of fear and thus it is found on the right side, while the Torah stands in the middle, between the two "higher" attributes. This is an uncommon type of symbolism, some aspects of which will be discussed in chapter 10 below. Also this understanding of the Torah as a median entity may reflect a theosophical view that identified the Torah with the *sefirah* of *Tiferet* that stands in the middle of the two other divine powers. This seems to be the meaning of the median place of the Torah here. Interestingly enough, truth and fear are not conceived of as conducive to deeds, a quality reserved solely to the Torah.

What is shared by the last two quotes is the common status of the Torah as a median entity, which is expressed by using different forms of imagery, philosophical, and theosophical. An important question should be asked in this context: what do we understand from Abulafia's use of theosophical imagery? Is there a structural homology between the triad of divine attributes, and the human feelings, which means that Abulafia believed in the first triad as a blueprint for the second, human triad within the lower world, or alternatively, does the Kabbalist interpret allegorically, what he conceives to be an *imaginaire* found in a theosophical literature that he did not accept its conceptual basis? Given the fact that his main concern, as seen above, was the median place of the Torah, that is illustrated by a variety of examples from other realms: two trees in the Paradise, the intellectual and the sensual, the knowledge of God – which means also the love of God – and the fear of God, which implicitly does not assume knowledge, we may try to extrapolate from these examples as to his major interest.

Someone may read the homologies as having some form of sympathetic affinities between distinct pairs of entities, affinities that would include both a theosophical and a potentially theurgical valence – in a manner reminiscent of Mircea Eliade's magical universe,[625] while

625 See Eliade, "The Cosmical Homology and Yoga," *Journal of the Indian Society*

another reading would see the homology as just rhetorical, or just analogous structures, and assume the existence of one basic pair that is found within the human being, which is the basis of the allegorization of the meaning of the other pairs, some of them of cosmic nature. That parallelism between different triads does not mean, according to such a reading, that there is a sympathetic or theurgical affinity between them, we may learn from a lengthy passage from *'Otzar 'Eden Ganuz.*[626]

I propose to adopt the second interpretation, since Abulafia is repeatedly speaking about the need to free, namely to unknot the intellectual element from its immersion within the material realm, this being one of the targets of his techniques. It is not a harmonious universe that the ecstatic Kabbalist inhabits but one based on a deep dualism that distinguishes between the intellect, on the one hand, and matter, imagination or desires, on the other, a disjunctive approach also true insofar as his anthropology was concerned. This is the reason why he is less interested in learning about the divinity from the divine acts, or natural phenomena, as philosophers do, but from divine names, which provided a shorter access.[627] To be sure: this is much more a Platonic type of dualism than a Gnostic one.

This second reading means that for Abulafia taking literally the imagery of the divine attributes would be a misunderstanding, since, as he put it once, God has no attributes, but solely what we do attribute to Him in order to understand Him.[628] According to another statement, probably stemming from Ismailiah sources, though found also among other Kabbalists,[629] God cannot be described as being or even

of Oriental Art, vol. v, (1937/1938), pp. 188–203. Neither do I believe that for Abulafia the noetic awakening of the individual has an effect on the external universe, in the manner that Eliade describes as the principle of meaning of homology in some Yoga practices, as he articulated it in his *Yoga, Immortality and Freedom*, (Princeton University Press, Princeton, 1971), pp. 108, 251–252, 254–255, 341. See also Idel, *Mircea Eliade: From Magic to Myth*, pp. 4–14.

626 See pp. 199–200, translated in Wolfson, *Venturing Beyond*, pp. 71–72.

627 See, e.g., *'Or ha-Sekhel*, pp. 108–109, and "Sheva' Netivot ha-Torah," pp. 14–15.

628 See *Shomer Mitzwah*, p. 42.

629 See Idel, *Old Worlds, New Mirrors*, pp. 163, 288 n. 22.

not as non-being.[630] The dyadic opposition of attributes is important not for conveying his theosophy but only in order to understand the special status of the Torah as standing in the middle. According to an additional source, the Torah is conceived of as median between God and man, again another instance of mediation.[631] However, what is crucial in this status of the Torah as occupying a median position is explicated in another passage from the same book, where the approach in the last two passages finds an explanation.

Let me turn to a complex discussion of the meanings of the *middot*. Without expressly saying it, Abulafia surveys three meanings of this term in one passage:

> "[a] And many of the attributes[632] are synonymous, and they are all called and comprised in the attribute of compassion. [b] Every perfect Kabbalist should know the secrets of the *middot*, and their rules and their laws, since they are the essence and the root of all the sciences. [c] And it is impossible for the illuminati to know the *middot* according to their quintessence but by means of his knowledge of the commandments found in the Torah, since the commandments were not promulgated but for the purpose of purifying the people.[633] And unless the issue of the *middot* we would not need the Torah, and without the issue of the Torah we would need no commandments that refer to the *middot*. And the Torah is something borne on the heart and imprinted on it with the thought, but the commandment depends on limbs."[634]

630 Ms. Oxford-Bodleiana 2047, fol. 68b and see also Wolfson, *Abraham Abulafia*, p. 161 n. 182.

631 *Sefer Gan Na'ul*, p. 2.

632 Abulafia mentions beforehand attributes like *shalom, 'emmet, tzedeq*, and the *Middah* of Pinehas and Elijah. Thus, they are forms of human acts rather than divine powers.

633 See, e.g., *Bereshit Rabbah'* 44:4.

634 *Shomer Mitzwah*, p. 37:

והרבה מהמדות משתתפות וכולם נקראים ונכללים בשם מדת רחמים. וצריך לכל מקובל שלם לדעת סתרי המדות ודינם ומשפטם, מפני שהם עיקר ושרש לכל החכמות והמדות

According to [a] *middah* means a specific concept, that *prima facie* is similar to the theosophical arrangements of many disparate terms under one category, as part of the process of reorganization of religious knowledge. However, it is also connected to the manner of behavior of some individuals, so that the theosophical meaning is less conspicuous, if at all. Then, the Kabbalist sees in measures the basis for sciences, according to [b]. It is in this context that, following Abraham ibn Ezra, Abulafia conceives the *sefirot* in many places in his writings, as another term for number, to be understood in a rather Pythagorean manner, as referring to the essence of reality.[635] According to one of his statements, the *sefirot* stand for the forms of the entity.[636]

However, most of the remainder of the quoted passage [c] deals with *middot* as referring to human modes of behavior, which are connected to the commandments. Interestingly enough, the Kabbalist distinguishes quite sharply between the commandments, that are organic acts, and Torah, that is a matter of thought. Thus the *middot* are corporeal acts that are shaped by the commandments, a view that is corroborated by the passage from *Sefer Ḥayyei ha-Nefesh*, pp. 81–82 to be quoted immediately below, where the attributes are expressly related to the attributes of compassion and judgment. So, for example, in his untitled treatise he recommends that one should:

> "Contemplate the secret of the shape of the letters within the phylacteries that are donned on the head [and] hand [sic]. The

לא יתכן שידעם המשכיל באמתתם כי אם בדעתו סתרי המצות שבתורה. כי לא נתנו המצוות אלא לצרף בהן את הבריות. ולולי עניין המדות לא הוצרכנו אל תורה, ולולי עניין התורה לא הוצרכנו אל המצוות שהן מורות על המדות. והתורה הוא עניין נשוא על הלב וחקוק בו עם המחשבה והמצוה תלויה על האיברים .

635 I assume that he refers to the concept of measure that is quintessential for the sciences. See also Abulafia's view of mathematics, *ḥeshbon*, as the basis for Kabbalah in *'Imrei Shefer*, a passage that has been discussed in Idel, "R. Menahem Mendel of Shklov and R. Avraham Abulafia," pp. 173–175 as well as its later influence. See also *'Otzar 'Eden Ganuz*, pp. 141–142. On a similar discussion of *ḥeshbon* in Gikatilla, see Morlok, *Rabbi Joseph Gikatilla's Hermeneutics*, p. 100.

636 See *Perush Sefer Yetzirah*, p. 26.

sign is Tefillah.[637] And you should find [the numerical valence of] my head and my hand [*Roshiy we-Yadiy*] where the commandments[638] are, and you will say: "the attribute of judgment is on my head[639] YHWH,[640] that is 'the attribute of compassion in [or on] my hand.'"[641]

Like in other cases, Abulafia creates new texts by amagramation of consonants and interprets the new texts.[642] This vision of the two attributes as related to limbs, though not to the heart, is characteristic of Abulafia's general attitude. Those human acts can be contradictory, and thus the acts related to them, as potentially dangerous:

"And whoever merits to realize the *sefirot* should be careful of the contradictory attributes unless he will die in the war of the urges, and the entire *Shemirah* depends on the entering the secret of every *sefirah* referring to the letters of creation, his entire mind should be [fixed] on the noble and numinous divine name, for the sake of heaven alone."[643]

One way of understanding this passage is to assume that within each of the *sefirot*, there are two opposite attributes, as seen above in the theosophical Kabbalah. However, this is not a contemplation of the powers that constitute the supernal structure, but much more part

637 *Tefillah* means here not prayer, as regular, but phylacteries. Its defective spelling, without a yod, amounts to 515 = ראש יד

638 541 = ראשי וידי = המצות

639 513= מדת הדין = בראשי Two times 513 = 1026, is reminiscent of YHWH = 26.

640 יהוה = 26 = בידי

641 Ms. Firenze-Laurenziana 11, 48, fol. 76b:
ועתה דע לך להתבונן בסוד צורת האותיות אשר בתפילין המונחים על ראש יד. סימן תפלה ותמצא ראשי וידי שבהם המצות ותאמר מדת הדין בראשי יהוה שהוא מדת רחמים בידי.

642 See, e.g., *Messianic Mystics*, pp. 295–307.

643 See *Gan Na'ul*, p. 16:
והזוכה להשגת הספירות צריך שיזהר מן המדות ההפכיות פן ימות במלחמת היצרים והשמירה כולה תלויה בכך שישים הנכנס בסוד כל ספירה בענין אותיות היצירה כל דעתו בשם הנכבד והנורא לכבודו לבד לא זולת זה

of the inner war in human consciousnes. This seems to be the case also in another, quite seminal passage, for a proper understanding of Abulafia's view of the two attributes:

> "[a] The human being possesses opposites, namely, it is possessing powers that no one is worthwhile to exist more than the other, and his two powers are his two urges[644] and this is the reason why they were called two dominions, indubitably, and they were called cherubs that invert by the flame of the inverting sword,[645] and they see face to face,[646] and the intellect decides between them. And they are like two verses that contradict each other, until a third verse will come and decide between them,[647] and they are called the accompanying angels, good and bad,[648] and one compels the other since all the time they are struggling with each other and they were created for this purpose.[649] ... Despite the fact that they are two brothers born from the same father and mother and it is impossible for the two to exist in actu in force in an equal manner, since the powerful and the weak, like the hard and the soft, and from it you should realize that they are not two substrata but one and it receives the opposites, and two opposites cannot coexist in one substratum at the same time. This is the reason why when one is operating *in potentia*, the other is operating *in actu*,[650] and the lower world depends on those two possible powers.

644 Compare, especially to Abulafia's passages analyzed in Idel, *The Mystical Experience*, pp. 24–27, where his technique is understood as overcoming the "attribute of *Gevurah*," and the human urge, both conceived of as inner powers. On the two urges in human being, and a remarkable parallel to the two divine attributes, see Rosen-Zvi, *Demonic Desires*.

645 Cf. Genesis 3:24. See also *Shomer Mitzwah*, p. 18.

646 See the description of the two cherubs in the Holy of Holiest, according to *BT Yuma'*, fol. 54a. See also the passage discussed in Idel, *The Mystical Experience*, p. 27.

647 Cf. *Sifra'*, Leviticus, chapter 13, A.

648 Cf. *BT Sabbath*, fol. 119b.

649 For the importance of inner struggle in Abulafia, see above n. 566.

650 A similar view is found in R. Nathan ben Sa'adyah's *Sha'arei Tzedeq*, p. 17,

This is the reason why the Torah was given to us, because these two attributes[651] are delivered under the dominion of our supernal soul and it is ruling over the two, and it is bringing always each of them out from potentia to in actu, time after time, and they were called by the supernal soul [by the name] of the attribute of judgment and the attribute of compassion, and by us they are called 'the scale of acquittal and the scale of guilt.'[652] And the supernal soul is called *Knesset Yisrael,* whose providence is over us always, over our species and over our individuals in actu from its perspective, and *in potentia* from our perspective, since it is impossible that one should be righteous and wicked at the very same time. [b] This is why God is [Exodus 34:7] "compassionate and gracious, long suffering" despite the fact that He is [ibidem] 'One who punishes sons and grandsons, etc.,' as the Rabbi mentioned in part I, in the secret of *Peqiydah.*[653]"[654]

though the terminology is somewhat different.

651 See abve the passage from *Shomer Mitzwah,* p. 37.

652 Cf. *Sefer Yetzirah,* ed. Hayman, p. 50 par. 23, p. 110. Compare also to similar comparisons between scales and attributes in *Mafteah ha-Shemot,* p. 164 and *Gan Na'ul,* p. 39.

653 Maimonides' *Guide of the Perplexed,* I:54. This secret is discussed in an elaborate manner in his three commentaries on the secrets found in Maimonides's *Guide*. It is the fourth secret in part I of Abulafia's list found in his commentaries. See, e.g., *Ḥayyei ha-Nefesh,* pp. 24–28, 47, 73, 88, 100, *Sitrei Torah,* pp. 34–47.

654 *Ḥayyei ha-Nefesh,* pp. 87–88:

ועל כן האדם בעל הפכים כלומר בעל כוחות אשר אין כח זה ראוי להמצא יותר מכח זה. וב׳ כוחותיו הם ב׳ יצריו, ועל כן קראם הקורא שתי רשויות בלא ספק, ונקראו כרובים מתהפכים בלהט החרב המתהפכת, רואים פנים אל פנים והשכל מכריע ביניהם. והם כשני כתובים המכחישים זה את זה עד שיבוא הכתוב השלישי ויכריע ביניהם. ונקראו מלאכים מלווים טוב ורע, זה מכריח את זה. כי כל ימיהם נלחמים זה עם זה, כי לכך נבראו... ואע״פ ששניהם אחים מאב ואם, ואי אפשר לשניהם שימצאו בפעל הגבורה בשווה, כי הגבור והחלש שני הפכים, כמו הרך והקשה. ומזה תכיר שאינם שנים נושאים כי אם נושא אחד והוא מקבל ההפכים, ולא יימצאו שני הפכים בנושא אחד בעת אחד. ועל כן בעת שזה פעל בכח זה פעל בפעל, ובשני הכוחות האפשריות האלה כל העולם הזה השפל תלוי. ועל כן נתנה התורה לנו מפני ששתי המדות האלה מסורות תחת רשות

Abulafia actually denies the coexistence of opposites in the same substratum, namely coincidentia oppositorum: they do not coincide within the divine, since there is no ontological distinction, but in the different reception of the recipients and in the recipients there is not coexistence since opposites cannot be together in the same substratum at the same time. The passage is built upon a strong opposition between the nature of the divine [b] and that of the human [a]: The former does not change since it is always in actu, being purely intellectual, the latter's nature is based on a dichotomy of states, which contradict each other and cannot coexit. The two states are referred by a long series of biblical and Rabbinic themes, conceived by him as opposites: the biblical ones are two types of two cherubs, the Rabbinic ones are two dominions, two urges, two scales, two angels, and finally, two attributes. By inserting the two attributes in such a list, their divine nature is implicitly denied[655] and they should better be understood as referring to human powers.[656]

Let me clarify the meaning of two terms used in [a]: the supernal soul and *Knesset Yisra'el*. In the ordinary uses of the two terms, they convey extradivine entities: the Neoplatonic soul of the world and the representative of the people of Israel in the supernal world in Rabbinic literature, respectively. Such a reading would mitigate the contrast between [a] and [b]. However, in Abulafia's nomenclature, they have been understood as related to a power within the humans. As to the first, in the above passage the Kabbalist uses not just the term

נשמתינו העליונה והיא המנהיגה את שתיהן והמוציאה כל אחת ואחת מהן מכח לפעל תמיד עת אחר עת, ונקראו אצל הנשמה העליונה מדת הדין ומדת הרחמים, ואצלנו נקראו כף זכות וכף חובה. והנשמה העליונה נקראת כנסת ישראל, אשר השגחתה בנו תמיד בכללינו ובפרטינו בפעל מצדה ובכח מצדינו, כי לא יתכן שיהיה האדם צדיק ורשע יחד בעת אחת, ע"כ השם 'נושא עון ופשע וחטאה' ואע"פ שהוא 'פוקד עוון אבות על בנים ועל שלשים' וכו', כמו שנזכר הרב בחלק א' בסוד פקידה.

655 Compare also to the other opposites in the passages analyzed in my *The Mystical Experience*, pp. 111–112

656 See *Ḥayyei ha-Nefesh*, p. 95: "The human being is compounded from cherubs and the flame of the inverting sword."

האדם מורכב מן הכרובים ולהט החרב המתהפכת

neshamah 'elyonah, but also *nishmatenu ha-'elyonah*, namely our supernal soul. Another occurence of this term in Abulafia's writings deals explicitly with a supernal soul found in the body,[657] and elsewhere the Kabbalist uses the related syntagm *nefesh 'elyonah* in order to refer to Moses's soul that attempts to adhere to the supernal world.[658]

On the other hand, *Knesset Yisra'el* is related here to the "Hebrew soul,"[659] the human feminine partner of God,[660] the result of one's comprehending himself and becoming a "perfect man,"[661] the female entity that is once virgin and once possesed,[662] and especially important is the discussion where the term *Knesset Yisra'el ha-'elyonah* occurs, meaning the collective of the speeches under the rule of the intellect.[663] Thus, despite what someone would imagine that the two terms are referring to transcendental entities, they relate to a power within the humans, probably in a manner reminiscent of the presence of the Agent Intellect within the humans, in the vein of the theory of Averroes.[664] This means that the two attributes are part of the human

657 *Hayyei ha-'Olam ha-Ba'*, p. 81:
לפי החכמה האלוהית לתת שפע שכלי אלוהי על הנפש לגומלה ולהענישה על כל מעשה הגוף המתנהג ממנה וגם על הבנתה בעניינים המושכלים כולם להבינה מה שאפשר להבינה לפי טבעה אחרי רדפה ההשגה בבחירה תגמול גמול עליון אלוהי עליה ואם בהיפך תהפוך עליה הכוונה והגוף שיש לנשמה עליונה והנשמה נבראת לעבוד את קונה ולהכירו ואם לא היה השם נותן הבחירה בידה ודעת תורה לא הייתה ראוייה לענוש ולגמול על כן נתן לנו השם ברחמיו תורה ומצוות חוקים ומשפטים צדיקים להורות לנו תכלית האנושיות בכלל ובפרט והודיענו הדרך אשר נלך בה לטוב לנו כל הימים.

658 See *Sitrei Torah*, p. 11. See also the anonymous treatise belonging to Abulafian Kabbalah, *Ner 'Elohim*, p. 85, to be discussed later on in this chapter.

659 See *Mafteaḥ ha-Tokheḥot*, his commentary on Deuteronomy, p. 113: נפש עבריה כנסת ישראל

660 *Gan Na'ul*, p. 24. See Idel, *The Mystical Experience*, pp. 184–190.

661 *'Imrei Shefer*, p. 121.

662 *Sefer ha-Melitz*, p. 26.

663 *Sitrei Torah*, p. 139. See also Idel, *The Mystical Experience*, p. 211 n. 36.

664 See also the syntagm שכל אלוהי that is related to the human intellect that is actualized in *Mafteaḥ ha-Shemot*, p. 154. See also Idel, *Studies in Ecstatic Kabbalah*, p. 9 and in particular in the Abulafian treatise *Ner 'Elohim*, p. 72,

constitution and not divine transcendental powers. Indeed, in one case the term "attributes" is used in a context that assumes a somehow negative dimension that someone should escape.[665]

Paragraph [a] is built on the assumption of the centrality of triads, constituted by two lower members and a higher one that determines the relations between the two, and this concerns also the two attributes. The determination of the third is indubitably identical to the intellect that determines between the body and the soul.[666] The main role played by the intellect notwithstanding, it does not mean that this Kabbalist conceived philosophy as the highest mode of perception. Insofar as the understanding of the divine attributes are concerned, the philosophers are conceived of as being inferior:

> "And we know that just as reality easily shows the philosophers the essences of things, all the letters, too, represent to us the essence of things in an even easier manner. This is why we have [esoteric] traditions which represent more easily the attributes of God, blessed be He, and His governance and providence, and His influx, and the existence of His actions, and what he [the Kabbalist] hears from it is something that the philosophers cannot attain even after a long toil, and after lengthy times and many studies, because about holy names you will hear [here]."[667]

The main argument here is that by resort to Abulafia's technique someone can transcend the mode of the philosophical understanding and get access to profound insight easier and in a shorter time. This is

(whose views will be discussed later on in this chapter): השכל האנושי הנאצל מן השכל האלוהי הנדבק בנו בטבע. "The human intellect that emanated from the divine intellect that is united with us by nature." The term "divine intellect" recurs many times in the writings of R. Isaac of Acre, under the impact of ecstatic Kabbalah.

665 See *Gan Na'ul*, p. 41, Idel, *The Mystical Experience*, p. 144.

666 *Otzar 'Eden Ganuz*, p. 167, where the same verb is used *KR'*.

667 *Sitrei Torah*, Ms. Paris BN, 774 fol. 163a, p. 160, and ibidem, pp. 20, 52, 183. See my *Absorbing Perfections*, p. 259.

a leitmotiv in his writings.[668] Thus, the attributes can be understood better by resorting to knowledge and a manipulation of divine names, which are the core of Abulafia's techniques.

Let us summarize my reading of Abulafia's treatments of the two divine attributes: he interiorized them and offered an allegorical understanding to both the Rabbinic and the theosophical understandings of these attributes, shifting the center of interest of the theosophical Kabbalah in the divine activities and personality to the human ones. This shift means not the coexistence of two sets of attributes – a metaphysical one and psychological or noetic one – but the reinterpretation of the Rabbinic and earlier Kabbalistic discourses as meaningful solely on the human level. This anthropocentric propensity is part of a wider tendency found in his writings to offer a psychological interpretation to the sefirotic realm as understood by theosophical Kabbalists.[669] Such an interpretation of the attributes and of the *sefirot*, which is characteristic of Abulafia's school, though not totally absent also in other Kabbalistic schools, contributed much to the later anthropocentric mode in Jewish mysticism, a topic that deserves much more investigation[670] and some such examples will be discussed also in the following pages.

The nature of the anthropocentric turn, however, deserves a special attention. Done in the framework of the Aristotelian worldview, it

668 See, e.g., *Mafteaḥ ha-Ra'yon*, pp. 13, 69, *Sefer ha-Melitz*, p. 12, *Sefer ha-Ḥesheq*, pp. 3, 6, 7, 38, 40, 58, 64, *Ḥayyei ha-Nefesh*, pp. 53–54, *Sheva' Netivot ha-Torah*, pp. 96, 122, *'Imrei Shefer*, pp. 71, 96.

669 See, e.g., my *Kabbalah: New Perspectives*, pp. 146–155, *Ben*, pp. 276–376, *Hasidism: Between Ecstasy and Magic*, pp. 16, 41, 45–47, 82, 104, 113–114, 130–131, 134, 146–153, 171–172, 227–238, and for later developments, Jonathan Garb, "The Psychological Turn in 16th century Kabbalah," eds. G. Cecere, M. Loubet, S. Pagani, *Les mystiques juives, chrétiennes et musulmanes dans l'Égypte medievale, (VIIe–XVIe siècles)*, (Institut Francais d'Archeologie Orientale, 2011), pp. 108–124, and Ron Margolin, *Inner Religion, the Phenomenology of Inner Religious Life and Its Manifestation in Jewish Sources*, (Bar Ilan University Press, Hartman Institute, Ramat Gan, 2011) (Hebrew).

670 Idel, "R. Menahem Mendel of Shklov and R. Avraham Abulafia," pp. 173–183.

should be seen as much more universalist than we may learn from recent studies of this Kabbalist. So, for example, we read in his last book *'Imrei Shefer*:

> "However, according to the path of truth, that is the Kabbalah that is specific to our nation, none of the philosophers reached it, and it is the secret of the divine *middot* that govern the human species, and our nation and their communities and their individuals, and the unique feature of our community and our nation and our people and our language and our script, since this has been revealed to us from the revelation of our Torah, that we have been elevated, in particular, by means of it over all nations and all languages. And we have the root and the branches and the fruit[671] that is selected from all the fruits, together with the 613 commandments, the 365 and the 248, since all [astral] cycle is revolving on them according to the sign *BYW TQTzH*,[672] which secret is *Beiyt '[o]LaMiYM*, since the secret of *Rosh ha-Shanah*[673] is the secret of *Beit ha-Miqdash*."[674]

Prima facie, this is one of the most particularistic understandings of Judaism in Abulafia's writings: all the major issues of this religion are depicted as superior to those of the other nations: Torah, language and script. However, for Abulafia, the nation of Israel is not defined in a genetic manner, but as the collective of persons who are intelligent, namely those who actualized their intellect.[675] This is the matter

671 For fruit as intellect see *Ḥayyei ha-'Olam ha-Ba'*, p. 108.

672 *BYW TQTzH* = *BeiYT '[O]LaMmYM* = 613 = 248 + 365.

673 *Rosh ha-Shanah* = *Beit ha-Mikdash* = 861. Is this figure related to the addition of 248 to 613?

674 *'Imrei Shefer*, p. 194:

ואמנם על דרך האמת כי עניין הקבלה המיוחדת לאומתינו לא השיגה אחד מן הפילוסופים והיא סוד המדות האלוהיות המנהיגות מין האדם ואומתינו וקהילותיהם ואישיהם וסגולת קהילתנו ואומתינו ועמינו ולשוננו ומכתבינו. כי זה נגלה לנו ממתן תורתינו שנתעלינו בה ביחוד על כל אומה ועל כל לשון ולנו השרש והעלים עם ענפיהם והפרי המובחר מכל פרי, עם תרי"ג מצוות השס"ה עם הרמ"ח שכל מחזור מתגלגל עליהם בסימן בי"ו תקצ"ה שסודם בי"ת עולמי"ם, כי סוד רא"ש השנ"ה הוא סוד בי"ת המקד"ש.

675 See my *Ben*, pp. 276–376, and in particular in *Ḥayyei ha-'Olam ha-Ba'*, p. 108.

also of the Hebrew language, which is understood as the natural language.[676] Moreover, the Kabbalah is understood here not just as limited to the Jews but to the entire human species, part of his much more universal approach than most of the other Kabbalists.[677] This is the reason why the term *Middot 'Elohiyyot* does not necessarily stand here for some form of theosophy, but for supernal intellectual powers, as we learn, for example, from the parallelism between three human *middot* and three cosmic ones, found in his *'Otzar 'Eden Ganuz*: the former are described as natural, spiritual and intellectual, the latter as earthy, celestial and divine.[678] This triad seems to inform also another discussion in this book, where the term "divine attributes" occur, but on the other hand the terms *Ḥesed, Gevurah, Raḥamim, Tzedeq,* and *Mishpat* as separate powers occur.[679] The series may point to the terms found in theosophical systems and may refer to the fourth, fifth, sixth, ninth and tenth *sefirot*. Moreover, there is nothing theurgical that transpires from those discussions. A Kabbalist using theosophical terms in a non-theosophical manner is no more a theosophist than someone who uses Rabbinic material in an allegorical manner qualifies him to be a Rabbi.

However, the proper understanding of the 613 commandments is connected here by means of gematria to the calculations related to the hallowing of the month and the impregnation of the year that depend on the combined cycles of sun and moon. I see this connection as part of the process of naturalization of Rabbinic Judaism according to the

676 See my *Language, Torah and Hermeneutics*, pp. 16–27.

677 See my *Abraham Abulafia's Esotericism*, pp. 163–166.

678 See "Preface," pp. 1 and 165, 200. This seems to be the case also ibidem, p. 34, and see also my "Commentaries on *Sefer Yetzirah*," p. 488 and n. 96. When dealing with "human *middot*" Abulafia acknowledges the impact of R. Shlomo ibn Gabirol's *Sefer Tiqqun ha-Middot* on his discussion. See ibidem, p. 165. The term "divine attributes" מידות אלהיות – which occurs also in two other cases in his writings, seems to reflect the influence of R. Yehuda ibn Tibbon's Hebrew translation of R. Bahya ibn Paqudah's *Hovot ha-Levavot*, Sha'ar ha-Yihud, chapter 10.

679 *'Otzar 'Eden Ganuz*, pp. 141–142.

interpretation of the ecstatic Kabbalist, in the vein of what we have seen already at the beginning of this chapter.

Let me turn now to three followers of Abulafia's ecstatic Kabbalah. The first one is R. Nathan ben Sa'adyah Ḥar'ar, the author of *Sha'arei Tzedeq*.[680] In my opinion, this treatise has been written in the late eighties of the 13th century in Sicily, perhaps in Messina[681] and there it is written:

> "During the time of the Exile, the activity of the names has been obliterated,[682] and prophecy has been cancelled from [the people of] Israel, because of the hindrance of the attribute of judgment. This state will go on until the coming of that whom God has chosen, and his power will be great because of what has been transmitted to him related to their power and God will reveal the name to him, and transmit to him the supernal keys. Then he will stand against the attribute of judgment... and the attribute of compassion will guide him. The supernal [entity] will become lower, and the lower will become supernal,[683] and the Tetragrammaton, which has been concealed – will be revealed, and 'Adonay – which was revealed[684] – will [then] be concealed. Then it will happen to us

680 Gerhard G. Scholem, "*Sha'arey Zedeq*, a Kabbalistic Text from the School of R. Abraham Abulafia, attributed to R. Shem Tov (Ibn Gaon)?" *QS* 1 (1924–1925), pp. 127–139 (Hebrew), "Eine Kabbalistische Erklaerung der Prophetie als Selbstbegenung," *MGWJ* vol. 74 (1930), pp. 285–290, *Major Trends*, pp. 147–155, and Idel, *Le Porte della Giustizia*.

681 Scholem was confident, on the ground of a colophon, that the book had been written in the land of Israel. However, in this book that is uncommonly autobiographical, the arrival to the land of Israel or any experience there, is not mentioned at all.

682 This view may have some affinity to the Midrashic vision of the change of the names of the angels by God at the time of the destruction of the Temple, in order to prevent invocation of Jewish masters, or Magicians, who would attempt to oppose the destruction of the Temple.

683 This view is similar to that expressed by Abulafia in a passage from his apocalyptic *Sefer ha-'Ot*, p. 69.

684 See *Sefer ha-'Ot*, p. 79 where the opposition between this name and the Tetragrammaton is also explicit.

> what has been written [Jeremy 31:33]: 'For they shall all know Me from the least of them to the greatest of them.' Then the natural, philosophical sciences by now unknown to us, will be revealed, because their [supernal] power is gradually enhancing. Then 'the Jews will have light and gladness,' [Esther 8:16] and sadness and worry will be [the part of] the deniers, and 'many of the people of the land become Jews' [ibidem, 8:17] and [Yoel 3:1] 'our sons and daughters will prophesy.'"[685]

Elsewhere in the same book we read that the change of the attribute of judgement into one of compassion will culminate in "the spread of the diadem of the kingdom of Israel in the world."[686] Again we read elsewhere in R. Nathan's book:

> "The entire world is governed [now] in accordance with [the laws of] nature, which indicates the attribute of judgment.[687] Thus, the world of Names is [now] suspended and obscured, and its letters and combinations and its virtues are not understood by those who conduct themselves in accordance with the attribute of judgment… and this is the secret [meaning] of the cessation of prophecy in Israel; [for prophecy] inhibits the attribute of judgment. [And this continues] until the one whom God desires will arrive, and his power will be great and will be increased by being given their power. And God will reveal His secrets to him… and the natural and philosophical wisdoms will be despised and hidden, for their supernal power will be abolished. And the wisdom of the letters and Names, which now are not understood, will be revealed."[688]

685 *Sha'arei Tzedeq*, p. 17. Significant parallels to some aspects of this passage can be found also ibidem, pp. 16, 20. See more about the background of this passage in Idel, *Language, Torah and Hermeneutics*, pp. 17–18.

686 Joel 3:1

687 See earlier in this chapter the quote from *Get ha-Shemot* and in *Sha'arei Tzedeq*, p. 21.

688 *Sha'arei Tzedeq*, p. 17; corrected according to Ms. Leiden, Warner 24, fol. 127a; Ms. Jerusalem 80 148, fol. 47ab; the text in the second manuscript is missing in those lines. See also Idel, *Absorbing Perfections*, p. 364.

Nature is therefore identified with the attribute of judgment, and both are regarded as obscuring the more intellectual world of the names and thus also prophecy that depends on divine names. In my opinion, this is an appropiation and a polemic with the view of Nahmanides, that claimed that there was another order, or arrangement of the text of the Torah, composed of divine names, which was lost, while the present order deals with commandments.[689] No doubt the figure mentioned here is reminiscent of the Messiah according to a Talmudic text.[690] The specific nature of this figure is depicted in a similar manner on the same page:

> "'This is his name that will be called *YHWH* our righteous' [Jeremy 23:6], and this is his matter: [Exodus 32:34] 'Behold my angel will walk before you' and He said, [ibidem 23:21] 'Provoke him not because My name is in him.' Moses did not want to be under its dominion, namely to invert and become the attribute of compassion underneath the attribute of judgment, and this is the reason why he said, [ibidem, 33:15] 'If thy face go not with me, carry us not up from here.' This is a very distinguished issue that many doubts will be removed regarding [what is written in] the Torah, and this is the reason you should pay attention and understand it in depth, and you will be saved from doubts."[691]

Moses or the righteous are not just historical persons living in the past or in the future: they are paradigmatic figures that are looking

689 See my "On Angels in Biblical Exegesis," pp. 227–230.

690 *BT Babba' Batra'*, fol. 75b, Idel, *Ben*, pp. 114–116. The Messiah is mentioned in Nathan's *Sha'arei Tzedeq*, p. 16.

691 *Sha'arei Tzedeq*, p. 20:

'וזה שמו אשר יקראו ייי' צדקנו' [ירמיהו כג:ו]. וזהו ענין 'הנה מלאכי ילך לפניך' [שמות לב:לד] ואמ'[ר] 'אל תמר בו כי שמי בקרבו' [שמות כג:כא]. ומשה לא רצה להיותו תחת רשותו כלומ'[ר] להתהפך ולהיות מדת רחמים תחת מדת הדין, ועל כן ענה לו 'אם אין פניך הולכים אל תעלינו מזה' [שמות לג:טו]. וזה עניין נכבד מאד יותרו בו כמה ספקות מן התורה ועל כן שים לבך עליו ותבינהו מאד ותצא מכל ספק.

See also my *Enchanted Chains*, pp. 90–91.

for the transformation into a divine power characterized by the Tetragrammaton, by the metanoia of their intellect – and refused to subsume to an angelic power, understood as a reference to the attribute of judgment. From the immediate context, the philosophical meaning of the latter attribute is the power of imagination whereas that of compassion stands for the intellect.[692] Moses is imagined to prefer the face of God – namely the attribute of compassion – rather than His back, the angel. Both, however, should be understood according to another discussion found in this book, the two attributes refer to an inner distinction within the ten *sefirot*, conceived of as two parts of a sphere.[693] Elsewhere in this book it seems that the terms face and back are related to the two attributes.[694] Therefore, though two hemispheres, they are part of a sphere.

Let me pay attention to the verb "invert" translating the Hebrew התהפך. It recurs several times in the small book.[695] Since it is related to the two attributes, it reflects elements from the two variants of model [E]. However, while the mythical element is conspicuous in the Rabbinic and theosophical discussions, here the change is related to the human search for apotheosis, namely shifting from a type of cognition that is imaginative, to one that is intellectual as much as possible. Like in Abulafia's treatments of the two attributes, also his student moved the locus of the main event from the inter-divine world to the human metanoia. Moreover, the two Kabbalists were concerned with the inversion of the activity of the divine names, as the main change from the spiritual point of view.[696] Indeed, Abulafia believed that his technique is based on manipulations of letters and divine names, and that he, qua Messiah, reveals the yet unknown divine name.[697] The inversion in the activities of names is to be

692 See my analysis in *Le Porte della Giustizia*, p. 194 n. 4.
693 See *Sha'arei Tzedeq*, pp. 28–29.
694 Ibidem, pp. 11–12.
695 Ibidem, pp. 16, 17, 29.
696 See *'Or ha-Sekhel*, p. 30.
697 See my *Abraham Abulafia's Esotericism*, pp. 244–254.

understood as a major part of a spiritual reform, which is done by deepening Maimonides' axiology and applying it also on topics about which the Great Eagle did not do so. In short, the Kabbalists adopted the Maimonidean speculative code, of ultimately Greek origin, that moved the place of the main religious event from the deity and the cosmos, to the human psyche.

Let me turn to the redemptive aspects of some of the passages adduced above. They can be read on the historical level as dealing with an external event, affecting a certain people that will change the mode of cognition from imaginary to intellectual. This would be a combination of the popular eschatology with an intellectual shift, in the vein of Maimonides's eschatology. However, it can be read on another level, the personal one, which means that redemption of an individual process, of pure cognitive nature, which has nothing to do with history or with a certain nation. According to such a reading, which I would call noetic eschatology, the eschatological conversions and the victory of Jews and Jewesses mentioned in R. Nathan's *Sha'arei Tzedeq* should be understood as allegories for intellectual powers. Those two forms of redemptive reading are found also in other instances in Abulafia's thought.[698] Though not necessarily exclusive, those constitute two different modes of thought.

Probably a colleague of R. Nathan, an anonymous Kabbalist from the circle of Abulafia, composed a small treatise entitled *Ner 'Elohim*, which has been mistakenly attributed to Abulafia himself.[699] In good Abulafian terms he wrote:

> "And this war is found within the heart[700] ... and it was born out of the first *sefirah* which in man, a good thought and an evil

698 See Idel, *Messianic Mystics*, pp. 77–79, "The Pearl, the Son and the Servants".

699 On the question of the authorship of this work, see Idel, *Abraham Abulafia's Works and Doctrines*, pp. 72–75, where I discussed the views of Moritz Steinschneider and Gershom Scholem as to Abulafia's authorship. Meanwhile, the book has been printed as Abulafia's book and even translated in English under his name.

700 See above n. 566.

> thought...and the persons who think it is wise to do by means of wisdom, good and evil, and so on in the case of the understanding and knowledge, good and evil, and the person that understands should understand, discern between good and evil...and the *sefirot* emanate into the heart and the influx is divided into many kinds...'The Compassionate wants the heart'[701] which means that the Compassionate wants the heart that pursues His attributes, just as He is compassionate, so also you should be compassionate, and so also in the case of other attributes, and the transitions of the attributes,[702] you should hear them in accordance to the secrets of the commandments."[703]

The struggle that is connected to the first *sefirah* is expressly related to an inner experience, in the vein of Abulafia's appropriation of the inner war. The attributes of man are regarded as modi of assimilation to God's attributes.[704] I assume that the secrets of the commandments should again be understood in the way Abulafia hinted at them in a passage adduced above, as related to limbs rather than to the heart.

Quite interesting is also another passage of this Kabbalist, where he describes the First Cause as follows:

> "It[705] has no *middah*, but Its *middot* are influxes and emanations and spiritual *Hawayyiot* that were created with the world and they were revealed since they were qualities within Him, and they were actualized when the world was actualized but It caused their influxes, their essence together with the world, since they are necessary for the world and it is impossible to our mind to understand how it was, since just as we do not comprehend It so we do not comprehend the essence of Its *middot* that are emanated from It and It governs over all. But we shall know by our mind that they are ten *middot*

701 See Rashi on *BT Sanhedrin* fol. 106b.
702 *Gilgulei ha-middot*. Compare to Abulafia's *Ḥayyei ha-'Olam ha-Ba'*, p. 65.
703 *Ner 'Elohim*, pp. 5–6. For a translation of a fuller context of this passage see Idel, *Kabbalah in Italy*, p. 147, and *Primeval Evil in Kabbalah*, appendix 2, pp. 383–384.
704 See also Idel, *Kabbalah: New Perspectives*, pp. 149–150.
705 Namely the divinity.

> which are divided in world, time, and man, ten to ten, and they are in total YY,[706] and this is the reason why Its name is so... and God was them... And according to our mind there is no essence beside them and they have no reality but It, since God is them and they are it, but It emanated their powers upon the creatures and It put them [the *middot*] in them [the creatures]... and all this is explained in the writings of the philosophers and this is the reason why I shall not elaborate on it."[707]

The *middot* are conceived of as created together with the world, as governing it, and for its purpose alone. The anonymous Kabbalist even defines the *middah* as follows:

> "It stems from *medidah* [measurement] and *shi'ur* [size] so that the *middot* are sizeable from God [or the name] upon His creatures... and It is not perceived of as having a size, namely He does not have a measure and His size, namely the size that is His,[708] and He gives a size to His world, in accordance to the known measures [*middot*] and constant sizes."[709]

706 Two letters of YY are one of the forms of an abbreviation of the Tetragrammaton.

707 *Ner 'Elohim*, p. 74:

רק ההתחלה והצור לכל שהוא הסבה הראשונה לכל נמצא, אין לו מדה, אבל מדותיו הם שפעים ואצילות והויות רוחניות נמצאו במציאות העולם ונתגלו לאשר היו איכויות בו בכח ויצאו לפעל בצאת העולם לפעל, אבל עצמותם השפיעם עם העולם, כי הם דברים צריכים לעולם. וזה לא יתכן שיצוייר בשכלינו איך הוא, כי כמו שלא נשיג עצמו כן לא נשיג אמיתת מדותיו הנאצלות מעצמו ובהן מנהיג הכל. אבל נדע אנחנו בשכלנו כי הן עשר מדות ונחלקות בעולם ובשנה ובנפש לעשר עשר, ויהיו בכללם י״י, על כן שמו מכונה כך... ובדעתנו כי אין לשם עצם זולתם ואין להם מציאות אלא השם, כי השם הוא הם והם הוא, אלא שהוא האציל כוחותיהם על הברואים ושמם בהם... וכל זה מבואר בספרי החכמה, על כן לא נאריך בו הנה, אבל נפסוק.

708 This is a polemic with the famous concept of *Shi'ur Qomah*, the title of an anthropomorphic book belonging to the Heikhalot literature, dealing with the sizes of the divine limbs. The naturalistic interpretation of this concept in Abulafia's school is a desideratum.

709 *Ner 'Elohim*, p. 72:

מדה מלשון מדידה ולשון שיעור ואם כן המדות משוערות מהשם על מדותיו... אם כן

The inner structure of the divinity does not concern this Kabbalist, neither the correlative theory. The ruler within the human personality is his intellect, and from it the judgment is emanated, either the stern or the soft one.[710] Elsewhere the Kabbalist resorts to Abulafia's parallelism between the ten human *middot* and the ten divine ones, which he calls as "spiritual" but without elaborating on it.[711]

Let me turn now to some quotes from a fourth Kabbalist, who wrote a *Commentary on the Pentateuch* found in an anonymous manuscript, at the beginning of the 14th century, and related to ecstatic Kabbalah:[712]

> "*Mezuzah* ... the intelligibles, which is the *mezuzah* of the heart,[713] [the pericope of][714] *shema'* which is the attribute of *Ḥesed*, which is the attribute of compassion, and [the pericope] *we-hayah* that is [the attribute of] *Gevurah*, which is the attribute of judgment which has two matters that should always be in the innermost part of his heart,[715] and he should look at them always, in order to walk

אינו משוער בעל שיעור כלומר אינו בעל מדה אבל שיעור ורוצה לומר השיעור שהוא שלו שהוא משער בו עולמו במדות ידועות ובשיעורין קבועין.

It should be mentioned that the term *middah* in order to refer to a size that is not necessarily a constant dimension of the deity, is found in early Kabbalah, like R. Asher ben David, as seen in chapter 5 above, and in his contemporary R. Eleazar of Worms, as he was quoted by R. Abraham ben Azriel, *'Arugat ha-Bosem*, ed. Urbach, I, p. 202, implying that the size is solely for the sake of the creatures.

710 *Ner 'Elohim*, p. 72.

711 Ibidem, pp. 17–18.

712 More on different passages from this commentary, see Idel, *Messianic Mystics*, p. 393 n. 28, *Kabbalah in Italy*, p. 146, and "The Jubilee in Jewish Mysticism," in *Shilḥei Me'ot – Qitzam shel 'Idanim*, ed. J. Kaplan, (Merkaz Shazar, Jerusalem, 2005), p. 82 (Hebrew).

713 I did not find the source for the Aramaic syntagm *Mezuziyta' de-Libba'* – translated here as the *mezuzhah* of the heart.

714 The Kabbalist refers to the two biblical portions inscribed in the parchment of the *Mezuzah*.

715 This phrase is found also in Ms. Oxford-Bodleiana 1920, fols. 10a, 55a.

> in the intellectual and negotiate with the attribute of compassion, and he should not walk after materiality, and negotiate with the attribute of judgment."[716]

This is an internalized interpretation of the two attributes, and their identification with the intelligibles and materiality.[717] There can be little doubt that the two attributes are also related to the two human urges, as we learn from another discussion in this commentary.[718] This means that the internal allegorization is not just a matter of two Kabbalists, whose names we know, as seen above in this chapter, but it penetrated also two other anonymous authors, and the depth of this internalized allegorization deserves additional inquiries.

Last but not least: In an anonymous and quite interesting treatise, entitled *Sefer ha-Dorban*, that appears in different versions in two manuscripts and whose content is very close to Abulafia's thought, we find a lengthy discussion of the meaning of the attribute of *Shalom*. I am not sure if we can identify the author with any of the Kabbalists mentioned in this chapter. Perhaps it belongs to an additional member of Abulafia's school.[719] He claims that a sage that does not possess the "attribute of *Shalom*" – the best of the three attributes *Ḥesed, Paḥad* and *Shalom* – did not study the names that are enscribed in the letters of *Shalom*, since from them *Shalom* comes into the world. However, the real sages are those whose first religion is the "attribute of *Shalom*." This statement is predicated on the permutation of the consonants of *MDT* – *middat* – to *DTM* – *dattam* – their religion.

716 Ms. Oxford-Bodleiana 1920, fol. 60a:

עניין המזוזה... המושכל שלה והוא מזוזיתא דליבא ששמע הוא מדת החסד והוא מדת רחמים והיה הוא גבורה והוא מדת הדין לו שני העניינים שצריכי׳ שיהיו תדיר במפתחות לבו של אדם וישתכל בהם תדיר שילך במושכליות ויתדיין במדת רחמים ולא ילך אחרי החומריות ויתדיין במדת הדין.

For another quote from this commentary see in the next chapter.

717 See also ibidem, fol. 2a.

718 Ibidem, fol. 10a.

719 On the affinity between this treatise and Abulafia see, e.g., Idel, *Studies in Ecstatic Kabbalah*, pp. 11–12.

He goes on to permutate the letters of *middat ha-Shalom* and create the phrase *Shem ha-Talmud* – the name of the Talmud – and *Lamed Shemot* – study names or thirty names – and by the dint of gematria *Nefesh ha-Shamayyim* – the soul of heaven and the perfection of a human – *Tashlum ha-'Adam*.[720] According to him, the permulation of letters are "the attributes of *Shalom*" and the "fruit of the soul and the body" by dint of the holy language, since this attribute is similar to "the attributes of the name" – *middot ha-shem*.[721] It is obvious that true sages are those who study the names and permutate letters, and thus they imitate the attribute of God by developing their mind to the perfection which is alluded here by the phrase "the fruit of the soul and the body" and perhaps also by the "soul of heaven."

These four or perhaps five authors analyzed in this chapter represent the existential situation of a belated Kabbalist writing at the end of the 13th century and early 14th century, after the powerful impact of Jewish philosophy and the somehow less widespread though significant presence of the theosophical Kabbalah, not to speak about the earlier forms of Jewish literatures. Their views are even more complex than the theosophical treatments of the two divine attributes, since they had to take in consideration a greater diversity of earlier treatments: Rabbinic, philosophical and theosophical. The question is what of the three conveyed the opinion of the Kabbalist and I am confident that the proper answer to this quandary has been supplied above. These belated Kabbalists had to respond to the mythical

720 *Middat ha-Shalom* = 826 = *Lamed Shemot* = *Shem ha-Talmud* [825] = *Tashlum ha-'Adam* = *Nefesh ha-Shamayyim* = *koḥot ha-lashon* = *koḥot ha-Tzeruf*.

721 Ms. Oxford-Bodleiana 1649, fol. 202b–203a:

כי כל תלמיד חכם שאין מדתו מדת השלום לא למד השמות החקוקים באותיות החקוקים שמהם שלום בא לעולם אך החכמי' האמתיים דתם הראשונה מדת השלום גם היא מדתם האחרונה שנ' 'יבא שלום ינוח על משכבותם הולך נכוחו' והנה מדת השלום, שם התלמוד, וסודו 'למד השמות' שהם 'נפש השמים' ומי שזהו 'מדתו שלמה' כי אין שלמות מדה למעלה ממדת השלום שהיא 'תשלום האדם' שנ' 'וישם לך שלום' והנה 'כחות הלשון' שהן 'כוחות הצירוף' 'באותיות' הם 'מדות השלום' על כן הוא 'פרי הנפש והגוף' 'בכוח לשון הקודש' מפני שזאת המדה המעולה דומה 'למדות השם' וכן מי שהוא 'שלום הדמות' ו'שלם מהדת' וממנו 'מדת הלשון' המחייבת מדת השלום.

treatments of the attributes by other Kabbalists, writing as the former were within the framework of a theology profoundly informed by Maimonides' explicit denial of such attributes.

Later on, some Kabbalists, especially in some forms of Safedian Kabbalah that belong to the theosophical schools, like Moshe Cordovero and Ḥayyim Vital, had to take their views into consideration, producing an even greater type of complexity, to which 18th century Hasidism reacted by a certain simplification of those theosophical syntheses, and by adopting allegorical readings.[722] However, in comparison to the earlier stages of ecstatic Kabbalah, the later psychological understandings of the attributes did not contribute fresh angles of looking at the divine attributes as referring to allegories of inner states.

722 See above n. 580.

TEN
On Three Divine Attributes

The emergence of the theory of two attributes in Judaism had important hermeneutical implications, as seen in chapter 2 above, which attempted to harmonize the fixed linkage between these attributes and the divine names, and the context that is found de facto in some cases in the Hebrew Bible, that not always conforms the detail of this linkage. This is especially evident in the cases when two divine names occur together in the same verse as seen in that chapter. However, there are few instances in the Hebrew Bible where three divine names occur together, as is the case in the verses Psalms 50:1, or Joshu'a 22:22. By the dint of the importance of the correlation between names and attributes, the question arose as to the possible meaning of the third divine name, that occurs together with the Tetragrammaton and *'Elohim*. The answer found in a Midrashic discussion is the assumption as to the existence of a third attribute, which corresponds to that third name. In the vein of the Rabbinic theory of cooperation between the two attributes, as seen in model [B] in chapter 2, such an attribute may be related to the other two attributes or not. When commenting on Psalm 50:1, a Midrashist asks, probably putting this question in the mouth of *minim*,[723] namely some form of heretics, perhaps Christians, the following question:

723 See, e.g., Segal, *Two Powers in Heaven*, passim, Naomi Janowitz, "Rabbis and

"A Psalm to Asaph. *'El 'Elohim H'*, "*'El 'Elohim H'* spoke and called the earth.' The minim asked R. Samlay: "Why it is written *'El 'Elohim H'* spoke? He said to them; "It is not written, 'They spoke and they called' but He spoke and he called.' His disciples told him: "Our master, you have responded to those by a broken stick, but to us what do you respond? He said to them 'all are one name.' Why did he[724] mention the name of God three times? In order to teach you that by means of these three names the Holy One, blessed be He, His world, corresponds to three attributes by means of which He created the world. And they [the latter] or the *Ḥokhmah*, and the *Da'at* and the *Tevunah*.[725] "What is [the prooftext] for *Ḥokhmah* [Wisdom]? Because it is said [Proverbs 3:19]: "YHWH in wisdom founded the earth." What is [the prooftext] for *Tevunah* [understanding]: [ibidem] "And by understanding He set the heaven in their place." And what is [the prooftext] for *Da'at* [knowledge] [ibidem]? "By His Knowledge the depths burst forth." Similarly, it is said [Exodus 20:5], "For I [am] *YHWH, 'Eloheikha, 'El Qano'*," behold they are three, corresponding to the three [names] by which the world was created. Likewise the sons of Gad and the sons of Reuven said [Joshu'a 22:22], "*'El 'Elohim YHWH, 'El 'Elohim YHWH*." Why did they see as worthwhile to mention it twice? But because by means of them the world has been created. *'El 'Elohim*" by means of which the Torah has been promulgated. It is possible that each of them operated by itself [alone]." No! But the two of them have been created together. And it is said [Isaiah 48:13], "With My own hands I founded the earth, with My right hand I formed the expanse of sky. When I summoned them they sprang together into being.""[726]

their Opponents: The Construction of the "Min" in Rabbinic Anecdotes," *Journal of Early Christian Study*, vol. 3 (1998), pp. 449–462.

724 Namely David, the alleged author of the Psalms.

725 See also Exodus 31:3, 1 Kings 7:14; Proverbs 24:3. Compare also to another Midrash, *Pirqei de R. Eliezer*, chapter 3, and Scholem, *Origins of the Kabbalah*, p. 124.

726 Midrash on Psalms 50:1, ed. S. Buber, (Wien 1891), pp. 278–279:

We may assume that the sequel of the three Names in Psalm 50:1 and Joshu'a 22:22, *'El 'Elohim YHWH*, does not exactly correspond to *Ḥokhmah, Tevunah* and *Da'at*. The point made by the homelist in the fuller context of the passage is that the three attributes work together and at the same time, as well as the view that the Names are synonyms. In any case, this is an exegetical issue that is related to a theological dispute with Christian trinity. Let me refer again to my hypothesis formulated in chapters 2 and 3 as to the possibility that a list of ten *middot* emerged before the written articularion of theosophical Kabbalah, perhaps by a combination of lists of three and seven divine attributes.

I shall address now some medieval passages sometimes attributed to a Midrash, which, however are not identical to the above passage. In an anonymous commentary on the Pentateuch, perhaps written in

מזמור לאסף. אל אלהים ה׳ אל אלהים ה׳ דבר ויקרא הארץ. שאלו המינין את ר׳ שמלאי: מהו דכתיב אל אלהים ה׳ דבר? אמר להן: דברו ויקראו אין כתיב כאן אלא דבר ויקרא. אמרו לו תלמידיו: רבינו לאלו דחית בקנה הרצוץ אבל לנו מה אתה משיב? אמר להם שלשתן שם אחד. למה הזכיר שמו של הקב״ה ג׳ פעמים. ללמדך, שבשלשה שמות הללו ברא הקב״ה את עולמו, כנגד שלשה מדות שבהן נברא העולם. ואלו הן - החכמה והדעת והתבונה. חכמה מנין, שנאמר (משלי ג:יט) ה׳ בחכמה יסד ארץ. תבונה, (שם) כונן שמים בתבונה. דעת, (שם, כ) בדעתו תהומות נבקעו. וכן הוא אומר, (שמות כ:ה) כי אנכי ה׳ אלהיך אל קנא. הרי שלש, כנגד שלש שבהן נברא העולם. וכן בני גד ובני ראובן אומרים, (יהושע כב:כב) אל אלהים ה׳ אל אלהים ה׳ הוא יודע. ומה ראו להזכיר שני פעמים, אלא, שבהם נברא העולם. אל אלהים, שבהן נתנה התורה. יכול אחד לעצמו ואחד לעצמו. לאו, אלא שניהם ביחד נבראו. וכן הוא אומר, (ישעיה מח:יג) אף ידי יסדה ארץ וימיני טפחה שמים קורא אני אליהם יעמדו יחדו.

See also the several parallels pointed out by Buber in the footnotes, and *Yalqut Shim'oni* on Joshu'a 22, par. 31. For a Kabbalistic quote of a part of this passage see R. Meir bn Gabbai, *'Avodat ha-Qodesh* 1:14, fol. 16c. The correspondence between three Divine names and three *middo*t is found also in R. Asher ben David, ed. Abrams, p. 65. See also Hames, "Ramon Lull, Solomon ibn Adret, and Alfonso of Valladolid Debate Trinity," p. 209. Compare also to the passage attributed to the book of *Bahir*, printed and discussed by Ronit Meroz, in *Kabbalah* vol. 7 (2002), pp. 319–326 (Hebrew) and the discussion from this book discussed in chapter 3.

the late 13th century or early 14th one, found in a unique manuscript we read:

> "What is stated in the Midrash: "With three attributes [*middot*] God created His universe, with the attribute of judgment, with the attribute of compassion and with the mediating attribute, as it is written [Psalm 50:1], *'El, 'Elohim Yah* appeared and called to the earth," for with one of them the world could not exist. For were there only the attribute of judgment, which is the name *'Elohim*, alone, the world could not exist, and were it only the attribute of compassion, the name *Yah*, then there would be no divine retribution. Therefore He created it with *'El 'Elohim Yah*, which is the combination,[727] and of this it is written [Deuteronomy 6:4], "Hear O Israel , the Lord is God, the Lord is One," that is, whether in the attribute of judgment , whether in the attribute of compassion, or whether in the mediating attribute, He is One. This is also what is written in the thirteen attributes[728] [of compassion] [Exodus 34:6], "*YHWH YHWH, 'El*, that is compassionate and full of grace." For the first divine Name is read as it is written and that is the attribute of compassion, and the second is read [traditionally] as *'Adonai*, and it is the mediating attribute, and *'El* is the attribute of judgment. But when a man returns to God they are all compassionate and they are all for good."[729]

727 The Hebrew form is *mazug*, which is reminiscent of the content of the discussion in *Genesis Rabbah'* 12:15 that is the basic representative of model [A].

728 Thirteen is also the gematria of *'Eḥad*, namely One.

729 Ms. Oxford-Bodleiana 1920, fol. 16a:

במדרש בג׳ מדות ברא הש׳ עולמו במדת הדין ובמדת רחמים ובמדת ממוצעת כדכתי׳ אל אלהים י׳ דבר ויקרא ארץ כי באחד מהם לא יוכל העולם להתקיים שאם היה מדת הדין והוא אלהים לבד לא יתקיים העולם ואם יהיה במדת רחמים בי׳ לא יהיה עונש לפי״כ בראו באל אלהי י׳ שהוא מזוג וזהו שכתו׳ שמע ישראל י׳ אלהינו י׳ אחד כלומ׳ בין במדת הדין בין במדת רחמים בין בממוצע הוא אחד והיינו שכתו׳ בי״ג מדות יי׳ יי׳ אל רחום וחנון כי האחד ככתבו והוא מדת רחמים והשני בקריאתו אדני והיא מדה ממוצעת אל הוא מדת הדין כשהאדם שב לשם הם כולם רחמים והם כולם לטובה.

I surmise that this commentary has been written in Italy or Sicily. See also in the previous chapter.

It is obvious that though using similar proof-texts, the two quoted passages do not depend on each other. What is new in the latter passage in comparison to the earlier one, is the introduction of the concept of a mediating attribute, *middah memutza'at,* which asserts that the two others are opposite.[730] This new phrase, nonetheless, it seems that this Midrash is part of a lost Rabbinic discussion.

Many years ago on the ground of this last passage and some others I published then, I drew the conclusion that a theory of three attributes predated the emergence of Kabbalah. This view is sustained by the passage from *Sefer ha-Bahir* we have discussed in chapter 3, and by R. Asher ben David's references to three attributes, as mentioned in chapter 5, and has been endorsed subsequently in two studies on the basis of new material found in an inedited Zoharic manuscript.[731] This means that a theory of three attributes predates the last third of the 13th century.

Let me turn now to a third passage, attributed again to a Midrash. It comes from a responsum of R. Shlomo ben Abraham ibn Adret, known as the Rashba', a late 13th and early 14th century major Halakhic and Kabbalistic figure active in Barcelona:

> "[a] And as to what the Rabbis said in the *Midrash,* that God created the world with those three attributes, [namely] with the attributes of *'El, 'Elohim* and *YHWH,* you should know that there are three attributes: judgement, compassion and a third being a combination [*mezugit*][732] of judgment and compassion. [b] And know that that it is impossible for the world to persist in its perfection by the two first attributes alone, since if it is created by the attribute of judgment alone it would not persist for a moment... and if the

730 See also the passage from Avner of Burgos, discussed in "Notes in the Wake of Medieval Jewish Polemic," pp. 58–59, and my footnotes there, where the preponderant third *sefirah* is described as mediating. See also R. Ezra of Gerona, *Commentary on the Song of Songs,* on the *sefirah* of *Tiferet,* p. 477: מדה... ממוצעת והשוה

731 See Ronit Meroz, "Zoharic Narratives and their Adaptations," *Hispania Judaica,* vol. 3 (2000), pp. 38–39, 44 and n. 137, 60 and Liebes, *God's Story,* pp. 123–157.

732 Or mixture.

world was created with the attribute of compassion alone, everything would be equal[733] because of the multiple sins … [c].This is the reason why it is impossible for it [the world] to stand on the true intention that it was created from an attribute comprising[734] these two attributes so that He will not extend His anger … And the name *'Elohim* represents the attribute of complete judgment, and the name *YHWH*, [represents] the attribute of complete compassion and the name *'El* is a comprised and combined attribute."[735]

733 Namely, righteous and wicked persons will be the same.

734 I preferred the version *kelulah*, found in a manuscript mentioned by the editor in the varia, to what is printed as בלולה. The latter is an obvious mistake – it does not exist in Hebrew – and especially since immediately afterwards the form מדה כלולה is found, and also elsewhere in his writings, and because this syntagm is a technical Kabbalistic term in Isaac the Blind's school and in Nahmanides' one. See also the next footnote. As a description of the relations between *sefirot*, the term related to the root *kll* occurs also in R. Mose de Leon, whose views do not depend on ibn Adret. See, e.g., his *Commentary on Ten Sefirot*, in ed. G. Scholem, in "Two Treatises of R. Moshe de Leon," *Qovetz 'Al Yad*, (1976), (NS), vol. 8, p. 372 (Hebrew).

735 *Teshuvot ha-Rashba'*, ed. Ch. Z. Dimitrovsky, (Mossad ha-Rav Kook, Jerusalem, 1990), vol. 1, p. 218:

מה שאמרו במדרש אל אלהים ה׳ דבר וגו׳ שבאותן שלש מדות ברא הקב״ה את עולמו במדת אל ואלהים ה׳. די כי שלש מדות יש מדת הדין ומדת הרחמים ומדה מזוגית בין הדין ובין הרחמים. ודע כי אי אפשר להיות העולם עומד על שלמותו בשתי המדות הראשונות לבד. שאם נברא במדת הדין בלבד אי אפשר לו התקיים רגע...וכן אם נברא במדת הרחמים היה הכל שוה ברוב החטא...על כן אי אפשר להיות לו עמידה על הכונה האמיתית שנברא עליה עד שנברא במדה כלולה משתי מדות האלה להאריך אפו...ושם אלהים מדת הדין הגמורה ושם ה׳ מדת הרחמים הגמורה ושם אל מדה כלולה ומזוגה.

See Hames, "Ramon Lull, Solomon ibn Adret, and Alfonso of Valladolid Debate Trinity," pp. 199–204. Compare to Hames's translation ibidem, pp. 210–211, where also the Hebrew original sources have been adduced. I corrected the Hebrew text and its translation. See also ibidem, p. 212, where Hames printed another passage of ibn Adret from a manuscript, where the form מדה מזוגה כלולה occurs. This passage had an impact of a longer discussion found in the anonymous *Sefer Ma'arekhet ha-'Elohut*, fol. 88b, an important Kabbalistic treatise written in ibn Adret's circle, and probably under its influence also in R. Meir ibn Gabbai's *Derekh 'Emunah*, p. 82.

I assume that while [a] is indeed replicating a Midrash, as seen in the two passages above, [b] is closer to the rationale found in the version from Ms. Oxford-Bodleiana 1920, while paragraph [c] contains a concept absent in the two other passages translated above: *middah kelulah*, translated as a "comprised attribute." As seen in chapters 5 and 6 above, this phrase refers to a fundamental Kabbalistic concept found many times in R. Asher ben David, and especially in Nahmanides' writings and in his school, to which ibn Adret belonged, though it occurs in slightly different form already in the book of Bahir. This cardinal term does not appear in Hames' translation of ibn Adret's text. Moreover, on the basis of his translation of the adjective *mezugit/mezugah* – which I translated as mixed or combined – as if pointing to a "total conjunction," Hames claims that ibn Adret has been influenced by a view of Ramon Lull, who used the terms *conjunctio* and *composta* in the context of his discussions of the trinity and of the divine powers he calls *dignitates*.[736] However, the Hebrew form *mezugah* does not mean "conjunction" but rather a combination, or a mixture between two attributes, sometimes envisioned as two types of liquids, one hot and another cold. Its sources are much earlier in Judaism and they may be even as old as Philo, who *inter alia*, has also resorted to a triad of divine attributes.[737]

Let me point out that also Abraham Abulafia, writing in Sicily, mainly in Messina, in the eighties of the 13th century, resorted to some forms of the root *MZG*.[738] Therefore, there is not a special reason to assume that this theme occurs for the first time in ibn Adret's texts, but in that of his master Nahmanides and other members of his school[739] and should, according to Hames, consequently be explained by resorting to the theory of an external influence.

736 See Hames, p. 211. See also his *The Art of Conversion*, pp. 258–265.
737 See Idel, "Notes of Medieval Jewish-Christian Polemics," p. 692.
738 See Abulafia's *Shomer Mitzvah*, p. 28, where he speaks about *middot memuzagot*. For the resort to the term *memuzag*, in order to describe the result of the union between a male and female, namely the offspring, that is related to two equal members of a couple, see his *'Otzar 'Eden Ganuz*, 1:3, p. 140.
739 See Nahmanides' discussion of the relations between the divine attributes

En passant, let me point out that the occurrence of the root *MZG*, together with the question of the concept of a combination between the divine attributes, is found at least twice in R. Menahem Recanati's *Commentary on the Pentateuch*, written sometime at the beginning of the 14th century in Italy.[740] Its contemporary, the anonymous Kabbalistic classic *Ma'arekhet ha-'Elohut*, a book that stems from the circle of Kabbalists around R. Shlomo ibn Adret in Catalunia, which has been written sometime early in the 14th century, describes the sixth *sefirah*, *Tiferet*, as *middah mezugah*,[741] combining as it is the two higher *sefirot*. Though it is not impossible to reduce these two discussions to a common earlier source, hypothetically found solely in ibn Adret's Kabbalistic school, I see it as much less plausible alternative to my assumption that there were earlier Jewish sources, independent of ibn Adret's passages, as adduced above and those that were influenced by them.

The recurrence of the terms *mezugah* and *mazug*, in various Kabbalistic contexts is the main reason why, unlike Hames's hypothesis that ibn Adret's discussions of the three attributes have been influenced by Ramon Lull's views on this point, it is much more economical and plausible, in my opinion, to assume the possibility of an inverse direction of the impact. The variety of Hebrew sources, from Zoharic material to early 14th century written in Spain and in Italy, and in the eighties of the 13th century in Sicily, some of which even referring to a "Midrash," may be easier understood as stemming from an earlier

in his commentary on Leviticus 23:17, ed. Chavel, vol. II p. 150 and use of the phrase דברים מזוגים. See also R. Shem Tov ibn Gaon's *Keter Shem Tov*, in ed. *'Amudei ha-Qabbalah*, p. 55. If we do not assume that the passage was influenced by Ibn Adret, which I do not see as a necessary assumption, then we may speak of the two authors active at the same time, drawing from a common source. For a later resort to the adjective *memuzag* in the context of a third *sefirah* that mediates between two others see R. Moshe Cordovero in, e.g., *'Or Yaqar*, (Jerusalem, 1970), vol. 5, p. 18, as well as pp. 194, 245, ibidem, vol. 11, (Jerusalem, 1981), p. 113 and n. 502 above.

740 Fols. 25d, 66a.

741 fol. 86b.

common source in Hebrew, similar to the Midrash translated at the beginning of this chapter. This means, in my opinion, that also Lull's resort to the terms *conjunctio* and *composta,* may reflect, like his doctrine of *dignitates* in general, a Jewish, basically Kabbalistic influence on this point.[742] Without being acquainted with the available Jewish sources in the Middle Ages and the pertinent bibliography on the three attributes, it is indeed difficult to deal with the sources of the late 13th century Kabbalists.

Moreover, it should be mentioned that the impact of Nahmanides' theory of several types of *kavod* or divine glories, on Lull's views on *dignitates,* may be related to the theory of the mixed third *sefirah* in ibn Adret's discussions, since he belonged to Nahmanides' Kabbalistic school. I am not confident that this is indeed the case since I did not sufficiently study the topic. However, on the ground of the available sources as they have been brought by Hames, this direct of influence seems to be *prima facie,* a more plausible solution. As it is known, Ramon Lull was in contact with ibn Adret, and with the latter's companion in Barcelona and Abulafia's former student, R. Yehudah Salmon that was mentioned above and, in my opinion, we may better assume that also in this case the direction of influence was from Jewish sources to Christian ones, not vice-versa.[743]

However, let me mention that Hames' major point in his article, namely to show that the addressee of ibn Adret's discussions is to be identified with Ramon Lull, is well-taken, since it includes a convincing testimony for a certain – implicit – dialogue between the two contemporary authors even if – in my opinion – the direction of influence should be changed, and see Kabbalah as one more source for Lull. My own view as to the direction of influence is sustained also by the fact that Nahmanides, when speaking on the thirteen divine attributes mentioned in Exodus 34:6, was quoted to the effect that the first three terms are the essence of the divine name[s] – *'Atzmutam* – or

742 See M. Idel, "*Dignitates* and *Kavod*: Two Theological Concepts in Catalan Mysticism," *Studia Luliana,* vol. 36 (1996), pp. 69–78.

743 Idel, "Ramon Lull and Ecstatic Kabbalah."

of the theosophical divinity in general, which he describes as the third *sefirah*, the sixth and the tenth, while the remaining ten terms as implicitly referring to ten *sefirot*.[744] Thus, some form of triunity is found already in a version of Nahmanides' commentary on the Pentateuch.

Last but not least: in a polemical work written by an anonymous author in Ashkenaz, a contemporary of ibn Adret, known as *Sefer Nizzaḥon Vetus*, the Christian is imagined to have said to the Jew in the context of trinity: "You say of the two attributes judgment and compassion that the attribute of mercy that preponderates and mediates between them."[745] This statement, most probably formulated by a Jew, operates with a triad that differs from the classical Kabbalistic one that identifies the attribute of compassion – *raḥamim* – with a synthesis[746] between mercy – *ḥesed* – and judgment – *din*. This view is found already in the *Book of Bahir* and became widespread later on and runs against the Rabbinic form of duality of the two attributes as mentioned above in so many cases.[747] Here, however, compassion changes place with mercy. This is indeed quite a rare type of triad but, nevertheless, not an exceptional one, as I have pointed out elsewhere.[748] I would like to not return to those examples, some of them found already in an English translation, but refer another small piece of information.

In a context of a quotation of this view of Nahmanides, R. Baḥya ben Asher, a disciple of ibn Adret, mentions the term *Ḥesed*,

744 This is a version of Nahmanides' commentary on Exodus 34:6, as quoted in R. Baḥya ben Asher's commentary *ad locum* that differs, however, from Nahmanides' printed commentary. See ed. Ch. D. Chavel, (Mossad ha-Rav Kook, Jerusalem, 1967), II, p. 352.

745 D. Berger, ed., *The Jewish-Christian Debate in the High Middle Ages – A Critical Edition of Nizzahon Vetus*, (JPS, Philadelphia, 1979), p. 3: אתם אומרים משתי מדות דין ורחמים ומדת חסד מכרעת וממצעת

746 Nota bene the linguistic form *mematza'at*, that corresponds to *memutza'* in the passage translated from Ms. Oxford-Bodleiana 1920.

747 See above chapter 3.

748 "Notes of Medieval Jewish-Christian Polemics," pp. 690–695, 219–222.

compassion, as being related to the third *sefirah* of a lower triad, that of *Tiferet*, in a manner paralleling some of the triads I discussed in my brief comments above.[749] Also in a book of R. Abraham Abulafia it is possible to discern an uncommon arrangement of the three *sefirot* under scrutiny here[750] as it is the case also in the book of his student, R. Nathan ben Sa'adyah Ḥar'ar.[751] This means that as late as the end of the 13th century, the sefirotic system as we know it since the 14th century was not totally stabilized and earlier traditions still competed with each other, as we can discern also in the writings of R. Isaac of Acre, the disciple of R. Nathan.

749 See R. Baḥya's commentary on Exodus, 34:6, ed. Chavel, II, p. 352.
750 See in the previous chapter, the quote from *'Or ha-Sekhel*, p. 20.
751 *Sha'arei Tzedeq*, p. 6, discussed in Liebes, *God's Story*, p. 150 n. 104. More on his views see in the previous chapter.

Some Concluding Remarks

As mentioned in some instances above, I propose to see in theosophical-theurgical schools of Kabbalah more the result of an evolution of traditions found within the orbit of Rabbinic elites rather than a Gnostic revolution. The situation that I attempted to portray above is that of a conceptual and institutional affinity between some aspects of Rabbinic theology and early Kabbalah, that excludes the emergence of a totally different axiology that Kabbalists were aware of, or an attempt to reform the allegedly "hypertrophical" Rabbinism by means of adopting hypothetical Gnostic myths.[752] Most of the Kabbalists surveyed above exposed mythical theories that were consonant with Rabbinic texts, in fact, by elaborating on some of the latter, a fact especially evient in R. Ezra of Gerona. Indeed, some of the important legalistic figures mentioned above were at the same time also Kabbalists.

The special concern of many Kabbalists with the Rabbinic literatures and worldviews has been duly noticed already by Alexander Altmann[753] and Gershom Scholem.[754] Nevertheless, when looking for the main clues for explaining the emergence of Kabbalah, those

752 See Scholem, *On the Kabbalah and Its Symbolism*, p. 120 and my "Kabbalism and Rabbinism," pp. 281–296. See also Sendor, *The Emergence of Provencal Kabbalah*, 1, pp. 263–270.

753 *Was ist Juedische Theologie*, (Frankfurt a/M, 1933), p. 15.

754 See *Major Trends*, pp. 28–29. See also Tishby, *Studies*, vol. 1, pp. 31.

concerns have been marginalized, especially in the manner that Scholem attempted to account for the phenomenology of early Kabbalah as substantially informed by Gnostic impulses. This is especially the case by his ignoring the topic of *middot* as a significant category for early Kabalists. The conceptual continuity is, in my opinion, not just a matter of drawing on earlier authoritative texts as mere prooftexts for new ideas, but is connected to the fact that it was done by persons either belonging to elites whose authority is strongly related to those texts as springboards for their speculations, or living in their entourage.

This rule has some interesting exceptions, one of the most important of them being Abraham Abulafia's critique of some Rabbis, a critique which is, in some instances in his later writings, indeed very sharp.[755] Our discussions in chapter 9 show the profound differences between his and his followers's psychological vision of the attributes and the more mythical and hypostatic perceptions of the Rabbis and of other Kabbalists. In fact, the more mythically oriented Kabbalists were more conservative while the more philosophically oriented school of Abulafia's was more in tension with the Rabbinic traditions. Thus, it would be a simplification to reduce the relations between Kabbalah as a whole and Rabbinism to any simple statement. The tensions mentioned there are related to the large-scale adoption of philosophical themes that differ from those adopted by the theosophical-theurgical Kabbalists. It may well-be that details of those critiques of Rabbinic Judaism found in Abraham Abulafia's writings were known by Johann Reuchlin, the early 16th century eminent Christian Kabbalist, who actually mentions books of Abulafia, without, however specifying their titles.[756] In my opinion, the approach to Kabbalah and Rabbinism as formulated by Reuchlin – what I call Christotrophia – had a deep impact on scholarship of Kabbalah, including the earlier Kabbalah, and I would like to elaborate on this point below.

The stark dichotomy between the Talmudists and the Kabbalists

755 This aspect of Abulafia's thought still waits a separate analysis.
756 *On the Art of the Kabbalah*, p. 92.

as proposed by Reuchlin in several instances[757] reflects a distinctly Christian, rather negative, attitude toward Rabbinic Judaism, an example of a transfer of categories from one culture to another. The view of the Talmudists as worshiping God out of fear, while the Kabbalists do it out of love, is mirroring the famous Christian distinction between Jews and Christians. In fact, Kabbalah is conceived of in modern scholarship in terms that are very close to the way the Christians understood Christianity. This attitude, already found in Giovanni Pico della Mirandola, become much more elaborate in Reuchlin. He has exploited even distinctions that are indeed found in the Jewish tradition between topics like the account of creation and that of the chariot, or the perfection of the body and that of the soul, as if they reflect the dichotomy of Talmudists versus Kabbalists.[758] In this case we may discern how the cultural hermeneutical grid of a Christian Kabbalist changed dramatically the sense of some distinctions found already in the Jewish tradition.

This Christian orientation is peculiarly evident in the different attitudes toward the Messiah in the Talmudic, versus the Kabbalistic camp.[759] While the former emphasizes the corporeal salvation, the latter is alleged to stress the spiritual one, which means also the world's redemption from sins by the Messiah in a clearly Christian manner. A similar claim is made also in the context of the presentation of a passage of R. Azriel of Gerone; for the Jewish Kabbalist the disappearance of sin is conditioning the advent of the Messiah.[760] I cannot enter here into the interesting details of Reuchlin's treatment of this passage, but it suffices to say that this is a fine example for the Christian turn he gives to the cited text since Reuchlin claims the very opposite, namely that the knowledge of the Messiah will put an end to sin.[761]

757 See, e.g, *On the Art of the Kabbalah*, pp. 96, 98, 100, 106.
758 Ibidem, p. 96.
759 Ibidem, p. 106.
760 Ibidem, p. 108. The text is found in Ms. Halberstamm 444, (New York JTS, 1887), fol. 66a, and was printed by Scholem, "New Remnants."
761 Ibidem, p. 108.

Interestingly enough, a short piece belonging to ecstatic Kabbalah made a very similar distinction, though an inverted one, according to which it is the Christ who stands for the corporeal Messianism, while the Jewish Messiah stand for the spiritual redemption.[762] More were the Kabbalists portrayed by Reuchlin as spirituals, more were the Talmudists conceived by him as immersed in a basically corporeal kind of life.

To a certain extent, Reuchlin, the most learned Christian author in matters of Judaica of his generation, continued nevertheless the much older religious polemics between Christianity and Judaism, by using classical clichés. What is new in the Renaissance transformations of the older confrontation is that instead of using Midrashic and Talmudic material in order to combat Judaism, as it was the case in the polemics in Middle Ages, some Renaissance Christian authors resorted to Kabbalistic material, especially exegetical strategies, which was put in the service of the new polemics.[763] Curious and willing to learn about the Jewish mysteries as they were, from the theological point of view, there are not great differences in the relationship to Judaism between the Renaissance and medieval Christian theologians as far as the validity of Judaism as a religious way of life.[764] When writing *De arte cabalistica*, immediately after his fierce controversy against the call for destruction of Jewish books, Reuchlin is defending a perception of Kabbalah that, in many cases, is not only far away from the original texts he quotes but, in some instances, it also con-

762 See Reuchlin, *On the Art of Kabbalah*, p. 110, Idel, *Studies in Ecstatic Kabbalah*, p. 54, *Messianic Mystics*, pp. 77–79, and "The Pearl, the Son and the Servants."

763 This is rarely the case of Christians but of Jewish converts to Christianity, like Avner of Burgos. On Pico's attitude to the Jews see my "Kabbalah and Hermeticism in Dame Frances A. Yates's Renaissance," *Esoterisme, Gnoses & Imaginaire Symbolique: Melanges offerts à Antoine Faivre*, eds. R. Caron, J. Godwin, W.J. Hanegraaf, J-L. Vieillard-Baron, (Peeters, Louvain, 2001), pp. 71–90.

764 See also Heiko A. Oberman, *The Roots of Anti-Semitism in the Age of Renaissance and Reformation*, tr. J.I. Porter, (Fortress Press, Philadelphia, 1984), pp. 24–31.

tradicts their main messages. Reuchlin's appeal to Baruchias earlier in *De Verbo Mirifico*: "Turn away from the Talmud"[765] is reverberated, conceptually if not literally, in many discussions in the later *De Arte Cabalistica*. This call is indeed bizarre for a scholar acquainted with the nature of Kabbalah in general, but it is especially staggering for a student of a Kabbalistic codex that mirrors the content of Ms. Halberstamm 444, (now Ms. New York JTS 1887), where long folios contain Kabbalistic interpretations of Rabbinic legends, as found in R. Ezra of Gerona's *Commentary on the Talmudic Aggadot*.[766] The cultural and theological hermeneutics of the Renaissance thinkers was much stronger than the philological and historical inclinations of their humanist contemporaries. Philology was good enough to fathom the original sense of the ancient classical, mainly of pagan culture, but it failed, rather systematically, when confronting the contents and the contexts of the Hebrew theological texts. Reuchlin failed to perceive the importance of the theurgical element in the main line of Kabbalah, strongly connected as it is with the meaning or the performance of the commandments.[767]

This dissociation of Rabbinic literature as an important conceptual background for the explanation offered to emergence of Kabbalah – which actually drew important modes of thought from Rabbinic texts – penetrated not just Christian Kabbalah but also Jewish modern research in the field. This is especially conspicuous from the great impact Reuchlin's theory of symbolism and his view of Kabbalah as

765 See Oberman, ibidem, p. 27.

766 See Isaiah Tishby's description of the relevant Geronese material found in the Halberstamm manuscript, especially fols. 25a–39b, in his introduction to R. Azriel's *Commentary on the Talmudic Legends*, p. 15. See also my introduction to Reuchlin's *On the Art of Kabbalah*, pp. XVI–XIX.

767 See my *Representing God*, pp. 142–148, and compare to the different definition of theurgy adopted by Elliot Wolfson, "Language, Secrecy, and the Mysteries of Law: Theurgy and the Christian Kabbalah of Johannes Reuchlin," *Kabbalah*, vol. 13 (2005), pp. 20–21, which differs from those he used in other, non-polemical contexts. This inversion of meaning of theurgy as used by him elsewhere is a tactic fascinating from the psychological point of view.

receptio symbolica, had on Scholem's view of Kabbalah.[768] However, even deeper and more influential is this Christian Kabbalist's perception of the conceptual disparity between the two types of Jewish literature, that has been adopted by Scholem and his followers. All this despite the fact that early Kabbalah has been endorsed by eminent Halakhic figures that were also leaders of their quite traditional communities, and by their disciples.

Indeed, as Reuchlin pointed out insightfully, there are affinities between R. Azriel's views and Christian thought, as Scholem has also duly pointed out, and I assume that this is an important insight that is helpful for understanding some few aspects of early Kabbalah. However, without diminishing this insight, we shall nevertheless pay attention also to other sources of early Kabbalah, including probably also Philonic thought. In addition to taking into consideration in a more serious manner the profound and recurring contribution of Rabbinic texts, one should pay attention also to other possible sources, in addition to Gnosticism and Neoplatonism, one of which are Pythagorean elements. However, the prevailing trend today can be conceived of as Christotropic, as it is evident from the introduction of new categories as Mariology and incarnation, as pertinent for a new scholarly interpretation of Kabbalah.

In this context let me point out that not always is the problem related to misinterpretation of texts. Scholem's suggestion, following Reuchlin, as to the impact of Erigena on R. Azriel, is not faulty, but when scholars avoid pointing out also the role of other decisive elements in the latter's writings, like theurgy, the picture that emerges as to his thought is, phenomenologically speaking, problematic. Moreover, overemphasizing the thought of R. Azriel in the more comprehensive picture of early Kabbalah, is also problematic . One should just compare the amount of discussions concerning the thought of R. Ezra and Nahmanides, in comparison to R. Azriel and Pseudo-R. Isaac

768 See my *Representing God*, pp. 128–137 and Scholem, *Die Erforschung der Kabbalah von Reuchlin bis zur Gegenwart* (Selbstverlag der Stadt, Pforzheim, 1969), p. 7.

the Blind, as done in Scholem's *Origins of the Kabbalah*, and one can easily discern the bias toward the more philosophical aspects, which indeed exist, but their role in the overall picture of early Kabbalah has been exaggerated. Moreover, some writings of Kabbalists which played a greater role, as testified by numbers of extant manuscripts, remained inedited, while books found in a unique manuscript, are printed, as is the case with R. Azriel of Gerona's *Commentary on the Talmudic 'Aggadot*, edited in a fine edition by Isaiah Tishby, while R. Ezra's commentary, which inspired much of Azriel's, is still extant only in manuscripts, more numerous than Azriel's commentary. This scholarly predilection is part of what I called in the introduction, the Romantic approach.

However, it should be pointed out that though the Neoplatonic ideas of early Kabbalah, pointed out by Reuchlin and Scholem, are the most significant among philosophical sources, there were also some other, that still require detailed investigations. To a certain extent some earlier Greek speculative, astronomical/astrological and magical materials arrived to Al-Andalus some decades before the arrival of Aristotelian material, and those elements were adopted by Jewish thinkers in different proportions, like R. Shlomo ibn Gabirol, R. Abraham ibn Ezra, R. Moshe ibn Ezra or R. Joseph ibn Tzaddiq, for example, and Kabbalists drew from that earlier stage of penetration of Greek material via Arabic translations and elaborations, in their attempts to offer a more comprehensive religious alternative structure to the later adoptions of the Neo-Aristotelian material by Jewish thinkers.[769] The appropriations of some Pre-Socratic theories

769 For the presence of Pseudo-Empedocles's quite substantial fragments translated from Arabic into Hebrew, probably in late 13th century in Castile, which were preserved solely in Kabbalistic writings, though only somewhat later ones, since early 14th century, see David Kaufmann, *Studies in Hebrew Literature of the Middle Ages*, tr. I. Eldad, (Mossad ha-Rav Kook, Jerusalem, 1965), pp. 78–125 (Hebrew), and Scholem, *Origins of the Kabbalah*, pp. 327–328 n. 264. Another book translated from Arabic, which had a significant impact on Jewish literature, including Kabbalistic ones, is ibn Sid Al-Bataliyusi's *Imaginary Circles*, that has been translated three times in Hebrew. This is a

of opposites are only one example for this penetration of Greek and Hellenistic materials: Hermetical, Pythagorean,[770] astrological and magical to Jews in medieval Europe.[771] The various doxographies

late 11th–early 12th century Neoplatonic-Pythagorean treatise, which has been printed and studied by Kaufmann. See his *Die Spuren al-Batalyusi's in der Judischen Religionsphilosophie* (Budapest, 1880), Alexander Altmann, "The Ladder of Ascension," in his *Von der Mittelalterlichen zur Modernen Aufklaerung: Studien zur Juedischen Geistgeschichte* (Mohr, Tuebingen, 1987), pp. 34–59 and my *Ascensions on High*, pp. 170–185.

770 See Franz Rosenthal, "Some Pythagorean Documents Transmitted in Arabic," *Orientalia* (NS) vol. 10 (1941), pp. 104–115, 383–395; idem, *The Classical Heritage in Islam* (Routledge, London, 1975), p. 40 and D.J. O'Meara, *Pythagoras Revived* (Oxford University Press, Oxford, 1989), pp. 230–232. On Nemesius of Emessa, John of Damascus and Shahrastani, who all mentioned Pythagoras, see Harry A. Wolfson, *Studies in the History of Philosophy and Religion*, eds., I. Twersky & G.H. Williams (Harvard University Press, Cambridge, 1973), vol. 1, p. 357 and see also Sa'id al-Andalusi, *Tabaqat al-umam*, tr. G. Blachere (Paris, 1935), pp. 57–62, Bernard R. Goldstein, "A Treatise on Number Theory from a Tenth Century Arabic Source," *Centhaurus*, vol. 10 (1964), pp. 129–160. For the impact of a central Pythagorean view, of *tetraktis*, on Abraham ibn Ezra and R. Azriel of Gerona see M. Idel, review of Sed-Rajna's translation of R. Azriel's commentary on prayerbook, in *QS*, vol. 50 (1975), 284–287 (Hebrew), as well as my "*The Sefirot above the Sefirot*," p. 261 n. 110. This theme occurs several times also in Abraham Abulafia and Joseph Gikatilla. See also Farber, "*The Shell Precedes the Fruit*," pp. 121 n. 14, 130–131 n. 69. For the possibility that *tetraktis* is found alredy in *Sefer Yetzirah* see Phineas Mordell, *The Origin of Letters and Numeral, According to Sefer Yetzirah* (Philadelphia, 1914), in fact Breslau 1914, printed by H. Fleichmann. The text had already been printed, to a great extent, in *JQR* [NS] vol. 2 (1912), pp. 557–583; vol. 3 (1913), pp. 517–544.

771 See, e.g., Sarah Stroumsa and Sara Sviri, "The Beginnings of Mystical Philosophy in Al-Andalus: Ibn Masarra and His *Epistle on Contemplation*," *Jerusalem Studies in Arabic and Islam* vol. 36 (2009), pp. 201–252, Sarah Stroumsa, "The Thinkers of "This Peninsula" – Toward an Integrative Approach to the Study of Philosophy in Al-Andalus," in ed. D. Freidenreich – M. Goldstein, *Beyond Religious Border: Interaction and Religious Exchange in the Medieval Islamic World* (University of Pennsylvania Press, Philadelphia, 2011), pp. 44–53. See also above n. 35. In this context the various topics of the epistles of the so-called "Brethren of Sincerity," are examples of mixtures of different types of Hellenistic views, which were one of the conduits of older material to Spain.

extant in Greek and Arabic were instrumental in transmitting ancient views to the High Middle Ages.[772] In this context also the significant influence of astrology on some Kabbalists should be mentioned again.[773] Interestingly enough, the interest in occult material is evident in the late 13th century king of Castile, Alfonso Sabio. Jewish scholars were very prominent in translating for him treatises from Arabic. It is in Castile that the most important floruit of Kabbalah is quite evident since the sixties of the 13th century, as some form of Jewish renaissance rparalleled by the Castilian renascence in the circle of the erudite king.[774]

This mixture of material can be labeled "occultist" and it contributed significant components for the articulations of various Kabbalistic systems and practices, which have also other, and often much more substantial sources.[775] The existence of this variety of accessible speculative sources is one of the reasons for the diversification of the conceptual structures of Kabbalistic literature already in its earliest phases, and even more so since the second part of the 13th century. Unlike the more stable *modus vivendi* of the most of the Kabbalists, the diversity of Kabbalistic theologies, informed by a wide variety of intellectual sources, more evident in the sometimes sharp controversies between the Kabbalists, precludes generalizations.

See also Goldreich, "The Theology of the Iyyun Circle," and Shlomo Pines, "Shi'ite Terms and Conceptions in Judah Halevi's *Kuzari*," *Jerusalem Studies in Arabic and Islam*, vol. 11 (1980), pp. 165–251, and Idel, "Sefirot Above Sefirot," pp. 269–272.

772 See, e.g., *Musserei ha-Filosofim*, ed. A. Loewenthal, (Frankfurt am/Main, 1896) and the various philosophical encyclopedias in Hebrew since the second part of the 13th century and especially in the various writings of R. Shem Tov ibn Falaquera.

773 See above in the Introduction.

774 See my *Kabbalah: New Perspectives*, pp. 210–218 and "On European Cultural Renaissances and Jewish Mysticism".

775 I hope to dedicate to this hypothesis a separate study. See, meanwhile, my "Anamnesis and Music, on Kabbalah as Renaissance Before the Renaissance," *Rivista di Storia e letteratura religiosa*, XLIX.2, (2013), pp. 383–405, and Sendor's earlier valuable remarks in *The Emergence of Provencal Kabbalah*, pp. 279–285.

APPENDIX:
From Rabbinic Model [A] to Lurianism

We have seen above a long series of topics in early Kabbalah that continue Rabbinic views about the two divine attributes, and elaborated and reinterpreted them in novel and sometimes surprising ways. I concentrated mainly on the 13th century Kabbalists, while later developments were mentioned only sporadically. In this appendix, however, I would like to address some texts written sometime in the last decades of the 16th century, by R. Joseph ibn Tabul Mugrabi, and R. Ḥayyim Vital Calabrese, two main disciples of R. Isaac Luria Ashkenazi, and mention shortly the third one, R. Israel Sarug. The importance of these passages is mainly their contribution for revisiting a certain scholarly theory dealing with the emergence of evil as part of the primordial withdrawal or retreat of the divine light, which regards the view included in the passage as the allegedly esoteric meaning. This scholarly theory imagines that such a Kabbalistic view was obfuscated by the most widespread depiction of this theory in the writings of R. Ḥayyim Vital, Luria's major disciple, which avoided, so it is alleged, expressing it in the incomparably more extensive presentation of Lurianic Kabbalah.[776]

776 Tishby, *The Doctrine of Evil*, pp. 17–18, 56–57. This version of withdrawal was

The major question addressed in it is the manner in which evil emerged out the perfect Infinite, and this explanation, described in scholarship as cathartic, has been conceived in scholarship as a doctrine to be hidden even from Kabbalists. Also Luria's views have been described in scholarship as Gnostic, in the manner the early Kabbalistic writings have been imagined by scholars.[777] I propose to see the discussions below as part of an inner development in Kabbalistic theosophy that started already at the end of the 13th century, and gradually became more concerned with the pre-sefirotic processes.

Let us start with a passage of R. Joseph ibn Tabul, where he describes the situation of the Infinite before the act of withdrawal, *Tzimtzum*:

> "[A]nd that power [of judgment] was mixed in the entire [realm] of His existence, blessed be He... and when He decided to emanate His world, He collected all the roots of judgment that were absorbed in Him, namely He disclosed them gradually... For example, the grain of dust within the great sea does not generate mud, and is not visible, but when the water is distilled the dust that was mixed there, will be found and revealed. This is also the case here, the extreme of compassion and of judgment are absorbed, and when all the power of judgment was collected and assembled to one place, it became gross, and because of it the light of the Infinite, blessed be He, was removed and there remained the *reshimu*[778] of light with the power of judgment."[779]

presented as the classical form of Lurianic thought also by Scholem in *Major Trends in Jewish Mysticism*, p. 267, idem, *On the Kabbalah and Its Symbolism*, pp. 110–111, and idem, *Kabbalah*, pp. 129–130. I dealt with this topic already earlier in my studies, cf. Idel, *Primeval Evil in Kabbalah*, pp. 282–285, but I return to it here in the context of my discussions of the divine attributes, starting with the Rabbinic model [A], an issue I did not engage in earlier.

777 Tishby, ibidem, pp. 16–18, idem, "Gnostic Doctrines."

778 Namely the vestiges of light that remain after the act of withdrawal.

779 *Derush Ḥeftzi Bah*, printed in *Simḥat Kohen*, by R. Mas'ud ha-Kohen el-Ḥadad, (Jerusalem, 1921), fol. 1cd,

Though the term "attribute" is not mentioned here, the resort to two entities described as compassion and judgment, points in this direction, and I assume that the term *middah* has been substituted by the word power: *koaḥ*. What seems to me pertinent for the topic of the present study is the similarity hetween the situation depicted in this passage and what I labeled above as model [A] in Rabbinic literature: In both cases two divine entities have been associated to water. However, while for the Rabbinic author the main concern was to address the mixture of attributes as strictly necessary for creation, for the Kabbalist the main concern is to show that the differentiation between these attributes that are depicted as initially mixed, is the clue for understanding the beginning of creation. In such a manner, he adopts the Rabbinic view that the world was created by the two attributes, but elaborates much beyond what is found in Rabbinic literature, especially insofar as the emergence of evil is concerned. Earlier in this sermon ibn Tabul says:

> "What caused the removal[780] was the power of judgment since all that is below is by necessity, its root is on high in the outmost [power of] compassion. If we do say that the root of judgment was not there it may be a deficiency in the nature of God, Blessed be He, that is not called perfect in outmost perfection, but [only]

ואותו הכח היה מעורב בכל מציאותו יתברך...וכשעלה ברצונו להאציל עולמו קבץ כל שרשי הדין שהיו מובלעים בו פי׳ שגלה אותם מעט בו...ונתקבץ האור אל מקום אחד ובמרום אותם השרשים נסתלק הרחמים דרך משל גרגיר עפר בתוך ים הגדול אינו עושה עכירות ואינו נרגש וכשיסתתנו המים ימצא ויתגלה העפר שנתערב שם. כך בכאן תכלית הרחמים והדין נבלע וכשנתקבץ ונאסף כל כח הדין למקום אחד מתעבה ומחמתו מסתלק אור א״ס יתברך ונשאר שם רשימו של אור עם כח הדין.

See also Tishby, *The Doctrine of Evil*, p. 57, Meroz, *Redemption in the Lurianic Teaching*, p. 248. For other important discussions of this vision of mixture see *Commentary on 'Idra' Rabbah* by R. Joseph ibn Tabul, ed. I. Weinstock, in *Temirin*, (1982), vol. 2. p. 137. See also Yonathan Garb, "The Kabbalah of Rabbi Joseph ibn Sayyah as a Source for the Understanding of Safedian Kabbalah," *Kabbalah* 4 (1999), p. 287 (Hebrew).

780 Of the divine light found in the *reshimu*.

if nothing is missing, God forefends, but certainly the power of judgment is found there."[781]

Let me start with the obvious observation that ibn Tabul did not consider this theory as an esoteric doctrine. Neither is the parallel found in Vital's seminal exposition of Luria's view assuming a hidden type of knowledge. He writes that "within water there is mud in a great occult manner, and this is the reason it is called *'Elohim*."[782] Later on in this context it is said that "the mud of water has been revealed since it is known that the shells seize the name *'Elohim*."[783] I assume that by a comparison to ibn Tabul's passages it will not be adventitious to assume that also Vital had in mind the attribute of judgment, related to the name *'Elohim*. This means that this attribute is found already in the space where the act of withdrawal of the divine light, known as the act of *tzimtzum*, takes place.

781 *Derush Ḥeftzi Bah*, fol. 1c:

ומה שגרם להסתלק הוא כח הדין שכל מה שלמטה מוכרח שיהיה כחו למעלה בתכלית הרחמים ואם לא נאמר שיהיה שם דין נמצא חסר ח"ו בחוקו יתברך שאינו שלם בתכלית השלימות א"כ שאינו חסר בו שום דבר ואם לא נאמר שהיה שם דין נמצא חסר ח"ו.

The passage was discussed by Tishby, *The Doctrine of Evil*, p. 57, Meroz, *Redemption in Lurianic Teaching*, pp. 186–191, and Yoram Jacobson, 'The Problem of Evil and Its Sanctification in Kabbalistic Thought,' in eds. H.G. Reventlow, Y. Hoffman, *The Problem of Evil and Its Symbols in Jewish and Christian Tradition*, (T. & T. Clark, London, New York, 2004), pp. 97–100. Jacobson did not point out the discrepancy between the concept of perfection and the cathartic thesis of Tishby and Meroz, neither Tishby's attempt to present the position of ibn Tabul in this passage as apologetic. On this Kabbalist see Zviah Rubin, "The Zoharic Commentaries of Joseph ibn Tabul," in Elior-Liebes, *Lurianic Kabbalah*, pp. 363–387 (Hebrew).

782 *'Etz Ḥayyim*, Gate 39, chapter 5, 11, fol. 71b:

מים יש בו עכירות בהעלם גדול לכן נקרא אלקים

Compare also to Vital's discussion at the very beginning of *Mevo' She'arim*, (Jerusalem, 1988), pp. 1–2, discussed briefly in Tishby, *The Doctrine of Evil*, pp. 20–21. The term "occult" here means that it is not discernable, not that it is esoteric.

783 *'Etz Ḥayyim*, Gate 39, chapter 5, 11, fol. 71c:

ונתגלה עכירות המים כי הקלי' נודע שנאחזין בשם אלהים

A similar approach is found also in a tradition adduced by another Kabbalist, R. Israel Benjamin, in the name of his master R. Joseph ibn Tabul, where it is written:

> "Since [the light of the circular *sefirot*] exited from the light within which the [act of] withdrawal took place, which is the returning light, and there is no returning light but out of the power of judgment, and despite the fact that *'Ein Sof* is a simple one, in outmost perfection of the unity, in any case it should be believed that it is perfect as much as possible in the quality of perfection, and you should believe that there was within it the very subtle and pure root of judgment, so that out of its extreme purity it is not distinguished, since there is no one called perfect but someone who comprises in it some existence of all the things that ascended in the thought and knowledge."[784]

I assume that light plays here a role similar to that of water in the other statements. It should be mentioned that also in other cases ibn Tabul articulated a similar view in the context of the two attributes.[785] I see therefore no reason to assume that there is a covering of the more mythical-cathartic view also in this passage. Tishby's methodological assumption as to the apologetic nature of this treatment is not necessary, even in accordance to his own premises. In order to discover the cathartic principle, which is absent in the largest corpus of Lurianic writings as edited by R. Ḥayyim Vital, Tishby relied on the view of the above-mentioned R. Joseph ibn Tabul, as reflecting the "authentic" theory of Luria, allegedly hidden in Vital's numerous and voluminous writings.[786] In my opinion, mentioning the simple and perfect nature

784 Printed by Avivi, *Kabbalat ha-'Ari*, vol. 1 p. 153, from Ms. London, British Library, Or. 10627, fols. 208b–209a. Compare also to R. Meir ibn Gabbai's *Derekh 'Emunah*, p. 82, where he claims that there is no light that is not mixed with darkness, and no darkness that is not mixed with light.

785 See Lawrence Fine, *Physician of the Soul, Healer of the Cosmos, Isaac Luria and His Kabbalistic Fellowship* (Stanford University Press, Stanford, 2003), pp. 126–127.

786 See *The Doctrine of Evil*, pp. 26–27. Meanwhile Avivi has printed a treatise of R. Ḥayyim Vital where the theory of the evil as mixed in the *tehiru* is quite similar

of the Infinite occurs in the context of dealing with the emergence of both good and evil, in the vein of some of the discussions above as to the opposition to the Aristotelian principle that only one and simple entity emerges from a simple perfect entity.[787]

However, beyond the question of alleged esotericism that was attributed by scholars to this theory, another major question should be addressed: was the cathartic model described above an original contribution of ibn Tabul to theosophical thought in Kabbalah, as Isaiah Tishby and Gershom Scholem claimed? As mentioned above, these discussions are better understood as part of an elaboration of Rabbinic model [A]. In my opinion the Rabbinic view served as a springboard, not just as a prooftext. However, between the late antiquity discussions and those of Luria or his disciples, we can discern traces of a development that culminated in Luria's disciples, but certainly did not start with him.[788] So, for example, we read in a late 13th century classic of Kabbalah, R. Joseph Gikatilla's *Sha'arei 'Orah*:

> "The dross of judgment[789] and its shells and they are the powers that exited when it ascended/occurred in His thought, blessed be He, to create the world by [means of] judgment, and the thought of the Holy One, blessed be He, does not turn vain, and they exited and [afterwards] were posited on the back of the holy emanation."[790]

Here judgment and dross were related to the beginning of creation, as part of a divine plan. There can be little doubt that this book was known to many Kabbalists, including the Safedian ones.

to that of ibn Tabul. See his *Kabbalat ha-'Ari*, p. 1012, and Meroz, *Redemption in Lurianic Teaching*, pp. 190–191. Let me point out that I do not accept the view that there is an "authentic" Lurianic view, but just different versions found among different disciples, that compete between themselves.

787 See above, *Some Concluding Remarks*.

788 Compare also my discussion of another version of Lurianic Kabbalah, that of R. Israel Sarug, as depending on the primordial existence of the two attributes as part of the theory of withdrawal, in *Absorbing Perfections*, pp. 38–39.

789 Compare to *Zohar*, II, fols. 191a, 267b, III, fols. 28a, 172a etc, and R. Meir ibn Gabbai, *'Avodat ha-Qodesh*, IV:4, fol. 116b.

790 *Sha'arei 'Orah*, fol. 6b.

However, even closer to Luria is a passage found in his teacher in matters of Kabbalah, R. Moshe Cordovero. In his book *Shi'ur Qomah*, the leading Safedian Kabbalist, wrote as follows:

> "It is explained in *Sefer Pardes Rimmonim* in the Gate of *Temurot*[791] that the *temurot* are found from the mud of the water and the dross of the holy *Hawayyiot*[792] ... and this is the reason why each *Hawayyiah* that emerges, is by necessity a remainder of what passed from that *Hawayyah* from one [level of] existence to another, and when the *Hawayyiot* passed for the sake of this world that emerged, a remainder remained there, and those remainders were emanated from the secret of that which causes the emergence of the lower *Hawayyiot*."[793]

Cordovero resorted to the phrase *'akhirut ha-mayyim*, which is identical to what we have seen in the two short sentences quoted above from R. Ḥayyim Vital's book. To be sure, Cordovero is not the first Kabbalist who used this syntagm in the connection to the theogonic process, as we shall see immediately below. However, it seems that he envisioned it in a manner closer to the Lurianic texts than earlier. Cordovero's vision implies some form of catharsis that assumes that the remainders remained on high and constitute the *temurot*, in a manner that explains how evil can emerge from a perfect entity. This means not only that the roots of evil are found within the supernal world, just as mud in water or dross within wine, but that it also remained there in some hypostatic manner.

Let me point out that the term *motarot*, translated as remainders, is compounded from the same consonants like *temurot*, and in the

791 See Gate XXV, chapter 1.

792 This is a polivalent term in Kabbalah in general, and especially in Cordovero, that means basically, an entity, divine or extra-divine.

793 *Shi'ur Qomah*, fol. 67b:

שפי׳ בספ״ר בש׳ התמורות כי התמורות נמצאו מעכירות המים ושמרי ההויות הקדושות כדפי׳ בפ׳ תרומה סי׳ ( ) ולזה כל הויה שיתהוה בהכרח ישאר מותר ממה שיעתק ההויה ממציאות אל מציאות וכאשר נעתקו ההויות לענין העוה״ז שנתהוה היה שם מותר למעלה ואותם המותרות היו נמשכות מסוד המהוה ההויות התחתונות.

specific context these *temurot* mean powers of evil.[794] The simile should be compared to that of the seed found in Cordovero's *Pardes Rimmonim* XXV:1, II, fol. 53c, since in both cases a fluid is conceived of as containing a component that is separated from it at a certain point. We may, therefore, conclude that this Kabbalist is one of the most plausible sources for the passages in Lurianic Kabbalah. Let me point out that though mentioning a secret, Cordovero does not intend the very theory of the source of evil as an esoteric topic but refers to some form of transcendence of the divine realm, which constitutes the source of the emanated entities.

Let me turn to a passage from the anonymous *Ma'arekhet ha-'Elohut*, an early 14th century treatise from the Kabbalistic school of Nahmanides: The book was in print twice in mid-16th century (Mantua and Ferrara in 1556) and thus available to all the Lurianic Kabbalists and plausibly also to Cordovero. In the context of the use of the syntagm "the Mud of the water" this Kabbalist mentions other Kabbalists – identified by Efraim Gottlieb as R. Shem Tov ibn Gaon's *Keter Shem Tov*[795] – according to whom the first *sefirah, Keter,* is designated as "Primeval Air, Nihil, Absolute Compassion, without any mixture of judgment."

This *sefirah* is posited vis-à-vis the second one, *Ḥokhmah,* described as "Judgment, since He created this versus the other, fire, justice, earth... and the third [*sefirah*] is preponderating [between them][796]

794 Compare also to Cordovero's *Tefillah le-Moshe,* fols. 167a, 192b.

795 See his *The Kabbalah in the Writings of R. Bahya ben Asher ibn Halawa,* pp. 250–251, corresponding to ed. *Ma'or va-Shemesh,* fol. 25b, (instead of 28b as mentioned in Gottlieb's book), or Ms. Paris BN 774, fol. 74b. In the edition of *'Amudei ha-Qabbalah,* p. 4, some of the words that are critical for my point here, do not occur.

796 Namely it is in the middle and mediates between the two first *sefirot,* envisioned as found on the same level. *Makhri'a,* as a technical term, recurs in Nahmanides' school for two lower *sefirot* found in the middle of two couples of higher *sefirot.* The first *makhri'a* stands for *Tiferet,* also called the equal line, cf. ibn Gaon, *Keter Shem Tov,* ed. *'Amudei ha-Qabbalah,* pp. 6, 7 while the second *makhri'a* is *Yesod.* See ibidem, p. 7.

and is called water."[797] This means that the third *sefirah* is a synthesis between the two, which means a sort of compassion combined with judgment, the latter being represented also by earth. In any case this vision of water as preponderating between two opposites is quite exceptional. According to ibn Gaon, in a passage that was not quoted in *Ma'arekhet ha-'Elohut,* when water is poured in a vessel and it settles there, dust is descending.[798] This is certainly an assumption that some form of purification is taking place as part of the theogonic process. It is in this context that he mentions the "mud of water," as stemming from *Binah,* which is considered by many Kabbalists as the beginning of the theo-cosmogony. It seems that the third *sefirah* is conceived of as occupying a median position between the two higher *sefirot,* in a manner reminiscent of a passage found in R. Abraham Axelrod of Koeln's *Keter Shem Tov,* written long before the other texts mentioned in this appendix.[799] Most probably the first occurrences of the syntagm *'akhiyrut ha-mayyim* in a theosophical context, are found in R. Azriel of Gerona's *Commentary on Sefer Yetzirah.*[800] Interestingly enough it is this Kabbalist that presupposes the existence of good and evil within the theosophical system prior to the attributes of compassion and judgment.[801]

This is indubitably an example for the projection of the Rabbinic duality of attributes not just in the lower levels of the sefirotic realm, but actually within the highest one, opening the way to the much later

797 Fol. 164b:

אויר קדמון ונקרא׳ אין והם רחמי׳ גמורים בלי תערובת דין...והשנייה היא דין זה לעומת זה ונקרא אש צדק ארץ...והשלישית מכריע נקרא מים...כי מעכירות המים יצא העפר.

798 *Ma'or va-Shemesh*, fol. 25b, Ms. Paris BN 774, fol. 74b:

ויסוד הד׳ שהוא יסוד העפר מעכירות המים נעשה וזה אות שאין העפר מתקיים בלא מים. וגם המים כשהם מתיישבים בכלי יורד מהם עפר בשולי הכלי.

For "the mud of the water" see also ibidem, fol. 78a: כי מעכירות המים נמצא העפר "from the mudiness of the water dust emerges."

799 *Keter Shem Tov*, p. 9.

800 *Kitvei ha-Ramban*, II, pp. 457, 460.

801 *Commentary on the Talmudic Legends*, ed. Tishby, p. 85, and compare to ibidem, pp. 100–101.

Lurianic speculations, that telescoped the duality on a higher level, as seen above in this appendix. This is part of a broader phenomenon of the gradual growth of interest in pre-sefirotic processes in the history of Kabbalah. In any case, we have here an attempt to offer an answer to the question of the relationship between the two attributes: that of judgment as emanated from that of compassion, by resorting to both a theory of the concatenation of the *sefirot* and by a more naturalistic assumption, following the pre-Socratic view of the Air of Anaximenes, as the source of other elements by condensation and rarefaction. Also the emergence of earth/dust from water by condensation is found in this philosopher.

Quite different is a discussion in the late 13th century anonymous treatise *'Eshkol ha-Kofer*, very close conceptually to R. Joseph Gikatilla's early writings.[802] Though not dealing with the parable of mud and water, the anonymous Kabbalist mentions the concept of Glory, identical with the *Nivra' Rishon*, the first creature,[803] as a place where the "attributes of compassion and attributes of judgment are found" – the plurals are in the original – that correspond to right and left, to face and back, and as the source of all the opposites, *hafakhim*.[804] Thus these attributes were envisioned as situated already before the theogonic processes. On the other hand, this treatise does not resort

802 See Gottlieb, *Studies in Kabbalah Literature*, p. 115 n. 44.

803 On this concept and its sources see S.O. Heller Willensky, "The "First Created Being" in Early Kabbalah and Its Philosophical Sources," in eds. S.O. Heller Willensky – M. Idel, *Studies in Jewish Thought*, (Magnes Press, Jerusalem, 1989), pp. 261–276 (Hebrew). See also Morlok, *Rabbi Joseph Gikatilla's Hermeneutics*, p. 215, and Orna Rachel Wiener, *The Gate of Punctuation, Joseph ben Abraham Giqatilla*, (Idra Publishing, Tel Aviv, 2016), p. 109 (Hebrew).

804 Ms. Vatican 219, fol. 7a:

וא"כ נמצא הכבוד הנברא ראשון שבו מדות רחמים ומדות הדין שהן ימין ושמאל ומאלו נמשכים כל ההפכים וזהו סוד את וארמוז לך פנים ואחור.

The secret of *'ET*, should be understood in the sense of Alpha and Omega, namely the *'Aleph* and *Tav*, the first and the last letter of the Hebrew alphabet, namely as comprising everything, found within the First Creature. See also ibidem, fol. 6b.

to theosophical understandings of the *sefirot,* though the term is used, rarely, in a more numerical sense. Last but not least, as seen in the passage of R. Isaac of Acre translated above beside n. 497, the two attributes are depicted as stemming directly from the *sefirah* of *Keter.*

Thus, we may have an additional case, where the term *middah* played an important role still at the end of the 13th century, more than a theosophical understanding of the *sefirah,* in a sort of Kabbalah much closer to Aristotelian philosophy, as this Kabbalist interprets the opposites as referring to the concept of privation and existence.[805]

The Kabbalistic treatises quoted above never mentioned the doctrine of the emergence of evil as a secret doctrine and there is no reason to assume that this doctrine was not known by Kabbalists long before Luria and his disciples, and subsequently there is not a reason to assume that he invented it or decided to hide it from other Kabbalists. Interestingly enough the two scholars who regarded Luria's theory of catharsis and evil as originating with him, are among the very few scholars that ever wrote in their generation studies about *Sefer Ma'arekhet ha-'Elohut,* where this theory has been alluded.[806] This is an outstanding example of the divorce of a scholarly theory from available primary texts, the latter being regarded, if at all, as just an illustration for the fascinating scholarly theory, formulated by thinkers who were not acquainted with Kabbalah at all, and imported then by scholars in the field of the study of Kabbalah.

The total separation by modern scholars of Luria's discussions of the topic of two attributes and the primordial water from the earlier Kabbalistic treatments is part of the propensity to explain some Kabbalistic views as the result of conceptual ruptures and radical

805 See ibidem, fols. 6b–7a.

806 See Gershom Scholem, "To the Problems of *Sefer Ma'arekhet ha-'Elohut* and Its Commentators," *QS,* vol. 21 (1944/45), pp. 284–295, and Isaiah Tishby, "Passages from *Sefer Ma'arekhet ha-'Elohut* in *Sefer Tzioni,*" *QS,* vol. 19 (1942/1943), pp. 55–57 (Hebrew). The latter's study was printed in the very same year when his monograph about *The Doctrine of Evil* had been printed and he did not refer to this article in the additions to the several editions of this book that he reprinted over the years.

turns, which were imagined to produce new and quite original forms of thought, and subsequently they underestimate the role of continuities in traditional societies that Kabbalists were part of them.[807] This proclivity is characteristic of modern scholarship of Kabbalah, as we have seen above also in the our discussions of the emergence of some aspects of this lore.

807 Compare also to my "Zimzum," as well as *Primeval Evil in Kabbalah*, pp. 270–274. Also the concept of breaking of the vessels that is related to the process of catharsis, is far from being a Lurianic innovation. See Liebes, *Studies in the Zohar*, p. 125, idem, *Studies in Jewish Myth*, pp. 85–86; M. Idel, "An Anonymous Commentary on *Shir ha-Yihud*," *Mysticism, Magic and Kabbalah in Ashkenazi Judaism*. eds. K-E Groezinger and J. Dan, (de Gruyter, Berlin, New York, 1995), pp. 151–154; Ronit Meroz, "R. Joseph Angelet and his 'Zoharic Writings'," *New Developments in Zohar Studies*, [= *Te'uda*, vol. XXI–XXII] Ed. R. Meroz, (Tel Aviv University Press, Tel Aviv, 2007), pp. 336–338 (Hebrew).

Abbreviations

Journals

HTR – Harvard Theological Review
HUCA – Hebrew Union College Annual
JJS – Journal of Jewish Studies
JQR – Jewish Quarterly Review
JSJT – Jerusalem Studies in Jewish Thought
JSJ – Journal for the Study of Judaism
JJTP – Journal of Jewish Thought and Philosophy
JSRI – Journal for the Study of Religions and Ideologies.
MGWJ – Monatschrift fuer Geschichte und Wissenschaft des Judentums
PAAJR – Proceedings of the American Academy for Jewish Research,
QS – Qiryat Sefer
REJ –Revue des études juives

Primary Sources

'Aggudat 'Aggadot – 'Aggudat 'Aggadot, ed. Ḥayyim Meir Horowitz, (Berlin, 1881).

'Amudei ha-Qabbalah – 'Amudei ha-Qabbalah, (Makhon Nezer Shraga, Jerusalem, 2001).

'Arugat ha-Bosem, ed. Urbach – R. Abraham ben Azriel, *'Arugat ha-Bosem,* ed. E.E. Urbach, (Mekize Nirdamim, Jerusalem, 1939–1963) (Hebrew) four volumes.

Asher ben David, Complete Works, ed. Abrams – *R. Asher ben David, His*

Complete Works and Studies in His Kabbalistic Thought, ed. Daniel Abrams, (Cherub Press, Los Angeles, 1996) (Hebrew).

'Avodat ha-Qodesh – R. Meir ibn Gabbai, *Sefer 'Avodat ha-Qodesh* (Jerusalem, 1973).

Berayyita' de-Yosef ben Uzzie'el – ed. Naama ben Shahar, *Berayyita' de-Yosef ben Uzzie'el*, in *Qovetz al Yad*, vol. 23 (33) (2015), pp. 145–187.

Commentary on Bereshit Rabba', ed. Hallamish – R. Joseph ben Shalom Ashkenazi, *Commentary on Bereshit Rabba'*, ed., M. Hallamish, (The Magnes Press, Jerusalem, 1985) (Hebrew).

Ba'alei ha-Nefesh – R. Abraham ben David of Posquières, *Sefer Ba'alei ha-Nefesh*, ed. J. Qapih, (Mossad ha-Rav Kook, Jerusalem, 1978),

Commentary on 'Idra' Rabba' – R. Joseph ibn Tabul, *Commentary on 'Idra' Rabba'*, ed. I. Weinstock, *Temirin*, 11, (1982), pp. 123–167.

Commentary on Sefer Yetzirah – [Pseudo-] R. Isaac Sagi Nahor, *Commentary on Sefer Yetzirah* ed. Gershom Scholem, printed as an appendix to his lectures published as *ha-Qabbalah be-Provence*, ed. R. Schatz (Akademon, Jerusalem, 1964).

Commentary on Sefer Yetzirah – R. Isaac of Acre, *Commentary on Sefer Yetzirah*, ed. G. Scholem, *QS*, vol. 31 (1956), pp. 379–396 (Hebrew).

Commentary on Sefer Yetzirah – R. Joseph Ashkenazi, *Commentary on Sefer Yetzirah*, (Jerusalem, 1961).

Commentary on the Song of Songs – R. Ezra of Gerona, *Commentary on the Song of Songs* printed in *Kitvei ha-Ramban*, ed. Chavel, vol. 11 pp. 476–548.

Commentary on Ten Sefirot – R. Shem Tov ben Shem Tov, *Commentary on Ten Sefirot*, printed in *Sefer 'Amudei ha-Qabbalah*, (Jerusalem, 2001).

Commentary on the Talmudic Legends – R. Azriel of Gerona, *Commentary on the Talmudic Legends*, ed. Isaiah Tishby, (Jerusalem, 1945) (Hebrew).

Commentary on Prayers and Blessings – R. Yehudah ben Yaqar, *Commentary on Prayers and Blessings*, ed. Shmuel Yerushalmi (Jerusalem, 1979), two parts.

Commentary on Daily Prayer – R. Azriel of Gerona, *Commentary on*

Daily Prayer, ed. Martel Gavarin (M.A. Thesis, Hebrew University, Jerusalem, 1984) (Hebrew).

Commentary on the Pentateuch – R. Baḥya ben Asher, *Commentary on the Pentateuch*, ed. Ch. D. Chavel, (Mossad ha-Rav Kook, Jerusalem, 1967), three volumes.

Commentary on the Pentateuch – R. Menahem ben Benjamin Recanati, *Commentary on the Pentateuch*, (Jerusalem, 1961).

Derekh 'Emunah – R. Meir ibn Gabbai, *Derekh 'Emunah*, ed. M. Shatz, (Jerusalem, 1997).

Kitvei ha-Ramban, ed. Chavel – *Kitvei ha-Ramban*, ed. Ch. D. Chavel, *Kitvei ha-Ramban*, (Mossad ha-Rav Kook, Jerusalem, 1964) 2 volumes.

Derush Ḥeftzi Bah – R. Joseph ibn Tabul, *Derush Ḥeftzi Bah*, printed in *Simḥat Kohen*, by R. Mas'ud ha-Kohen el-Hadad, (Jerusalem, 1921)

'Etz Ḥayyim – R. Ḥayyim Vital, *'Etz Ḥayyim* (Warsau, 1891).

The Guide of the Perplexed, tr. Pines – Moses Maimonides, *The Guide of the Perplexed*, tr. Shlomo Pines (Chicago University Press, Chicago, 1963) 2 volumes.

Ḥayyei ha-Nefesh – R. Abraham Abulafia, *Sefer Ḥayyei ha-Nefesh*, ed., A. Gross, (Jerusalem, 2001)

Ḥayyei ha-'Olam ha-Ba' – R. Abraham Abulafia, *Ḥayyei ha-'Olam ha-Ba'* ed. A. Gross, third edition, (Jerusalem, 1999).

'Imrei Shefer – R. Abraham Abulafia, *'Imrei Shefer*, ed. A. Gross, (Jerusalem, 1999).

Kad ha-Qemaḥ, – R. Baḥya ben Asher, *Kad ha-Qemaḥ* in ed. Ch. Chavel, *Kitvei Rabbenu Bahya*, Mossad ha-Rav Kook, Jerusalem 1970).

Keter Shem Tov – R. Abraham Axelrod of Koeln, *Keter Shem Tov* printed in *'Amudei ha-Qabbalah*.

Kitvei ha-Ramban – *Kitvei ha-Ramban*, ed. Ch. D. Chavel, (Mossad ha-Rav Kook, Jerusalem, 1964) 2 volumes.

The Liturgical Poems of Rabbi Yanai, ed. Rabinovitz, – *The Liturgical Poems of Rabbi Yanai*, ed. Z.M. Rabinovitz (Bialik Institute, Jerusalem, 1987), 2 volumes (Hebrew).

Ma'arekhet ha-'Elohut – *Sefer Ma'arekhet ha-'Elohut*, (Mantua, 1558).

Mafteaḥ ha-Ḥokhmot – R. Abraham Abulafia, *Mafteaḥ ha-Ḥokhmot*, ed. A. Gross (Jerusalem, 2001).

Mafteaḥ ha-Ra'yon – R. Abraham Abulafia, *Mafteaḥ ha-Ra'yon*, ed. A. Gross, (Jerusalem, 2002).

Mafteaḥ ha-Sefirot -– R. Abraham Abulafia, *Mafteaḥ ha-Sefirot*, ed. A. Gross (Jerusalem, 2001).

Mafteaḥ ha-Shemot – R. Abraham Abulafia, *Mafteaḥ ha-Shemot*, ed. A. Gross (Jerusalem, 2001).

Mafteaḥ ha-Tokhehot – R. Abraham Abulafia, *Mafteaḥ ha-Tokhehot* ed. A. Gross (Jerusalem, 2001).

Ma'or va-Shemesh, – *Ma'or va-Shemesh*, ed. Yehudah Qoriat, (Livorno, 1939).

Matzref la-Kesef, – R. Abraham Abulafia, *Matzref la-Kesef ve-Kur la-Zahav*, ed. A. Gross, (Jerusalem, 2001).

Me'irat 'Einayyim, ed. Goldreich – R. Isaac of Acre, *Sefer Me'irat 'Einayyim*, ed. A. Goldreich, (Hebrew University, Jerusalem, 1984) (Hebrew).

Meshiv Devarim Nekhoḥim, ed. Vajda – R. Jacob ben Sheshet, *Meshiv Devarim Nekhoḥim*, ed. Y.A. Vajda (Israeli Academy for Sciences and Humanities, Jerusalem, 1968).

Migdol Yeshu'ot, ed. Cohen – R. Yehoshu'a ben Shmuel Naḥmias, *Migdol Yeshu'ot*, ed. R. Cohen (Jerusalem, 1988).

Ner 'Elohim – *Ner 'Elohim*, anonymous, though attributed in print to Abraham Abulafia, ed. A. Gross (Jerusalem, 2002).

Novelot Ḥokhmah, – R. Joseph del Medigo, *Novelot Ḥokhmah*, (Basle, 1631).

'Or Yaqar – R. Moshe Cordovero's *Commentary on the Zohar*, *'Or Yaqar* (Jerusalem, 1963–2009), 28 volumes.

'Otzar Ḥayyim – R. Isaac ben Shmuel of Acre, *'Otzar Ḥayyim* ed. A. Gross, (Jerusalem, 2020).

'Otzar ha-Kavod – R. Todros ben Joseph ha-Levi Abulafia, *'Otzar ha-Kavod*, (Warsau, 1879).

Pardes Rimmonim – R. Moshe Cordovero, *Sefer Pardes Rimmonim* (Muncasz, rpr. Jerusalem, 1962), two parts.

'Otzar 'Eden Ganuz – R. Abraham Abulafia, *'Otzar 'Eden Ganuz,* ed. A. Gross, (Jerusalem, 2000).

Reshit Ḥokhmah – R. Elijah da Vidas, *Reshit Ḥokhmah ha-Shalem,* ed. H.J. Waldman, (Jerusalem, 1984), three volumes.

Pardes Rimmonim – R. Moshe Cordovero, *Pardes Rimmonim* (Muncasz, rpr. Jerusalem, 1962), two parts.

Perush Sefer Yetzirah, ed. Weinstock – R. Abraham Abulafia, *Perush Sefer Yetzirah,* ed. I. Weinstock, (Mossad ha-Rav Kook, Jerusalem, 1984).

Sefer Bahir, ed. Abrams – *Sefer ha-Bahir,* ed. D. Abrams, (Cherub Press, Los Angeles, 1994).

Sefer ha-'Emunot – R. Shem Tov ben Shem Tov, *Sefer ha-'Emunot,* (Ferrara, 1556).

Sefer ha-Melitz – R. Abraham Abulafia, *Sefer ha-Melitz* printed in Abulafia's *Matzref ha-Sekhel,* ed. A. Gross, (Jerusalem, 2001).

Sefer ha-'Ot – R. Abraham Abulafia, "Sefer ha-Ôt. Apokalypse des Pseudo-Propheten und Pseudo-Messias Abraham Abulafia vollendet in Jahre 1285," edited by A. Jellinek, in *Jubelschrift zum Siebzigsten Geburstage de Prof. Dr.H. Graetz,* (Breslau, 1887), pp. 65–88.

Sefer Yeṣira, ed. Hayman – A. Peter Hayman, *Sefer Yeṣira, Edition, Translation and Text-Critical Commentary* (Tübingen: Mohr Siebeck, 2004).

Sha'ar ha-Razim, ed. Kushnir-Oron – R. Todros ben Joseph ha-Levi Abulafia, *Sha'ar ha-Razim,* ed. Michal Kushnir–Oron, (Mossad Bialik, Jerusalem, 1989) (Hebrew).

Sha'ar ha-Sho'el, – R. Azriel of Gerona, *Sha'ar ha-Sho'el,* printed as *Be'ur 'Eser Sefirot,* ed. M. Schatz, (Jerusalem, 1997).

Sha'arei 'Orah – R. Joseph Gikatilla, *Sha'arei 'Orah,* (Warsau, 1883).

Sha'arei Tzedeq- R. Nathan ben Sa'adyah Ha'rar, *Sefer Sha'arei Tzedeq,* ed. J.E. Porush, (Jerusalem, 1989)

Sheqel ha-Qodesh, ed. Mopsik – R. Moshe de Leon, *Sefer Sheqel ha-Qodesh,* ed. Ch. Mopsik, (Cherub Press, Los Angeles, 1996).

Shomer Mitzvah, – R. Abraham Abulafia, *Shomer Mitzvah,* ed. A. Gross, (Jerusalem, 2001).

Shi'ur Qomah, – R. Moshe Cordovero, *Sefer Shi'ur Qomah,* (Warsau, 1883).

Sitrei Torah – R. Abraham Abulafia, *Sitrei Torah,* ed., A. Gross, (Jerusalem, 2002).

Tefillah le-Moshe – R. Moshe Cordovero, *Tefillah le-Moshe,* (Przemysl, 1892)

The Book of the Mirrors, ed. Matt – ed. D. Ch. Matt, *The Book of Mirrors: Sefer Mar'ot ha-Zove'ot by R. David ben Yehudah he-Hasid,* (Brown Judaic Studies, Scholars Press, 1982).

The Rule Scroll, ed. Licht – *The Rule Scroll, A Scroll from the Wilderness of Judaea,* Text, Introduction and Commentary by Jacob Licht (Bialik Institute, Jerusalem, 1965) (Hebrew).

Tiqqunei Zohar – *Tiqqunei Zohar,* ed. R. Margoliot, (Mossad ha-Rav Kook, Jerusalem, 1978).

Tzafnat Pa'aneaḥ – R. Joseph Alashqar, *Tzafnat Pa'aneaḥ,* ed. M. Idel, (Misgav Yerushalayim, Jerusalem, 1998).

Zohar – *Zohar,* ed. R. Margoliot, (Mossad ha-Rav Kook, Jerusalem, 1978), 3 volumes.

Zohar Ḥadash – *Zohar Ḥadash,* ed. R. Margoliot, (Mossad ha-Rav Kook, Jerusalem, 1978).

Who Is the Heir of Divine Things – Philo of Alexandria, *Who Is the Heir of Divine Things, and on the Division into Equals and Opposities,* trs. F.H. Colson – G.H. Whitaker, (Cambridge, Mass., – London, 1985), vol. IV

Studies

Abrams, *Kabbalistic Manuscripts and Textual Theory* – Daniel Abrams, *Kabbalistic Manuscripts and Textual Theory,* second edition, (Jerusalem-Los Angeles, Magnes-Cherub, Press 2013).

Abrams, *The Female Body of God* – Daniel Abrams, *The Female Body of God in Kabbalistic Literature* (Magnes Press, Jerusalem, 2005) (Hebrew).

Abrams, "Chapters from an Emotional and Sexual Biography of God" – Daniel Abrams, "Chapters from an Emotional and Sexual

Biography of God: Reflections on God's Attributes in the Bible, Midrash and Kabbalah," *Kabbalah*, vol. 6 (2001), pp. 263–286 (Hebrew)

Afterman, *Devequt* – Adam Afterman, *Devequt; Mystical Intimacy in Medieval Jewish Thought*, (Cherub Press, Los Angeles, 2011) (Hebrew).

Afterman, "From Philo to Plotinus" – Adam Afterman, "From Philo to Plotinus: The Emergence of Mystical Union," *The Journal of Religion*, vol. 93 (2013), pp. 177–196,

Altmann, "The Motif of the 'Shells'" – Alexander Altmann, "The Motif of the 'Shells' in Azriel of Gerona," *JJS*, vol. 9 (1958), pp. 73–80.

Altmann-Stern, *Isaac Israeli* – Alexander Altmann and Samuel M. Stern, *Isaac Israeli, A Neoplatonic Philosopher of the Early Tenth-Century*, (Oxford University Press, Oxford, 1958).

Arieli, *On the Source of the Doctrine of the Sefirot* – Shemer Arieli, *On the Source of the Doctrine of the Sefirot in Kabbalistic Theosophy: Comparative Study of Kabbalah in the Middle Ages and the Religion of Mesopotamia* (Ph.D. Thesis Bar Ilan University, Ramat Gan, 2014) (Hebrew).

Avivi, *Kabbalat ha-'Ari* – Joseph Avivi, *Kabbalat ha-'Ari*, (Makhon ben Tzvi, Jerusalem, 2008), 3 volumes (Hebrew).

Baer, "The Service of Sacrifices in the Second Temple"- Yitzhak Baer, "The Service of Sacrifices in the Second Temple," printed originally in *Zion* vol. 40 (1975), pp. 95–153, and reprinted in *Studies in the History of the Jewish People*, (Historical Society of Israel, Jerusalem, 1985), vol. 1 pp. 399–457 (Hebrew). The quotes are from the later edition.

Bar-Asher, "Illusion versus Reality" – Avishai Bar-Asher, "Illusion versus Reality in the Study of Early Kabbalah: The *Commentary on Sefer Yeṣirah*, attributed to Isaac the Blind and Its History in Kabbalah and Scholarship," *Tarbiz* 86 (2019), pp. 269–384 (Hebrew).

Ben Sasson, *The Divine Name* – Hillel H. ben-Sasson, *The Divine Name YHWH: Its Meaning in Biblical, Rabbinic and Medieval Jewish Thought*, (Ph. D. Thesis, Hebrew University, 2013) (Hebrew).

Ben Sasson-Halbertal, "The Divine Name YHVH and the Measure

of Mercy" – Hillel ben-Sasson – Moshe Halbertal, "The Divine Name YHVH and the Measure of Mercy," in J. Garb, R. Meroz, M. Niehoff, *And This is For Yehudah, Studies Presented to Our Friend, Professor Yehuda Liebes* (Hebrew University, The Bialik Institute, Jerusalem, 2012), pp. 53–69 (Hebrew).

Ben Shalom, "Kabbalistic Circles" – Ram ben Shalom, "Kabbalistic Circles Active in South of France (Provence) in the Thirteentn Century," *Tarbiz*, vol. 72 (2004), pp. 569–605 (Hebrew).

Ben-Shalom, *The Jews of Provence and Languedoc* – Ram Ben-Shalom, *The Jews of Provence and Languedoc: Renaissance in the Shadow of the Church* (Open University, Ra'anana, 2017), (Hebrew).

Boyarin, "Once Again: "Two Dominions in Heaven" in the Mekhilta," – Daniel Boyarin, "Once Again: "Two Dominions in Heaven' in the *Mekhilta*," in eds. M. Kahana, Ch. Turniansky, I.J. Yuval, *Studies Presented to Professor Yaakov Sussman*, [=*Tarbiz*, vol. LXXXI] (Jerusalem, 2013), pp. 87–102 (Hebrew).

Bréhier, *Les idées philosophiques* – Émile Bréhier, *Les idées philosophiques et religieuses de Philon d'Alexandrie*, (Vrin, Paris, 1925).

Brody, 'Human Hands Dwell in Heavenly Heights" – Seth Brody, "'Human Hands Dwell in Heavenly Heights: Contemplative Ascent and Theurgic Power in Thirteenth-Century Kabbalah," in ed., R.A. Herrera, *Mystics of the Book*, (New York 1993), pp. 123–158.

Dan, *History of Jewish Mysticism* – Joseph Dan, *History of Jewish Mysticism and Esotericism*, vol. VII (Zalman Shazar, Jerusalem, 2012) (Hebrew).

Dauber, "Competing Approaches to Maimonides" – Jonathan Dauber, "Competing Approaches to Maimonides in Early Kabbalah," in ed. J. Robinson, *The Cultures of Maimonideanism, New Approaches to the History of Jewish Thought* (Brill, Leiden, Boston, 2009), pp. 57–88

Dauber, 'Pure Thought' – Jonathan V. Dauber, 'Pure Thought' in R. Abraham bar Hiyya and Early Kabbalah, *JJS*, vol. LX (2009), pp. 185–201.

Eliade, *Images & Symbols* – Mircea Eliade, *Images & Symbols, Studies in Religious Symbolism* tr. Ph. Mairet, (Sheed and Ward, New York, 1969).

Eliade, *The Two and the One* – Mircea Eliade, *The Two and the One* tr. J.M. Cohen (Harper and Row, New York, Evanston, 1965).

Elior-Liebes, eds. *Lurianic Kabbalah* – eds. R. Elior, Y. Liebes, *Lurianic Kabbalah* (Jerusalem, 1992) (Hebrew).

Farber, "The Shell Precedes the Fruit" – Assi Farber, "The Shell Precedes the Fruit, to the Question of the Source of the Metaphysical Existence of Evil in Early Kabbalistic Thought," *Myth in Judaism*, ed. H. Pedayah, (Beer Sheva, 1996), pp. 118–142 (Hebrew).

Farber-Ginnat, *The Concept of the Merkabah* – Assi Farber-Ginnat, *The Concept of the Merkabah in the Thirteenth-Century Jewish Esotericism* (Ph. D. Thesis, Hebrew University, 1986) (Hebrew).

Fishbane, *Biblical Myth and Rabbinic Mythmaking* – Michael Fishbane, *Biblical Myth and Rabbinic Mythmaking* (Oxford University Press, Oxford, 2003).

Fishbane, 'The "Measures" of God's Glory in the Ancient Midrash' – Michael Fishbane, 'The "Measures" of God's Glory in the Ancient Midrash,' in eds., I. Gruenwald, S. Shaked, G.G. Stroumsa, *Messiah and Christos, Studies in the Jewish Origins of Christianity Presented to David Flusser on the Occasion of His Seventy-Fifth Birthday* (Mohr/Siebeck, Tuebingen, 1992), pp. 53–74, reprinted in his *The Exegetical Imagination, on Jewish Thought and Theology* (Harvard University Press, Cambridge, 1998), pp. 56–72.

Fishbane, *As Light Before Dawn* – Eitan P. Fishbane, *As Light Before Dawn: The Inner World of a Medieval Kabbalist* (Stanford University Press, Palo Alto, 2009).

Freudenthal, "The Theory of the Opposites" – Gad Freudenthal, "The Theory of the Opposites and an Ordered Universe: Physics and Metaphysics in Anaximander," *Phronesis* vol. 31 (1986), pp. 197–228,

Garb, *Manifestations of Power in Jewish Mysticism* – Jonathan Garb, *Manifestations of Power in Jewish Mysticism*, (Magnes Press, Jerusalem, 2005), (Hebrew).

Gavarin, "The Problem of Evil" – Martelle Gavarin, "The Problem of Evil in the Thought of Rabbi Isaac Sagi Nahor and His Disciples," *Daat* vol. 20 (1988), pp. 29–50 (Hebrew).

Goldreich, "The Theology of the Iyyun Circle" – Amos Goldreich,

"The Theology of the Iyyun Circle and a Possible Source of the Term *'Aḥdut Shava',*" in ed. J. Dan, *The Beginnings of Jewish Mysticism in Europe* (Jerusalem, 1987), pp. 141–156 (Hebrew).

Goodenough, *By Light, Light* – Erwin Goodenough, *By Light, Light: The Mystic Gospel of Hellenistic Judaism* (Yale University Press, New Haven, 1935).

Gottlieb, *Studies in the Kabbalah Literature* – Ephraim Gottlieb, *Studies in the Kabbalah Literature*, ed. J. Hacker, (Tel Aviv University, Tel Aviv, 1976) (Hebrew).

Gottlieb, *The Kabbalah in the Writings of R. Bahya ben Asher ibn Halawa* – Ephraim Gottlieb, *The Kabbalah in the Writings of R. Bahya ben Asher ibn Ḥalawa* (Kiriat Sepher, Jerusalem, 1970) (Hebrew).

Halbertal, *Concealment and Revelation* – Moshe Halbertal, *Concealment and Revelation* tr. J. Feldman, (Princeton University Press, Princeton, 2007).

Halbertal, *By Way of Truth* – Moshe Halbertal, *By Way of Truth, Nahmanides and the Creation of Tradition*, (Shalom Hartman Institute, Jerusalem, 2006) (Hebrew).

Hames, *The Art of Conversion* – Harvey Hames, *The Art of Conversion, Christianity & Kabbalah in the Thirteenth Century*, (Brill, Leiden, 2000).

Hames, "Ramon Lull, Solomon ibn Adret, and Alfonso of Valladolid Debate Trinity" – Harvey Hames, "It Takes Three to Tango: Ramon Lull, Solomon ibn Adret, and Alfonso of Valladolid Debate Trinity," *Medieval Encounters*, vol. 15 (2009), pp. 199–224.

Heller Wilensky, "Isaac ibn Latif – Philosopher or Kabbalist?" – Sara O. Heller Wilensky, "Isaac ibn Latif – Philosopher or Kabbalist?" in ed. A. Altmann, *Jewish Medieval and Renaissance Studies* (Cambridge, Mass., 1967), pp. 185–223.

Huss, *Sockets of Fine Gold* – Boaz Huss, *Sockets of Fine Gold: The Kabbalah of Rabbi Shim'on ibn Lavi* (Magnes and Ben Zvi Presses, Jerusalem, 2000) (Hebrew).

Hyman, "From One and Simple" – Arthur Hyman, "From One and Simple only What is One and Simple Can Come to Be," in ed.

L.E. Goodman, *Neoplatonism and Jewish Thought,* (SUNY Press, Albany, 1992), pp. 111–135.

Idel, *Abraham Abulafia's Esotericism* – M. Idel, *Abraham Abulafia's Esotericism, Secrets and Doubts* (de Gruyter, Berlin, 2020).

Idel, *Abraham Abulafia's Works and Doctrine* – M. Idel, *Abraham Abulafia's Works and Doctrine* (Ph.D. Thesis, Hebrew University, Jerusalem, 1976) (Hebrew),

Idel, *Absorbing Perfections* – M. Idel, *Absorbing Perfections: Kabbalah and Interpretation* (Yale University Press, New Haven, London, 2002).

Idel, *The Angelic World* – M. Idel, *The Angelic World: Apotheosis and Theophany* (Yediyot Sefarim, Tel Aviv, 2008) (Hebrew).

Idel, *Ascensions on High* – M. Idel, *Ascensions on High in Jewish Mysticism, Pillars, Lines, Ladders* (Central European University Press, Budapest, New York, 2005).

Idel, *Ben* – M. Idel, *Ben: Sonship and Jewish Mysticism* (Continuum, London, New York, 2007).

Idel, "The Commentaries of R. Nehemiah bar Shlomo to the Piyyut" – M. Idel, "The Commentaries of R. Nehemiah bar Shlomo to the Piyyut '*Ha-Ohez be-Yad Middat Mishpat*'," *Kabbalah* vol. 26 (2012), pp. 165–202 (Hebrew).

Idel, "Commentaries on the Secret of Impregnation" – M. Idel, "Commentaries on the Secret of Impregnation in the Kabbalas of Catalunia and Their Significance for Understanding of the Beginning of Kabbalah and Its Development," *Da'at*, vol. 72 (2012), pp. 5–49, vol. 73 (2012), pp. 5–44 (Hebrew),

Idel, "Defining Kabbalah" – M. Idel, "Defining Kabbalah: The Kabbalah of the Divine Names," *Mystics of the Book: Themes, Topics & Typology,* ed. R.A. Herrera (Peter Lang, New York, 1993), pp. 97–122.

Idel, "Differing Conceptions of Kabbalah" – M. Idel, "Differing Conceptions of Kabbalah in Early 17th Century," *Jewish Thought in the Seventeenth Century,* eds. I. Twersky – B.D. Septimus, (Harvard University Press, Cambridge, Mass., 1987), pp. 137–200.

Idel, *Enchanted Chains* – M. Idel, *Enchanted Chains: Techniques and Rituals in Jewish Mysticism* (Cherub Press, Los Angeles, 2005).

Idel, "On European Cultural Renaissances and Jewish Mysticism" – M. Idel, "On European Cultural Renaissances and Jewish Mysticism," *Kabbalah* 13 (2005), pp. 43–64.

Idel, "The Evil Thought of the Deity" – M. Idel, "The Evil Thought of the Deity," *Tarbiz*, vol. 49 (1980), pp. 356–364 (Hebrew).

Idel, *Golem* – M. Idel, *Golem, Jewish Magical and Mystical Traditions on the Artificial Anthropoid* (State University of New York Press, Albany 1990).

Idel, *Hasidism: Between Ecstasy and Magic* – M. Idel, *Hasidism: Between Ecstasy and Magic* (SUNY Press, Albany, 1995).

Idel, "Higher than Time" – M. Idel, "Higher than Time" – Some Observations on Concepts of Time in Kabbalah and Hasidism," in ed. B. Ogren, *Time and Eternity in Jewish Mysticism*, (Leiden, Brill, 2015), pp. 179–210.

Idel, "The Image of Man Above the *Sefirot* " – M. Idel, "The Image of Man Above the *Sefirot*: R. David ben Yehuda he-Hasid's Theosophy of the Ten Supernal *Sahsahot* and Its Reverberations," *Kabbalah* vol. 20 (2009), pp. 181–212.

Idel, "In a Whisper" – M. Idel, "In a Whisper: On Transmission *of Shi'ur Qomah* and Kabbalistic Secrets in Jewish Mysticism," *Rivista di storia e letteratura religiosa*, XLVII/3 (2011), = *Il mantello di Elia. Tradizione, innovazione nella cabala*, pp. 477–522.

Idel, "Interpretations of the Secret of Incest in Early Kabbalah," – M. Idel, "Interpretations of the Secret of 'Arayyot in Early Kabbalah," *Kabbalah*, vol. 12 (2004), pp. 89–200) (Hebrew).

Idel, "Jewish Kabbalah and Platonism" – M. Idel, "Jewish Kabbalah and Platonism in the Middle Ages and Renaissance," in ed. L.E. Goodman, *Neoplatonism and Jewish Thought* (SUNY Press, Albany, 1993), pp. 319–352,

Idel, "Kabbalistic Prayer in Provence," – M. Idel, "Kabbalistic Prayer in Provence," *Tarbiz* vol. 62 (1993), pp. 265–286 (Hebrew).

Idel, *Le Porte della Giustizia* – Natan ben Sa'adyah Har`ar, *Le Porte della Giustizia,* intr. and ed. M. Idel, tr. M. Mottolese, (Adelphi, Milano, 2001)

Idel, "Leviathan and Its Consort" – M. Idel, "Leviathan and Its Consort: From Talmudic to Kabbalistic Myth," in eds. I. Gruenwald – M. Idel, *Myths in Judaism: History, Thought, Literature,* (Merkaz Shazar, Jerusalem, 2004), pp. 145–187 (Hebrew).

Idel, *Kabbalah & Eros* – M. Idel, *Kabbalah & Eros* (Yale University Press, New Haven, London, 2005).

Idel, "Kabbalistic Material" – M. Idel, "Kabbalistic Material from R. David ben Yehudah he-Hasid's School," *JSJT* vol. 2 (1983), pp. 169–207 (Hebrew).

Idel, *Kabbalah in Italy* – M. Idel, *Kabbalah in Italy, 1280–1510, a Survey* (Yale University Press, New Haven, London 2010).

Idel, "Maimonides and Kabbalah" – M. Idel, "Maimonides and Kabbalah," in *Studies in Maimonides,* ed. I. Twersky (Harvard U.P., Cambridge, Mass., 1990), pp. 31–81

Idel, "Maimonides' *Guide of the Perplexed* and the Kabbalah," – M. Idel, "Maimonides' *Guide of the Perplexed* and the Kabbalah," *Jewish History,* vol. 18 (2004), pp. 197–226.

Idel, *"Male and Female"*- M. Idel, *"Male and Female": Equality, Female's Theurgy, and Eros – R. Moshe Cordovero's Dual Ontology* (in preparation).

Idel, *Messianic Mystics* – M. Idel, *Messianic Mystics* (Yale University Press, New Haven, 1998).

Idel, *Mircea Eliade: From Magic to Myth* – M. Idel, *Mircea Eliade: From Magic to Myth* (Peter Lang, New York, 2014).

Idel, *The Mystical Experience* – M. Idel, *The Mystical Experience in Abraham Abulafia,* tr. J. Chipman, (SUNY Press, Albany 1987).

Idel, "Maimonides and Kabbalah" – M. Idel, "Maimonides and Kabbalah," in ed. I. Twersky, *Studies in Maimonides* (Harvard University Press, Cambridge, Mass., 1990), pp. 31–81.

Idel, "The Mystical Intention of the Eighteen Benedictions" – M. Idel, "The Mystical Intention of the Eighteen Benedictions by R. Isaac Sagi Nahor," in eds., M. Oron and A. Goldreich, *Massu'ot, Studies in Kabbalistic Literature and Jewish Philosophy in Memory of Prof.*

Ephraim Gottlieb, (Mossad Bialik, Jerusalem, 1994), pp. 25–52 (Hebrew),

Idel, "Notes of Medieval Jewish-Christian Polemics" – M. Idel, "Notes of Medieval Jewish-Christian Polemics," *JSJS*, vol. 3 (1983/1984), pp. 689–698, 219–222 (Hebrew).

Idel, "Notes in the Wake of Medieval Jewish Polemic," English translation in *Immanuel*, vol. 18 (1984), pp. 54–63.

Idel, *Old Worlds, New Mirrors* – M. Idel, *Old Worlds, New Mirrors: On Jewish Mysticism and Twentieth-Century Thought*, (University of Pennsylvania Press, Philadelphia, 2010).

Idel, "On R. Nehemiah ben Shlomo the Prophet's Commentaries on the Name of Forty-Two" – Moshe Idel, "On R. Nehemiah ben Shlomo the Prophet's Commentaries on the Name of Forty-Two and *Sefer ha-Ḥokhmah* Attributed to R. Eleazar of Worms," *Kabbalah*, vol. 14 (2006), pp. 157–261 (Hebrew).

Idel, "On the Identity" – M. Idel, "On the Identity of the Authors of Two Ashkenazi Commentaries on the Poem *ha-'Aderet ve-ha-'Emunah*, and on the Views of Theurgy and *Kavod* in R. Eleazar of Worms," *Kabbalah*, vol. 29 (2013), pp. 67–208 (Hebrew).

Idel, "On the Performing Body" – M. Idel, "On the Performing Body in Theosophical-Theurgical Kabbalah: Some Preliminary Remarks," in eds., M. Dielmling, G. Veltri, *The Jewish Body, Corporeality, Society, and Identity in the Renaissance and Early Modern Period* (Brill, Leiden-Boston, 2009), pp. 251–271.

Idel, "On Angels in Biblical Exegesis" – M. Idel, "On Angels in Biblical Exegesis in Thirteenth-Century Ashkenaz," in D.A. Green and L.S. Lieber (eds.), *Scriptural Exegesis, Shapes of Culture and Religious Imagination, Essays in Honour of Michael Fishbane*, (Oxford University Press, Oxford 2009), pp. 211–244.

Idel, "On the Theosophy at the Beginning of Kabbalah" – M. Idel, "On the Theosophy at the Beginning of Kabbalah," in *Shefa Tal: Studies in Jewish Thought and Culture Presented to Bracha Sack*, eds. Z. Gries, Ch. Kreisel, B. Huss (Ben Gurion University Press, Beer Sheva, 2004), pp. 131–147 (Hebrew).

Idel, "The Pearl, the Son and the Servants" – M. Idel, "The Pearl, the

Son and the Servants, in Abraham Abulafia's Parable," in ed. A. Grossato, *Quaderni di Studi Indo-Mediterranei, Le Tre Anella*, vol. VI (2013), pp. 103–136.

Idel, *Primeval Evil in Kabbalah* – M. Idel, *Primeval Evil in Kabbalah: Totality, Perfection and Perfectibility* (Ktav, New York, 2020).

Idel, *R. Menahem Recanati* – M. Idel, *R. Menahem Recanati: The Kabbalist* (Schocken Books, Jerusalem, Tel Aviv, 1998), vol. 1 (Hebrew).

Idel, "R. Menahem Mendel of Shklov and R. Avraham Abulafia" – M. Idel, "R. Menahem Mendel of Shklov and R. Avraham Abulafia," in eds. M. Hallamish, Y. Rivlin, R. Shuhat, *THE VILNA GAON and His Disciples*, (Bar Ilan University Press, Ramat Gan, 2003), pp. 173–183 (Hebrew).

Idel, "Rabbinism versus Kabbalism" – M. Idel, "Rabbinism versus Kabbalism; on G. Scholem's Phenomenology of Judaism," *Modern Judaism*, vol. XI (1991), pp. 281–296.

Idel, *Representing God* – Moshe Idel, *Representing God*, eds. H. Tirosh-Samuelson – A. Huges (Brill, Leiden, 2015).

Idel, *Saturn's Jews* – M. Idel, *Saturn's Jews: On the Witches' Sabbat and Sabbateanism*, (Continuum, London, New York, 2011).

Idel, "The Secret of Impregnation" – M. Idel, "The Secret of Impregnation as Metempsychosis in Kabbalah,'' in eds. A. and J. Assmann, *Verwandlungen, Archaeologie der literarischen Communication* IX, (Munich, 2006), pp. 349–368.

Idel, "*Sefer Yetzirah* and Its Commentaries" – M. Idel, "*Sefer Yetzirah* and Its Commentaries in the Writings of R. Abraham Abulafia, and the Remnants of R. Isaac Bedershi's Commentary and Their Impact," *Tarbiz*, vol. 79 (2011), pp. 471–556 (Hebrew).

Idel, "The Sefirot Above the Sefirot" – M. Idel, "The Sefirot Above the Sefirot", *Tarbiz* vol. 51 (1982), pp. 239–280 (Hebrew).

Idel, "Some Remarks on Ritual and Mysticism" – M. Idel, "Some Remarks on Ritual and Mysticism in Geronese Kabbalah," *Jewish Thought and Philosophy*, vol. III (1993), pp. 111–130.

Idel, *Studies in Ecstatic Kabbalah* – M. Idel, *Studies in Ecstatic Kabbalah* (SUNY Press, Albany, 1989)

Idel, "On the Theologization of Kabbalah" – M. Idel, "On the Theologization of Kabbalah in Modern Scholarship," in *Religious Apologetics – Philosophical Argumentation*, eds. Y. Schwartz and V. Krech, (Mohr, Tuebingen, 2004), pp. 123–174.

Idel, "The Triple Family" – M. Idel, "The Triple Family: Sources for the Feminine Perception of Deity in Early Kabbalah," in eds., E. Baumgarten, A. Raz-Krakotzkin, R. Weinstein, *Tov Elem, Memory, Community & Gender in Medieval & Early Modern Jewish Societies, Essays in Honor of Robert Bonfil*, (Mossad Bialik, Jerusalem, 2011), pp. 91–110 (Hebrew).

Idel, "We Have No Kabbalistic Tradition on This" – M. Idel, "We Have No Kabbalistic Tradition on This," in ed. I. Twersky, *Rabbi Moses Nahmanides (Ramban): Explorations in His Religious and Literary Virtuosity* (Cambridge, Mass. 1983), pp. 51–73.

Idel, "Zimzum" – M. Idel, "On the Concept of Zimzum in Kabbalah and Its Research," in eds. R.

Elior, Y. Liebes, *Lurianic Kabbalah* (Jerusalem, 1992), pp. 59–112 (Hebrew).

Kaplan, "Faith, Rebellion, and Heresy" – Lawrence Kaplan, "Faith, Rebellion, and Heresy in the Writings of Rabbi Azriel of Gerona," in *Faith: Jewish Perspectives*, edited by Avi Sagi and Dov Schwartz, (Boston: Academic Studies Press, 2013), pp. 278–301.

Kister, "The Manifestations of God" – Menachem Kister, "The Manifestations of God in the

Midrashic Literature in Light of Christian Texts," in eds. M. Kahana, Ch. Turniansky, I.J. Yuval,

Studies Presented to Professor Yaakov Sussman, [=Tarbiz, vol. LXXXI] (2013), pp. 103–142

(Hebrew).

Knohl, *The Divine Symphony* – Israel Knohl, *The Divine Symphony: The Bible's Many Voices* (JPS, Philadelphia, 2003).

Levenson, *Creation and the Persistence of Evil* – Jon D. Levenson, *Creation and the Persistence of Evil: The Jewish Drama of Divine Omnipotence* (Harper and Row, San Francisco, 1988).

Liebes, "De Natura Dei," – Yehudah Liebes, "'De Natura Dei', On the Jewish Myth and Its Metamorphosis," in eds., M. Oron and

A. Goldreich, *Massu'ot, Studies in Kabbalistic Literature and Jewish Philosophy in Memory of Prof. Ephraim Gottlieb,* (Mossad Bialik, Jerusalem, 1994), pp. 243–297 (Hebrew).

Liebes, "*Sefer Yetzirah* in R. Shlomo ibn Gabirol" – Yehuda Liebes, "*Sefer Yetzirah* in R. Shlomo ibn Gabirol and a Commentary on the Poem *'Ahavtikha,*" *JSJT*, vol. 6 (1987), pp. 73–123 (Hebrew).

Liebes, *God's Story* – Yehuda Liebes, *God's Story, Collected Essays in the Jewish Myth* (Carmel, Jerusalem, 2008) (Hebrew).

Liebes, *The Cult of the Dawn* – Yehudah Liebes, *The Cult of the Dawn, the Attitude of the Zohar toward Idolatry* (Carmel, Jerusalem, 2011) (Hebrew).

Liebes, *Sections of the Zoharic Lexicon* – Yehuda Liebes, *Sections of the Zoharic Lexicon* (Ph. D. Thesis, Hebrew University, Jerusalem, 1976) (Hebrew).

Liebes, "The Kabbalistic Myth of Orpheus" – Yehuda Liebes, "The Kabbalistic Myth of Orpheus," *Shlomo Pines Jubilee Volume on the Occasion of His Eightieth Birthday,* eds. M. Idel, Z. Harvey, E. Schweid, (Jerusalem, 1988), vol. 1, pp. 425–446 (Hebrew).

Liebes, *Studies in Jewish Myth* – Yehuda Liebes, *Studies in Jewish Myth and Jewish Messianism,* tr. Batya Stein (SUNY Press, Albany, 1993).

Liebes, *Studies in the Zohar* – Yehuda Liebes, *Studies in the Zohar,* trs. A. Schwartz, S. Nakache, P. Peli, (SUNY Press, Albany, 1993).

Liebes, "The Messiah of the Zohar" – Yehuda Liebes, "The Messiah of the Zohar" in *The Messianic Idea in Israel* (Jerusalem, 1982) pp. 87–234 (Hebrew).

Liebes, *Ars Poetica in Sefer Yetsira* – Yehuda Liebes, *Ars Poetica in Sefer Yetsira* (Schocken, Jerusalem, Tel Aviv, 2000) (Hebrew).

Lorberboim, *Image of God, Halakhah and Aggadah* – Yair Lorberboim, *Image of God, Halakhah and Aggadah* (Schocken, Tel Aviv, 2004) (Hebrew),

Marmorstein, *The Old Rabbinic Doctrine of God* – Arthur Marmorstein, *The Old Rabbinic Doctrine of God,* vol. 1, *The Names and the Attributes,* (Oxford University Press, London, 1927).

Meroz, *Redemption in the Lurianic Teachings* – Ronit Meroz, *Redemp-*

tion in the Lurianic Teachings (Ph. D. Thesis, Hebrew University, Jerusalem, 1988), (Hebrew).

Meroz, "R. Joseph Angelet and his "Zoharic Writings" – Ronit Meroz, 'R. Joseph Angelet and his "Zoharic Writings"' in ed. R. Meroz, *New Developments in Zohar Studies*, [= *Te'uda*, vol. XXI–XXII] (Tel Aviv University Press, Tel Aviv, 2007), pp. 303–404 (Hebrew).

Morlok, *Rabbi Joseph Gikatilla's Hermeneutics* – Elke Morlok, *Rabbi Joseph Gikatilla's Hermeneutics* (Mohr, Tuebingen, 2010).

Mopsik, *Les grands textes de la cabale* – Charles Mopsik, *Les grands textes de la cabale, Les rites qui font Dieu* (Verdier, Lagrasse, 1993).

Mottolese, *Analogy in Midrash and Kabbalah* – Maurizio Mottolese, *Analogy in Midrash and Kabbalah, Interpretive Projections of the Sanctuary and Ritual* (Cherub Press, Los Angeles, 2006).

Naeh, "He Does Peace and Creates Everything," – Shlomo Naeh, "He Does Peace and Creates Everything," in ed. E. Naeh, *Zikhron Moshe* (Jerusalem, 2005), pp. 293–230 (Hebrew).

Naeh, "Philo and the Rabbis on the Powers of God" – Shlomo Naeh, "*Poterion en cheiri kyriou*: Philo and the Rabbis on the Powers of God and the Mixture in the Cup," in eds., H.M. Cotton, J. J, Price, D.J. Wasserstein, *Scripta Classica Israelica*, XVI (= *Studies in Memory of Abraham Wasserstein* II), (Jerusalem 1997), pp. 91–101.

Oron, "The Literature of Commentaries to the Ten *Sefirot*"- Michal Oron, "The Literature of Commentaries to the Ten *Sefirot*," in eds. Y. Ben-Naeh, and alia, *Studies in Jewish History Presented to Joseph Hacker*, (The Zalman Shazar Center, Jerusalem, 2015), pp. 212–229 (Hebrew).

Pachter, *Roots of Faith and Devequt* – Mordechai Pachter, *Roots of Faith and Devequt, Studies in the History of Kabbalistic Ideas* (Cherub Press, Los Angeles, 2004).

Patai, *The Hebrew Goddess* – Raphael Patai, *The Hebrew Goddess*, (Discus, New York, 1978).

Pedaya, "'Flaw' and 'Correction'" – Haviva Pedaya, "'Flaw' and 'Correction' in the Concept of the Godhead in the Teachings of Rabbi Isaac the Blind," in *The Beginning of Jewish Mysticism in Medieval Europe*, ed. J. Dan, (Jerusalem, 1987), pp. 157–286 (Hebrew).

Pedaya, *Nahmanides* – Haviva Pedaya, *Nahmanides, Cyclical Time and Holy Text* ('Am 'Oved, Tel Aviv, 2003) (Hebrew).

Pedaya, *Name and Sanctuary* – Haviva Pedaya, *Name and Sanctuary in the Teaching of R. Isaac the Blind* (Magnes Press, Jerusalem, 2001) (Hebrew).

Pedaya, "Sabbath, Sabbatai, and the Diminution of Moon" – Haviva Pedaya, "Sabbath, Sabbatai, and the Diminution of Moon: The Holy Conjunction, Sign and Image," in ed. H. Pedaya, *Myth in Judaism = Eshel Beer-Sheva*, vol. 4 (1996), pp. 143–191 (Hebrew).

Pines, "And He Called Out to Nothingness and It was Split"- Shlomo Pines, "And He Called Out to Nothingness and It was Split – A Note on a Passage in Ibn Gabirol's *Keter Malkhut*," *Tarbiz*, vol. 50 (1980–1981), pp. 339–347 (Hebrew).

Pines, *The Collected Works* – Shlomo Pines, *The Collected Works*, (The Magnes Press, Jerusalem, 1979–1996), 5 volumes.

Pines, "Points of Similarity" – Shlomo Pines, "Points of Similarity Between the Doctrine of the Sefirot in the *Sefer Yetzirah* and a text from the Pseudo-Clementine Homilies: The Implications of This Resemblance," *The Israel Academy of Sciences and Humanities*, vol. VII, no. 3 (1989), pp. 63–142.

Porat, *"Founding of the Circle"* – Oded Porat, *"Founding of the Circle": Rudiments of Esse and the Linguistic Creation in the Book 'Fountain of Wisdom' and its Related Treatises* (Ph. D. Thesis, Hebrew University, Jerusalem, 2012) (Hebrew).

Porat, *The Works of Iyyun* – Oded Porat, *The Works of Iyyun, Critical Editions* (Cherub Press, Los Angeles, 2013), (Hebrew).

Reuchlin, *On the Art of Kabbalah* – Johann Reuchlin, *On the Art of Kabbalah – De Arte Cabalistica*, trs. M. and S. Goodman (University of Nebraska Press, Lincolm – London, 1994).

Rosen-Zvi, *Demonic Desires* – Ishay Rosen-Zvi, *Demonic Desires: Yetzer Hara and the Problem of Evil in Late Antiquity* (University of Pennsylvania Press, Philadelphia, 2011).

Rowland – Morray-Jones, *The Mystery of God*, – Christopher Rowland and Christopher Morray-Jones, *The Mystery of God, Early Jewish Mysticism and New Testament* (Brill, Leiden, 2009).

Runia, *Philo of Alexandria: On the Creation of the Cosmos* – David T. Runia, tr. and commentator, *Philo of Alexandria: On the Creation of the Cosmos According to Moses* (Brill, Leiden, 2001),

Sack, *The Kabbalah of Rabbi Moshe Cordovero* – Bracha Sack, *The Kabbalah of Rabbi Moshe Cordovero,* (Ben Gurion University Press, Beer Sheva, 1995) (Hebrew).

Sagerman, *The Serpent Kills* – Robert J. Sagerman, *The Serpent Kills or the Serpents Give Life: The Kabbalist Abraham Abulafia's Response to Christianity,* (Brill, Leiden 2011).

Schaefer, *Mirror of His Beauty* – Peter Schaefer, *Mirror of His Beauty, Feminine Images of God from the Bible to the Early Kabbalah* (Princeton University Press, Princeton, 2002).

Schaefer, *The Origins of Jewish Mysticism* – Peter Schaefer, *The Origins of Jewish Mysticism* (Princeton University Press, Princeton, 2009).

Schneider, *The Appearance of the High Priest* – Michael Schneider, *The Appearance of the High Priest: Theophany, Apotheosis and Binitarian Theology, from Priestly Tradition of the Second Temple Period through Ancient Jewish Mysticism* (Cherub Press, Los Angeles, 2012) (Hebrew),

Schneider, "The Myth of the *Satan* in the *Book Bahir*" – Michael Schneider, "The Myth of the *Satan* in the *Book Bahir*," *Kabbalah,* vol. 20 (2009), pp. 287–343 (Hebrew).

Schneider, *Scattered Traditions of Jewish Mysticism* – Michael Schneider, *Scattered Traditions of Jewish Mysticism* (Cherub Press, Los Angeles, 2012) (Hebrew).

Scholem, *Devils, Demons* – Gershom Scholem, *Devils, Demons and Souls, Essays on Demonology,* ed. E. Liebes, (Ben Zvi Institute, Hebrew University, Jerusalem, 2004) (Hebrew).

Scholem, *Jewish Gnosticism* – Gershom Scholem, *Jewish Gnosticism, Merkabah Mysticism and Talmudic Tradition,* (JTS, New York 1965).

Scholem, *Kabbalah* – Gershom G. Scholem, *Kabbalah* (Keter, Jerusalem, 1974).

Scholem, *The Kabbalah in Provence* – Gershom Scholem, *The Kabbalah in Provence,* ed. R. Shatz, (Akademon, Jerusalem, 1986), (Hebrew).

Scholem, *Lurianic Kabbalah* – Gershom G. Scholem, *Lurianic Kab-*

balah, Collected Studies, ed. D. Abrams (Cherub Press, Los Angeles, 2008) (Hebrew).

Scholem, ed., *Mada'ei ha-Yahadut*, – Gershom Scholem, ed., *Mada'ei ha-Yahadut*, vol. II (Jerusalem, 1927), pp. 165–290 (Hebrew).

Scholem, "Mafteaḥ le-Perushim" – Gershom Scholem, "Mafteaḥ le-Perushim 'al 'Eser *Sefirot*," *QS*, vol. 10 (1933/1934), pp. 498–515 (Hebrew)

Scholem, *Major Trends* – Gershom Scholem, *Major Trends in Jewish Mysticism* (Schocken Books, New York, 1960).

Scholem, "New Remnants" – Gershom Scholem, "New Remnants from Rabbi Azriel of Gerona's Writings," in *Asher Klein and Samuel Gulak Memory Volume* (Jerusalem, 1942), pp. 201–222 (Hebrew).

Scholem, *On the Kabbalah and Its Symbolism* – Gershom Scholem, *On the Kabbalah and Its Symbolism*, tr. R. Manheim, (Schocken Books, New York, 1969).

Scholem, *On the Mystical Shape* – Gershom Scholem, *On the Mystical Shape of the Godhead*, tr. J. Neugroschel, ed. J. Chipman, (Schocken Books, New York, 1991).

Scholem, *Origins of the Kabbalah* – Gershom G. Scholem, *Origins of the Kabbalah*, tr. A. Arkush, ed. R.J.Z. Werblowsky, (JPS, Philadelphia, and Princeton University Press, 1987).

Scholem, "R. Moshe mi-Burgos," – Gershom Scholem, "R. Moshe mi-Burgos: The Student of R. Isaac," *Tarbiz*, vol. 3 (1932), pp. 258–286, vol. 4 (1933), pp. 207 224, vol. 5 (1934), pp. 54–60, 180–198, 305–322 (Hebrew).

Scholem, *Reshit ha-Kabbalah* – Gershom Scholem, *Reshit ha-Kabbalah*, (Schocken, Jerusalem-Tel Aviv, 1948) (Hebrew).

Scholem, *Sabbatai Sevi* – Gershom Scholem, *Sabbatai Sevi, the Mystical Messiah* tr. R.J. Z. Werblowsky, (Princeton University Press, Princeton, 1973).

Scholem, "Schoefung aus Nichts" – Gershom Scholem, "Schoefung aus Nichts und Selbstverschraekung Gottes," *Eranos Jahrbuch* vol. XXV (1956), pp. 87–119.

Scholem, *Studies in Kabbalah* – Gershom Scholem, *Studies in Kabbalah*

(1), eds. J. ben Shlomo – M. Idel, ('Am 'Oved, Tel Aviv, 1998) (Hebrew).

Schremer, *Male and Female He Created Them* – Adiel Schremer, *Male and Female He Created Them, Jewish Marriage in the Late Second Temple, Mishnah and Talmud Period* (Merkaz Shazar, Jerusalem, 2004) (Hebrew).

Sed-Rajna, *Azriel de Gerone, Commentaire sur la Liturgie Quotidienne* – Gabrielle Sed-Rajna, *Azriel de Gerone, Commentaire sur la Liturgie Quotidienne,* (Brill, Leiden, 1974).

Segal, *Two Powers in Heaven* – Alan F. Segal, *Two Powers in Heaven: Early Rabbinic Reports about Christianity and Gnosticism,* (Brill, Leiden, 2002).

Sendor, *The Emergence of Provencal Kabbalah* – Mark Sendor, *The Emergence of Provencal Kabbalah: R. Isaac the Blind's Commentary on Sefer Yetzirah,* (Ph.D. diss., Harvard University, 1994), two parts.

Stroumsa, *Hidden Wisdom* – Guy G. Stroumsa, *Hidden Wisdom, Esoteric Traditions & Roots of Christian Mysticism* (Brill, Leiden, 1996).

Tishby, *The Doctrine of Evil* – Isaiah Tishby, *The Doctrine of Evil and the Shells in the Lurianic Doctrine,* (Magnes Press, Jerusalem, 1942) (Hebrew).

Tishby, "Gnostic Doctrines" – Isaiah Tishby, "Gnostic Doctrines in Sixteenth-Century Jewish Mysticism," *JJS*, vol. 6 (1955), pp. 146–152.

Tishby, *Paths of Faith and Heresy* – Isaiah Tishby, *Paths of Faith and Heresy,* (Masada, Ramat Gan, 1964) (Hebrew).

Tishby, *Studies in Kabbalah and Its Branches* – Isaiah Tishby, *Studies in Kabbalah and Its Branch* (Magnes Press, Jerusalem, 1982–1993) three volumes (Hebrew).

Tishby, *The Wisdom of the Zohar* – Isaiah Tishby, *The Wisdom of the Zohar: An Anthology of Texts,* tr. D. Goldstein, (Littmann Library, London, Washington, 1991), 3 volumes.

Travis, *Rabbi Ezra of Gerona* – Yakov Travis, *Rabbi Ezra of Gerona: On the Kabbalistic Meaning of the Mizvot* (Ph. D. Dissertation, Brandeis University, 2002).

Twersky, *Rabad of Posquières* – Isadore Twersky, *Rabad of Posquières, a*

Twelfth-Century Talmudist, (Harvard University Press, Cambridge, Mass., 1962).

Urbach, *The Sages* – Ephraim E. Urbach, *The Sages, Their Concepts and Beliefs*, tr. I. Abrahams, (Magnes Press, Jerusalem, 1979), 2 volumes.

Urbach, "The Traditions about Merkabah Mysticism" – E.E. Urbach, "The Traditions about Merkabah Mysticism in the Tannaitic Period," *Studies in Mysticism and Religion Presented to Gershom G. Scholem* (The Magnes Press, Jerusalem, 1967), pp. 1–27 (Hebrew).

Vajda, *Le commentaire* – Georges Vajda, *Le commentaire d'Ezra de Gerone sur le cantique des cantiques* (Aubier, Paris, 1969).

Vajda, *Recherches* – Georges Vajda, *Recherches sur la Philosophie et la Kabbale dans la pensée juive du Moyen Age* (Mouton, Paris, 1962).

Valabregue-Peri, *Concealed and Revealed* – Sandra Valabregue-Peri, *Concealed and Revealed, 'Ein Sof in Theosophic Kabbalah* (Cherub Press, Los Angeles 2010) (Hebrew).

Verman, *The Books of Contemplation* – Mark Verman, *The Books of Contemplation, Medieval Jewish Mystical Sources* (SUNY Press, Albany, 1992).

Weinstock, *Studies* – Israel Weinstock, *Studies in Jewish Philosophy and Mysticism* (Mossad Harav Kook, Jerusalem, 1969) (Hebrew).

Weiss, "Most of the Errant Err in *Malkhut*" – Tzahi Weiss, "Most of the Errant Err in *Malkhut*:" The Worship of the *Shekhinah* in Early Kabbalah," *Tarbiz*, vol. 82 (2014), pp. 319–334 (Hebrew).

Weiss, *Cutting the Shoots* – Tzahi Weiss, *Cutting the Shoots: The Perception of the Shekhinah in the World of Early Kabbalah*, (Magnes Press, Jerusalem, 2015) (Hebrew).

Wolfson, *Abraham Abulafia* – Elliot R. Wolfson, *Abraham Abulafia: Hermeneutics, Theosophy, and Theurgy* (Cherub Press, Los Angeles, 2000).

Wolfson, *Aleph, Mem, Tau* – Elliot R. Wolfson, *Aleph, Mem, Tau*, (University of California Press, Berkeley, 2006).

Wolfson, *Along the Path* – Elliot R. Wolfson, *Along the Path: Studies in Kabbalistic Myth, Symbolism, and Hermeneutics* (SUNY Press, Albany, 1995).

Wolfson, *Circle in the Square* – Elliot R. Wolfson, *Circle in the Square*,

Studies in the Use of Gender in Kabbalistic Symbolism (SUNY Press, Albany, 1995).

Wolfson, "Kenotic Overflow and Temporal Transcendence" – Elliot R. Wolfson, "Kenotic Overflow and Temporal Transcendence: Angelic Embodiment and the Alterity of Time in Abraham Abulafia," *Kabbalah*, vol. 18 (2008), pp. 133–190.

Wolfson, *Language, Eros, Being* – Elliot R. Wolfson, *Language, Eros, Being, Kabbalistic Hermeneutics and Poetic Imagination*, (Fordham University Press, New York, 2005).

Wolfson, "Light through Darkness" – Elliot R. Wolfson, "Light through Darkness: The Ideal of the Human Perfection in the Zohar," *HTR*, vol. 81 (1988), pp. 73–95.

Wolfson, "The Tree That Is All" – Elliot R. Wolfson, "The Tree That Is All: Jewish-Christian Roots of a Kabbalistic Symbol in *Sefer ha-Bahir*," *JJTP*, vol. 3 (1993), pp. 31–76.

Wolfson, *Through a Speculum* – Elliot R. Wolfson, *Through a Speculum That Shines, Vision and Imagination in Medieval Jewish Mysticism* (Princeton University Press, Princeton, 1994).

Wolfson, *Venturing Beyond* – Elliot R. Wolfson, *Venturing Beyond, Law & Morality in Kabbalistic Mysticism* (Oxford University Press, Oxford 2006).

Wolfson, 'The Theosophy of Shabbetai Donnolo' – Elliot Wolfson, 'The Theosophy of Shabbetai Donnolo with Special Emphasis on the Doctrine of Sefirot in His *Sefer Hakhmoni*', *Jewish History*, vol. 6 (1992), pp. 281–316.

Wolfson, *Philo* – Harry A. Wolfson, *Philo: Foundations of Religious Philosophy in Judaism, Christianity, and Islam*, third edition (Harvard University Press, Cambridge, Mass., 1962), two volumes.

Yahalom, *Between Gerona and Narbonne* – Shalem Yahalom, *Between Gerona and Narbonne, Nahmanides' Literary Sources* (Makhon ben-Zvi, Jerusalem, 2012) (Hebrew).

INDEX